POLYSITUATEDNESS

MANCHESTER
1824
Manchester University Press

ANGELAKIHUMANITIES

editors
Charlie Blake
Pelagia Goulimari
Timothy S. Murphy
Robert Smith

general editor
Gerard Greenway

Angelaki Humanities publishes works which address and probe broad and compelling issues in the theoretical humanities. The series favours path-breaking thought, promotes unjustly neglected figures, and grapples with established concerns. It believes in the possibility of blending, without compromise, the rigorous, the well-crafted, and the inventive. The series seeks to host ambitious writing from around the world.

Angelaki Humanities is the associated book series of
angelaki – journal of the theoretical humanities.

Already published

The question of literature: the place of the literary in contemporary theory
Elizabeth Beaumont Bissell

Absolutely postcolonial: writing between the singular and the specific
Peter Hallward

Late modernist poetics: from Pound to Prynne
Anthony Mellors

The new Bergson
John Mullarkey (ed.)

Subversive Spinoza: (un)contemporary variations
Timothy S. Murphy

Disclosed poetics: beyond landscape and lyricism
John Kinsella

ANGELAKIHUMANITIES

POLYSITUATEDNESS

A poetics of displacement

John Kinsella

Manchester University Press

Published by Manchester University Press
Altrincham Street, Manchester M1 7JA
www.manchesteruniversitypress.co.uk

British Library Cataloguing-in-Publication Data
A catalogue record for this book is available from the British Library

Library of Congress Cataloging-in-Publication Data applied for

ISBN 978 1 5261 1334 4 *hardback*

First published 2017

The publisher has no responsibility for the persistence or accuracy of URLs for external or any third-party internet websites referred to in this book, and does not guarantee that any content on such websites is, or will remain, accurate or appropriate.

Typeset by
Servis Filmsetting Ltd, Stockport, Cheshire
Printed in Great Britain
by TJ International Ltd, Padstow

For Tracy and Tim

I wish to acknowledge the traditional custodians and owners of country I write – the only 'ownership' of land I recognise.

CONTENTS

List of figures   *page* x
Acknowledgements   xii
Preface/synopsis   xiii
A polysituated ode with occasional, demi-Boustrophedon   xvi

1 **On place itself**   1
A personal introduction on practice and context including some
    external considerations of 'place'   3
Polysituated(ness): international regionalism   18
Agoras   21
Redefining or maybe replacing 'place': towards a theology of
    presence? Consequences and responsibility   27
Application   36
For beauty's sake   40
Overhearing: poetics of place with brief reference to
    Jack Davis's poetry   43
Concretion and damage: a pre-manifesto (though written after)   49
De-mapping – Jam Tree Gully 4 Concretions Manifesto 1   59
Concreted protest poem against bauxite mine at Morangup   62
Further Jam Tree Gully concretions   65
Near Goomalling: Oak Park concretions   70
Living with Moondyne Joe: *points de repère*   82

2 **Where we are**   89
A polysituated manifest (with an incomplete circle 'o'),
    on Jack Davis, Tennyson and Socrates   91

3 **Displaced acts of writing**   149
Displaced acts of writing   151
Anti-'craft' in the context of Western capitalist cultures   159
A brief look at the avant-garde and 'Western' spirituality   162

Contents

Rereading 166
The eternal work-in-progress 169
I'll tell you a story 173
Uses of knowledge/data/detail in writing and reading 177
Where I sit in the process: working with Ali Alizadeh to produce
    an anthology of Persian poetry 181
Auguste Lacaussade 186
On the track of desiring and absence: a letter to McKenzie Wark
    on his email correspondence with Kathy Acker 196

4 **Sublimated displacements in read texts** 205
On sublimated displacements in read texts (including a gesture
    towards a thread in the definition of 'displacement') 207
A rage for verse: the case for Charles Walker as the author of
    the first volume of verse published in Western Australia
    (1856) 211
Further reconstruction: coda or prologue? 217
Henry Lawson: national displacements 222
On Peter Carey's *True History of the Kelly Gang* 229
The collapse of space: on Lisa Gorton's *The Life of Houses* 238
Inevitability and searching in John Mateer's *Elsewhere* 245
Tales of place: Barbara Temperton's *Southern Edge* 248
On *Contemporary Asian Australian Poets* 251
On the poetry of Janet McAdams 255

5 **Emplacement** 259
Corthna, Carraiglea, Anchor Lodge – from Schull Journals 261
More from a Schull Journal 268
On the trauma of writing 'Seeing' and the urge to create
    a poem after journeying out on the Mizen 277
Further extracts from a Schull Journal 281
On painting and poetry 286
Also from a Schull Journal 288
More 'ways of seeing' 292
From a Schull Journal 295
Terms and conditions of writing place? 302
Irredentism 306
Being back: place, storage, waste and (un)belonging 309
Storage 312
From storage towards waste 317
Finding belonging? 322
The place of reading: the geographical context of (re)reading
    The Jindyworobaks and self – from Schull to an imaginary
    Australia 325
Harvesting the grass (from a Schull Journal) 334

Last entries in Volume Three of a Schull Journal 337
Coda: changing route (October 2015) 342

6 Weirding place/Anti-bucolic 349
'Below the surface-stream, shallow and light' – transferences of
   weirding place 351
Working with Thurston Moore on the poems of a *Remarkable*
   Grey Horse 361
Eclogue failure or success: the collaborative activism of poetry –
   working with Charmaine Papertalk-Green 366

7 Appendices 387
1: Some answers to missing questions 389
2: Manifesto against rapacity 399
3: Landfill: a conversation between John Kinsella and
   McKenzie Wark 401
4: Notes on globalisation and neo-Luddism 410
5: Graphology mutations 11: reclaiming 'dwell' 414

Bibliography 421

FIGURES

1   Under Walwalinj concretion poem installation – gravel rocks, shadecloth, and 'civilise falsehoods' intact on paper   *page* 50

2   Under Walwalinj concretion poem installation – heat cracks and an abandoned bungarra hole and torn 'civilise falsehoods' on paper   50

3   'Tunnelling spiders' charcoal on concrete pathway concretion poem installation   51

4   Literal concrete … was already there – added charcoal   54

5   Literal concrete again … charcoal washed off after a week   54

6   Paper was recycled afterwards   55

7   Stick-writing on firebreak at JTG   55

8   Weighted down in high wind   56

9   Christmas spider came along of its own accord, after I placed the poem between 2 trees!   56

10   Another graphology in a different form   57

11   One of many gravel concretions that change shape over days   58

12   No Bauxite Mining at Morangup!   62

13   Where the north-east ant colony centres itself   66

14   Plato's Cave is rarely locked and secured. The Red Shed   66

15   Raingauge, witness to the fading green   66

16   On the firebreaks colour is queried. Someone has passed over. Tread. Trod.   67

17   Carried by the wind from firebreak (though 'secured') to wild oats   67

18   Logo – not! JTG, acronym for…?   67

19   Firebreak scratchings poem – Loss Rarity Bird Gully…?   67

20   Oak Park – resides: saline walk   70

21   Oak Park – trees as bare bones 1   71

22   Oak Park – trees as bare bones 2   71

23   Oak Park – trees as bare bones 3   72

24   Oak Park – dry lake bed aghast   72

25   Oak Park – calling the absent birds   73

26   Copy of Randolph Stow's handwritten draft (obtained by
     John Kinsella from Stow's sister Helen in 2011)   352

ACKNOWLEDGEMENTS

Most of this book has been written over the last few years with the singular purpose in mind of challenging and reconstructing notions and versions of place, and it has not seen the light of day until this publication. Even the personal journal material was written in the context of creating this book. However, I have drawn relevant material that I have written over the years in other contexts into the orbit of the overall text, and wish to acknowledge the publishers of those pieces. Further, some of the work has been extracted and published in journals and books (primarily the poems), and other pieces have appeared on the blog I share with Tracy Ryan, *Mutually Said*, and a website of 'mine' that hasn't been updated for many years. Thanks to *Southerly* (journal and *Southerly* blog), Penguin Books, Arc Publications, McKenzie Wark, Tracy Ryan, my twelve-year-old son Tim, Gerard Greenway, Matthew Frost, Andrew Kirk, Phil Mead (eternally good advice and input on pieces here and there but also as a vital and supportive force), Niall Lucy (I miss you and I miss your brilliance), Fremantle Press, the 'blind' referees/readers of this text (I listened always, addressed where I felt I could without losing my intent or altering my strange way of seeing, and hurtled headlong where I felt impelled, and take responsibility for this!), *New England Review* (which carried a short extract from my Lacaussade essay along with some of my translations of his poetry), *Poetry* (Chicago) online, *Australian Book Review*, BBC 3, *Cordite* (online poetry journal), *Index on Censorship*, Work & Tumble, *The Kenyon Review*, Picador Books and *Denver Quarterly*.

PREFACE/SYNOPSIS

This book is concerned with the complexities of defining 'place', of observing and 'seeing' place, and how we might write a poetics of place. From Kathy Acker to indigenous Australian poet Jack Davis, the book touches on other writers and theorists, but in essence is a hands-on 'praxis' book of poetic practice. Using essay, journal entry, 'review', and *commentary* on writing and ecology, it examines issues of belonging and displacement from many angles. Arguing for a 'polysituatedness' of presence in which all places we have been part of (lived in, visited, 'stayed in', 'inherited' through parents and grandparents, even imagined) become enmeshed with a sense of belonging (or not), the book posits an alternative model for participation in community and landscape. It does this in the context of a worldview of 'international regionalism', in which international lines of communication are seen to enhance regionality. Considering modes of belonging and community ('agoras') in conjunction with issues of isolation, the book traces a journey from 'home'[1] at Jam Tree Gully in wheatbelt Western Australia, via a range of personal experiences and intertextual interactions/readings with other works, to Schull, in West Cork, Ireland, where a consideration of belonging and land is read through ancestral displacement via famine and the politics of empire. However, this is not a work of history, but of subjectivity as it affects 'ways of seeing'. It is also about the 'making' of poems out of 'place', and questions the politics of making and the politics of place. Displacement, but with constant, renewing and 'replacement'.

The book attempts to create new ways of writing and reading place, without getting stuck in the mud – that is, it's a 'real-world' take that crosses field-guide and critique. Subtextually, the book is an enactment of my well-documented process/belief/theory known as 'international regionalism'. How do we belong to a place? How do we communicate with where we've come from?

---

1 In Robert Frost's 'The Death of a Hired Man' from *North of Boston*, Mary says: 'Home is the place where, when you have to go there,/ They have to take you in.' But Warren responds 'I should have called it/ Something you somehow haven't to deserve.' I cannot answer for the veracity of either comment!

The book is in seven sections:

1. **On place itself** – this section presents a series of definitions and personal backgrounding of research and creative endeavour in the field. Place, agoras, 'international regionalism', displacement, collaboration, activism, 'polysituatedness', theoretical underpinnings are all considered and contextualised. Further, a redefining – even rejection – of the word 'place' itself is explicated in detail. Activism in the context of the Noongar writer Jack Davis and a personal move towards concret(ion) poetry are discussed. This section finishes with a personal 'encounter' with the nineteenth-century Western Australian bushranger Moondyne Joe, in whose zone of influence we live and on whom I collaborated on a book with the late Professor Niall Lucy.

2. **Where we are** – a manifesto of polysituatedness with considerations of Alfred Tennyson's poem 'The Kraken', an extensive and 'close' reading of Jack Davis's life and poetry texts in the context of *the polysituated*, and a tangential but relevant engagement with Socrates and animal rights. This section also con/tests aspects of Marc Augé's *Non-Places: An Introduction to Supermodernity*.

3. **Displaced acts of writing** – this section is not about definitions but about illustration. Why craft is an ineffective measure of the poem, how spirituality and the poem dialogue, a series of commentaries on 'reading' texts from childhood to the present day with an emphasis on creating an experimental novel when I was a teenager, and tracing its unusual history through to its recent publication as it moved through different zones of intactness and rehabilitation, an 'introduction' to collaborating on a collection of Persian poetry and how not being in Iran affects this process, a biographical overview of the nineteenth-century poet Auguste Lacaussade (La Réunion and France), and finally a long piece on McKenzie Wark's and Kathy Acker's intense email correspondence that came out of a brief physical interaction and the displacements (alluded to) that emerge from this.

4. **Displacements in reading texts** – this section includes reading of writers of place such as Ouyang Yu (historical-social-cultural geographies), the mysterious and elusive Charles Walker, the great Australian short story writer Henry Lawson, Peter Carey (*True History of the Kelly Gang*), Lisa Gorton (*The Life of Houses*), Western Australian poets John Mateer and Barbara Temperton, a reading of an anthology of Asian-Australian poetry, and a brief comment on Native American poet, Janet McAdams.

5. **Emplacement** – issues of migration, 'return' and belonging are explored through the Irish-Australian nexus, with a focus on animal rights, 'nature' and human presence in 'landscape'. This is what I see as the gravitational (off-) centre of the book. Journal entries are interspersed with essays considering diverse but interconnected issues, always coming back to the idea of 'place',

ranging from questions of 'storage', 'irredentism', the Australian Jindyworobaks (white appropriators of 'Aboriginal Australia' in the 1930s–1950s), Travellers and 'nomadism', and the issues behind writing 'local' poetry from 'outside' and 'reversioning' *The Táin*.

6. **Weirding place/Anti-bucolic** – 'Below the surface-stream, shallow and light' – transferences of weirding place: through the eye of Randolph Stow's 'Still Life with Amaryllis Belladonna' we approach and reproach the pastoral and arrive at a reading of *STILL Moving* by Marc Atkins and Rod Mengham; *and* Working with Thurston Moore on the poems of *A Remarkable Grey Horse* and 'New Stuff': *Et in Arcadia ego*, not; *and* Eclogue failure or success: the collaborative activism of poetry – working with Charmaine Papertalk-Green.

7. **Appendices** – a radical ecological manifesto and 'answers' to 'deleted questions'. This section contains background 'data'.

A POLYSITUATED ODE WITH OCCASIONAL, DEMI-BOUSTROPHEDON

'Odeshock'
   Walter Murdoch

We're all in it together, this place, that one too: passing through,
born here, born there, overlays and more: tangential butterfly effect
out of the flailed hedge, the Romanware they lift from the development site
to validate the new-build, historically contextualised, coprolite – dinosaur shit.

I am never in once place when I am here. A composite. Hup two hup two
hup two three four, the beat tattooed on walkways and paths, squaddies
behind the copse, the burgeoning coppiced growth, the white butterfly
seen here and simultaneously flitting across the top paddock

at Jam Tree Gully 14 600 kilometres away. I fixate on the shott, my eyeline
dragged out to plumb the shallow chalky soil: I see shapes – letters even –
and the write is up and down and kerned. Or from a different angle
wrapper chip a and trees hollowed dead from bats rabbits envisage I.

So taking the longhandle to the bridle path, to the footpath, to the highway,
I trudge my way across the shire. At home. The percussion of shot, the rapid
expansion of gases, so much kinetic energy, the falling body equation dug
up from memory, the hole all the way to China. I chit-chat along the way –

some welcome me, some turn away, some concentrate on a speck on the ground
!moment the share me let they'd only if them as much as me fascinates which
swap notes, learn ground and air and water by rote, make metaphysical leaps.
I could drop dead mid-stride, and unless they cart me 'back', I'll lie in this soil,

in their soil, with generations and shifting texts, written in and forgotten,
but there. I would listen for the tawny frogmouth in my insomnia: sound a dark
vision on my event horizon, the blooms heavy in the York gums but not
so spectacular as: barn owl ripping out of the halflight or, say, a deer

nosing at the window of a house – our house temporarily – on the edge
of Gambier village, with stalagmites of ice doing their threat thing, nailing
us down as if we've no choice: never to step outdoors, to become cold dust
in a house so characteristic of mid-Ohio. Here, back from my walk

into the fens, I say this. I know it. I hear all the voices, and can pick out
each and every one: those passing through, those lodged deep, those visiting
and determined to say. Magpies, white swans, grey heron, pigeons, mallards,
foxes, badgers, all the birds that will leave when summer passes. Return.

PART I

On place itself

A PERSONAL INTRODUCTION ON PRACTICE AND CONTEXT INCLUDING SOME EXTERNAL CONSIDERATIONS OF 'PLACE'

I am concerned with issues of presence and their cost but also affirmations. My prognosis is that we all occupy many spaces at once, and that no 'place' in human terms is a place isolated from others. Since moving to Jam Tree Gully, 'our place' on the edge of the Avon Valley and on the edge of the Victoria Plains wheat-growing area of the Western Australian wheatbelt, and arguably on the very north-eastern nub of the Darling Range, we have been much concerned with issues of belonging, possession (and its antithetical dispossession – our presence *costs*), 'property' (which I reject) and, indeed, being on the edge of community.

In the main, we don't 'fit in' due to environmentalist, anarchist, pacifist and vegan politics, but we co-exist with neighbours and community, and work to encourage respect for the spatiality of other living things. Our work here is about the agency of the non-human as much as the human. Yet the picture is not of locality, but of a number of locales and 'locals'. There's the town of York and its environs about 80 km from here where we previously lived in the shadow of Walwalinj, there's Cambridge and the fens with which we've had a long association, but also the Mizen Head Peninsula of West Cork, Ireland, where we lived for just under a year and which has strong ancestral associations for both me and my partner, Tracy Ryan. The complex policy of heritage comes into play, and is put to the test in many ways. The 'polysituated' model of place I developed there is a subset of the 'international regionalism' I have subscribed to for twenty years.

All of this book is about the 'making' of poems out of 'place', but it's also a book questioning the politics of making and the politics of place. Displacement, but with constant renewing and 'replacement'. In an essay entitled 'Pastoral and the Political Possibilities of Poetry' (published in *Southerly* in 1996, but later collected in *Spatial Relations*),[1] I wrote, 'What I find particularly fascinating is the

---

1 John Kinsella, 'The Pastoral and the Political Possibilities of Poetry', *Southerly*, 56.3 (1996), pp. 227–9; reprinted in John Kinsella, *Spatial Relations. Volume 2: Essays, Reviews, Comments and Choreography* (Amsterdam and New York, Editions Rodopi, 2013), p. 74.

displacement of the lyrical "I" with the externalized, supposedly non-referential "I".' In a poem published in *The Hierarchy of Sheep*[2] entitled 'Displacements', 'Each tree' is a 'totem for a dead soldier' (trees planted in King's Park, Perth, in memory of soldiers who died on battlefields thousands of miles away) – the sense of connected disconnection has been at the core of my modus operandi for a writing lifetime.

It is worth noting that recently, in a review of three poetry titles including my own *Vision of Error: A Sextet of Activist Poems*,[3] the brilliant linguist, poet and critic Javant Biarujia pinpoints 'displacement' as the nexus of the three titles he was reviewing. He observes: 'Displacement is apparent both geographically and textually', and later notes, 'Expatriation as a kind of displacement.'[4] Displacement is an echo in this book, not an 'unpacked' (hideous term) word or idea: it's a gesture towards the issue of belonging or desire to belong, or, prevalently, an 'inability' to belong or a *loss* of connection. The aim of this book is to show place, belonging and 'international regionalism' alive in negotiations with writing location, social and biological environment, and 'space'. It's a poetics of polyvalent connectedness and disconnection.[5]

---

2 John Kinsella, 'Displacements', in *The Hierarchy of Sheep* (Newcastle upon Tyne, Bloodaxe Books, 2001).

3 John Kinsella, *Vision of Error: A Sextet of Activist Poems* (Melbourne, Five Islands Press, 2013).

4 See Javant Biarujia, 'X Marks the Parataxis: Louis Armand, John Kinsella and Jessica L. Wilkinson', *Cordite Poetry Review*, 1 May 2014, http://cordite.org.au/essays/x-marks-the-parataxis/ (accessed 18 March 2016).

5 This book has been written out of a compulsion to tell a story, to collect together strands of thought about a crisis of (un)belonging and a sense that one's place-identification is polyvalent, as people are themselves in having multiple subjectivities – there are few unities in life. Thus, it is not a survey of all the works on 'displacement' and 'place' out there. In fact, in running through the final typescript, and reading an essay of Seamus Heaney's in which he discusses 'displacement' (Seamus Heaney, 'Place and Displacement: Recent Poetry of Northern Ireland' [Grasmere, Trustees of Dove Cottage, 1984]), I came across a book by Stan Smith entitled *Poetry and Displacement* (Liverpool, Liverpool University Press, 2007) in which definitions of displacement run contrary to what I argue, but unsurprisingly have distinct overlaps with it in theory if not practice. That book is on my to-read pile, but I have looked at the pages of the introduction available on Google Books (a wonderfully truncated perversion of intention which is a displacement, in my sense, in itself, though maybe not in Smith's), and I feel compelled both to respect his purpose and to differentiate mine in many if not all ways. In the reworking of spatiality that follows the mass displacements of the twentieth century in Europe, a particular consideration of belonging and exclusion necessarily 'evolves'. It's a sophisticated argument I haven't considered yet, but will, though I will take a quote from the introduction to establish my approach in contraindication. Smith writes: 'Contemporary poetry repeatedly transforms the physical and demographic displacements of modern history into a "poetics of exile", metaphors for the very condition of the human in a decentred cosmos and an increasingly and ironically centralised world order, offering a vision of what might be called metaphysical and ontological displacement – displacement as a condition of being itself. By and large, this poetry of displacement has sought to make accommodations with its predicament, forging manageable, if predictable, identities from the shifting allegiances of a globalised culture, where no claims on loyalty and allegiance can be seen as absolute'

I am always searching for new ways of seeing the poem because the poem, for me, ultimately escapes into an aesthetic curatorial space I deeply doubt, and see as materialistic. I am looking for the poem that divests itself of its own value as art and works as a conduit for change, as a nodal point for activist motivation and outcome. The poem of place I write to divest itself of Place. The capitalisation is important here. While looking for specificity and integrity and the value of the local – the pantheistic – I am also looking for the universal signifier, the ground rules for conservation, preservation and tolerance. Specific templates that apply everywhere. Place, for me, has become a paradoxical condition of presence.

(pp. 9–10). I hope in what follows I show that it is possible to create a non-'manageable, if predictable' identity/ies by refusing to be incorporated into global paradigms because of historic, social, or cultural compulsion. This doesn't mean it doesn't happen, but it does mean I refuse. Smith then moves into a brief discussion of the Seamus Heaney essay that led me to a search in the first place (because I did not have a copy of the book with me in my present translocation), an essay which I strongly contested, in which Smith notes, citing Heaney's essay: 'Poetry now, he argued, sought to speak from what Carl Gustav Jung called "a displaced perspective", in which the self could move beyond particularised allegiance while managing to "keep faith with … origins", "stretched between politics and transcendence … displaced from a confidence in a single position by [the] disposition to be affected by all positions, negatively rather than positively capable"' (pp. 10–11). In this I identify something of the polysituated ('all positions') but am wary to identify the (nation-) affirming ends it's put to. A critique must contest the problems of origins themselves – and Smith notes earlier that '[n] eighbourhood can also provoke mass murder, inter-communal pogroms, ethnic cleansing, as in the "great hatred, little room" which Yeats attributed to his native Ireland' (p. 8) – and all that comes between a 'start' and a 'finish', but there are many ways of reading origins and there are many potential finishes. A polyvalent reading of all movements of self and what constitutes the self (including its 'others'), and maybe an acceptance that a poetry text is never as fixed as we might imagine, changes the dynamics of these readings. Smith continues his comments on Heaney's essay with: 'Heaney's double sense of displacement, as both a physical and psychological condition, is central to the present study.' My sense is exponential – not of Heaney, but of all markings of place and placement in our lived lives and our expressions of those lives. There is a politics of reclaiming place that the capitalist-military machines of the state would control or from which they would exclude us. This is not a book about the choice or lack of choice around where and how we choose to live, but a consideration of what constitutes how we make place and are made by place. From a vegan, anarchist, pacifist point of view in which all monetary exchange, all tools of most societies utilised to engender 'stability' and appropriate behaviour are to be challenged, in which the basic exploitation of animals for human gain is seen as being morally wrong, the point of departure in such discussions is going to be different. I notice Smith uses the word 'unplace' – his usage is contextual; mine is generative from writing poems of unbelonging. Maybe it comes from living on stolen indigenous land and not knowing how to resolve the problem of restitution outside the personal? Displacement is a question of the agency of plants and animals, of human disruptions of the non-human, and of textual breakdown and reconfiguring. Heaney's is a model for the conditions he experienced and observed, but it is a human model and a local model that projects outwards, as most poetry of place and culturality regarding the 'self' does. But we need to break those anthropocentric ways of seeing, and we need to break colonial manifestation into its myriad, complex, often counteracting splinters: e.g. my Irish family escaping Famine conditions and British exploitation to become settler-pioneers who in a variety of ways re-enact the colonial modus operandi they experienced.

International regionalism: a personal case

International regionalism is an expression I coined some twenty years ago that gained traction in the mid to late 1990s. In essence, it entails facilitating international lines of communication while respecting regional integrity. I have written extensively about the nuances and applications of this 'ideology' in earlier books,[6] but in essence it is a way of enhancing an understanding of the local by opening up writing and conversation about that local/locale to comparison with other localities. I was developing these notions concurrently (I was to discover) with the Global/Local movement, and in fact found that my own poetry was being used by scholars such as Professor Rob Wilson of Hawaii Pacific University, who observed 'his poetics remains largely tied to the problematics of representing a more multicultural, multilingual vision of Australia and the Asia/Pacific region'.[7]

International regionalism includes the possibility of critique of the global; it does not confer legitimacy upon global economics and marketplaces, whether by approval or disapproval. While economics plays a necessary part in understanding place, it is secondary in this study to the need to create understanding through written and oral models that highlight what makes a place unique while contextualising with comparisons to other localities, thus highlighting difference as much as similarity. Not only a respect for difference, but a belief in its necessity, is a traceable outcome of poetry and other writing of place. There is a recognition of the 'other' as marginalised but legitimate voice in any given place. A multi-layered and cumulative picture of place emerges (historical, communal, changing environments). In this picture relationships between people, between people and animals and plants, people and the material of the land itself, necessarily change and alter hierarchies of interaction.

At the University of Western Australia, where much of the work I have been doing on place was facilitated (along with Curtin University, Western Australia, where I now work on issues relating to 'place'), there is a strong lineage of contextualising the local within the national and international. The literary journal *Westerly* was founded with the intention of presenting local writing within the framework of other Australian, as well as South-East Asian, writing. There have been focuses on the Indian Ocean, or innovative poetry, and indigenous Western Australia. Professor Bruce Bennett was a pioneer of Australian 'place' studies in literature and positioned Western Australian writing within the 'Australian Compass'. So much of the published writing of Western Australia

---

6 See John Kinsella, *Disclosed Poetics* (Manchester, Manchester University Press, 2007); Kinsella, *Activist Poetics: Anarchy in the Avon Valley*, ed. Niall Lucy (Liverpool, Liverpool University Press, 2010); Kinsella, *Spatial Relations. Volume I: Essays, Reviews, Commentaries and Chorography: 1 (cross/cultures)* (Amsterdam and New York, Editions Rodopi, 2013); and Kinsella, *Spatial Relations. Volume 2.*

7 Rob Wilson, 'From the Sublime to the Devious: Writing the Experimental/Local Pacific', *Jacket*, 12 (2000), http://jacketmagazine.com/12/wilson-p-pomod.html (accessed 18 March 2016).

has been concerned with the specificities of place, especially differentiating or qualifying experience in terms of the country as a whole, the region and the world. Peter Cowan's stories, Sally Morgan's *My Place*,[8] Kim Scott's break-through fictions of contact and its consequences,[9] Dorothy Hewett's Great Southern mythologies[10] and Jack Davis's political and social declarations and reclamations[11] are all part of a mosaic of identity-spatiality. At work are textual and intertextual poetics. This is the background from which my own concerns have emerged; when combined with a keen interest in literary theory, travel and a political *poetics*, an 'international regionalism' began to form.

I have carried such concerns with me to the various locales I have written and edited in/out of around the world. When I co-edited the British liter-ary journal *Stand* in the late 1990s/early 2000s with Michael Hulse (Leeds University), we had the task of retaining the journal's 'Northern' identity and increasing its international appeal and reach. We edited special issues on various countries and regions, from New Zealand to America to Africa, and on a variety of movements and ways of reading texts, 'postmodernism' through to various thematic groupings. The journal became a conduit for broader conver-sations and connections, building on its long history as a vehicle for translated literature. In my own creative practice I have for many years been recreating new poetry texts out of poems from other languages, in which poems function as completely original poems, informed by the place in which I worked on them, and also translations informed by the places embodied in the originals. This is a concrete and practical example of international regionalism at work: one place communing with another; the presence of both is relevant. The poem becomes a device for a comparative poetics, rather than a response or representation of a specific place (or set of places) experienced by one poet alone.

This extends further into collaborative work, such as that I have done with Ali Alizadeh in *Six Vowels & Twenty-three Consonants: An Anthology of Persian Poetry from Rudaki to Langroodi*.[12] This project produced translations of original works as well as an enhanced dialogue with Iranian poets and critical writing *on* this process. I see the creative and the critical as inseparable.

Editing has had a fundamental role in the pragmatics of my international regionalism. When I founded *Salt* magazine in Perth (first issue June, 1990) it was with a desire to create an overtly internationalist journal from the world's so-called most isolated (state) capital city. I saw no reason why the avant-garde movement of Language Poetry, for example, wasn't as relevant to those in the

8   Sally Morgan, *My Place* (London, Virago, 1982).
9   Kim Scott, *Benang: From the Heart* (South Fremantle, Fremantle Arts Centre Press, 1999) and *That Deadman Dance* (Sydney, Picador, 2010).
10   Dorothy Hewett, *Collected Poems* (South Fremantle, Fremantle Arts Centre Press, 1995) and a number of plays.
11   Jack Davis's collections of poems, plays and autobiographical writings (see bibliography) are all characterised by these qualities.
12   Ali Alizadeh and John Kinsella (eds), *Six Vowels & Twenty-three Consonants: An Anthology of Persian Poetry from Rudaki to Langroodi* (Todmorden, Arc Publications, 2012).

Perth suburbs or out in the Western Australian countryside as it was to New York and San Francisco. And this proved to be the case, with many of the luminaries of that movement publishing in *Salt* magazine. *Salt* eventually grew into a major international publisher of poetry, criticism and more recently fiction.

One might say the same regarding my international editorship of the *Kenyon Review*, based in Ohio. The point isn't being an editor but rather an 'international editor'. From wherever I am living, I act in that role. If I am out in the bush in Western Australia, surrounded by kangaroos and echidnas, I retain and carry out that role. More recently, in London, I agreed to sit on the ecological panel at the Parnassus International Poetry Festival because decisions made in, say, a heavily polluting country like the one I come from affect people's lives on low-lying islands where rising sea levels mean destruction. The regional affects the international, and vice versa. I lived for some time in the mid-1990s on the Cocos Islands in the Indian Ocean, islands only fifteen metres at their highest (sand-dune) point, and mostly not much above coral-reef level. Rising seas will have drastic implications there.

The creation of poetic texts is necessarily informed by many obvious external referents and many un-noted or undetected subtexts. An anti-war poem written in Afghanistan might be about a very local tragedy but it is also written against the backdrop of international relations. A local image is broadcast on a national and international screen. A poem of dispossession written by the great Aboriginal poet and playwright Jack Davis is also a poem of conflict told locally but inevitably read by those informed by other conflicts, immediate and historical. That's the practice of reading and no doubt was part of Davis's consciousness when writing his poem/s. A poem, a story, a novel or a piece of critical writing doesn't exist in a vacuum, and cannot be analysed as such. It will have a political and ethical charge to it.

To create genuinely interactive models of international regionalism I would also concurrently be writing poetry and stories of those places and entwining them in manuscripts that embody notions of 'regional integrity' and 'internationalism'. A poem of Ohio next to a poem of La Réunion: can they speak with each other? Is it only the (same) author who allows them to speak or are there linguistic and topological, political and ethical factors that over-ride these? Is it a question of knowledge and exposure? Does lack of knowledge of a place one is writing about impair or even lead to potential offence? How can one claim belonging to and with a 'place'? What of people passing through places, of migration, of displaced persons? Do we need to create new 'models' of what constitutes place to allow for these variables? The critical and the creative are woven together.

Templates

Though 'templates' are a vital component in my creation of poetic works, they are less so in my attempt to formulate alternative approaches to place. But though not specifically explored herein, I think it is vital to mention them because they certainly form a backdrop, a subject of consciousness for any consideration of place I make. By templates I mean pre-existing models such as earlier literary, scientific or cultural works and structures/formats, and templates customised and created for specific needs. The purpose of such templates is to create a temporal and spatial conversation across (often strongly) different cultural co-ordinates, that clarifies observation through slippage and stark contrast. Resetting Milton's *Comus* in the age of genetic engineering, for example, creates contrasts that are stark, deeply ironic and yet strangely apt. The adaptation of *Comus* I did for the Marlowe Society and Christ's College in Cambridge (later published as a book)[13] was performed with the original as part of the Milton 400th anniversary celebrations, and aimed to stimulate discussion of contemporary ecological issues.

To give further examples from my own writing and poetic practice: I have used pre-existing works such as Dante's *Divine Comedy*,[14] Milton's *Paradise Lost*,[15] Sir Philip Sidney's *The Old Arcadia* (The Countess of Pembroke's *Arcadia*),[16] Thomas Lovell Beddoes's *Death's Jest Book*[17] and Edmund Burke's *A Philosophical Enquiry into the Origin of Our Ideas of the Sublime and Beautiful*.[18] I have also used works such as *The Thousand and One Arabian Nights*[19] and Sherwood Anderson's *Winesburg, Ohio*[20] as looser templates or departure points for my prose fiction work, *In the Shade of the Shady Tree*.[21] Examples of templates created specifically for works are best found in my own practice in collaborative works, of which there are numerous examples.

Collaboration has informed what I do

Again, this does not directly concern the arguments of this book, but I think it is relevant to point out that so much of my thinking has developed out of working with others in creative projects. The anarchist communalism of collaboration is essential to me. Further, most of what I write has been read and often discussed with my partner Tracy Ryan, whose own writing practice so interests me.

Collaboration in the creation of texts is a cornerstone of my poetics. In the ten-year collaborative project *Synopticon*,[22] written with Louis Armand,

---

13 John Kinsella, *Comus: a dialogic masque* (Todmorden, Arc Publications, 2008).

14 I consulted *most* translations (into English) in print, plus various editions of the original Italian.

15 John Milton, *Paradise Lost* (Oxford, Oxford University Press, 2008).

16 Sir Philip Sydney, *The Countess of Pembroke's Arcadia: The Old Arcadia* (Oxford, Oxford University Press, 1999)

17 Thomas Lovell Beddoes, *Death's Jest Book* (1829), ed. Michael Bradshaw (Manchester, Carcanet, 2006).

18 Edmund Burke, *A Philosophical Enquiry into the Origin of Our Ideas of the Sublime and Beautiful* (Oxford, Oxford University Press, 1998).

19 *The Arabian Nights: Tales from a Thousand and One Nights*, trans. Richard Burton (New York, Modern Library Classics, 2004).

20 Sherwood Anderson, *Winesburg, Ohio* (Toronto, Dover, 1995).

21 John Kinsella, *In the Shade of the Shady Tree: Stories* (Athens, Ohio University Press, 2012).

22 Louis Armand and John Kinsella, *Synopticon* (Prague, Litteraria Pragensia, 2012).

principles of over-writing and rewriting meant the text remained unstable until a given section was completed, with each of us reworking and extending the piece of poetry emailed by the other. The template in essence was a set of principles. More recently I have collaborated on a work of ecological poetics with the American poet and theorist Forrest Gander, *Redstart*.[23] This is an interactive, interdisciplinary, cross-genre work of which Joan Retallack has written: 'It should and does raise important questions about poets' ventures into textual and extra-textual ecologies.'[24]

The collaboration is built around an email exchange of poems written *in situ* in our various locales and mapping the topography of our 'seeing' – creating poems of spatiality. The exchange digressed into commentaries on process, essays on the notion of an 'ecopoetics', and in my case an essay on writing poetry out of tracking the movements of a group of yellow-rumped thornbills on 'our' West Australian wheatbelt/bush block over a year ('The Movements of Yellow-Rumped Thornbills: Twittering Machines'). The essay and associated poetry, which appears separately in my *Jam Tree Gully* book,[25] templated on Thoreau's *Walden*,[26] investigates the thornbills' patterns of interaction, movement and territoriality, bringing into question human notions (and impositions) of property and ownership. Special focus is given to a comparison between the territoriality of thornbills (as observed) and that of magpies. Substrata of 'theories of presence' referenced through Bachelard's 'desire lines', and Proudhon on property, bring into question rights of 'ownership'. This is set against a background of colonisation, indigenous dispossession and the politics of 'mapping'. The outcome is an expression of desire to apply these observations to a poetry of place in which prosody is a direct outcome of that observation.

But though the Thornbills essay was my work, the book was also intrinsically a collaborative expression in the same way the proposed project would be. In an interview with Andy Fitch of *The Conversant* I noted:

> *Redstart* only could be completed collaboratively, for the very reasons Forrest outlined. The whole concept of so-called Western subjectivity gets imbued with concerns of ownership and possession. But here we've attempted to broaden the scale of our collective responsibility. Personally, I don't think there's much purpose to a poetry that doesn't try to make things happen. This world is damaged, and becoming rapidly more damaged. Though I've never felt that's irreversible. Individual components may be sadly irreversible. Still in a general sense, things always can get better. This book provides a blueprint for identifying problems – not only how they present themselves in ecologies, but how we actually talk about them. Because how we talk leads to how we change and rectify problems. Forrest's poetry always has offered an active textuality. The active world gets embodied in

23 John Kinsella, *Redstart: An Ecological Poetics* (Iowa City, University of Iowa Press, 2012).
24 Joan Retallack, reader's report for Kinsella, *Redstart*.
25 John Kinsella, *Jam Tree Gully* (New York, W.W. Norton, 2012).
26 Henry David Thoreau, *Walden and Civil Disobedience* (London, Penguin, 1986).

the words of his poems. These words aren't just representations of things. They almost become organic matter, be they rock or be they vegetable. This organicism extends across all existence. Ideas of the 'I' or the self long have been challenged in poetry. That's nothing new. But the way we've described our relationship to place ... I think we do need a new language. Not saying we've found that new language, but we've explored new parameters of representation.[27]

Up-close: the local and spatial poetics

With my work *Divine Comedy: Journeys Through a Regional Geography*,[28] I argued in poetry and introductory essays that I was using an 'up-close' approach to place – to observe in great detail a specific area (5.5 acres) over a long period (three years). Furthering the use of the 'up-close', the minutiae of the local, I argue that every detail of one's surroundings when writing affects the text itself. In essence, we cannot understand a poem without at least considering (or searching for) the conditions of its creation. In the essay 'The Poetics of Gradients', I track the effect 'hills' and 'slopes' have on the poet and the making of poems:

The poem 'Red Hill' from Bronwyn Lea's *The Other Way Out: New Poems*[29] combines a clarity of affirmation offset by a haunting sense of threat that comes no matter the familiarity of climbing the same hill over a long period of time. It's a poem that has the language of gradient (though it doesn't specifically use that more mathematical descriptor/definition), poised to a point of absolute concision:

>   – the acute
> angle of the world
> to my cheek
> rising as if to slap or kiss me
> even to lie
> down I am near
> vertical & filled with steep
> inclination –
>   ('Red Hill')

The physicality of both body and spirit and the intellectual processing of the co-ordinates are deftly handled. The hill *we* live on would not 'slap or kiss me' – it is too stony and too 'defiant' to register me/us in that way. Strangely, I know no matter how long I walk its slopes, it will resist me, but do so with indifference. Such 'gradient' poems will always deploy words like 'steep', 'incline', and terms related to angles ('acute', 'obtuse', 'right' ...) but the point is how these terms

---

27   Forrest Gander and John Kinsella with Andy Fitch, *The Conversant*, October 2012, http://theconversant.org/?p=1469 (accessed 18 March 2016).
28   John Kinsella, *Divine Comedy: Journeys Through a Regional Geography, Three New Works* (New York, W.W. Norton, 2008).
29   Bronwyn Lea, *The Other Way Out: New Poems* (Sydney, Giramondo, 2008).

relate to the emotional, social, political, and ethical space of the poem. The specificity matters and brings different impressions. An acute angle makes for a very different tension to an obtuse angle: not only in the different description of place, but also, obviously, in the effect the angle has on how the reader 'feels' the description.[30]

But the methodology I am proposing also demands praxis. This poem from my *Jam Tree Gully* collection serves as an example:

> You choose which inclines you show a friend,
> or which inclines your friend might favour –
> but he makes his own way through the stones
> and up the steepest parts and is interested
> in what happens when water runs and cuts.
> He is interested in gradients and erosions,
> in the pair of eagles that come at dusk
> before shutting down, in the echidnas
> eating the termites that hollow York gums
> that '28' parrots nest in. He is interested
> in bringing his boys up here to plant trees,
> to labour. I offer to pay them and him
> but he declines, saying he would like them
> to labour where the steepness sharpens
> seeing and their work will grow without end.[31]

Because I live and write on a hillside bush block, the land's gradient is a dominant factor. The book *Jam Tree Gully* is full of 'slope', 'incline', 'gradient' and so on, and these actualities dictate the way one behaves inside and outside the poem. From these 'earlier' experiments in applying the topology and topography of 'place' to the creation of literary texts and considering both how they affect the prosody and content of a poem, and how the poem in turn influences future consideration of and relation to that place, I am developing an interactive spatial model through which poetics becomes 'active' rather than merely 'aesthetic' and 'responsive'. In turn, this feeds back into conceptualisations of 'place' the poems come out of and evoke. The practice of thinking the poem is inseparable from the place it comes out of (I would argue, no matter the subject matter).

Poetry as activist agent: intervention and negotiation of public and private spaces

In previous books I have argued that poetry is a form of activism and can act as an intervention or space for negotiation in day-to-day life and issues, and I maintain that stance here. Poetry that works in both public and private spaces as

---

30 John Kinsella, 'The Poetics of Gradients', in Kinsella, *Activist Poetics*, pp. 146–8.
31 John Kinsella, 'An Elective of Gradients', in Kinsella, *Jam Tree Gully*, p. 32.

a means for change and discussion can be used as a tool of 'policy' through which pragmatic, non-invasive and egalitarian outcomes are possible, even essential. Writing and art have a debt of duty to improve the wellbeing of people's lives and the health of the environment as much as feeding a sense of 'cultural worth'.

I think poetry and other creative writing can be *directly* interventionist (at the *moment* of event, not only by *gradually* changing opinion). A single or communal poetic action (poetry can be so deeply communal) can alter public opinion over, for example, an ecological issue, by bringing public awareness – but also by 'discovering' a language that articulates what is often lost in hard science or diluted by journalism. In essence, poetry or any creative writing becomes a tool of immediate change and also long-term diplomacy (which might well be how most writing is configured by scholars). In my essay 'Poetry as Means of Dialogue in Court Spaces'[32] and a keynote speech, 'I Am Not a Bagman for the State-run Justice System' delivered at the Supreme and Federal Courts Justices' Conference in Perth, 2007, I made an argument for the 'liberation' of public space through the use of poetic texts. In the essay I wrote,

> [a]s one dedicated to 'openness' in public architecture, I see courts as places of communication and exchange more than as places of control … It seems essential to me that if there is to be any reconciliation in Australia between Indigenous peoples and migrant Australians (all other Australians), it needs to start with the court buildings themselves and, obviously, the law. These are places, and this is an issue of place. All zones of cultural activity wherever they are in the world take on the qualities of 'place' in terms of presence and the denial/refusal of presence. Government institutions can become non-place if we wish access and they refuse, and place if they open themselves; they can be deadening in terms of orientation and their apparent non-place status (though all cultural activity and history they overlay cannot be deleted, however much their makers and operators desire it, but this is all semantics [I contest Marc Augé's work in so many ways]). The oral and written poetry of Indigenous Australian poets is constantly concerned with law and justice and should be incorporated into all legal buildings in consultation with the traditional owners of the land.

I have been engaged in various public arts projects in which poetry presented in public space is used to offer avenues for reflection, affirmation and liberty even when the nature of that environment (such as a court building) is naturally perceived as oppressive.

Challenging national identity through the regional: an environment of discussion

A critique of nationalism has always informed my poetics. This critique is centred on nationalism's propensity towards exclusion, domination and

---

32 John Kinsella, 'Poetry as Means of Dialogue in Court Spaces', *Cultural Studies Review*, 13.2 (2007), pp. 98–114.

colonialism. My identity comes out of the place I write, and the place I feel a responsibility to conserve and write out of, and in some ways write to. A conversation with place. I feel in a similar way about the fens of England, where I have also lived. There is a conversation to be had between the wheatbelt and the fens, the dry and the wet.

Departures from pre-existing models and new nomenclature

In order to create an environment of discussion around local and 'national', regional and international issues of literary language usage, one requires a model to work through and against. I have engaged with Gaston Bachelard's *The Poetics of Space*[33] in critical and creative ways for the last decade. Bachelard's landmark work is necessarily configured through a Eurocentric *way of seeing* that I find inadequate when looking at space through wheatbelt Western Australian experience. In questioning not only how we 'position' an object with regard to a referencing object, but even what might constitute that referencing object itself, the entire notion of spatiality is shifted. When we consider how 'prospect' and 'refuge' are contingent on the landscape in question (forests, open/cleared land, hills, salt scalds) our sense of how we approach the intimate changes. In exploring the 'desire lines' of sheep, kangaroos and humans, the flight paths of birds, the variable nature of dwelling[34] depending

33 Gaston Bachelard, *The Poetics of Space*, trans. Maria Jolas (Boston, Beacon Press, 1964).
34 As with Augé's discussions of (non-)place(s), so I refute Heidegger's notion(s) of dwelling, from its foundations to its application. It is not within the scope of this book to demonstrate that challenge (that will be the subject, in part, of a future work), but when one operates from a different language of belonging and exclusion, in colonial, ecological and vegan-ethics distress, inevitably even the origins of terminologies become distorted and displaced. Language is polysituated, and my meanings absorb any readings I encounter, and in this deployment of words and knowledge I stand as a distorted representative, but I also overtly refute. For my review and engagement with Heideggerian 'dwelling', especially with regard to poetry and the poetic, please see Appendix 5 of this book.
    As an aside, for the time being, consider these lines from the lecture 'Building Dwelling Thinking': 'The truck driver is at home on the highway, but he does not have his lodgings there; the working woman is at home in the spinning mill, but does not have her dwelling place there; the chief engineer is at home in the power station, but he does not dwell there. These buildings house man. He inhabits them and yet does not dwell in them, if to dwell means solely to have our lodgings in them.' Martin Heidegger, 'Building Dwelling Thinking', in *Basic Writings*, ed. David Farrell Krell (rev. edn, London, Routledge, Kegan and Paul, 1996), pp. 347–8. In a literal sense, the sleeping cab has become an integral part of the Australian long-distance truckie's life: 'his' home on wheels. The caravan, the motorhome, all become building *and* dwelling (filled with their own transient-permanent 'poetry'). In the war between Ukraine and separatists, an engineer/plant operator has set up home in a power station to keep it going and because his own home has been shelled. Slave labour often means the spinner sleeps in the basement factory he or she 'lives' in (most Western clothing is sourced from such conditions of production!) Though Heidegger might take us to a closer understanding of dwelling, to dwell, dwellers and the relationship to the built and the cultivated, of belonging, the analogies mentioned in the quote displace purpose and praxis (even if I take out of context). Heidegger says, 'We do not dwell because we have built, but we build and have built because we dwell,

on conditions (heat, flood, lack of rain, not being on the power grid) an entirely different imaging of space evolves. In conjunction with indigenous knowledges of 'country's' temporal and spatial configurations, we create a model for a radically different *language* of spatiality.

Acknowledging (and engaging with) the work of Paul Carter, I politically and ethically differentiate my practice in numerous ways. For me, the intactness of the thing-in-itself, as autonomous entity with agency, is primary, even in the contexts of its communal functionality. For instance the 'natural' world can be considered outside human uses of it or interactions with it. I have long been writing poems *in situ*: poems created at the moment of 'event', poems that could only be written at the time of 'witness'. In her introduction to a special issue of *Southerly* entitled *shared space brokered time: paul carter*, Jennifer Rutherford notes, 'Carter's theoretical and speculative thought unfolds in a poesis *in situ*.'[35] While I do not challenge this (and, rather, affirm it), for me the creation of a poetic text at the moment of event is both part of the residue of that event or place in a material sense, and also operates outside its temporal reality. In other words, the poem transforms and removes as much as it records, comments or negotiates. The poem itself becomes a space for the regional and the international as part of 'timeless' human endeavour. The question of what constitutes an image and how images are made is pivotal. Does the image have a 'dynamism' of its own, as argued by Bachelard, or is the image always integral to the space of its creation?

A further 'evolving' and continuing innovation is a more straightforward one: to contest the use of terminologies such as 'nature writing' and 'landscape' in spatial poetics discourse. In an interview with *Overland* magazine (online) with reference to my book *Jam Tree Gully*, I said:

> I consider myself a writer of the environment – an ethically and politically motivated writer who perceives each poem, each text I write, as part of a resistance against environmental damage. 'Nature writing' is a concept too tied up with validating the relationship with the (Western!) notion of self, of egotistical sublime, of the gain the self has over the 'nature' s/he is relating to. This privileging is a problem. Which is not to say I have a problem with the inevitabilities of the anthropomorphic, if that necessarily brings about greater respect for 'nature' than would arise without it. So once again, it's relative.[36]

---

that is, because we are dwellers' (Heidegger, 'Building Dwelling Thinking', p. 350). Yes, but what of the politics and ethics of dwelling and having knowledge of the implications of our dwelling (and being dwellers)? Heidegger was a member of the Nazi Party until 1945 – his utterances are lost in this, before and after.

35 Jennifer Rutherford, 'Editorial', *Southerly: Shared Space Brokered Time*, 66.2 (2006), pp. 5–6.

36 Clare Strahan, 'Writing is Always a Political Act: An Interview with John Kinsella', *Overland*, 21 September 2011, https://overland.org.au/2011/09/writing-is-always-a-political-act/ (accessed 18 March 2016).

Reconsidering 'landscape'

Approaching the issue of 'landscape' in terms of human markings, signatures and intrusions, contesting configurations of 'seeing' in poetry and painting necessitates reconsidering oral poetries and songs in local traditional and indigenous cultures. A commentator such as Chris Fitter in *Poetry, Space, Landscape: Towards a New Theory* rightly conveys the differences between 'landscape' and 'landskip' and uses each for very different modes of 'conceptualising and perceiving natural space'.[37] How does his work, for example, function as a template for very different conditions of art and poetry in a different time and different part of the world (Fitter tracks landscape painting from the fifth century BCE to seventeenth-century England in poetry and painting)? For all his acuity, Fitter essentially *limits* his model by conditioning 'landscape-consciousness' through 'nature-sensibility', which as he notes has 'broader, historically local structures'[38] and other confinements of terminology, such as 'ecological', which I would argue are category errors. Even historically and geographically specific models need to be applicable to the ecological/'landscape' conditions/crisis of the modernity in which they are written/constructed, especially when millenarianism is prevalent and a 'landscape of action' is part of the consciousness.[39]

It is neither possible nor desirable to separate a poetics of space from the broader (and ever multiplying) considerations of space in human geography and society. Neither is it desirable to ignore basic philosophical questions around the subject, such as, say, contesting or confirming Leibniz's point that space is 'an order of co-existences, as time is an *order* of successions'.[40] John Urry's essay 'Social Relations, Space and Time'[41] is as much a departure point for an analysis of the phenomenological questions around the making and interpreting of poetry and poetic texts as it is for the 'human sciences'. Urry draws on John Berger for his purposes of arriving at an argument regarding the 'spatial-temporal' 'supported by considering the processes of capitalist accumulation within the sphere of production',[42] just as the poet might draw on Berger in considering the social (and environmental) conditions of a poem's subject. Extending the application here is part of the innovation.[43]

---

37 Chris Fitter, *Poetry, Space, Landscape: Towards a New Theory* (Cambridge, Cambridge University Press, 2005), p. 10.

38 Fitter, *Poetry, Space, Landscape*, p. 9.

39 Fitter, *Poetry, Space, Landscape*, p. 302.

40 Gottfried Wilhelm Leibniz, *Political Writings*, ed. Patrick Riley (Cambridge, Cambridge University Press, 1988), p. 13.

41 John Urry, 'Social Relations, Space and Time', in *Social Relations and Spatial Structures*, ed. Derek Gregory and John Urry (Basingstoke, Macmillan, 1985), pp. 20–48.

42 Urry, 'Social Relations, Space and Time', p. 31.

43 Reading David Harvey's *The Condition of Postmodernity* (Malden, MA, and Oxford, Blackwell, 1990), I am struck by the usefulness of the terms 'temporal displacement', 'spatial displacement' and 'time-place displacements' as anti-colonial paradigms in considerations of over-accumulation under capitalism. This is obvious enough, but it is his use of the term

Whether engaging with de Certeau or Marc Augé, with *The Táin*[44] or *Buile Suibhne*,[45] I seem to trace the impact of the idea of *place* on place itself. Stories, the marks and impacts we make on country/land, the living and the dead, the accumulation and tabulation of data of observation, passing through and staying – all are variables in the account we make to ourselves of belonging, and, disturbingly, exclusion. The poem becomes a means of processing these often conflicting variables and of considering the de-mapping of constructions we impose on place (cartography is an overt, 'occupying' version of spatiality of place).

'spatial displacement' – which, Harvey tells us, 'entails the absorption of excess capital and labour in geographical expansion' (p. 183) – that particularly interests me in the context of this book. The horror of this reality (Harvey is one of Marx's more acute readers) might effectively parallel discourses on the displacements of peoples, language, marks and memorials of presence, and 'industry's' desire to create a monopoly of presence in which difference is fetishised as 'diversity' in the market to absorb possible subversion, threat and contrary interests. To keep growing profit.

So the polysituated self is 'permitted' to exist insofar as it adds *variety* to the market conceptualisation of the individual (of the participant in the market). Industry desires variety in the scope for the production of (different types of) goods, allowing for the ongoing expansion of capital (and labour), but only if this is contained within the social control such economics requires. The military, paramilitary, police and mechanisms of social policing will see to this, defending the capitalist modus operandi. The complex layering of place-in-self is not allowed full expression, as this involves a constant decolonising and reclaiming of the very space of 'geographical' expansion, and thus becomes subversive and anti-capitalist. Polysituatedness is an expression of pluralism that cannot be modelled from a 'central' point; neither can it be controlled by the defence mechanisms of an 'open market' that are ultimately about wealth accumulation for the few at the top of the production pyramid.

In displacing Harvey's observations as I do here, I enact a textual reterritorialising of space which I acknowledge is problematic. Harvey is on track when he further notes, 'And it also follows that the manner of prior occupation of the spaces into which capitalism expands, and the degrees of resistance encountered there, can have profound consequences' (p. 183). Indeed. And it's how we interpret these consequences that matters – and how we might prevent the intrusions in the first place, and non-violently support resistance to these grotesque expansions. The asylum-seeker detainees on Nauru, imprisoned by the Australian government, if they are ever released from their living hell, will probably (if legislation goes through parliament) be prevented from ever coming to Australia, though, of course, they could purchase Australian products wherever they are (outside Australia) and benefit Australian capitalism and the system that has rejected and oppressed them. As scholar Steve Mickler has said to me in private correspondence (16 November 2016): 'Brought to them by a "globalisation" that wants no limits on the mobility of profit-making but massive limits on the mobility of those dislocated by it (i.e. refugees).' Such rejection by industry, and by its proxy, the state, of a polysituating self that encompasses all the possibilities of who we are and who we might be inevitably leads to brutal othering and criminal abuse of fellow individuals and peoples. I am also thinking of Derrida's salient observations in *Spectres of Marx* here.

44 *The Táin*, trans Thomas Kinsella (Oxford, Oxford University Press, 2002).
45 *Buile Suibhne*, http://www.ucc.ie/celt/published/T302018/.

POLYSITUATED(NESS): INTERNATIONAL REGIONALISM

I was recently invited to an event to discuss 'home and away'. I think it is part of a series located in different cities. Anyway, that's an aside to my present point, which is not a critique of that event, but rather a comment that comes out of the issue central to my critique of the idea of 'place'.

I do not believe one is ever 'at home', because home is composed of so many variables, so many intersecting, bisecting and even parallel lines, that the expression only serves as a very general 'location' device that evokes certain sentiments around particular geographic co-ordinates. My problem with 'home' is that it is too often deployed as a term of ownership rather than belonging, and even when belonging is a passionate component, it is so as a declaration of exclusion, possession and security that necessarily denies such claims by (some) others. Who belongs 'at home'? Those with whom we grow up, whom we allow and admit, who came before us (and how far back)?

I argue that we can only discuss connection, belonging, participation and even visiting or departure in terms of polysituatedness. We are always polysituated. If we are talking of where we primarily live (though we might go away, travel, or relocate and return every now and again), we are talking about so many different notions of connection and alienation that 'home' simply doesn't answer the condition. At Jam Tree Gully we are talking of the idea of a 'block', the idea of fences or absence of fences, where a space begins and ends, overlaps with near and far neighbours, the act of accepting visitors, intrusion by the Shire (and its roadside herbicides), relationship with the town (some distance away) where we shop and collect mail, and the relationship of this town to the regional centre. Then there are animals and plants (endemic and 'introduced'), topographies and histories (dispossession, 'settler', 'claim' and so on), all of which create alternative configurations of that place.

Place is never static, and place is always defined in contradictory as well as complementary ways by outsiders and insiders, by those with vested interests and those indifferent. The horror of bauxite mining companies trying to develop their 'claim' south of Toodyay is a case in point: their configuration of a home that is not theirs in terms of dwelling (they can't live in their proposed excavation), and a home which is the colonial target of a multinational conglomerate, is redefined in terms of run-on 'local' benefits for those who claim it as their place of dwelling. Shires love such propaganda to fuel their own dreams of personal and collective profit focussed through improvement to living conditions (theirs). As such pressures come to bear on place, 'home' unravels into the polysituated: we take in information about our condition from sources far from our dwelling, well and truly outside locale. We create intersections with dialogues in Europe, Asia, Africa and North America. At the same time, racist and exclusionary forces are at work in confining and enforcing sub-communal notions of home (to keep it 'white' or to resist certain religions or to keep out 'greenies'). We polysituate where we sit, as much as when we travel or if we have more than one 'home-place'. I am never 'away' because I am concurrently present in a nuanced and polyvalent discussion of belonging and exclusion.

One is cast as 'UnAustralian' for opposing the mining industry; living in a corner of Europe you're asked, 'when will you be going home?' even if you have ancestry in that place. We live at a single point and all other points at once: the damage done locally affects the wellbeing of the entire biosphere. That's the core of international regionalism: respect for regional integrity (whether we claim 'region' as home or not) and a desire for international dialogue. I celebrate difference and respect the customs of the local, but I also know that 'home' is a construct that suits the coloniser, as the colonised are forced to have loss of dwelling become a definition of home where other ways of conceptualising connection (e.g. totemic) are re-hybridised to accord with Western colonial notions of participation, connection … and ownership or non-ownership.

This is the way the disgraceful intervention into indigenous communities worked in Australia: home security becomes security for the nation to control and exploit what it sees as its materials of presence (people, minerals, soil, air, animals, plants etc.). That's home. And then the complicit (so very many of us) leave and look back with nostalgia, judgement, new knowledge, and still the desire to own memories and even the future of where one is not literally. They, also, are polysituating. It's not always a generative and positive paradigm.

Polysituatedness works as a model within international regionalism for recollections and embodiments of earlier places of dwelling in one's life, a family's existence, or that of an entire community. When migrants describe their present 'home' as entailing aspects of their previous 'home', or refugees while embracing 'opportunities' in their new place/zone of enacting 'living' recall what they have been forced to leave behind and seek to recreate the complexities of that previous space in the new space, a polyvalent model of belonging is created.

Polysituatedness 'explains' these chronologies and spatialities, but takes things further by questioning the very nature of origins, birthplace, allegiance and loyalty, rights by soil, and other expressions (legal or conjectural) of connection to a particular set of geographical co-ordinates and their claimant communities. It also allows for a way of seeing entirely outside 'claim': connection through association, or even connection through 'place' itself making a claim on him/her/them. To occupy space and identify space are necessarily acts of definition, acts of establishing presence. To disrupt and twist Michel de Certeau's words (yet again – *unplanning* in my/this case!):

> The long poem of walking manipulates spatial organizations, no matter how panoptic they may be: it is neither foreign to them (it can take place only within them) nor in conformity with them (it does not receive its identity from them). It creates shadows and ambiguities within them. It inserts its multitudinous references and citations into them (social models, cultural mores, personal factors).[1]

It's the 'shadows and ambiguities' of 'home' that undo rather than reinforce its claims to certainty, permanence, and as a reference point, but they are also the generative, creative and spiritual values of any such desires. Dwelling resists these, place embodies them and space is the place of enactment.

From the city to the country, from pathways to trails, the rhetorical path is broken inside and outside the discourse. Parkour breaks the established paths and permissions through urban space; the sheep that breaks its desire line trails to the farm dam to escape, with its lamb, the predating fox, changes the rules it has established within the rules the farmer has established within the rules survey has established; and all the while there are preceding laws and rules of movement and belonging that are being negotiated without awareness (and sometimes with).

A brutal example of breaking the lines using 'freedom' as the outcome would be the trail-bike or four-wheel drive thrashing its way through bush, or following kangaroo trails and damaging peripheral vegetation. The 'freedom' of the place, of making use of, say, a broader definition of and catchment for 'home' (i.e. not where they dwell but within the region where the 'participants live') by these parties is an enhancement of their notion of freedom and belonging, adding value to their sense of home, while diminishing it in the animals and plants, in the ecos itself, and in those humans who live in something more akin to a symbiotic relationship with that place.

Movement through place becomes the constant in the polysituated equation as one leaves the dwelling in pursuit of food (or receives it via an online delivery service or has a friend pick up a take-away and bring it over, etc.), or as one contacts the water board or electricity company or phone company to bring in to one's space the allowances and opportunities of extended place, broader community. The lines are always alive, right to our transference to the funeral parlour in death, even if the ashes come back as a quasi-final statement of belonging.

1 Michel de Certeau, *The Practice of Everyday Life*, trans. Steven F. Rendall (Oakland, University of California Press, 1988), p. 101.

AGORAS

I have a poem in mind. A 'late' Jam Tree Gully poem. It will be entitled 'Agora' and I will get to writing its first lines shortly.

Why late? I haven't ceased being connected with Jam Tree Gully, nor have I ceased writing it. Maybe because I am thinking about its spaces in different ways now, from afar. I often write from 'afar', and as Thomas Bristow has highlighted, I write poetry 'in situ' and also 'at a distance', but as I have said to him, this is a complex equation and no binaries; they are both elements of the 'cloud' that makes up 'international regionalism'. And I am not simply co-opting a techno-fetish by saying 'cloud', though I might be ironising it. In essence, the ecologies I construct around the lens to biosphere collapse, the 'damage done' as I wrote in *The New Arcadia*,[1] are silhouetted through the costs of technologising. I have written 'neo-Luddite' texts in the past, deploring what I see as unnecessary technologies – especially those where 'product' takes precedence over 'necessity'. Under the rubric 'necessity' I would put certain medical advances, the basic technologies of sustaining human life (from the shovel and scissors through to, maybe, comparatively low-impact modes of transport that don't exploit animals). Advances in computer technology are largely driven by corporate capitalism, and change is interminably linked to sales and profit. All advances, all product developments, cost the biosphere. My aim is constantly to reduce the ironies of consumption – to own less, to 'change' product less, to resist the sales pitch. For me, place is entirely contiguous with how it is or isn't 'sold'.

Jam Tree Gully sits about fifteen km outside the town of Toodyay. There are no shops nearby and even the local wheatbin is no longer in use. It might, of course, come back into use, and is kept at the ready. Last season was a 'bumper' one, despite the ravages of climate change. Late, unseasonal rain and heat boosted the crops. The temptation to bring the bin 'back online' was probably strong. But the harvest could just as easily have been a disaster. From one extreme to the other.

---

1 John Kinsella, *The New Arcadia* (New York, W.W. Norton, 2005).

What's interesting about Jam Tree Gully and the other 'small rural holdings' in its locale is that they are gazetted 'rural residential'. This is to prevent large-scale agribusiness in the area. Of course, we are on the border of the shift in size in holdings, so within a very short distance are large farms with massive machinery. It's not a liminal zone, but the opposite. It's abrupt, and the vast wheat-growing area that is Victoria Plains tilts the psychology of those where we live into an anxiety about not being 'legitimate' big-scale farmers but rather small-scale hobbyists. The tension is rarely generative, and small bush holdings are readily cleared and cropped (though zoning-wise, such 'farmers' shouldn't be profiting from their land in such holdings), and industrial-scale poisons and other chemicals are readily used to 'control' the surveyed and apportioned spaces.

Jam Tree Gully sits alongside 'public space' (in essence a reserve). A couple of years ago the Shire, it its wisdom, 'control-burned' the area and destroyed stands of flooded gums that were hundreds of years old, with trunks wider than three or four or five people could link hands in a ring. The classic implosion of Australian fire 'protection' – the 'preventative' fires that destroy everything other than human homes, and sometimes (as in Margaret River a few years ago when over forty homes were burned to the ground), sometimes those as well. Fire is wielded as a weapon and is feared as the enemy. People build houses among trees, then pull the trees down because they are a fire risk. The irony is crushing and traumatising. We are all for fire-readiness and we practise it at Jam Tree Gully. In fact, I just wrote a poem about being absent when leaves need clearing from gutters, in case a spark or ember should ignite and thus destroy the house, if the horror of fire became a reality. Here's an extract, including the refrain, which is written in seven-syllable lines (because of the early Irish stanza in which I am working at present):

> Tomorrow, the Guru is going over
> to Jam Tree Gully to clear the gutters
> of dead, dry leaves. They congest
> without style, embellish with urge,
> the pragmatism of making a growth
> medium: in summer easterlies red dust
> falls as the true rain of modernity
> and tumbles into the leafy bed
> already set in aluminium conduits.
> If fire comes, a stray ember or spark
> will make rocket fuel of this process.
>
> No ember or spark has come
> to ignite dry-leaf coffins;
> No ember or spark has come
> to make heat that can melt steel;
> No ember or spark has come
> to leave soft beds of grey ash;
> No ember or spark has come

to the gutters, though it might;
No ember or spark has come
but you will clear leaves in case.

Thus even in absence, we are there. So 'late' isn't 'past', but something else.

At the dinner table Tim, just turned eleven, was talking with Tracy about Gaeltacht areas in present-day Ireland. He'd asked his teacher at school about whether the Irish dialect in Leinster was different from, say, in Munster. She pointed out that it didn't really have its own dialect, disturbingly, because that part of Ireland was so intensely colonised by the British (arable land as opposed to the rocky western areas that kept their Irish language to a greater degree). She was talking about a deletion of language right to the core. Indigenous language around what we call Jam Tree Gully was and is Ballardong Noongar. Noongar people are working to reconstitute Noongar language across the south-west, and in that process elements of Ballardong come into use, or are empha-sised by speakers with family background in the Ballardong language area.

Our neighbours at Jam Tree Gully are from many backgrounds, but mainly Anglo-Celtic or European 'stock', and loudly so. But no picture of ethnicity is that simple. What is simple, though, are declarations of rights and exclusion: those who object to 'boat people', those who make snide remarks about land rights, and those who differentiate on the basis of who is authentically rural and who is not. That's because a lot of land holdings in the region are 'weekenders', or belong to people who do a long commute to work in the city (about two hours' drive away), and those who live permanently local feel an 'investment' in having a 'say' that goes beyond paying land rates. But this rarely means conservation of bushland and native flora and fauna, or in fact any flora and fauna other than those which bring profit or pleasure (the pleasure of being a weekend farmer).

It's easy to accuse another of lacking authenticity, and it is common to find the accuser usually has a loathing of indigenous claims to land. The crisis of pos-session that haunts some of us certainly doesn't haunt others. Okay, a paranoid reading[2] of their day-to-day conversations would yield indicators of anxiety, but too often that's because of a fear of getting less than they feel they're owed. I have to point this out before talking about 'past' and 'present', about writing of the moment in the place ('*in situ*') and when absent ('at a distance'), which I've always found the most clarifying way of seeing. But not so much now. Absence is a lack of activism. And that's where 'late' comes in. I am writing from the Mizen Head Peninsula in County Cork, Ireland, in a retracing of origins that's tied up in readings of the 'rugged', less colonised/controlled, versus the arable colonised, an inversion I find necessary in order to complicate, not ease, my issues with dispossession and possession in Australia.

My paternal great-great-grandparents left after the Famine. Elsewhere I have written much on the dynamics of the oppressed becoming oppressors

2 Robert Ian Vere Hodge and Vijay Mishra, *Dark Side of the Dream: Australian Literature and the Postcolonial Mind* (Sydney, Allen & Unwin, 1991).

themselves. Here, in Cork's towns of the 'Anglo-Irish war', civil war and ambush, there are the unmarked graves of conflict's victims; there are also earlier Famine mass-burial pits, and the ghosts of British imperialism – and what amounted to a policy of genocide – emanate through local histories and Halloween, through gossip and national decision-making. The sanitising of colonisation is Australian default social policy. Jam Tree Gully of course is built on the bones of indigenous dispossession, and this can never be denied or minimised. So I am writing poems at a distance, but sometimes I dream terrible dreams and am actually at Jam Tree Gully, seeing the peripheral effects of poisonings by Shire and neighbours (herbicides, pesticides, rodenticides, fungicides), the shooting of roos, and the constant burning. A hallucinatory in-situ brought out of guilt of absence, ironic, since were I there at this moment, that's precisely what would be happening and what I would be resisting.

I write a lot about fences. And the removal of internal fences – we removed many (all) when we took 'custodianship' (temporary – the land is NOT ours and never can be) to allow free movement of wildlife, and to show our desire not to have 'property' marked by the keeping and control of animals. That's what fences do – they are a proto-capitalism. Interestingly, to prevent roos eating vegetables (hard to grow with the lack of water – we are not on mains water), we do 'fence' the plants in, but in such a way that the roos are not hindered in their passage, nor will they injure themselves if colliding with the barrier. Locals would say – rightly – kangaroos just jump the fences. However, having had to remove dying roos from fences when they have caught their legs hopping over and twisted/ broken their legs in the process, I have seen this theory come unstuck. Also, we had some very high fences at Jam Tree Gully when we moved in – built to prevent 'stock' climbing rocks and getting out. We removed interior fences (some of them were close together, which really traumatised local animals; they'd been put in by earlier occupants for coralling sheep and horses) and created entry points in external fences on the side of the reserve. Up front, roos move through two 'openings' between posts on the external fences running along the bitumen. It's interesting to note that they always select this mode of entry – a clear passage – rather than jumping fences, when given the chance. Now they will only leap the fences when startled – a fear reaction. So it's a complex picture!

Agora. How far I've strayed. Well, maybe not. You see, agora for me isn't just the meeting place of humans, the open space of the village or city where markets and political debate, arts moments and consensus might be enacted (an anarchist, I can only believe in consensus), but also a place of non-human interaction and consultation. There are many such agoras at Jam Tree Gully. Firstly, there are the insect meeting points: bees in the hollows of great York gums, or swarming and hanging in fuming teardrops from acacias before moving on to permanent residence; ants in their colonies with open spaces around their entrances/exits where conversations constantly take place when the colony is active; from which nuptial flights depart; in which fundamental decisions about threat and 'welcome' are enacted. There are bird agoras – down in the gully where the magpies define their territory in such auditory ways, tops of dead trees where pink and greys cluster before flying into the top right paddock to pick seeds between the replanted York gum saplings. There are the kangaroo day-sleeping places under trees, the open areas where they graze at twilight and just before dawn. These are agoras where decisions are made and we have moments and points within those interactions where we are permitted entry and even discussion. You learn to 'read' and be 'read' by ants, bees and roos. A colony of ants 'adapt' to your movements, and you to theirs. Roos learn that you won't hurt them, and come to the bedroom window at the same time and sniff through the flywire. They tell you things if you know how to listen. They will stay in their rest-place as I pass because the moment of passing is an agora-like moment.

At times I have suffered from agoraphobia. Not just being 'inside', but being inside Jam Tree Gully. Outside is threat, or rather, things I love and respect are threatened. Inside Jam Tree Gully, I feel roos and other animals, should they choose to rest or stay there, are safer than elsewhere. I have a crisis of boundaries and possession, of inside out (the name of the last book of my *Jam Tree Gully* trilogy):[3] I don't wish to own, but I wish to allow the agora its moments, its desire lines that bring all to the conversation which is safe ground, which is inside. This thinking is how my agora poem begins. I link it across to earlier years of addiction and being bullied, of anger and violent protest. I have been a pacifist for decades now, but when I was young I was aggressive in my objection to capitalism, to bullying, to imperialism, to greed. The agora was a place of confrontation for me. Sometimes I fear this kind of agora is always there to encroach on Jam Tree Gully.

I am not painting Jam Tree Gully as an island, it's not: really, I am talking about a concept of infinite space, of mutual respect, aid and sharing. Of the right of all animals. Of the biosphere to define its own terms outside the capitalist competition of human desire to thwart thanatos, to gain some kind of immortality. Hunters who blast away (illegally) in the reserve have the greatest lust for life. They have twisted ritual into greed for more-than-life. This is not 'living off the land' (which is a complex equation and is tied to totemic ancestral rights in so many ways), but making the land comply. It's about control: like the neighbour who, with green fingers, plants many new trees by poisoning and destroying vegetation and insect life already there.

Gardening is too often antithetical biosphere. Growth should be unhindered and define its own terms. Seeds should find their own beds. It's all about the seeds' access and rights to work it out! The threat to agoras. I have a reason. The 'neighbour' (some can be quite distant and rarely seen) who threatened to bury me (literally), because he thought I was one of those up-themselves, green, reading types who was probably from an inner-city suburb (whereas before living at Jam Tree Gully, I lived outside York, another wheatbelt town). I don't object to his anxieties, but I do object to his bragging about earning more

3 See John Kinsella, 'Inside Out', in *Firebreaks* (New York, W.W. Norton, 2016).

money than anyone else, and being able to bury people like me. He stood on my boots and had his face millimetres away from mine as he yelled it. I thought I was dead. The agora was bleeding, and not working for humans, the animals and plants were at risk as well. We negotiated our way out of the crisis and the result was a welcome to come on to 'his land' any time. The agora expanding? Probably not, but the crisis might mean that something survives out of it. The thinking is leading me somewhere. A poem about space and maps. I have been spatially configuring Jam Tree Gully to find my way around my own prejudices of location: privileging the 90,000-litre water tank we rely on, the granites from which I have a sublime view. Agora.

Here on Mizen Head Peninsula, it's the sea that preoccupies me. Crossing the sea, the cost of doing so, the distance between here and Jam Tree Gully, the power of water and swell. It is so dry at Jam Tree Gully, despite the burst of spring rain. Spring rain. There is only one season there now: it burns all year round. As I wrote in an early poem, 'things burn in rain'. But distance is not adequate in the configuring of place and belonging (or not, as I fear). Wedge tombs, stone circles, old red sandstone, passes through mountains, massive Atlantic swell, grey wagtails, dead hares on the roads. Each is a connector and each is an 'alienation'. The wedge tombs might be those of my ancestors; Australia, however close I feel to the land there, can be home only to my post-'settlement' ancestry.

I don't invest authority in ancestors (though I respect that others do), because it's a centralising of authority, but I do accept connection to place through inherited knowledge and experience. For me that's a deep science that matters: acquired knowledge. But knowledge that is trapped in a damage cycle is false knowledge. Knowledge needs knowledge and a map of awareness created: just because ancestors cut turf doesn't mean that it's a good thing to continue doing as the biosphere chokes on carbon! In the agoras of place, we need to meet with other knowledges, other life forms (as well as try to respect and read the inanimate). Each a co-ordinate for a psychotopology: a connecting through ancestors, literature, news, history, one's own life, with the passings through and the anchor points. I map here through there and vice versa. What else can I do? I belong nowhere. I live in my head but have obligations to the biosphere (I will respect as well as I can). I am writing agora poems. Not just a poem entitled 'Agora', but agora poems in which life draws up maps timeless and instantaneous. It's not Whitman's contradiction; that's too easy and lacks obligation. It's the contradiction of responsibility. To witness, to translate, to understand. To remove the fences. Open the agora; create a non-profit marketplace – a place of exchange.

REDEFINING OR MAYBE REPLACING 'PLACE': TOWARDS A THEOLOGY OF PRESENCE? CONSEQUENCES AND RESPONSIBILITY

> and the place has become part of us.
> Nettie Palmer (from *Fourteen Years*)

I have an intense dissatisfaction with the word 'place' and its definitions, as it applies to presence, location and spatiality when it is used outside poetic texts, and even, on occasion, if used 'uncritically' within poems. Though maybe it's impossible for 'place' to be used uncritically within a poem: a poem displaces language from its standard and 'user-friendly' contexts, and applies pressure to all words and their frameworks. The act of the poem leads us to question, whatever the intention of the poet. But is this in itself adequate? To question is not necessarily to act; to wonder is not necessarily to respond in a pragmatic, activist way.

Given that 'place' is a word highly flexible in application and meaning, and given that it's probably the word most repeated in my work since I started high school, this dissatisfaction seems to me worth my considering. The other day, I saw a real-estate sign outside a small rural property in wheatbelt Western Australia displaying the company name 'My Place'. I guess it works as a wish-fulfilment signifier, though one always has to wonder if there's a subtext of colonial reclamation, not only in the activity of buying and selling real estate, but also in acting as a rejoinder to Sally Morgan's well-known and important declaration of presence, belonging and identity in her story *My Place*. These things are never far below the surface out here.

'Place' for me, in my poetry, has been both an affirmation and denial of presence, but mostly an expression of uncertainty and discomfort regarding 'belonging'. I have explored its spatiality contingent on environmental, social and cultural variables, and I have used it as a tag of location. I won't note every usage as they run into the thousands. If 'snow', as the (fallacious) story/contrivance goes, has so many meanings to Inuits, 'place' is probably the most used, flexible and indeterminate while paradoxically being a specific term in all its versions in all languages.

Of course, specificity varies from language to language, and 'place' might have absolute totemic value in a particular language or dialect, only to become universalised or at least a little blurred when translated into another language, especially a language structurally very different. People of any culture that has 'named' a location, or a plant, or even replaced an animal's self-understanding with their own naming, will do so in a more informed manner if they and their family have a long-term connection with that place. Names come from seeing, listening and experiencing 'place'. The jiddy jiddy – Noongar name for willy wagtail – reflects the sounds made by the bird. You can hear 'jiddy jiddy' (or 'djiti djiti' or 'djidi djidi' or 'chitty chitty') as close approximations of a particular sound made by the wagtail (often described in broader terms as 'chatter'), and it seems to suit the bird's behaviour as observed by a human in close contact with its life cycle. The imposition of a Latin name might capture some characteristics (especially as they relate to larger connected groups), but always lacks some of the immediate, the local, the place of connection with that creature. Naming is intimately connected with the specificities of *place*.

In the light of this, I think the word 'place' should be constantly under review. Not only personally, but communally. It is the same, and it is different. For many years I have been hoping to establish wheatbelt forums in which indigenous people and non-indigenous 'locals' might meet in informal circumstances to discuss issues of presence and place. At the top of the agenda might be indigenous access to private property. In Britain, the network of public paths and bridleways across the counties allows a sense of belonging even when property laws exclude rights of abode and usage. Taking this as a starting point, one of the grim ironies of any discussion of rights of land when the colonial residues of the Crown need to be negotiated, rights of way might be developed into rights of non-intrusive usage. And maybe, hopefully, through negotiation, something further from there. This necessarily engenders new ways of thinking about property, ownership, traditional claims, moral presence and place.

Place is always less fixed than we imagine. That doesn't mean it's equivocal or non-measurable; this is the problem of the effete and not the pragmatic take on spatiality. Place is very real to those who know the co-ordinates and their content. No ambiguity, no doubt. But in a sense, that shows 'place' as a word and a concept as all the more limiting. Its strictures relate to the human. To the monadic and dyadic. To the self, the ego I, and the community in which many selves negotiate a collective presence. Place requires our presence, or an awareness that a human presence is possible. Even a place of animals is configured through a human understanding of connection. Sure, science fiction and fantasy, and literature in general, might seek to imagine place without human values, but in the end we are prisoners of the language we deploy.

I propose something very different. A portmanteau word necessarily falls into the trap of confinement relating to its constituent parts; an expression or sentence definition clearly relies on a reference to 'place' to differentiate. These are complicating problems. I detest looking at 'dictionary definitions' as the dictionary is the most subjective and limiting of devices (yes, think levers, pulleys etc.). But as an exercise, it might prove useful in this case. I have at hand the digitised *Oxford American Dictionary* of the early 2000s. Here are the noun definitions for 'place' with my 'challenges' listed immediately below each definition inside square brackets:

• place |plās|
noun
1 a particular position or point in space: *there were still some remote places in the world | the monastery was a peaceful place.*

[No matter how seemingly specific 'place' is, there are always a subset, subsets and points within those subsets. At best, it can only be a collective description of a point in space, as the 'point' in this context is not on a subatomic level, but on the visible level. Further, it suggests a static model of the universe, rather than one in which particles are not fixed. It's a steady state version of 'place'. A model of 'place' needs to be flexible, mobile and polyarticulate. But even that fails because 'place' is confining and any qualifications we add necessitate participation in the steady state theory of place. None of us is in or of one place. But neither are we a fuzzy inarticulate version of no-place in particular. We are literally and concretely all places. In this sense, there is a static quality to place: all points at a particular moment are locatable, though they won't stay there. So a paradox: place is fixed and moving at once. Yet in the end, we can't think of 'place' in the abstract – doing so allows us to relax while the planet burns and the biosphere collapses. Place has to be specific to particular points in time and space, and the consequences of 'being there' or noting it must be felt in what we write and how we act.]

• used to refer to an area already identified (giving an impression of informality): *we head to a disco – the place is pandemonium.*

[Though this is simply an example of a grammatical positioning, it nonetheless suggests connection, even belonging, and sharing that knowledge with others who either know that place or somewhere similar to create a comparative model of understanding, to 'get it'. Ironically, it relies on the fuzzy values of locality and connection – a bit like handing over one's rights in a Western democracy to representatives of the people – it relies on someone else's knowledge and identification of that place. Who defined the values attributable to that place, what their reasons were, and what kind of meaning is lost in the slippage over time and between individuals, is vague if present at all. Place (as in the example given!) resolves itself as a semi-familiar place of certainty, a hoodwink to lure you in.]

• a particular point on a larger surface or in a larger object or area: *he lashed out and cut the policeman's hand in three places.*

29

[More specific, though really a more up-close version of the first definition. Really, it becomes an issue of focus. How close do we focus?]

• a building or area used for a specified purpose or activity: *the town has many excellent eating places.*

[An issue of scale and focus, as we will discover most noun versions/definitions of 'place' are. So, are we talking about time, location, specificity and detail?]

• [informal] a person's home: *what about dinner at my place?*

[The informality belies the question of possession and property. Of accumulation of points in time and space, a set of co-ordinates of ownership. At one end of this scale we have greed; at another, rights of association that manifest in a spiritual connection.]

• a point in a book or other text reached by a reader at a particular time: *I must have lost my place in the script.*

[Time and location. Something measurable from point A to point B, a point along the way. We read at different paces under different conditions so the time taken to get to that place will vary, even for the individual reading/rereading.]

2 a portion of space occupied by someone: *he was watching from his place across the room.*

[The definitions in '2' are spatial and generally specific. In many ways, most of these prove pragmatic and functional usages of 'place'. The problems arise from the participation of the 'self' as opposed to the displacement, the area and volume occupied by a body. The notion that presence occludes other presences. Yes, 'you' are in that place, but you in yourself are the composition of many such places (cells, atoms, dust motes, clothes ... 'you' is all of these but also mutually exclusive). Once again, 'place' serves as a generalised non-specific variable of spatiality. Place is 'naturally' poly – it is already translocating, sharing, multifaceted, omnipresent, fuzzy, inconclusive. And that's the problem. There's no revelation in any of this – it's obvious as soon as we use the word 'place'. When I use it poetically it is to signify the polyvalent, but also the specific. It is inclusive. But in discussing its functionality outside the poem or literary text, we so often lose so much and subscribe to a politics of uncertainty and laxness. The reason we need to 'reinvent' the word is because in a time of extreme damage to the biosphere humans hide behind this generality, deploying it as a holdall and a certainty when it is in fact disguising hypocrisy, indifference or naivety. Place has to be activist in its very usage. Presence has implications. We need to associate presence with cause – place with intent and impact.]

• a portion of space available or designated for someone: *they hurried to their places at the table.*

[A marked point in space. The size of the designated area and of the entity intended to occupy it is roughly (at least) known. There is a causal relationship between the designated area and what's to fill it.]

• a vacancy or available position: *she won a place to study German at the university.*

[Along with the previous definition, this is a pragmatic and probably the most functional and least compromised usage of 'place'. Problems come in the context, not in the use of the term. And though one could say this of most usages of 'place', in this case it is regarding a particular point on a list/scale which is conceptually 'unoccupied'. It is a set of specific co-ordinates.]

• the regular or proper position of something: *lay each slab **in place**.*

[Specific, roughly or relatively accurately known quantities.]

• [often with negative] somewhere where it is appropriate or prudent for someone to be or for something to occur: *that street at that time was **no place for** a lady.*

[This is a case of 'place' as unresolved specificity. It is vague and its 'negative' implication is an extension of this unresolvedness (duplicity and intimation). One might argue that this is what makes the word 'place' so interesting in the poem: place's many meanings, its slippages, its failure to be what it claims. Rather than locating the specific, the word 'place' alludes and suggests. It functions as metaphor. It can also be the vehicle for bigotry and avoidance of 'consequences'. Whether this is good or bad is irrelevant to the argument; but in environmental writing, especially 'eco-poetry', this vagueness can become the speak-one-way-and-act-another school of poetics. So lament the loss of habitat and keep using the devices of modernity and consumerism that contribute to habitat decline. The computer and internet are glowing examples of this. Words are nothing without cause … and consequences. Otherwise they are entertainment attaching to zeitgeist. Think of the nature-writer who makes hunting and gun culture as one with the natural world. The environmentalist who shoots. I am sure they would readily put me in my place. And claim that during deer-hunting season the woods are **no place** for a vegan like me!]

• a chance to be accepted or to be of use: *the policy left no place for individual initiative.*

[Truly vague here. No room. No space. No slack. No place. How does place belong here? It does, of course. But place, when I write about being in Jam Tree

Gully at the same time as in Mohican, central Ohio, and the Cambridgeshire fens, and Schull in West Cork, is something more than 'place'. This versatile and fluid word serves polysituatedness well on so many levels, but I need another way of talking of such applications of place. Yet the echoes need to be there so all these place 'nouns' can resonate in the background. They are connected, but distant.]

• a person's rank or status: *occupation structures a person's place in society.*

[There are many versions of spatial place. An ordering, an arrangement, often an imposition, even a tyranny.]

• [usu. with negative] a right or privilege resulting from someone's role or position: *I'm sure she has a story to tell, but it's **not my place** to ask.*

[The social order. Place in my poetry is never about order; it's about rejecting the machinery that would create a list of definitions in the first place. It's about presence and obligation, cause and effect. The relationship between subject and object in this definition epitomises the flippant disregard with which place is treated. It is loaded with implication by context, not in itself. The use of 'place', in any version or meaning, doesn't fill us with trepidation at our impact on a point in time-space, its echoes outwards. It should.]

• the role played by or importance attached to someone or something in a particular context: *the place of computers in improving office efficiency varies between companies.*

[Hierarchies of functionality. To serve. To have serve you. To be servants of.]

3 a position in a sequence, in particular

[Variations on spatialities discussed. The hierarchies, desire for order – an underlying subjectivity (ordering the world as we desire it) threatens to well up and consume. Seemingly the most specific of definitions within the range of possible meanings, there's also this 'control' mechanism to negotiate and understand. Or at the other end of the 'scale', there is the point in space, the precise value. Place at its most orderly, even where applied to fractals!]

• a position in a contest: *his score was good enough to leave him in ninth place.*

[Space and value.]

• the second position, esp. in a horse race.

[Neither first nor third; it is what it is because it isn't what it's not.]

• Brit. any of the first three or sometimes four positions in a race (used esp. of the second, third, or fourth positions).

[Don't forget, this is the American version of the Oxford Dictionary. Cultural difference, cultural specificity, a sovereign state's difference from the originating cultural space of the dictionary (which is already a displacement of the 'original') at the time of writing. Something that might have bled across national boundaries, over the pond, that will pass through border checks and lurk in the murky recesses of Americana?]

• the degree of priority given to something: *accurate reportage **takes second place to** lurid detail.*

[Occupancy: the best room is taken. Someone better occupies the best place. Good management indicates you will be deprioritised. Space is accorded to the best possible placement. Place is interchangeable only insofar as one unit exceeds the usefulness or 'value' of another unit (of place).]

• the position of a figure in a series indicated in decimal or similar notation, esp. one after the decimal point: *calculate the ratios **to one decimal place**.*

[A known quantity. Resolvable within its own terms, or the terms we set for such actions and that remain consistent in their outcomes.]

4 [in place names] a square or a short street: *our new restaurant is in Hilliard Place.*

[Vague, but roughly a known quantity. We default into thinking we know what it is precisely, what value to attribute. We believe it, but aren't completely sure of what it entails until we see it. Not all 'places' are the same, but they are the same enough?]

• a country house with its grounds.

[In order to avoid calling Jam Tree Gully our 'property', as the government and authorities, as well as private industry, would define it, we call here (Jam Tree Gully) 'our place'. We don't mean to claim ownership, and only a form of custodianship – not in the sense of Ballardong Noongar people or individuals who might claim a custodial relationship to country, but in the sense of having an obligation to keep the space within a certain set of co-ordinates healthy and regenerative because no one else will, and, in fact, if we don't observe certain rules (paying rates, keeping firebreaks) the government and its enforcers would in the end not 'allow' our presence here. The irony is that our planting trees and encouraging flora and fauna and respecting the rights of the non-human do not garner respect or approval from those same policing bodies. This is a country house with grounds – a place – but one functioning in a very different way from the 'country house' we might read into this definition. It's a slim description, so why would we think of any particular 'country house'? Because this is a dictionary of the centre, of good human ordering, echoing from Oxford via America, old values made anew (though where the 'old values' emanate from requires a lot more legwork, and doesn't necessarily fit old-style colonial models or nation-making myths). This description, more than any other, epitomises why I am working towards not only a variant but an entirely different expression of 'place'. This can only be part of a book at least sub-titled 'Displaced Poetics', because I can't locate, and when I do, I realise the claims inherent in doing so. Furthermore, I am not buying into the having-your-cake-and-eating-it-too school of equivocation and fluid meaning that underpin so much 'place' theory. As I have said, for me all places I know (visited, read of, heard of, inherited, discarded) are the place of me. The place of me is part of the place of you and us. Set theory. Venn diagrams. Overlapping spirals. The areas in common and contiguous are only one plane of this interaction, this presence: without actively and constantly working through what makes us as we confront problems of environmental damage, we compromise the act of our resistance. The place/s from or out of which the rapacious themselves come are part of us, and we need to know them in order to resist and persuade. The common interest is place, the common interest is the biosphere (ironically the most precise and comprehensive of all 'places'.]

Leaving aside the verbs and adjectives (maybe aside from the 'derivative': 'placeless'!), we arrive at the origin of 'place', the word:

> ORIGIN Middle English: from Old French, from an alteration of Latin *platea* *'open space,'* from Greek *plateia (hodos) 'broad (way).'*

Inevitably defence and attack, *point de repère*, a militaristic subtext of protection and conquest underlie the origins of 'place', and one of control: public space/private space, right of way/*rite de passage* (the personal journey of discovery). Prospect and refuge, occupation and presence, colonisation and invitation, territory and confinement, freedom and restriction, immediacy and range, precedent and challenge, a priori and observation, security and risk, breathing space and snugness, the nest and the clearing. Location and access. Deterrent and vulnerability. Lists of association build and can go anywhere.

But this isn't my place because it's not yours. It can be our place if we work out terms, means, ways of sharing, crossing over, interacting. Retaining our identity. Noongar people are said to have offered to share with 'settlers' only to lose 'their place' in the material sense, but never in the spiritual sense. The whites began their pantheistic trick of spiritualising the new place they cleared and devastated and bonded to. Their place?

So, where do we head, what do we occupy, where do we dwell if not in place? Another word as substitute will necessarily lapse into the many definitions of place as well as have its own cascading meanings. Abode, dwelling … all have had their applications in the ways I am indicating. Presence, also. Zone is a favoured word in many poems I have written as it arises out of Tarkovsky and Apollinaire with his probable drawing on Ovid's Metamorphosis – *Prolem sine matre creatam*. Other poets favour it too. But what I am looking for is none of these. In some ways it's the unutterable as the name of God. To give it name, to define a meaning of 'place', is to offend and to diminish. This is an issue of respect. De-mapping, reconfiguring words into symbols on firebreaks, finding 'holes' in 'random' configurations of trees (I found another one recently – my first in years) and language-switching are all attempts to express the unutterable. They're all part of a concretion of sound and sight, or language and thought. Place becomes a void, an emptiness that is constantly being filled, that was never in fact empty. I am straying into the field of the figurative. Yesterday I saw an eight-foot-long mulga snake on the bitumen road, lifting its head and rearing as a car passed. Its inherent knowledge of place might have roads and even cars factored in, but cars aren't predictable, especially with local drivers who try to run snakes down. Spiralling and overlapping sets of space.

Am I suggesting 'place' is 'God'? In a way. But maybe more to the point I am saying we are place and all it entails. You, me, we … us. We are placed. And too often complacent. But we are emplaced and placing. Acts of placement. Inside and outside. Always fearing displacement. Being placeless. And many of us fear Godlessness. Many of us have no God. Many are placed by God to the decimal place. Place is a theology. It's a topography of presence. I … we … struggle towards light … a light broken open, too often cancer-causing, but a light we need nonetheless. The default is the poem, which is always an act of *témoignage*, if only in that it was created in a location in time/s that inevitably will inflect and reflect the conditions of its writing, its 'production'. Witness is about time and 'place', witness entails the reportable, the translated, the comparative and the inexplicable. What has been witnessed is often too horrific to be uttered.

The degradation of the biosphere by human activity ('place' rendered as habitus) is like witnessing an accident slowed down without anyone taking action. And what is said and written is slowed down too, syllables and consonants drawn out so that real speech, the expression of horror, becomes a subliminal message even to those who wrote it. Writing needs to be emphatic, immediate and terrifying.

Poetry is the unutterable transcription of 'place'. Too often when confronted with a reality of (eco) loss, the witness is too shocked to report, and/or readers/ listeners too shocked to receive. Poetry as criticism is too often forced into the space of the ineffable, into 'mystery' and intangibility, in order to prevent confrontation with reality. The poem becomes a secular prayer to give assurance, to gift back to its maker and reader, rather than declare a state of emergency and declare, irresolvably, a need for (pacifist) 'intervention' and change.

APPLICATION

In writing the non-human life of *where* we *live*, one might substitute 'class' with human denial of animal agency, and subscription to a hierarchy, a hierarchy between, say, the ant or beetle and the dog or horse, in their relationship with the human. Lately I have been reading Pierre Bourdieu, and though as usual I decontextualise and wander off at tangents (I like to wander), I wonder about the habitus of animals – its construction by humans, the carrying-over of habits from one 'class of human owner' to another (think of the stray dog starving and eating opportunistically, which retains its behaviour of 'eating everything in sight and not knowing when to stop' even when it is owned and well-fed by a wealthy leisured individual who pampers and perhaps substitutes it for a human family member).

In Bourdieu's analysis of 'Class Habitus and Political Opinions',[1] the carrying from one class to another of the markers of class origins can be figuratively extended to the way people treat animals, especially 'rescue animals'[2] or animals that have been given 'a better home', but also in the way humans treat animals as extensions of their own class's expectations (a small-holding farmer might 'understandably' wittingly or unwittingly handle the stock roughly because of

---

1 Pierre Bourdieu, *Distinction*, trans. Richard Nice (London and New York, Routledge, 2010).
2 I am not intimating that those who rescue animals aren't often impoverished; they do so frequently to their own social and 'financial' detriment. I would add that their experience of 'lack' and oppression would make them more amenable to caring, though the oppression of poverty can also lead away from animal rescue to a kind of resentful brutality. I also acknowledge that leisure and money are often not the variables at work in these relationships. However, I don't think any human–animal relationship is entirely free from the risk of exploitation in some form – that has to be discussed with the most ardent and committed activist (or just caring person). Of course, there is a massive difference between, say, 'using' an animal for emotional solace, and eating one! I think all of us who care about such things must be constantly vigilant about how we relate to those we protect. And it goes without saying that I fully support the rescuing of oppressed, deserted or at-risk animals. There are degrees. But human 'class' absorbs animals into its structures both real and conceptual.

stress, financial trouble and a lack of help, whereas the rich farmer with farm-hands doing the labour is more hands-off and has more time to pamper his gun dogs, as the cliché goes, with its seeds of dubious truth).

If what Bourdieu is suggesting is that the markers and imprints of class remain with us no matter how upwardly or downwardly mobile we might be, then it's worth considering the case of all animals in their relationships with humans. But I am taking the argument away from habitus and into issues of class oppression, though habitus is a marker of place, and so is class: a construct of social dynamics of place. No matter how well looked-after or even pampered a 'pet' might be, it will always be 'animal' to its owner's 'human'. The animal's habitus is constructed by humans for it, denying animal agency. Bourdieu writes, and I include more than I need to illustrate the point because I think there are rich grounds for further digression (which I intend to do at some future point, in some future place):

> The habitus integrates into the biographically synthesizing unity of a generative principle the set of effects of the determinations imposed by the material conditions of existence (whose efficacy is more or less subordinated to the effects of training previously undergone as one advances in time). It is embodied class (including biological properties that are socially shaped, such as sex or age) and, in all cases of inter- or intra-generational mobility, it is distinguished (in its effects) from class as objectified at a given moment (in the form of property, titles etc.), inasmuch as it perpetuates a different state of the material conditions of existence – those which produced it and which in this case differ to some extent from the conditions of its operation.[3]

For animals, the differentiation only accords with the conditions of tyranny under which they live as meted out by humans. The social conditions of the tyrant will only change the circumstances of their imposition, rarely the imposition itself; the animal remains unfree under all conditions. Cruelty and/or usage by those in less materially 'comfortable' conditions might well be the result of their own oppression, as opposed to the wealthier human with free time to lavish on their 'pets' (if not nature at large). Embodied class in my terms means the embodied human in their 'place', the zone they claim and locate, the expectation of control (over 'pests', over what is safe or desirable for them to allow). As we grow older, we are trained to progress from merely cuddling an animal to understanding that the teddy bear in real life can be life-threatening, that the pet dog can give you worms. A model of place that is human–animal 'class' aware is not part of the definitional array we have been considering. It needs to be. And the ineffable is as much part of animal self as it is human. And it carries the same problems in its being attributed to the (non-human) animal by the human. I think of pet cemeteries and pets living in their own shared funereal deathspace and the expectation of their own heaven, or if the human desire

3 Bourdieu, *Distinction*, p. 438.

holds sway, to join with their 'owner' in a larger, more accommodating heaven (where the earthly relationship won't become *déclassé* but *re-classé*).

In dealing with the habituations of 'place', in recognising the class structure of interactions between human occupiers of a space and the other life (seen and unseen) that is resident or passes through, we are confronted with the trauma of witness of our own prejudices, greed and denial. In Oldenquist's *Moral Philosophy: Text and Readings*,[4] we are introduced at the beginning to the terms 'Action Morality' and 'Agent Morality':

> *Action morality* is concerned with judging what people *do*, hence with the right-ness and wrongness of actions and with obligation, but it is not concerned with praise and blame, moral guilt or punishment. *Agent morality* is concerned with judging persons and therefore involves praise, blame, motives, intention, and perhaps punishment.[5]

In negotiating whether, in Oldenquist's words, '(a) people … mean well, but do harm that no reasonable person could anticipate' or '(b) people … mean well, but do harm because they are stupid and do not know that they are stupid' (I would prefer 'inept'!), we are engaging with what Oldenquist observes as being a case of our 'prais[ing] and blam[ing] people not only because they *deserve* it but also to *encourage or discourage certain types of behaviour*…'[6]

I bring these factors into the discussion because how we relate to our co-ordinates, variables and formulae for density, mass and volumes, the number of particles in a particular space, of area, that is, how we connect to unutterable 'place', is a moral equation. We judge ourselves and our neighbours by how clean and orderly they keep their abode, how their dwelling affects ourselves. The fire-hazard ramshackle house is a risk to our own, and so on. In some cases, intervention is called on: we publicly or to their face rebuke them, we praise them when they fix the problem, sometimes 'we' call on outside forces to rectify the problem. In extreme cases punishment is meted out. Action morality underpins what agent morality becomes. But when it comes to dealing with the disempowered in 'place' – animals and plants – we most often deploy an action morality that judges what people (ourselves) do, but does not attribute anything beyond the register of the case. We do not condemn ourselves for turning on the power switch, or for using aluminium whose extraction has meant the col-lapse of a jarrah ecosystem. But we are aware it's wrong. Insects live in our world of action morality. The well-intentioned person who is respected and judged as 'good' (treats their dogs well), is not considered immoral because they kill mosquitoes which most reasonable people would see as undesirable, even a threat. They are not judged as they would be if they killed a dog because it

---

4 Andrew G. Oldenquist, *Moral Philosophy: Text and Readings* (Prospect Heights, IL, Wavelands Press, 1978).
5 Oldenquist, *Moral Philosophy*, p. 2.
6 Oldenquist, *Moral Philosophy*, p. 3.

carried parasites and is a threat. One of these actions is encouraged, another discouraged. This is how we bend place to our social dominance, how we create the ultimate class system of oppression. We see our damage to the biosphere in terms of both action and agent morality, but mainly in terms of ourselves doing our best and therefore being less worthy of blame if not more worthy of praise.

Until an investigative and self-critiquing model of 'place', a new language of context, is created, these factors are written out. For such an expansive word, the definitions are limited and constraining. And humans would have it no other way, even drawing in the poem to give the impression of versatility, depth and ambiguity, to avoid culpability.

FOR BEAUTY'S SAKE

Poetry is so often less about 'Art' and more about 'activism' than many like to think. The poem that captures a glimpse of 'nature', or human loss, or reconstitutes a family memory through an object found while going through the belongings of a deceased relative, might seem to be little to do with activism but everything to do with art. That is, to do with the art of compacting, containing and adding 'depth'/layering/nuance to an idea so it creates conduits into other ways of seeing – creating the poem-object. But for me, rather than the 'artiness of art', I am interested in the poem's potential for resistance, not its compliance with a status quo, not as the production of what will become an *objet d'art*, a thing intended for wealth accumulation and pleasure. Of course, a piece of art can escape its creator's (or buyer's) intentions and become subversive through context. (Create its own place(ment) anxieties, interventions and distractions.)

Poetry works the contradictions, the paradoxes, and brings the incongruous and contiguous into alignment, rendering them into shape, pattern and interpretability. That's art, and this art is about aesthetics, about a hierarchising of perception into a spectrum of 'taste'.

I've never cared much for taste, and most of us would agree beauty is subjective, which doesn't have to lead us to say aesthetics can contain such difference, because the issue of 'beauty', to me, shouldn't come up in the first place. Or rather, 'beauty' as thing-in-itself. Because if our intent is to oppose beauty to, say, destruction, and use it as a symbol of integrity, liberty and agency, then it becomes something outside the limitations of taste – in fact, to the arbiters of taste, it might well be 'tasteless'. Beauty in this case becomes a political point, an act of defiance in the face of damage, destruction and disempowerment. Beauty becomes a symbol of resistance and possibly its paradox. That's a point-of-view issue, or maybe it's actually an issue of empowerment?

Does the mining company, such as Bauxite Alumina Joint Ventures, wanting to create a massive open-cut mine at Morangup that would reach to Wundowie almost 20 km away see the destruction of habitat that it will wreak in terms of destruction of beauty? Of course not. They see their promised 'rehabilitation' of land as a kind of beauty; they see the aluminium goods we consume as a kind of beauty; they see wealth-creation as a kind of beauty. No doubt, like Rio Tinto's collaboration with the Black Swan Theatre Company, they'll target 'the arts' in their desire to extend their largesse, to manufacture beauty that we can all digest as art.

And poetry? Poetry is *occasionally* offered funding directly and indirectly by such companies. It's easy to get caught out, so we need to be wary and understand where the money's coming from; often it's hidden. Business mostly wishes to take beauty and turn it into a form of capitalist activism, they wish to take art – all your arts – and make them subservient to this notion of beauty. It's called advertising ... or propaganda!

But if we accept that the integrity of land, that country itself is intrinsically beautiful, then in the name of beauty we might claim all evocations of natural beauty in poetry as an activist moment, as a resistance to the mining industry version. So poets describing a kangaroo paw, poets evoking a sunset (with or without pollution coloration), poets noticing a birdcall and implanting it in their own aubade, their own dawn love-poem, become activist in a way that resists the consuming of country enacted by these corporate miners.

So activism in poetry is often implicit, unless you celebrate goods, fetishise your possessions for the sake of them being your *possessions*. No amount of irony can save the poem that's built around the actual ordering and acquisition of material goods for the literal sake of *ownership*.

But the activism I am interested in is possibly more direct. It's a matter of working lyrical and rhetorical registers, of bringing the figurative and didactic into conversation. The activist poem can traverse the spatiality from 'celebratory nature poem' all the way to the damning rant, the poem that simply says, in essence, that 'All mining companies are fucked! They serve their own purposes. The rock they crush was a home to animals and plants. The rock they crush was a story...' and so on. A poem doesn't need to be stuck in the consistency of diction, in registers of display, in the packaging that more accords with Rio Tinto's glossy arts policy. And if it does deploy 'regular diction', 'predictable' metrics and a pat rhyming scheme, let its subject matter challenge the very conventions from which such approaches to poetry arise. Or let it connect with them, with the aural roots, the aids to memory that fomented the patterning of words into lyrics, into combinations of lines that become memorable.

Either way, let the poem protest against the constraints that industry, the military, religion and government would impose on poets, poetry and community. Poems speak for themselves however hard they might rant, and maybe that's what the governments and corporate cultures fear the most: their unpredictability, their capacity to make non-violent radical change.

It took the American poet Muriel Rukeyser in 1938 to help articulate in *The Book of the Dead* the horror of the deaths of hundreds of labourers from silicosis after they were forced to mine silica without masks when excavating the hydroelectric Hawks Nest Tunnel at Gauley Bridge, West Virginia, from 1927 to the late 1930s. That's poetry as direct, unremitting activism. Is there beauty in the poetry? – maybe of a sort touched upon above, but certainly not that packaged by Union Carbide, the company at the centre of the disaster, or any other prodigal of global corporate capitalism. The beauty of product, the beauty of modernity hawked by such companies is at variance with life, habitat and health of the biosphere. Rukeyser wrote, investigated, reported:

> The tunnel is part of a huge water-power project
>   begun, latter part of 1929
>   direction: New Kanawha Power Co.
>   subsidiary of Union Carbide & Carbon Co.
>   That company – licensed:
>   to develop power for public sale.
>   Ostensibly it was to do that; but
>   (in reality) it was formed to sell all the power to
>   the Electro-Metallurgical Co.
>   subsidiary of Union & Carbide Carbon Co.
>   which by an act of the State legislature
>   was allowed to buy up
>   New Kanawha Power Co. in 1933.
> –They were developing the power. What I am trying to get at,
>   Miss Allen, is, did they use this silica from the tunnel; did
>   they afterward sell it and use it in commerce?[1]

And let us consider a few lines from a poem entitled 'Mining Company's Hymn' from the 1977 collection *Jagardoo* by Aboriginal poet and playwright Jack Davis:

> The Government is my shepherd,
> I shall not want.
> They let me search in the Aboriginal reserves
> which leads me to many riches
> for taxation sake.
> Though I wallow in the valley of wealth I will fear no weevil
> because my money is safe in the bank
> vaults of the land,
> and my Government will always comfort me.[2]

The poem is activist in its place-specific critique, and also in its (em)placement in the world at large. It is polysituated in its creation and its publication – it is cross-referenced in the contexts of literature and the open, broad, ongoing conversation of different approaches and realities of human occupation of physical and conceptual spaces.

1 Muriel Rukeyser, 'Statement: Philippa Allen', in *The Book of the Dead* (1938), http://murielrukeyser.emuenglish.org/writing/the-book-of-the-dead/ (accessed 22 June 2016).
2 Jack Davis, 'Mining Company's Hymn', in *Jagardoo: Poems from Aboriginal Australia* (Sydney, Methuen, 1978), p 32.

OVERHEARING: POETICS OF PLACE WITH BRIEF REFERENCE TO JACK DAVIS'S POETRY

Sitting in a car outside a hospital, waiting to go in to see my partner and young son who was stricken with scarlet fever, an uncommon sickness in these times, echoing with the literary trauma of loss in nineteenth-century literary (and other) texts, I briefly heard an interview on the radio with a guy who'd won an essay competition. At the time, I felt welded to the car park, the place of the hospital, because of our son's inability to be anywhere but where he was. My place was his place, temporary, hopefully, as it was. I didn't catch much, but one line I did made me prick up my ears. The speaker said (claimed?) only indigenous peoples, certainly in Australia, could legitimately write of place. In essence, I wouldn't argue with this, as his essay was (it seemed) on trauma, dispossession and loss. And that is the legacy of colonialism, of the European attack on Australian Aboriginal people throughout the continent.

As I said, I didn't get much of the context and maybe I misheard, so I am obviously extemporising, but the point I wanted to pick up on was this idea of legitimacy of writing 'place'. Obviously the author in question (or the way I construct my memory of the soundbite) was using 'place' in a literal and absolute way, in terms of articulating (totemic?) connection to specific locations, and intimating that the non-indigene, in not being directly connected with the long-term negotiation of that space, must necessarily remain outside it. And does this extend to the artist or poet or writer (e.g. an essayist) seeing through the layers of presence (seen and hidden) and articulating them in 'art'? Is it an inclusive observation or does it set up a binary?

Now, whether the speaker on the radio meant this or not is not my issue. What I am taking as my point of departure is the frequent claim (whether from him or others), that only the indigenous can legitimately talk of place. Maybe it's a matter of definitions, or the agency we ascribe to a word, but 'place' will never (in English) work in such a specific and exclusive way. Place is a quantifiable register, not an ethical divider. One can argue that the dispossessed have more moral right, and inevitably a more experienced and more informed means of talking of 'place', but surely not the only way of talking of place. Anyone making contact with any co-ordinates on maps in any way is in a position to articulate a relationship to that place. Where the problems begin is when that contact denudes or deletes others' contact with that place. Really, if one pushes definition, just the deployment of a term like 'place' is a colonising or at least territorialising act. 'Place' is such a Western concept in its terminology. But not necessarily in its application. We can argue a more self-critical and deconstructive application of the term. When many of us write 'place', we do so aware of these problems of usage and application, and seek to use it as much as a term of resistance to that invasively possessive and occupying urge, as one of affirmation of the special, unique and particular (and overlapping, for that matter).

Place is the most effective means we have of defining agreement and disagreement on how a set of co-ordinates is related to. As I have written elsewhere (such as in *The Cambridge History of Australian Literature*,[1] *Disclosed Poetics: Beyond Landscape and Lyricism, Contrary Rhetoric*,[2] *Activist Poetics: Anarchy in the Avon Valley*), non-indigenous writing of place in Australia is necessarily anxious, and creates an instigational/causal anxiety. I have long subscribed to Hodge and Mishra's concept of the paranoid reading (see *Dark Side of the Dream*).[3] There can be little reading of place in Australia without an awareness of violent dispossession, but this does not preclude other readings of place, or even very different configurings of place that might be ignorant of the damage done, or intentionally avoid (thus the necessity of the paranoid reading, to reveal the hidden layers of denial and affirmations of an ongoing colonisation). In a sense, it is not in the interests of one trying to affirm indigenous rights and presence to deny alternative and/or other readings of place (in *their* place). Revelation, understanding and restitution will arise from being able to read and decode such a complex montage of ways of seeing and experiencing 'place'.

So, say, in the occupation of Noongar lands in what is now known as the Western Australian wheatbelt, to state only Noongar people have the right to claim and even discuss place is actually to obfuscate necessary conversations between occupiers and dispossessed, and between intruders and in some cases co-existent traditional owners. As mentioned earlier, in recent years I have been proposing something I call 'wheatbelt forums' in which indigenous locals and non-indigenous locals can discuss this very issue of 'place', create a comparative model that will allow for a more just use of space, and redress some of the issues of occupation. It should be added that there is documentary evidence to show that early contact between Noongar people and 'white settlers' showed

---

1 Peter Pierce (ed.), *The Cambridge History of Australian Literature* (Cambridge, Cambridge University Press, 2009).

2 John Kinsella, *Contrary Rhetoric: Lectures on Landscape and Language,* ed. Glen Phillips and Andrew Taylor (Mount Lawley and South Fremantle, Edith Cowan University and Fremantle Arts Centre Press, 2008).

3 Robert Ian Vere Hodge and Vijay Mishra, *Dark Side of the Dream: Australian Literature and the Postcolonial Mind* (Sydney, Allen & Unwin, 1991).

some leeway on Noongar people's part regarding the 'sharing' of 'space'. The whites were incapable of co-existence.[4]

As noted, *any* dictionary definition of place will have many alternative applications of meaning. It's a proliferating polysemic term. But when we speak of 'place' in literature in terms of cultural specificity, then a particular point in space becomes invested with experiential, material, spiritual, moral and survival factors. One who has been at particular points in space through generations of familial and spiritual connection is obviously in a better position to articulate the nature of that place. No question. And the moral impropriety of changing that relationship through intervention or theft is clear.

However, place is never static, and change is registered even within those domiciled in that place. This does not make change right, but change is a condition of place. Entropy, if nothing else. Further, the actions of those in neighbouring spaces necessarily affect the conditions of the reference-place itself. Factories (fuelled by materials taken from other places) in one place will still toxify even distant places. Human-induced climate change is the most overt example of the impossibility of separating ideas of place.

Interactions between people in any given place with others from elsewhere also change the conditions of that place. This does not alter the legitimacy of connection, but changes its nature. Further, it's not only humans who create languages of 'place': all living things do. Humans absorb (or exterminate) other life into their notions of 'place'; so do, for example, kangaroos. We live in the bush and see kangaroos most days. They come to our place because they know they will not be interfered with. They make clear choices about their (highly) violated space, and though I don't defend our presence here (for one thing, I *do* believe it's stolen land, and further, I don't believe in 'property'), I do claim that we live in agreement with the roos. They know our patterns and we know theirs. There are, I recognise, different forms of 'agreement'.

Our claim to this 'place' is certainly problematic, but in recognising this, we extend the meaning of place, of interaction, and in doing so create a polyvalent spatiality. Not one informed only by human presence and the crimes of occupation (though those, primarily), but also one in which the desire lines of animals are paramount, where remnant native vegetation guides are best on how to

---

4 This is not to suggest that non-resistance to invasion was the 'general' case. However, in stories of first contact between Noongar peoples and Europeans, the initial 'dialogue' is often pivotal. Consider the notion of the 'Friendly Frontier'. Neville Green, in *Broken Spears: Aboriginals and Europeans in the Southwest of Australia* (Perth, Focus Education Services, 1984), writes: 'The Aborigines must have regarded the activities of the settlers with great curiosity. They accepted the strangers without anger because they had rationalised them into the Nyungar universe as the Djanga, or the returning spirits of the dead, a word that became a synonym for the European settlers. At first the settlers found it rather disconcerting to be hailed as father, brother or mother, but after a while it was accepted with a great deal of humour and paternalism' (p. 53). Also see the brilliant Kim Scott novel *That Deadman Dance* (Sydney, Picador, 2010), and the author's note pp. 397–400. Further, cross-reference with Len Collard interviewing Dorothy Winmar: http://www.derbalnarrra.org.au/first-contact-and-timeline

replant and repair, and even the feral animal passing through is given rights to life: we are of its fate as well.

What brings me to this? Well, I started editing a collection of Jack Davis's poetry in 2013. It had me thinking a lot about overlaying claims to place and the simplistic views many well-meaning non-indigenous writers bring to the 'cause'. In recognising theft and damage, a necessary restitutive (though not always healing) act is taking place. But it might also fail to register the often-complex nature of indigenous–migrant heritage, skins, movement through the country of other indigenous peoples, personal agency and so on. It's not an anthropological picture! Mining companies seem to think it is, with patronising claims to 'education' (whose learning?), jobs (to contribute to the imperialism of companies) and 'health' (as in opening new uranium mines in Western Australia? That's the world's health at risk, as well as locals' health.)

Jack Davis was one of Australia's greatest poets, and Part 2 of this book will engage directly with his life and poetics. Four major books of poetry, as well as poetic interludes throughout his many plays and poetic prose among his other non-fiction works, provide us with a body of substantial achievement. This work has never been collected before and all of his poetry books are out of print.

Jack Davis was an intensely political poet. I aim to highlight his relationship to country, his north-west ancestry and south-west experiences with the Noongar people, and consider his personal biography in terms of Western Australian history, especially in terms of a 'black timeline'.

For example, Davis's early experience at Moore River, his work that led to him becoming director of the Aboriginal Advancement Council and the publication in 1970 of *The First Born and Other Poems*[5] are all deeply connected. Place is cross-hatched, interactive, with borders crossed and negotiated, and 'reports' of different places working in conjunction with places with which he self-identified (complex in itself). I want to trace those connections. Poems on Rottnest Island and John Pat don't exist as artworks separate from the history, stories and traumas that led to their creation: Davis always had a purpose.

The early colonial use of Rottnest Island as a prison camp for Noongar men changes the nature of the 'place' in so many ways. I find it a crime that people visit there with little care or even consciousness of this. Because Noongar people were taken from *their* place, a different kind of place was made, and for all those who come into contact with it, 'place' is altered, but still remains place. This is what's terrifying about place.

Those who died in Nazi death camps alter the nature of those places forever – their being taken there from elsewhere doesn't make them less implicated in those places of horror. They were murdered there. In a sense, they have nowhere else to go. One cannot deny place to the dead. Davis wrote:

> I look across at Rottnest
> in the far off haze

5 Jack Davis, *The First-born and Other Poems* (Sydney, Angus and Robertson, 1970).

> where my people
> breathed their last sigh
> for home the mainland
> to them the distant blue

In that last 'sigh' we overhear a truth, an absolute: the breath that is not life. The poem concludes with the knowledge that the dead/killed will always be part of that place:

> to be forever part of
> the island of the dead

At times, astonishingly, Davis was called a formally 'conservative' poet in how he wrote his poetry (the forms used); I challenge this – the opposite is true. He was a radical poet in so many ways: technically, politically and thematically, especially in the volume *Black Life: Poems*.[6]

I have a life-commitment to land rights issues and have written/spoken much about this. I believe that only through dialogue and respect can due acknowledgement of rights over land and culture be consolidated, and presenting poetry to the world is one way of achieving this. But I feel, as part of this, it is important for me to write and discuss my own notions of the 'place' I occupy, the 'places' I negotiate – there's a primary home and many other places I connect with (on a somewhat different tangent, and with somewhat different implications, Glen Phillips has written interestingly of people's birth and 'second' landscapes etc. in terms of his own experiences in Australia, Italy and China).

I did not know Jack Davis well. I met him in Fremantle a couple of times with Noongar mates, and 'hung around' a bit when I was very young. But for someone like me who has spent a lot of his life around the wheatbelt, Davis's poems and plays have special meaning. Further, I lived in Yarloop when I was 23, and my notions of that 'place' necessarily give me an insight into Davis's articulations of the same place (he grew up there), if in a narrow and limited way.

In recent times, I have been offering what support I can to the Yindjibarndi people in their resistance to the divide and conquer tactics of Andrew Forrest and Fortescue Mining.[7] The issues of place are so entangled in the mining companies' duplicity of recognising native title and yet doing everything in their power to get rights over the materials of the place itself. Now, I understand and respect that place is spirit of, through and beyond these materials, but they are still part of a whole, and their removal is a crime. In the case of uranium in the Wiluna area, the lands of the Martu people, the removal has consequences for the health of the entire world. Uranium doesn't respect any boundaries or co-ordinates of place.

---

6 Jack Davis, *Black Life: Poems* (Brisbane, University of Queensland Press, 1992).
7 Yindjibarndi Aboriginal Corporation (YAC) website. Note, this site was accessed throughout 2015 but as of 19 April 2016, the YAC is in the 'hands of receivers'. This is the colonisation by capital of indigenous space, however you look at the situation. http://yindjibarndi.org.au/yindjibarndi/?p=2556

Jack Davis wrote a deadly and precise poem regarding 'place' and iron ore mining. It's entitled 'Iron Ore', and goes:

The ship slips in
ore fills her gut
I know it will all
come back one day
In the form of –
So – come on man
let's blow
let's go I say
let's split and pray
then vet it
dust our knees
hold a protest
before we regret it

Jack Davis and I are completely different people, with largely different heritages and life experiences, and no doubt substantially different readings of place. But he would recognise the places I 'paint' in my poems, as I recognise his. A dialogue is created through reading and writing. Dorothy Hewett writes similar 'areas' (in some cases), but again is different. But passing through Wickepin on one occasion, Tracy and I couldn't help wishing that if the local Shire was calling it Facey Country, they might also acknowledge it as Hewett space. But of course, it's many others' country, and many of those lost access to their place, and even died in the colonisers' assault on it.

'Country' is such a mediated word now, and pivotal in terms of a semantics of belonging: it is used in a way that best equates to an intimacy of place. To call anything someone's 'Country' takes this with it, and I am sure Dorothy would have baulked at such a description. Wickepin is better not being called Hewett Country, though it is vital to recognise that it was an important place for Hewett, and part of her mapping of life, a mapping understood for what was stolen, and an implied knowledge of the required restitution. As Hewett writes (in *Wheatlands*)[8] her construction of 'one place seventy-three years in the making – the story of the Great Southern of Western Australia' is a place shared, but it is a colonially constructed space categorised as 'place'. It's not all places, nor does it defeat the places that it claims. And to my mind, no overlays or augmentations on Noongar Boodjar (country) can ever change the relationship between indigenous people and their country, their land.

In fact, its claims are the loudest call and prompt for other, more emphatic and long-term readings and claims of place. We can all hear that if we listen, and even partially hearing it or overhearing it is enough to trigger our own participation, our own contribution to a manifesto of place that means liberty, respect and restoration – a polysituatedness of place.

8 Dorothy Hewett and John Kinsella, *Wheatlands* (Fremantle, Fremantle Arts Centre Press, 2000).

CONCRETION AND DAMAGE: A PRE-MANIFESTO (THOUGH WRITTEN AFTER)

Following this commentary is a short 'manifesto' piece on creating 'concrete' texts in 'natural' environments or environments in which the 'natural world' intervenes, 'intrudes', or defines the conditions of viewing. This necessitates a lot of scare quotes because of the problem of mediating the 'natural' in the context of human seeing, perception and activity. All human activity is contingent on the 'natural world', regardless of how much it attempts to distance itself from the materials and variables of its construction. In the case of the images below, it might entail a spider or some other creature walking over a sheet of paper displaying a poem – the poem/sheet placed on the ground (or elsewhere) in the expectation that something will cross its path, literally. The patience is in waiting to capture the photograph, to watch the patterns of place fluctuate.

The series of poem-texts on sheets of A4 was done near Walwalinj in York between 2005 and 2008. The poems were written and printed and no copy kept (digital or otherwise). They were then photographed *in situ* and the paper recycled. These poems exist somewhere between installations and *concretions*.

Over the last nine or so years I have been accumulating poems that exist as expressions in landscape – accepting that landscape is a mediated term in itself, and relates to human presence and intervention with varying levels of impact. Whether printed paper placed among rocks and scrub, or lines written in charcoal on a concrete path between York gums, or words scratched into a firebreak, none of the creations had more than a temporary presence in the environment outside being captured in photographs. The aim is always minimal impact on the 'natural'. As we located ourselves mentally (as well as physically) at Jam Tree Gully, as we travelled away and returned, a real sense of concretion developed. The words written on the page, often while looking through a window, typed to shape on a manual typewriter, written in journals, seemed to be one part of a locution of place, an articulation of presence and the politics of this. The aim was to plant (literally trees, but also words) and repair, and to record.

Even 'healing' brings its costs, and all impacts generate change and loss. I started forming words on the obligatory firebreaks with sticks, scratching short

1 Under Walwalinj concretion poem installation – gravel rocks, shadecloth, and 'civilise falsehoods' intact on paper

2 Under Walwalinj concretion poem installation – heat cracks and an abandoned bungarra hole and torn 'civilise falsehoods' on paper

3 'Tunnelling spiders' charcoal on concrete pathway concretion poem installation

poems in the gravel driveway with its steep gradient (see my earlier chapter on the poetics of gradients). Sometimes I photographed these; mostly I didn't. And in other places, in other countries, I did the same, recording the concretions in poems: describing activities but with no other record. Walking became a concretion for me, and I stepped the lines across roadways and pathways, through fields and paddocks and along fence-lines, up mountains (literally) and across bodies of water. All of these (from various locations around the world) feed into what is formulating as *Jam Tree Gully 4* – a conceptualisation of concretion, a 'de-mapping'[1] of presence that shows the costs of even the lightest impact, and contemplations of alternatives and consequences. They are works of 'place', displaced in their presentation.

I have always been interested in handwriting and drawing, and since the mid-1990s have been writing 'graphology' poems. *JTG4* is part of that project, and separate. In absence, as the grass is cut by a family member who helped

1 See John Kinsella, 'De-mapping & Reconnoitring Notions of Boundaries – Mutually Said: Blogging & Acting', in Kinsella, *Activist Poetics: Anarchy in the Avon Valley*, ed. Niall Lucy (Liverpool, Liverpool University Press, 2010), pp. 137–62.

build our house at Jam Tree Gully, I have been drawing word 'maps' of the cutting and tree growth to 'be there'. They are mental maps, conceptual maps in lieu of. The absentee reconstruction so when we return I can compare the imagined with the reality, and based on something I've done year after year, and bear the calluses on my hands to inform the cartography. But these are 'de-maps' because even absent-presence comes at a cost, and the polysituated self absorbs so much – a consciousness that giving back, sharing and restoring even when away has to be built into the texts.

Which brings to mind someone else's recent project of connecting with place in Wales where a poem was painted on to rock faces in the Snowdonia National Park, intended to be temporary, to be washed away by the rains, but ended up being baked by a warmer than expected September and proved indelible. There are a number of issues here. One is the desire to mark place beyond the moment, which is problematical. But even more so is to miss the fact that climate change will necessarily alter conditions of interaction and presentation. So many of these things are ill thought-out – a nice notion, but no depth in understanding of causality. So much 'eco-art', intended to be of a place and meld with it, merge with it, do no damage, leaves a permanent mark. I recall river installations made from 'local materials' that damaged microenvironments then floated down into the sea to join the suspended wastes that are changing the biosphere. The artist's desire to leave a mark is understandable, but ephemerality has its worth in such contexts. Speaking words that won't be heard, scratching words in sand that will blow over in a day ... there are millennia of such acts. They are more durable than felled trees and carved rock (damaged or 'used' in the name of art and knowledge) in so many ways. They enter language and ritual, they inform our movements and day-to-day activities in ways we are rarely aware of.

But I am talking about a form of *the concrete*. A dissolvable, non-toxic concrete. That's thinking about materials used and where they are from, what will happen to them afterwards, the ink used, the electricity used, the manufacturing implications – everything. In a global-capitalist world that is consuming itself, that glorifies the soldier in war but not the janitor who cleans up the body wastes of Ebola victims, we need to recognise the art of the moment, the poetry that is survival without damage. We don't need to write out words in places revered for their natural beauty, but we can speak them there and even hold up a sheet of paper with those words, backdropped by the sublime or whatever you want to call it. The marks must be temporary because any more than that and the place will be changed irrevocably.[2] And that it was altered in such ways in the past doesn't mean we need to continue doing so. All borders are artifices. How we connect to a place is informed by so many variables. We don't need to mark our connection by undoing the stone of it, itself.

---

2 We can memorialise without damaging – in fact, a memorial to loss or injustice is best served by not replicating a damaging act. Memorials can be – *are* – in word *and* reception, and can be passed by word-of-mouth as much as being fixed by markers – *in* place.

The creation of a text in a *natural environment*, a concretion, brings into question how close you are/were to the event. I suggest that those performing an act of damage probably have it subliminally or overtly 'written into' their poetic language. And in their practice overall. These things are highlighted or hidden depending on how conveniently we can distance ourselves from the impacts we make, the damage we do. In poems of place we inevitably implant 'locators' – 'co-ordinates'/spatial reference points (tree, rock, mountains) that relate to the terrain of the place out of which the language comes. Without those topographical reference points, sense of place is lost. Or is it? One could create simulacra in a poem on the page that seemingly have nothing to do with the place they refer to…?

This applies to one of the tenets of polysituatedness and its larger set, international regionalism. The influx of many other geographical and topographic knowledges doesn't undermine the fact that any place will have long-associated presence/experience and (spiritual) connectedness that has generated a specific language of that place, that loses something (or something is changed) in its being translocated or invested with new presence. The globalisation of economies (that is, imposing a mode of trade and finance centred on major economic power clusters but consuming and smothering smaller and less robust communities in the process) is vanguard military-capitalist self-empowerment, which is about ensuring that all the conduits feed the wealth of the few. Constructing a shop that sells mobile phones in place of a stand of trees, one might very well lessen communication rather than extend or 'create' it. It's not about egalitarianism or caring, but about wealth-accumulation and control. To go into an impoverished space and create texts in the physical materials of that place (human-made or 'natural'), without a personal connectedness with that place, is clearly exploitative on many levels; but it might be generative if, say, it brings awareness of issues that leads to self-empowerment. That would be a thread of polysituatedness that is conscious and self-critiquing. Does the end justify the means? That depends…

Poems implanted into the natural world are always about intrusion. They alter the co-ordinates of the 'poetry'/poetics that pre-exist their intrusion. And there's always a poetry ('constructed' and utilised in various forms and manifestations by people, animals, birds, plants). To leave your mark is to occlude other marks, equally and maybe more necessary (codes to survival and understanding). If we start from that knowledge, then we can lessen the negative impact and increase the generative (awareness, different ways of seeing, respect). Also, we need to stop thinking of 'poetry', or rather the gestural substance of poetry, as a purely human activity. What we might call a 'found' poem or 'artwork' in nature (from a flower through to a burnt stump in the shape of something we think we recognise) is also nature in-itself.

Listening to a rare bird recently, I was conscious of taking its song for my purposes. It is its song. It's not an installation. It's not my poem (though I will make it mine, then altruistically share with other humans), but it might well be the bird's poem. It's *not* a concretion. But it might be something

4 Literal concrete … was already there – added charcoal

5 Literal concrete again … charcoal washed off after a week

6 Paper was recycled afterwards

7 Stick-writing on firebreak at JTG

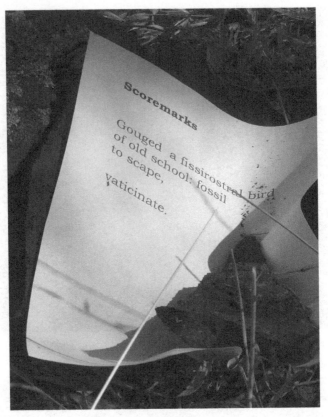

8 Weighted down in high wind

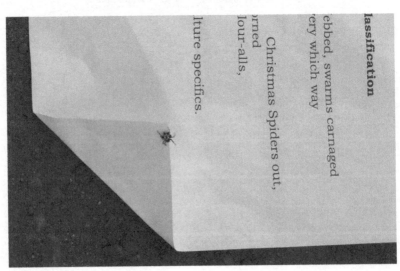

9 Christmas spider came along of its own accord, after I placed the poem between 2 trees!

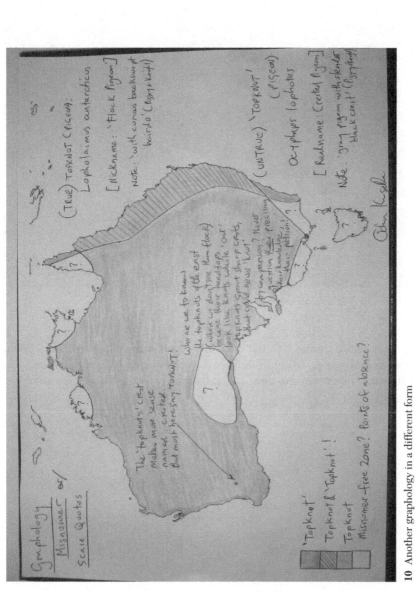

10 Another graphology in a different form

11 One of many gravel concretions that change shape over days

akin, something similar. It's not all utility, I am sure. When placing a poem in the natural world, we could think of it as collaboration … with nature? But what is the 'other' getting out of it, rather than yourself and your audience (people)?

DE-MAPPING – JAM TREE GULLY 4
CONCRETIONS MANIFESTO I

Jam Tree Gully 4 is a visual accretion of concrete poetry/visual poetry material, sound files and other materials from the last decade of creating artworks *in situ* – that is, at the place of conception and awareness. In essence, Jam Tree Gully 4 can only come into being in a public space – I see this 'book' as a curated art space rather than the conventional printed page (though a catalogue would work well to accompany the installed materials).

The map poems are part of a 'concrete' line of work that I have been investigating for many years. They include poems written and printed (and then deleted from the electronic 'record' – these large-font printed poems only exist in this form), poems photographed 'in terrain'/*in situ* (including rocks, clay, even ants 'randomly' walking across them) at my mother's place below Walwalinj (Mount Bakewell) in York, Western Australia; literal maps of Australia with text inserted; and poems created from text that 'map' a place – i.e. the words working as figurative and representative acts – standing for, and spatially in relation to, the place itself. I have also included images of texts scraped into the dirt and word poems ('graphology') made from sticks laid out on a firebreak at our place (Jam Tree Gully in the Western Australian wheatbelt). I am now working on concretions in the south-west of the Republic of Ireland which will become an extension of the Jam Tree Gully scenario – an ironic 'annexe' to the place of 'home'.

I am particularly interested in materiality of 'presentation' – the 'etho'/'ethical' politics of deploying waste materials; of using, say, charcoal taken from a bushfire that went through the zone years before, of writing on concrete scribbled out on rough ground as a track when the rains (eventually!) come, the yellow sand brought in from elsewhere to break up soil for a vegetable garden or laying a driveway. Equally important is a respect for the intactness of rocks and eucalypts, the passing insects and animals – these are 'caught' in photographs and in textual imaging, but left unhindered in their place of origin.

This all fits into a politics of what I term 'de-mapping' colonised spaces and looking to different ways of configuring space outside of survey (indigenous Australians have numerous traditional and post-traditional methods – verbal and visual). When I say 'etho-political' I am playing on ethical, ethos, ecological and so on. In creating 'spatial poems' in which I 'map' our place at Jam Tree Gully, I enact 'return' as well as retrieval: this is stolen land which cannot be 'owned', and by acknowledging that the colonising language is overlay, I also acknowledge that other languages exist/pre-exist as well, and are indeed primary. I do not use *strings* of indigenous words in order not to appropriate. The act of concretion is a recognition of the totemic, of the indigenous, and of the fact that I cannot lay claim to the material, spiritual or conceptual co-ordinates of this space. But I can witness, observe and 'present' (not 'represent').

So the 'mapping' poems become a process (even 'methodology') of/for breaking away from the constraints of mapping for control, occupation, dispossession

Humane Traps Release Map (John Kinsella)

old arena
sandy revegetating
nooks and crannies
first release zone   TOP PADDOCK
hop over into reserve   (too vulnerable to raptors)
in shadows cast by moon
through a GREAT York gum

RESERVE

York gum / jam tree
old and new growth
        granite boulders
            ecotonality: a better option
                than house dwelling (briefly considered
                    as release zone)

RED SHED (alive with mice
        in old hay bales)

                        HOUSE:
        90 000-litre   mice humanely trapped
        tank   herein!

BOULDERS

second release zone
(multiple visits)

                                        Bird Gully
RESERVE   (never an option)
(third release zone
in effort to get distance,
reduce liminality)

and other power-ploys. The map defies its own purpose, its own subservience to 'usage'.

Jam Tree Gully 4 is curated space. A curator 'spatialises' it within the conceptual (and real) gallery. In essence, it is an exhibition of the creation of 'the book' in curatorial space.

Spatial Realignment of Jam Tree Gully (John Kinsella)

```
                          asphalt
                              asphalt  asphalt  asphalt  asphalt
        RESERVE                        ant empire 1

        false fence      false fence  crossover

        distended boundary        wattlefestgate             caltrop  outbreak
                                     crossover                rounded corner

        arena reclamation        gravel drive runoff          cluster of quartz
        York gum saplings           erosion                    rock dragons
           free-ranging

              ant empire 2          seedling sandalwood in sluices
              wattles               latching on to York gum roots
              roos sheltering
                                                 paddock plantings (thriving)

  Granites interwoven jam tree saplings ridge

                      ancient wind-bent
                      gnarled York gums
 RESERVE           dead trees              ant empire 3
                                           RED SHED

                                        ant empire 4

    granite boulder overlooking       terrace
      granite boulder protecting
        echidna balled and projecting          roos grazing
          potent quills               terrace
                                          well 1

          den             90 000-litre
          holes           tank (life)      HOUSE                well 1
                          terrace / bank
                                                 lemon tree
              GREAT YORK GUMS
                                                          bird gully
                                                          bird gully
                                                          bird gully
    dead territory          GREAT YORK GUM with bees       bird gully
    drought residues                                       bird gully
    greyed trunks                                          bird gully
                                                           bird gully
                                                           bird gully
                          bent trees / run-off damage /    bird gully
                            slalom from gradient           bird gully
                            filled with rocks              bird gully
                              to slow erosion    ant empire 5   bird gully

          dense tangle of confused trunks (living and dead), termite-ridden
                          stubble quail sheltering         STEEP BANK

    fence    fence   fence  fence  fence  fence  fence  fence  fence  fence clutter of detritus fence

                          NEIGHBOUR


                RESERVE
```

CONCRETED PROTEST POEM AGAINST BAUXITE MINE AT MORANGUP

12 No Bauxite Mining at Morangup!

These photos are taken outside the office of the mining conglomerate seeking to establish a massive bauxite mine at Morangup, just south of Toodyay. The conglomerate is inculcating itself into the community, as many mining companies do, mixing notions of beneficence and largesse, and suggesting that the local people's standard of living will rise without illustrating the long-term costs. The destruction of habitat is not correctable, despite what is all too often claimed, and what is left is an emptied shell of place and space.

The photos here are protest poems. They are words on an A4 page, working as protest slogan and concreted poem. I used this size paper rather than a larger 'poster-size' format to capture the printed working page, to show the dynamism of the poetry page as space. The text on the page is inseparable from the context in which it is written, within the moment and location of protest, but its message is polyvalent and polysituated.

NO BAUXITE MINING AT MORANGUP!

WHEN IT'S GONE IT'S GONE

THIS IS MORE THAN A POEM

The idea of the 'temporary local' (only here when it suits) that underpins the mining conglomerate, its incursions into local social and business bodies, its making of a politics of extraction into a vanguard-of-benefits modus operandi, is typical of the industry.[1] The proffered wealth attracts the greedy and the needy alike – such companies require both, and the anodyne middle ground who will hold opinions (either way) and do nothing. (I am not demeaning or challenging the needy here. I use the expression 'greedy and needy' in the context of how mining companies perceive their access points to community. Obviously I am using the expression within this 'diegesis'. The expression is glib because of the glib nature of the mining company's take on their potential employees and the communities in which they operate.)

The poem/text in these photos is a prompt to take the discussion out of its

---

1 I differentiate (or nuance) here between what I have come to call 'temporariness' and what I am discussing here. Regarding 'The multiplicities of polysituatedness, the echoes, nuancing, and "stains" of temporariness', see: http://poetsvegananarchistpacifist.blogspot.com.au/2016/03/temporariness-2-photography.html. In this discussion I consider the generative nature of the 'temporary', the additions to place and what is taken away. Gain and loss.

niches, to join with many other conversations and protests. I recall once being told my services were not required in a pro-refugee protest because someone already had the ground covered – as if I would be taking their 'protest air'. When such cadre politics and politics of personality overtake the cause, the cause is damaged. The poem should be about the cause, to my mind, and in this case the minimalism of the text is an attempt to achieve this. Including myself in the photo is a registering of personal protest against the mine in dialogue with the text I created, but also working independently of it. It is also assuming responsibility for the views expressed (as is Tracy's taking of the photos). There are many vectors to any position we take and they all need to come into consideration.

FURTHER JAM TREE GULLY CONCRETIONS

These concretions were carried out in late 2014. It was an extremely windy day, which became part of the process – the wind altering the way the text could be 'secured' and thus conveyed to a reader, and even to myself as creator and participant.

As installations, they were obviously highly unstable and 'temporary', but as I have walked their placement points and zones since, the experience of movement is marked by that earlier engagement. There could have been an accompanying soundtrack – the wind, a variety of birds, my discussing the dynamic with young Tim who followed me around making comments at salient moments … and reading the pieces aloud, or reciting them in my head.

In a place where we've been trying to lessen human 'intervention', these are reminders of the crossover and conversations of being 'living things' that share space (which we do, of course). They also help remind (me at least) that our withdrawal from space is probably a consequence of trying to balance a very overdetermined 'ledger' (pure metaphor here, no fiscal actuality!) that has resulted in such massive colonial human imposition that flora and fauna struggle to maintain agency.

Though there is noise all about us (machinery, guns …), the reinstatement of flora, and the fauna that arrive searching out this growing refuge, create walls of 'silence' around the space from which we view and attempt to comprehend. I am reminded of Gomringer's 'silencio' – wishful thinking or metaphor? In terms of the texts themselves, their 'shape' is a reflection of the 'ambience' and way one interprets moods of place (a distorted anthropomorphics), and in this they are concrete representations.

But ultimately, they are unmappings of co-ordinates, an unfixing of points on the maps we create to control. The scratchings in the red-brown 'dust' of the firebreak work as markers of associations, parodies of 'logos' and ownership (Naomi Klein got over her childhood love of labels!)[1] The more we try to fix the

---

1 Katharine Viner, 'Hand-to-brand combat', *The Guardian*, 23 September, 2000, http://www. theguardian.com/books/2000/sep/23/society.politics (accessed June 2015).

picture, the more unstable becomes the language we use to describe it. And the language that is woven into the picture is at the mercy of the wind, of atrophy. What follows is a selection of concretions from around a dozen texts emplaced and photographed in a variety of ways at the time.

13 Where the north-east ant colony centres itself

14 Plato's Cave is rarely locked and secured. The Red Shed

15 Raingauge, witness to the fading green

16 On the firebreaks colour is queried. Someone has passed over. Tread. Trod.

17 Carried by the wind from firebreak (though 'secured') to wild oats

18 Logo – not! JTG, acronym for…?

19 Firebreak scratchings poem – Loss Rarity Bird Gully…?

Two of the texts exist as poems 'in themselves', outside concretion, outside installation. They are different viewed as such:

THE RED SHED

is changing shape; not Plato's Cave

though many sheds within the region

might be

it changes shape in the heat,

but also with cooling

passerines

take generational records

and score them

the tawny frogmouth is not lost in the York gum branches

though if I don't give directions – point it out – you're lost

the branches cradle the shed

though don't each over it entirely,

not completely

GUTTERS ARE THE MEASURE

Where the wild oats are left uncut

possibilities abound – of, with, and

When the cliché is deployed

we might mostly lament

the loss of texture

nothing too vigorous

in the extreme heat?

sparks? conflagration?

or the tremors of insect dominance:

conflicts predation, nesting, egg-laying,

the materials of aesthetics

rejected elsewhere

NEAR GOOMALLING: OAK PARK CONCRETIONS

CASE 1: These concretions were prepared in late spring and displayed in early autumn. The gap was part of the process between text as conceptual and text as installation. *In situ*, they become integral parts of place, if temporary ones. After the fact, they are representational: of that moment, of the history of Oak Park. Between preparing text and displaying it came the devastating summer. There are no more edges, no more ecotones – the blurring is not liminal, but sharp lines of demolition. No benefits and richness and plethoras where habitats contact and overlap, but the scribble of damage. What is given way to is the reality of the vestigial or the remnant. Not a condition of healthy and unhealthy, but of different states of decay. It's a brutal reality – the land set aside is dying, and rehabilitation is a gesture. The farmed land feeds the nature-reserve land with its residues. Does that mean one should resign oneself to this? Of course not. But the edges need to be unmapped, need to be denied, to grow over into an ambiguity, which is what the romantic ecologists wish as edge and liminality. 'Habitat' is extinct as useful terminology – its colonial residues are toxic.

20 Oak Park – resides: saline walk

CASE 2: In photographing the words, one had to be careful to avoid the couple who were come across on a bench installed near the saline (dry) lake, caught *in flagrante*; one turns away. Nature walking. Nothing of Manet's *Le déjeuner sur l'herbe*, though you might think the couple thrill to the idea, nature in decay around them. But there is life: swamp sheoaks, bobtails, bush flies, mosquitoes, rabbits, roos, willy wagtails playing the trickster in acacias nearby: all the transliterations of their name (djitty djitty, jiddy jiddy…). All the perching birds watch on suspiciously, as we won't watch, as we avoid and scuttle away, giving the realm of place to the lovemakers.

21 Oak Park – trees as bare bones 1

22 Oak Park – trees as bare bones 2

CASE 3: To mention an edge doesn't give us an edge. To note the gnamma hole worked over centuries to make deep water-storage now full of beer cans and cigarette packets, the granite a radon machine, is not to participate in custodial presence. It is not scenic, and visiting is not participatory. The machine of the water place is altered with the ticking-off of points on the walk. Journey to the centre of the earth. Discovery wearing down to bare bones.

CASE 4: This spiral of husbandry taking us far away from a source point at any given moment. The wild-oats scenario: chokes out native grasses, and then the poisons used to eliminate it alter the biochemistry of the soil, the place as a whole. Metaphor and data overlap, compete, leave blank dead areas and the sand in a state of unrest, vulnerability, as unstable as the texts printed with industrial ink on recycled commercial paper with the costs imposed on environment far away. The slippage of textual activism, the polyfilla that is poetry. Yet this is not a denial of the living world but rather an affirmation. As Shelley

23 Oak Park – trees as bare bones 3

24 Oak Park – dry lake bed aghast

writes in *Prometheus Unbound* (IV, Ione):[1] 'How every pause is filled with undernotes,/ Clear, silver, icy, keen, awakening tones/ Which pierce the sense and live within the soul...' We might have an inversion of seasons and basic climatics, but the same resolution life has to find a way is what drives this act of witness, presence and participation.

CASE 5: For some, and maybe for many of those whose land this is and will eternally be (going forward, going back, in the depth and dimensions of here and now), place is a location (technically, a set of co-ordinates, a specifically quantifiable and locatable set of points using the planets, the stars ... a wider sense of time and place) that cannot be erased by the destruction wrought through colonial invasiveness. The texts are not sonorous, but they might be words plucked from a song, or sounds from those words might form harmonics with words from the song of place. That's wishful supposition, but it's also aspiration. It seeks to appropriate nothing, and will leave no discernible physical mark. The desire behind these concretions is to leave little signature, to do little or no damage, to acknowledge and maybe vicariously participate in a health of locality, place, timelessness. But a conceptual imprint is left and is magnified by the images being blogged or published or displayed, even if they are ignored. And that is an imposition the poet and the reader/viewer must process and be accountable for.

25 Oak Park – calling the absent birds

---

1 Percy Bysshe Shelley, *Shelley's Poetry and Prose* (New York, W.W. Norton, 2002).

Chitty Chitty

Jiddy Jiddy

Djity Djity

Djidy Djidy

Willy Wagtail

Willie Wagtail

Black-and-white fantail

Rhipidura leucophrys

passerine

Probability is   HIGH
                   MEDIUM
                   LOW

of seeing: Bungarra
               Bobtail
               Dugite
               Mulga Snake
               Ornate Rock Dragon
               Sun Skink

or of seeing: Wedge-tailed Eagle
               Elegant Parrot
               Mulga Parrot
               Pink and Grey Galah
               Ringnecked Parrot
               Spoonbill
               Black-shouldered Kite
               Bronzewing Pigeon

or of also seeing: Grey Kangaroo
                      Red Kangaroo
                      Wallaby
                      Echidna
                      Possum
                      Fox
                      'Feral' Cat

The capitalisation of presence has nothing to do with certainty. Are we mapping living examples. Are they samples? What sets and subsets do they form, and where do we see from given anticipation? Removing data (of evidence), what do we leave in its place? The extracted image makes holes: we've seen them, I've recorded them in photographs. Which are not images. The consequences of science.

Sheoak voices but no 'Casuarina
obesa' which is interpolation
to the songs.

In the salty quagmire, the Swamp Sheoak
chatters against the grain. Fly-catchers dart
from its nodal points. The needles carpet.

Jam Tree provisions

Wolyamuury though *wolya* (or
woylie?) are gone (deletion)? Wetlands
as euphemism. Picture a Kangaroo Rat.
Not interchangeable. Namings collapse.
Identify.

Lake Walyormouring is easy to dismiss
as a deadzone. The living
take offence.

Gnamma holes: granite reactor
of water processing plant. Sundews
shine at the right time. Away for
a couple of years and you can predict
beer cans tossed into the holes.
Statements and less than *this*.

Waterbirds in the demi-

in the dry

quasi

making do

resetting   centre offset
edging

'PARK'
(resonances of English naval oak... ancient timbers)

denotes ecological
indifference, even failure,

on so many

levels:

it's the triumph of leisure

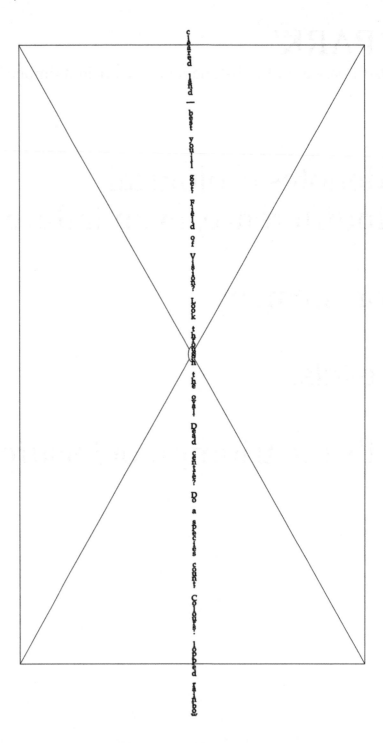

cleared land — best you'll get. Field of vision? look through the oval. Dead centre? Do a species count Colours. lopped rainbow

Uncleared land —
best you'll get.
Field of Vision?
Look through an
oval. Dead centre?
Do a species count.
Colours: lopped
rainbow the closer
you get. Visit:
less consequences?
Concretions every
step.

LIVING WITH MOONDYNE JOE: *POINTS DE REPÈRE*[1]

for Niall Lucy

When the ticket-of-leave convict Joseph Bolitho Johns escaped the Toodyay West lock-up in 1861, his history as 'Moondyne Joe' began, though the nickname came later. The location name 'Moondyne' probably came from a coloniser/ settler re-pronunciation of a Whadjuk Noongar place name. Moondyne is near Julimar Brook where Johns had set up his horse cage in the bush, where he'd originally trapped the 'clean-skin' horse and marked it with his own brand that led to his first colonial (re)incarceration and that first escape of 1861. This escape certainly encouraged the building of the Newcastle Gaol (which was to become the Toodyay Gaol), a building of stone, wood and metal which is now a popular tourist destination in Toodyay, often associated with the bushranger probably more than it should be.

Our postcode is 6566. The postcode of the location of Moondyne is 6567. There's a land sale on there now – lots being surveyed, parcelled up and sold off. Development. Moondyne is in the district of Toodyay. Those of us who dwell in the district are by proxy integrated into the mythology of Moondyne Joe, whether like us you're up on Toodyay Brook, or like many (not that many) others, close to the banks of Julimar Brook, to the west of the Avon River that runs down through the hills, over the Darling Scarp into the Swan River as it winds across the Swan River coastal plain to the Indian Ocean.

Our lives in the Toodyay area are saturated in an active awareness of Moondyne Joe's 'exploits', as well as the sales pitch of his 'good bushranger'

---

1 I collaborated with Niall Lucy over a couple of years on the book *The Ballad of Moondyne Joe* (North Fremantle, Fremantle Press, 2012). A hybrid work of history, cultural criticism, poetry, memoir and much else, the piece reprinted here is my personal account of (literally) living in and near 'Moondyne territory'. Niall's astonishing research and creativity is to be found throughout the book, but especially in his genre-defying essay 'Preface (The Many Skulls of Edward Kelly)' and his 'Timeline'.

identity. My familiarity with him goes back to childhood days, visiting York town from my uncle's and aunt's farm at Wheatlands, out off the Goldfields Road. The myth of Joe was also part of the psychology of the oldest inland town in Western Australia, though he spent comparatively little time there. However, many police searches were focussed through York, and the town was a specific legal co-ordinate in the story of Joe's struggle to escape the authorities. How much truth was attached to the stories I heard as a child is anyone's guess. It is a 'given' that Moondyne Joe stories are often either apocryphal or highly embellished. So many of the incidental details are of dubious status, and apparently necessary to the myth-urge of an invader-settler society. The making of the contradictory, ironic, everyman, anti-hero (even a *commedia dell'arte* harlequin figure at times) is writ in colonial desperation for separation and independence, and yet ongoing certainty of connection with the mother culture/s.

That Joe was a mixture of the rough'n'ready, the gentleman, the wildman, the skilled carpenter and even something of the entertainer provides the European-invader trickster-figure through which broader tales of occupation and legitimising presence in the 'new land' may be made. Because Joe could eloquently state the unfairness of his treatment in letters to the Governor, could point out that a deal to ensure his freedom had been ignored and an injustice done to him, another quality of the effective hero/anti-hero in a young society is established: that of a literate intelligent man who has been oppressed for the danger of his libertarian thinking, his ability to stand up for his rights.

He was popular among colonists, who enjoyed the ironic reporting of his constant evading and embarrassing of colonial authorities (the foundations of independence!); songs were sung praising his cleverness. And although Joe's letters are no statement of refusal and resistance like Ned Kelly's Jerilderie letter, they nonetheless entered the popular imagination as records of being wronged by authorities. What's more, in the west, people are conscious of differentiating themselves, of almost seceding at times, from the stories (historic facts *and* colonial myths) of eastern Australia. Convicts came late to Western Australia and were brought in at the request of settlers to provide labour – as over-compensation for this utilitarian exploitation, there is inevitable communal investment in a trickster-figure like Moondyne Joe.

In my 1995 book *The Silo*,[2] which was written over many years and really encompasses my life of deep association with the wheatbelt, from Mullewa through to the Great Southern, but especially the region around York and Northam, I included this small poem:

Moondyne Joe

Bugger Moondyne Joe –
there was a bloke
from our mob

2 John Kinsella, *The Silo: A Pastoral Symphony* (Todmorden, Arc Publications, 1997).

who jumped roofs
in towns from
Northam to Narrogin
just for the hell of it.

This is a poem about myth and apocrypha, but also about restating ownership of the land's stories. The use of 'our mob' suggests an indigenous narrator-protagonist and the lives of incarceration and evading the
new agri-military-'settler' complex that had been forced on their lands.
Moondyne Joe has been quasi-incorporated into this fact in so many ways.
He is almost a liminal figure, a crossover between colonial perceptions of
the 'wild' and what it should or shouldn't be, and the values of Old Europe
(especially later in his life). His eventual 'insanity' becomes symptomatic of
the perceived irreconcilable nature of these apparently opposing forces. He
embodied elements of the 'indigenous' (which, of course, he wasn't), and
the coloniser, a mix destined to collapse. It was noted on reports when Joe
was admitted to the Fremantle asylum that he had a tendency to remove his
clothes. This 'reversion' from civilised apparel fits with a desire to reinstate
him as 'wildman', a sense that the forces of the bush, of 'nature', took him back
in the end.

But as a convict in the first place, as a ticket-of-leave man, he was already in
the hazy world of non-settler settler. Like so many other men and women, he
didn't fit any model of belonging. Convicts, in all their varying states of incarceration and degrees of liberty, were originally landless and 'homeless', and if
they brutally took their opportunities to create status within the colony, they
did so with permanent records at their heels. Stories of the fair go, equal rights
and so on flounder in reality. Wherever hierarchies within the ranks of the disempowered are established, so that an ex-convict has, for example, power over
the life of a ticket-of-leave convict (e.g. working on a property for them), there
deep resentment and much abuse of authority are inevitable. The mythology of
Joe as a kind of liberator arises as much from this as from his pursuit of physical
freedom.

Moondyne Joe has long interested me because of these apparent contradictions. Over the years, I discovered that various of my ancestors were likely to
have had contact with him, but there's no hard evidence for it. Certainly during
the time from 1879, when he was working around the forests of the Vasse, he
may have worked with a number of my Irish Kinsella forebears. The verse
play in this book, 'The Tattoo',[3] is based on that possibility. Joe's lifelines, and
those of my great-great-grandfather, my great-grandfather and great-uncles,
are intertwined in many locations of the Vasse. The small Kinsella family farm
on the coastal wetlands, before the great tuart forests near Busselton, might
even have been one of his work-points, as it might have been close to where
John Boyle O'Reilly made his escape from the colony in 1869 on the American

3 'The Tattoo', in Kinsella and Lucy, *The Ballad of Moondyne Joe*.

whaler the *Gazelle*, to America, where he would eventually write the novel *Moondyne*.[4]

A personal connection through an aunt's marriage presents the possibility that one of the police who pursued Joe near the 19 Mile Inn on the road to York was indirectly related to me. Many south-western Australians could make similar claims, for affirmative or negative reasons. It ties in with a desire to juxtapose the massive physical area of 'here' with the relatively small population of colonists and the close links they shared, whatever their perceived origins or designated social position.

A few days ago our eight-year-old son, who attends Toodyay school, came home excited because his class was doing a project on the old Connor's Flour Mill in town, and on Moondyne Joe. He said he'd been able to fill in *pages* of 'facts'. That's the thing about Toodyay – it has made Moondyne Joe its identity. Shops are named after Moondyne, there's the annual Moondyne Festival, there are brochures and publicity items galore. But most vitally there's a real communal sense of connection with what Moondyne Joe has been 'made' to stand for. He represents a set of values that anyone who lives in the district will know are not just some stereotypical romantic cliché, but hard reality.

The front cover of the 2011 Toodyay Business and Community telephone directory carries the famous (if doubtfully 'authentic') image of Joe in his moleskins, with kangaroo skin cape and hatchet in hand, a sepia image oval-framed with smaller images at its four imagined corners: Connor's Mill, the town hall, the Anglican church and the old gaol (the one built a few years after Joseph Bolitho Johns's first escape). The icons of town architecture are in fixed elliptical orbit around the spirit of community as represented by the photo that has religious, municipal, feral and rebellious qualities all at once.

This is an area where small holdings of six to thirty acres mix with larger farms and tracts of forest reserve. There is, in fact, a Moondyne Nature Reserve. There is a strong culture of motorbikes, tattoos and 'outlaw' attitudes. You can make of that what you will, among the more middle-class aspirations that necessarily underpin any rural town. There's the folk festival and a drinking culture. Ballads and AC/DC. The recently-closed CD shop, Moondyne Records, delighted young Tim (and us) because of its vast collection of AC/DC recordings, posters, hats and other paraphernalia. We got Tim's blazing 'Bonfire' poster there, depicting Bon Scott on Angus Young's shoulders amid leaping flames. When AC/DC did their Black Ice tour gig in Perth, not only did many adults from this area make their way down through the hills to the city, but so did many children. It was the talk of school for months. The connection between Moondyne Joe and AC/DC seems a logical one around here – no explanation required.

This is a town which celebrates the convict and outlaw during its Moondyne Festival – redcoats and great landed families take a back seat. It's where

4 John Boyle O'Reilly, *Moondyne: A Story of Convict Life in Western Australia* (1879) (Australind, The National Gaelic Publications, 2010, being a facsimile edition of the George Robertson Publication, 1880).

colonising never really succeeded over the bush, though for us there's the grim irony that more could be done here to recognise that the bushranger ranged through indigenous lands; that this was and always will be Noongar land.

Moondyne Joe's *points de repère* are everywhere in the Avon Valley and the Avon catchment. Whether it's Joe's Cage across the Avon (from us), or the Walyunga Lookout, or York, or, say, Doodenanning (Joe was captured there at the end of 1865 – he'd been on the run for a month) where we sometimes take family excursions on the way to Quairading, Moondyne is everywhere. He is 'down south' when we visit my father in Bunbury, or the old family 'pioneer' graves in Busselton cemetery, or Karridale Cemetery, deep, deep down towards Augusta, or even driving up through the goldfields on the way to Adelaide, passing through Southern Cross, thinking how Moondyne had planned with his fellow escapees to make it east, to escape the west and start again, only to be recaptured. A free man, Joe would travel to the Yilgarn discoveries with his wife in 1887. And when we drive the 'back way' to Perth through Julimar Forest and Chittering Valley, we come out of the hills at Bullsbrook and drive past the school with its busy mural of Moondyne Joe. Bullsbrook is an airforce town, and the contradiction clashes and resonates every time I look at it. Joe as frontiers-man as much as law-breaker.[5]

The mythology of Moondyne is very adaptable. And as you drive on down the Great Northern Highway through Middle Swan, towards Midland and Guildford, you pass Dale Road and Houghton's winery, and the incident of the 'wildman' Joe swinging a 'waddy' (understandable defensive violence? we are so often assured he was caught unawares and reacted in surprise, not with malicious intent!), after being surprised stealing wine in the cellar, comes to mind like a formula, a mantra. It is written into the journey. There seems to be no escaping it…

Even when I lived in Clifton Hills and later Westfield, with Kelmscott our local centre, I was living in the shadow of Moondyne, who had been locally nicknamed 'Old Mad Moondyne' by then, apparently, and was charged with counterfeiting coinage.

Then there's Fremantle Gaol, both his nemesis and the site of his canonisation for outwitting all the system could throw at him in its attempt to prevent escape. There's nothing like a declaration of 'escape-proof', and its undoing, to get popular sentiment moving. Let's face it, his escape really *was* a great piece of strategy and tactics, the rejection of an imprisonment both absolutely physical and absolutely psychological (the cell was designed *just* for Joe). Joe's escape from the prison yard, from behind the heap of stones he had been forced to

---

5 Moondyne Joe, the great escape artist, becomes the embodiment of the polysituating self – he is all he was that led to his transportation (barbaric act that transportation was), his Welsh/British life, and all that is constrained, freed and re-constrained, and ultimately reconstructed in his future, our present. His polysemous name/naming – Joseph Bolitho Johns/Imperial Convict 1790/Moondyne Joe – and his quasi-mythical status create the blurring of identity that shifts boundaries of (un)belonging. There is also the element of the 'polymorphously perverse' in the place-myth-settler-renegade-maverick festishisation of him as outsider-insider.

break and pile, is more than symbolic of an undoing of the panopticon; it is the trickster's triumph over the penalising of the mind.

I have always refused to visit the Fremantle Gaol in its tourist manifestation, because of what it represents as a site of vicious oppression, not only historically but also for people I knew in my youth. It was never about rehabilitation, to my mind. But that refusal might change. Niall has tried to convince me to see Joe's cell, and in doing so to make a statement about refusing instead to be defeated by the machine of unjust punishment. Maybe.

Moondyne Joe returned to Newcastle (Toodyay, as it is called now, or more accurately – derived from Noongar – the area of Duidgee) with his wife Louisa in 1887. Even then he had issues with the law over the lack of a Bill of Sale, and he was incarcerated briefly in the Perth lock-up before the case was dropped. This further occasion of forceable removal of Joe from Toodyay seems to be key to the town's obsession with him as the symbol of its psyche. It is a resilient town that pulled together with monumental fortitude in the aftermath of the devastating fire that ripped through the southern parts of the town and district in late 2009 on a 46° centigrade day, with a strong northerly wind fanning the flames, destroying animals, plants, houses and sheds and anything else in its path. I suspect the spirit of Moondyne may have been invoked by many then as talisman, even as patron 'saint'. A secular saint. It's not unusual for authority to be challenged in and around Toodyay – be it over a building permit or dozens of other issues of 'rights'. But in the end there are close bonds that preserve the fabric of community, and Moondyne Joe is significant among these.

The poems, play, short prose pieces and 'texts' of mine in this volume are a dialogue of a life living with Moondyne Joe. But they are also a dialogue with my good friend Niall Lucy who, as a Fremantle person, has been living with Joe as well. We have conducted our conversation from the wheatbelt, the hills, the coastal plain and the waterside, connected by the Avon and Swan rivers. Joe seemed more than one person in so many ways, and it has certainly taken two of us (and the many others who have been part of our conversations), to come up with a verbal map of his stories, his mythology. I've never believed in closure, so I doubt this will be our final word on the subject, but it's certainly another point on our journey with Joe, and hopefully *for* Joe, and for all others who find him as fascinating and worthy as we do.

PART II

Where we are

A POLYSITUATED MANIFEST
(WITH AN INCOMPLETE CIRCLE 'O'),
ON JACK DAVIS, TENNYSON AND SOCRATES

1. (a) All places we have been part of, visited and *received* (via family stories, our reading, what we watch on television and film) are part of our sense of place. Place is not just where we are, but where we have been and where we can perceive ourselves as having been, or imagine ourselves being. Place is polyvalent and ever-increasing in its nodal points. This is polysituatedness, a process of growth of perception and a sense of multiple belongings that enhance our understanding and respect for the *here and now* by creating a comparative model we can use for decision-making and reflection on our condition of being, and the impact our actions might have on other people and the environment as a whole. It is a subset of international regionalism, in which regional integrity is respected while encouraging broader cross-'border' conversations with an ultimate aim of a borderless respect for presence. All presences (a feature of landscape, a village, a town, a network of tracks or roads, etc.) become in this contiguous, whatever physical distance separates them. It is essentially a communal anarchism.

(b) About six months ago, when we were in Cambridge and I was walking up to 30 km a day through the countryside around the city-town, I wrote in a letter to a poet friend, 'I am particularly interested in disturbance of soil and place, and the comparisons of the rural world I come from in Australia and differences with the rural world here. I am working on clod level – the chalky clay soil of the fens has always fascinated me. I have been investing these observations with a nodal system of connection and disconnection I term "polysituatedness" – a notion of polyvalent belonging, but one that critiques its cultural positioning and the problems of claim and desire in presence.' The poet responded with the question, 'Do you think there is a connection between composing poems while walking and writing work over time that is ongoing and unfinished?' And I replied, 'I do … and I know that when I can't walk I find the ongoingness of poem-making stifled and a different kind of unfinishedness comes into place – and unfinishedness that is not the generative sort that allows for the eternally open poem (tendency to create longer compiling works), but rather fragments searching for other fragments. And solitary walking creates its own companions – and making poems as you walk is a way of creating these "companions", the poem becomes the accompaniment, and if you walk with others, the poems become dialogic and multi-voiced.' And just now, reading through a flawed Poetry Foundation biography essay on Tennyson, pastiched and cobbled together from numerous biographical and critical sources, I read of Tennyson living on the Isle of Wight in Farringford from late 1853:

> Most of the time, however, he was content to walk on the great chalk cliffs over-looking the sea, composing his poems as he tramped, their rhythm often deriving from his heavy tread.[1]

The inculcation of not only the rhythms of his steps but the dialogue between those steps, his breath, the auralisation and visualisation of words in his mind's eye, and the movement of waves, seabirds and any other life, would have become integral to the creation of poem-texts. Not enough is made of the correlation between the 'heavy tread' of walking and how surface and ecology affect the step being made. Here at Jam Tree Gully, I lunge up steep slopes, I brace myself going down, hanging on to tree branches and working my footing (to avoid lichen patches) on granite rocks. The rhythms are not regular, even when we wish them to be so.

2. To understand the place we write from, to write outwards to others doing the same – i.e. writing outwards to us, criss-crossing lines of text and speech that create a multi-perceptual 'map' unravelling convention, survey-control applications of mapping which are about jurisdiction and possession (for example, even sea charts to prevent ships foundering on rocks historically find their knowledge applied to warfare). The mapping of conversations and lines of projection of belonging and passing through, of understanding that the sign indicating a landscape feature or historic landmark doesn't have to be empty governmental words in the 'non-place' sense of illustration and a sense of 'proximity' as conveyed by Marc Augé in *Non-Places*[2] but rather an understanding of the actual trace of the sign itself, the impact it has on place in a literal sense, and how it is interpreted by the many different people who pass through (there is no one way of reading a text), as well as how individuals may choose to break the 'contract' in interacting with signs (refusing to pay the toll, to vote, to do as the state tells us).[3] The conversation highlights similarities and differences and creates

---

1 Alfred, Lord Tennyson, biography at the Poetry Foundation, http://www.poetryfoundation. org/bio/alfred-tennyson (accessed 22 April 2015).

2 Marc Augé, *Non-Places: An Introduction to Supermodernity*, trans. John Howe (London and New York, Verso, 2008), p. 78.

3 Augé, *Non-Places*: 'There will be no individuation (no right to anonymity) without identity checks' (p. 83). True this might be, I question the very nature and need and desire of his 'individuation' and 'anonymity' – in the polysituated always-contiguous de-mapping of movement and conversation, place being primary offers both public and private levels of contact, is always anonymous and announced. We all *retain* our identity as we pass through

a set theory of belonging and alienation. Collaborative making of art and text is vital to me, especially when I am spending long periods of time relatively isolated from those outside my family. I am fairly eremitic at Jam Tree Gully, and poem collaborations that create axons (tail of the kangaroo) and dendrites (branches of York gums) to interact with the neurons of other poets become essential. Co-writing or co-enacting works helps clarify what I am seeing *here* through a glimpse into what my collaborator/s are seeing *there* (which is not an *elsewhere*!)[4] and what I am trying to articulate. Difference is generative; the greater the gap, the more energetic the bridging.

3. Place is an inadequate term even when used in conjunction with the axis of place. See earlier discussion of 'definitions of place'.

4. I have long been interested in the connections and interstices between poetry and mathematics – indeed, like poetry and music, or like poetry and visual art, one could argue that poetry and mathematics are inseparable. This is the case in the context of metrics, or in the 'shape' and form of a poem and also, in my view, in creating proofs of 'existence'. Further, I am interested in creating a figurative language out of curves, shapes and lines. For example, I am focussing on spirals at the moment – from the nautilus, through to 'dust devils', through to doodles on pages! I am particularly fascinated by the 'subsets' formed by overlapping spirals, and how they might be used figuratively/poetically – how they might go

---

any place and no government or military control or corporatism can extract this completely from us.

Even in the Nazi death-camps, language and memory persisted and the place was written with this as much as the tidal waves of blood drawn by the murderers. The place becomes so present as a testament to its crimes, its absolute haunting, that it defies any visitor not to feel culpable as a human for allowing such crimes to be performed by others acting in human bodies. Celan's 'Todesfuge' is an endgame in the trauma of writing, of speaking ... as John Felstiner has written, 'How to find words for "that which happened," as Celan called what we call Holocaust or Shoah' (*Selected Poems and Prose of Paul Celan*, trans. John Felstiner [New York, W.W. Norton, 2001], p. xxi) in which music collapses ('he shouts play death more sweetly') under the weight of the crime, but the poem awakens us to the evils art paradoxically hides and yet announces – the paradox at the utter breakdown and fragmenting of language itself.

'Non-places' in the Augéan sense sadly allow the exploitations of 'downtime' to be played out benignly by a kind of aware 'acceptance' (sorry, anthropological distance doesn't rub with me!), we need to resist – some believe texting, tweeting, phoning, watching movies ... interacting with the world 'out there' in real place/s helps with this as they're on the move, but an appreciation of where we actually are (including in the air in a plane ... who is around you, how we are all behaving ... what we are flying over ...; Augé's example of not drinking in Saudi airspace signifying 'the intrusion of territory into space' is ironic here, given he seems to miss any spiritual or cultural laterality and its broader implications in drawing that to our attentions as an 'afterthought' or, rather 'epilogiac' thought [p. 95]) and what we are passing through or over at any given time becomes an ethical, if exhausting occupation.

4 Necessary emphasis. I often wonder what would happen to Rosemary Tonks's poetry if one removed the exclamation marks (in all their profusion?) ... or, for that matter, if one removed them from my prose!

'beyond', say, the Venn diagram. Is there a 'solution' for this problem of shared area in overlapping spirals (especially where spirals oscillate/change)? Is it possible to create a nomenclature in maths *and* in poetry? The spiral is a way of configuring space and place within an active model of belonging. Yesterday we got caught in a dust devil and swayed and jostled and shifted from our intended path. It came rapidly and as a surprise, and we were part of the place as we expected it to be, as we had pre-processed, travelling the familiar, but this 'random' event temporarily changed the nature of that place and it looked and felt different. In fact, it was a threat to our expectations and could have permanently altered us and the place itself. Cause and effect.

5. I write out of where I am, even when I am writing a distant event and experience. In a sense, all writing is speculative, in that we can't entirely process what constitutes the place/s we write. Atrophy, growth, the consequences of chaos … there is no fixedness, no certainty. We can only observe change. There is no stasis, there is no 'fixed picture'. But there is no living picture as well, no *tableaux vivants* outside the arranging, the presenting. The truth is in the living, not in the capturing. All place is movement. Or Aristotelian motion. Change. I write change from *in situ*. We are at the centres of all events. We are affected by all events. We are the event. Place as event. It is a spectacle for something or someone and all of us, or we can choose to 'let it be', making it no spectacle at all. Spectacle is the fetishisation of event which is a fetishisation of place.

6. My 'Graphology 640' (Redback phantasma)[5] is an *in situ* poem that was literally written as the neurotoxin of a redback spider bite was 'coming on'. My

5 **Graphology 640: While awaiting the phantasma effects of a redback spider bite …
written for Tracy to give to the Dr should I pass out…**

It's weird typing this with one hand
and a couple of fingers, thumb out of action,
a redback having perched momentarily on the print
and a sharp, deep pain indicating a bite. It takes
some time before redback poison really gets hold –
I do feel nauseous and giddy and there's fire
flooding my palm, now extending to my wrist,
my full left hand, and pyrexia and paralysis
seem truisms. I have the flu anyway
so flashbacks – hallucinations –
are only a few memories away, and the swirl
I am caught up in promises the full son-et-lumière;
maybe I'll get the colour back into my visions.
Latrodectus. Do I imagine my lymph nodes
swelling? Ah, the glories of neurotoxins!
It is horrendously spiritual, this working up
a sweat I don't want to spill – glister
that might poison anything I touch.
I was clearing redbacks from Tim's playground.

first *overtly* (that is, meta-textual rather than purely situational) *in situ* poem
was written in 2000 in Cambridge.[6] I wrote it to make place 'alive' for Tracy in

---

I was searching out the comb-footed.
Catching the tripwires in bright daylight,
huddled up under shadecloth, nurtured
in window frames, collating exoskeletons,
strung out in the hot day where the hosts
won't go. My left hand aches
too much to type. The poem
is the order I try to impose
on my body. Proteins,
transmitters: excruciating
chemistry, electrics, déjà vu,
to flow through victim livestock
as blood product, as antivenene,
reaction against agony to stop the poem
in its tracks, muscling in on my apostasy,
its mismanagement of 2, 4, 6-trihydroxypurine,
its inevitability: the bite you have to have
to sign off on morbid fascination,
straight for a decade to slam dunk
an ultimate high: inosine, adenosine,
guanosine, all lit up as exit signs,
so fantastic seeing inside havoc
as exquisite as conscience,
dashing off lines without pause
when the body and its guidance systems
are being overloaded with syntax.

6   **Grantchester In Situ**

for Tracy, back in Australia

The river's soothed angles
scan with variegated light;
houses backdrop *in situ* –
twisted culverts
feeding the flow
that locals can't swim in;
infeudation of canola –
bright possessor
of its own light,
its own shape – stems
a map of an atmosphere's
delicate structure.
Roadside moisture
lifts out of hedges and drains,
undulations in the groundplan
complementing a dark cloud,
evoking expanse
and bleakness.
Rich cars and seasonal clothes

her 'absence' – she was in Australia at the time. Of course, it's how I've always approached the drafting of a poem ('in place' or *placed*), but I started to theorise it around 2000. The poems arising from *realtime* interaction with locality became a conversation with process as well as 'place'. Many poets have written *plein air* or *in situ* of course, but I think this is often a state of the poem itself, or of a particular poem's requirements, or even a series of 'outdoor' poems written as a group, rather than a *way of seeing* poetry writing as an act of presence and witness. For me, it's literally about an event and writing during, in and out of occasion and presence. An iteration. My *in situ* is a containment of the text within place and event, but also allowing it to speak out from this through sharing (e.g. giving to someone, or via publication where it becomes part of many other placements and timescales and spatialities). Which is not to say my *in situ* poems don't draw many 'external' and 'extraneous' factors into the poem at the time of making – of course one does and they do; that's metaphor, apart from anything else; but *in situ* immediacy tends to keep a focus on an immediate moment and locale, especially if it's *threatening* in any way (e.g. experiencing poisoning).

7. Others write of *us* writing place. When one uses figurative language in creating a 'sense' of place, it is assumed that this is not place itself. For the poet (in the broadest sense of the term), place certainly can be the text itself. For me, place is text and text is place. It's not a binary, but a code-sharing.

8. I accumulate place as I go.[7] Presence impacts, travel impacts (distributing the load and often creating residue, a third party of impacts), and as a consequence place as stability and conservation unravels. We deny the intactness of place by presence, temporary or 'permanent'. We can lessen impacts by being conscious of each step we take. As a vegan, that's quite literal for me, watching out for small creatures where my foot is about to make contact with surface. Breathing. Especially driving and its massive residues and extractions.

> defend *The Rupert Brooke* –
> designer pints and earthy jokes.
> Lord Archer raises
> the hair on their necks,
> but they're not sure why.
> Birds mimic their own songs,
> but are nowhere to be seen.
> All hangs in the air
> like brittle strands of wire.

7 Again, to refute Augé with whom I disagree more and more! When he says, 'a foreigner lost in a country he does not know (a 'passing stranger') can feel at home there only in the anonymity of motorways, service stations, big stores or hotel chains' (Augé, *Non-Places*, p. 86), this othering (and he should know!) is bizarre: the inclusive and absolutist deployment of the demographic category is part of an active attempt to delete the agency of place and the 'foreigner'. No two places are the same, no matter how much profiteers and social manipulators and social-spatial theorists try to make them so!

9. We all have our theories of how we occupy the space we inhabit or move through (we displace air and much else in being), and that is fine if they add together to lessen the strain on the biosphere. There is no ownership. There is no 'property', only a propaganda and enforcement of the notion of possession. True 'possession' is presence that doesn't delete or damage others' right of presence. To have occupied indigenous lands and denied the rights of presence to those people is wrong and essentially an act of perpetuated theft. Not a theft of something not *owned*, but a theft of presence, a theft of the very spirit and essence of country itself. *Terra nullius* is the tool of propaganda dressed up as Crown 'law' that was used to deny presence and to impose ownership. Now indigenous land rights claims are forced to use 'ownership' and 'property' as terms of discussion, using the 'enemy's' language to get back what amounts to a custodial presence. Presence brings knowledge, and that is to be respected always. But 'passing through' brings knowledge as well, and can distribute knowledge in generative and enhancing ways.

10. (a) An *in situ* example of polysituatedness – I write as I process an observation. Was just outside ('outdoors') seeing Tim and Tracy off on their journey to the city, and I looked down the hill maybe at a slightly different angle than usual, maybe in a different way because of the nature of temporary farewells, maybe because of the time of the year and the state of dry grass and the tinge of new green … and I noticed that a number of the small granites are arrayed in a semi-circle. It looks as if they have been 'arranged' in that way by human hands. I can see they go deep, like icebergs.[8] We didn't do it, and I doubt the previous occupant of the space did – not the kind of thing you'd expect, and the ground around them looks like it's been set for decades or millennia … and the lichen growth is old and set renewing and dying renewed and to die. Of course, I think much further back than 'settlement'. I have not heard of Noongar stone arrangements in this way, but that says nothing in itself. There's the unique occasion, or the acts of a group for its own reasons or a wider practice no longer discussed. Or I just don't know. What I do think of, rightly or wrong, in my polysituated self,[9] are

---

8 Igneous rock slowly revealed by weathering/erosion. But these look 'arranged'.

9 Augé writes: 'If Descombes is right we can conclude that in the world of supermodernity people are always, and never, at home…' (Augé, *Non-Places*, p. 87). I suggest that we are always and always belonging, present and part of. 'Home' is a construct of those wishing to deny belonging or to control their possession/s. And further, noting 'non-places' are often a target of terrorism, Augé writes, 'The non-place is the opposite of Utopia: it exists, and it does not contain any organic society' (Augé, *Non-Places*, p. 90), which in itself, is a terrorist overwriting of the organic fluidity of all the belonging that 'non-place' has overwritten, all the organics of those who work in such places and rely on them to support families (whatever I personally think of such places of employment), and claims other communities might be making to the land on which the edifice of 'non-place' is erected. This is not connected to land in the way Augé might think – it is often an attempt to delete local agency, but in the end it can't (see the Australian film *The Castle* as a utopian vision of resistance against the expansion of an airport's cargo-handling facilities).

the stone circles in Ireland, the sandstones and granites arranged for purposes unknown, related to the seasons, the calendar, to ritual. And a poem comes to mind that I wrote in late November in 2013 visiting the Drombeg Stone Circle in West Cork near the coast, on land 'owned' by one of Tim's schoolfriends' family. The degrees of separation. And the poem refers to the quartz of Jam Tree Gully where I write this now. I won't establish a discourse around the experience of the stones in West Cork and the realisation of the 'arrangement' of these granites I am near right now, but rather let this text and the text of the poem from 2013 prompt, refute or be left in a textual limbo. The evocation of the uncanny, the phantasm of wish-fulfilment that is part of a polysituated belief in omnipresence, the sharp-edged kerning of the visual and written texts, of memory and the here-and-now, of ethical responsibility in reporting (is it ethical to allow oneself to be affected by a spider's bite and write the experience rather than seeking immediate medical attention?) Poetry is responsibility, place is responsibility – both are ongoing acts of restitution and preparation. Both are/were welcomings but also affirmations of belonging.

White Quartz of the Drombeg Stone Circle

Fixating on a white quartz
seam in the grey standing stone
west of the recumbent stone
the megalithic becomes
geological; sunlight
in late November is free
of conjecture and ritual,
of blood and burial, teeth
of the portal, a desire
to offset cars, cameras,
roads, tractors, contrails, the lust
for electricity; white
quartz is not an uncommon
rock back at Jam Tree Gully,
largish chunks broken up by
heavy machinery, now
crystals in the schematics
of geomorphology.
Some come and hear the banshee.
Some leave quickly because 'bad
vibes' emanate; others will
believe they have made contact
with a primal truth, accessed
a subtle technology
far less damaging than their
arrival or departure.
On one stone a hair-clip rests,
simple object of complex
manufacture. The motive?

Such compulsions of white quartz
follow the sun. Tomorrow
a hair-clip will be called for.[10]

(b) *In situ* polysituatedness is about awareness and reception. To hear not just 'birds singing' as you write something unrelated to birds, but to be able to distinguish different bird songs, to hear the mice running over the ceiling, to notice a midgie inside the flywire, the warmth of the sun, the odour of smoke from burning-off, the distant rumbling of a grain train. All of this is active while you write; all of it is the space of curating of the text. Not as some pseudo-romantic 'beautiful world' subjectivity (a quasi-spiritual 'nature'-is-there-for-me take on existence), but as awareness we are not alone in anything. We are not anonymous to the ants we accidentally step on, the general cost of displacement (the space our bodies occupy, as a bird's body occupies, and so does an ant's). And readers will have their own set of concurrent experiences which will inevitably influence the way they read your text created under the influence (for, recognise variables or not, or make them generic, what goes on *in situ* as you write must enact its chaos on your agency!)

11. Profit is anathema to place if 'place' is taken as a value of intactness and integrity. If we manifest place as something desirable and holistic, then to profit from it and accumulate wealth as opposed to surviving or 'living off' it, we inevitably subtract from its substance and change it in such a way that it is diminished. In becoming a different place in *sudden* micro and macro ways (place is always becoming different, but I mean in a sudden and rapid way, as human-induced climate change is doing to the biosphere), contributing to the change of universal place in a cumulatively damaging way, it is not only the place/s it was but the emphasis becomes the place it is not and cannot be and inevitably will become. Entrepreneurs of place inevitably erode place rapidly. Custodians of place live, even prosper, as part of place without altering it too dramatically, without altering it in such a way that it can't self-heal. One *can* co-exist with a healthy and life-supporting place and change along with changes to place in a compatible and mutually aiding way. Once can also 'heal' damaged place and co-exist. And some places humans do not 'belong' in, and are best left to themselves. Humans do not have to inculcate themselves into every square metre of the planet. Taboo evolves for a reason. Taboo can be a form of self-protection for the inanimate made by the animate. An activist refusal to annexe and dominate.

12. Walking/inside and outside. Outside, it's not just a case of observation, but non-intrusive involvement. Field notes that are participatory through acknowledging the impact of one's presence, while trying to minimise that impact.

10 John Kinsella, *Firebreaks* (New York, W.W. Norton, 2016) – being parts 2 and 3 of the Jam Tree Gully cycle of books.

Inside, I am pacing back and forth over the ley lines of what was before and what still exists in my working east to west, west to east. An act of health and thinking. Tapping the barometer, checking the thermometer, I confirm what I feel the day is, and what might be coming. I confirm. I'd like to think I know it in my bones.

13. Is it possible to read Tennyson's 'The Kraken' as a polysituated *in situ* poem? How can we read a poem about a mythical creature contrived in as much of a non-'*in situ*' environment as one can imagine?

The Kraken

Below the thunders of the upper deep;
Far, far beneath in the abysmal sea,
His ancient, dreamless, uninvaded sleep
The Kraken sleepeth: faintest sunlights flee
About his shadowy sides: above him swell
Huge sponges of millennial growth and height;
And far away into the sickly light,
From many a wondrous grot and secret cell
Unnumbered and enormous polypi
Winnow with giant arms the slumbering green.
There hath he lain for ages and will lie
Battening upon huge seaworms in his sleep,
Until the latter fire shall heat the deep;
Then once by man and angels to be seen,
In roaring he shall rise and on the surface die.

Firstly, the particulars of *where* Tennyson wrote the poem, where he had been and what he had read, are obviously embedded and *mirrored* in the images and collocations ('Huge sponges'), even if the rhythms are part of a broader metrics Tennyson was developing by 1830 as a catch-all for his contemporary encounters with a heroic chthonic past. Christopher Ricks points out that it wasn't reprinted after *Poems, Chiefly Lyrical* until 1872 under the rubric 'Juvenilia'. He notes Tennyson commenting, 'See the account which Erik Pontoppidan, the Norwegian bishop, born 1698, gives of the fabulous sea-monster – the Kraken (*Biographie Universelle*) [1823]'.[11] Ricks also notes, 'Ian Kennedy suggests adding to the sources a dream in Lytton's *Falkland* (1827, p. 269), a book Tennyson knew (*Letters*, i 23)':

He was a thousand fathoms beneath the sea ... he saw the coral banks, which it requires a thousand ages to form, rise slowly ... and ever and ever, around and above him, came vast and misshapen things, – the wonders of the secret deeps;

---

11 Christopher Ricks, *Tennyson: A Selected Edition* (rev. edn, Harlow, Pearson Longman, 2007), p. 17.

and the sea-serpent, the huge chimera of the north, made its resting place by his side, glaring upon him with a livid and death-like eye, wan, yet burning as an expiring sun.[12]

Ricks mentions other reading by Tennyson that inevitably fed his mythopoetical landscape portraiture,[13] and other scholars have drawn on other sources. Indeed, one could go to Shakespeare's *The Tempest* for atmospherics, and we could consider any earlier source of Leviathan-like creatures from the early modern period back to ancient accounts of experience or belief to furnish a kraken. Tennyson was omnivorous with textual sources, as much as he was with his experience of being in the landscape and composing his verses *in situ*, as he walked.

Tennyson's imagination *was* inspired and drew on his polyvalent reading (his father's library at the rectory at Somersby, in Lincolnshire), but I would argue also that he drew on the various places[14] of habitation and visitation (the rectory at Somersby, its surroundings, the grammar school he attended for four years, Lincolnshire as a whole, especially his visits to the seaside, and later Trinity College and Cambridge – though we can't pin the writing of 'The Kraken' specifically to this time period), on the sights and sounds around him as do all poems, however and wherever they are constructed.

Even if we are dealing with sunlight and shadow through a window, or the effect of tree limbs and leaves on light streaming through or being blocked out, experience is a transcript of a language of place. While 'faintest sunlights' is generic, it is also made more specific in the pluralising of 'sunlight', a universal signifier in itself. We all might be assumed to know what sunlight is, unless kept ignorant and away from it since birth. One gets a sense of a nuancing of light across a small area, not across the world; the sunlight at this point of the garden being different from the sunlight at another. Walking through Trinity College, Cambridge, the buildings at certain times of year keeping green growth or bare trees and cobbles and certain windows in shadow, the influence of a cold and impenetrable (if shallow) greened surface of the Cam evoking a thunderous abysmal sea, as much as the seaside of his later 'Break, Break, Break'. Images by extrapolation. One can extend this example through the images of the poem, as one can through many of the

---

12 Ricks, *Tennyson*, p. 17, citing *The Letters of Alfred Lord Tennyson*, ed. Cecil Y. Lang and Edgar F. Shannon, I (1982), p. 23, and Ian Kennedy, 'Alfred Tennyson's *Bildungsgang*: Notes on His Early Reading', *Philological Quarterly*, 57 (Winter 1978), pp. 82–103 (p. 97).

13 An inadequate coinage on my part, but in this poem as in others Tennyson paints an image in which landscape and entity seem synonymous.

14 In a letter from Tennyson to Emily Sellwood of 'October or November 1838', we read: 'I have dim mystic sympathies with tree and hill reaching far back into childhood. A known landskip is to me an old friend, that continually talks to me of my own youth and half-forgotten things, and does more for me than many an old friend that I know. An old park is my delight and I could tumble about it forever.' *Alfred Tennyson: A Critical Edition of the Major Works*, ed. Adam Roberts (Oxford, Oxford University Press, 2000), p. 495.

poems that were to follow across his long life, even as it entered its entrenched imperialistic 'laureate phase'.

This fifteen-line poem is claimed as a 'sonnet' despite its 'extra' line, but is it intentionally *not* a sonnet because to package the imagined scenario so completely would be to consign it to 'illustration'? Maybe. Rather, Tennyson probably broke the convention to create a sense of the uncanny that is in this case an illogical but visceral connection to the real. With its apocalyptic awakening and death at the end, in the cataclysm of Edenic fall, corruption and revelation, we undergo a 'natural' occlusion of a religious theme.

Critics have latched on to what seem obvious correlations with Milton's *Paradise Lost*, Shelley's *Prometheus Unbound* and obviously *Revelation* 8.1[15] and Ricks notes that M.A. Lourie argues for 'a new kind of Romanticism' in Tennyson. If one believes, as I do, that Romanticism was less *plein air* than contrived from the experiences to fit a verse aesthetic of communal relations between consenting writers and readers, then it is both new and *the same* in enlivening the mythological through observations of nature (light and dark, growth and death…).

In the end, I would argue that Tennyson relied on what was immediately to hand – a 'slumbering green' of a garden (either blowsy with summer or hidden under bare branches in winter), 'sickly light' (the inside of a house), and a deep fear of the (female) abject expressed through a contraindicative use of grotesque male 'fertility': 'swell huge sponges' and 'enormous polypi' play about 'a wondrous grot and secret cell' in an exchange of terminal fructification. A youth's sex-death poem (possibly associated with a fear of epilepsy supposedly brought on by sexual 'overactivity' and 'madness' associated with excess in general … part of Tennyson's family's medical history, and Tennyson's own tendency to trances which he didn't stop fearing until after much water and other therapy later in life) speaks many presences and many *in situs*, from the onanistic to the walk through the garden to the reading of vivid mythologies by poor lights late at night.

The poem is full of a desire to resolve frustration of body as place enacted through the mythological 'imaginary' (which creates a safe distance from its core sexual place subjectivity). That's how poems are made. In this unsonnet, it's in the fourth and fifth lines with their caesura colons across which meaning and encounter leap that I locate myself, that is the space of viewing the place of writing, seeing and broadcast:

> The Kraken sleepeth: faintest sunlights flee
> About his shadowy sides: above him swell

If we are to take the approach of Tennyson's creating lines and snippets as he walked that would later find their 'setting' in the way the Poetry Foundation cast it in their extended 'biographical' note on the poet, we would be misguided:

---

15 Ricks, *Tennyson*, p. 18.

One peculiar aspect of his method of composition was set, too, while he was still a boy: he would make up phrases or discrete lines as he walked, and store them in his memory until he had a proper setting for them. As this practice suggests, his primary consideration was more often rhythm and language than discursive meaning.[16]

I would argue that such an activity is decisive evidence of a polysituated approach to place in poetry, that lines inspired by one point of a walk can conspire and converse with snippets from another point, or indeed, a different locale, and that adhere themselves to an imagined or perceived scaffolding of place: a template. The sublimation and 'dispersal' of place within text, reshaped (or shaped) by the tools of prosody, make it no less place! In apparent contradiction to the implication of the sentences from the Poetry Foundation biography, further on in the text we read more accurately:

> Nonetheless, in the Pyrenees Tennyson marked out a new dimension of the metaphorical landscape that had already shown itself in 'Mariana', and for the rest of his life the mountains remained as a model for the classical scenery that so often formed the backdrop of his poetry. The Pyrenees generated such marvelous poems as 'Oenone', which he began writing there; 'The Lotos-Eaters', which was inspired by a waterfall in the mountains; and 'The Eagle' which was born from the sight of the great birds circling above them as they climbed in the rocks.[17]

And I would make the same claim for the more 'mythological' and imagined apparently contrived dreamscape of 'The Kraken'. But we should also take to task the 'metaphorical landscape' and 'backdrop of his poetry', as these statements again reduce the agency of place in Tennyson's poetry – being a watercolour 'wash' makes it no less real and material, no less pressing on the vision and narrative created in the poem. A polysituated model critiques degree of engagement and expression of this engagement, but doesn't discount even the smallest amount of paint in the colouring. Place is more than a zone for the extraction of imagery ('He came again and again to walk in the valley, and it provided him with imagery until his death more than sixty years later'); it is an active part of the poetry and the part of the fabric of the *in situ* composition that is redrafted (mentally and graphologically), remade and reinvented. The traces remain and are a vital part of the poem within the poem.

On further considering artifice, place and polyvalent translation from the textual and the imagined in 'The Kraken', we *might* conclude that the embodiment of place in such a poem 'of the imagination' borders on the literal, never

16 Alfred, Lord Tennyson, biography at the Poetry Foundation, http://www.poetryfoundation. org/bio/alfred-tennyson (accessed 22 April 2015).
17 Alfred, Lord Tennyson, biography at the Poetry Foundation, http://www.poetryfoundation. org/bio/alfred-tennyson (accessed 22 April 2015).

mind the symbolic.[18] In popular renditions of Tennyson's biography, 'landscape' is formative and omnipresent. For example, the Wikipedia entry for Somersby is psychogeographically configured (or, maybe, configures its 'consensus' via par-anonymous authorship as its presentation to the world through this) through the notion that Somersby as place underpins the almost mythopoetic figure of Tennyson:

> Alfred, Lord Tennyson, Poet Laureate, was born and raised in Somersby, the son of the rector, and the fourth of twelve children. When he wrote *The Babbling Brook* he was referring to a small stream here. Other features of the local landscape are claimed as features mentioned in Tennyson's poetry, such as 'Woods that belt the grey hillside' and 'The silent woody places by the home that gave me birth'. In 1949 the copper beech was reported to be still standing at the former rectory which was mentioned in *In Memoriam*: 'Unwatched, the garden bough shall sway,/ The tender blossom flutter down,/Unloved, that beech will gather brown,/This maple burn itself away.' The same poem also mentions leaving 'the well-beloved place / Where first we gazed upon the sky'. In such poems as *The Lady of Shalott* Tennyson uses the word "wold" for a hill in a sense found in Lincolnshire.[19]

The sea may be quite a few miles from Somersby, but it was a fixture in Tennyson's constellation of place and a *racine caractéristique*[20] in his rotations through the conceptual and physical landscape his family home bordered on, and bled into. In another popular information source we read:

18 See visionary New Zealand poet James K. Baxter's sixteen-line poem 'The Kraken' for embodiment of place and the displacement of Euro-myth by the power of the place he is writing. Its almost matter-of-fact engagement with the sea, with the reality of 'cliff-top boulders and/ The abandoned gun-pit', resonates pointedly around Tennyson's (distant, curatorial?) version. But both, I argue, are poems of *place/s* (in Baxter's case possibly *against* an invasive sense of imperial poetics!) The last lines of this superb, highly visceral poem go:

> Out of the gulf's throat. Even the dead
> Who made this from dug earth, proud air,
>
> Something cruder than that they meant,
> Hang on museum walls. As night comes
>
> You will hear from the lighthouse the foghorn speak
> With a shuddering note, and watch how the kraken's wide
>
> Blinding tendrils move like smoke
> Over the rock neck, the muttering flats, the houses.

James K. Baxter, *Selected Poems*, ed. J. E. Weir (Oxford, Oxford University Press, 1982), p. 84.
19 'Somersby, Lincolnshire', http://en.wikipedia.org/wiki/Somersby,_Lincolnshire (accessed 16 May 2015).
20 See reference in 'Eigenvalue, eigenvector and eigenspace', http://www.cs.mcgill.ca/~rwest/link-suggestion/wpcd_2008-09_augmented/wp/e/Eigenvalue%252C_eigenvector_and_eigenspace.htm (accessed 16 May 2015).

At the lonely rectory in Somersby the children were thrown upon their own resources. All writers on Tennyson emphasize the influence of the Lincolnshire countryside on his poetry: the plain, the sea about his home, 'the sand-built ridge of heaped hills that mound the sea,' and 'the waste enormous marsh.'[21]

And more pertinently to the case in point, to the polysituated nexus of textual/imagined/geographical co-ordinates that form the template for 'The Kraken', we might consider Tennyson's recent biographer John Batchelor's statement regarding the 1827 publication of *Poems by Two Brothers*:

> On the afternoon of the publication Alfred and Charles hired a carriage with some of the money that Jackson had paid as their advance, and drove over the wolds and marshes to their favourite part of the coast, Mablethorpe, where they 'shared their triumph with the winds and the waves'.[22]

This was Tennyson's first book,[23] actually published with his two other brothers, Frederick and Charles, and containing a number of mentions of the 'sea' that are mostly what critics might term 'literary convention', but also, arguably, moments that feel underpinned with more *in situ encounter* than convention. Thinking of the volume as a *collective work* of family, rather than as the individual poems one would usually argue they properly are, we might consider 'We Meet No More'[24] as containing a sense of literal contact with 'sea' despite the love/loss/fate conventions of the poem. Note also a relevant engagement with Burke's 'The sublime always dwells on great objects and terrible' in 'Sublimity'.[25] And most relevantly, when thinking of possible texts we might 'connect' with 'The Kraken' and the geo-psycho-ecology around it, go to 'Love'[26] and the lines:

> The mighty sea-snake of the storm,
> The vorticella's viewless form,
>
> The vast leviathan, which takes
> His pastime in the sounding floods;

with its note on 'vorticella' saying, 'See Baker on animalculae'.

Some might rub their hands with glee at the prospect of crossing the liminal to reach the edge of the sea (see the Batchelor quote above), though I would argue that the marshes were not liminal but as integral as the sea is itself to Tennyson's

---

21 http://www.britannica.com/EBchecked/topic/587422/Alfred-Lord-Tennyson (accessed 16 May 2015).
22 John Batchelor, *Tennyson: To Strike, To Seek, To Find* (New York: Pegasus Books, 2013), p. 38.
23 My references are to Alfred and Charles Tennyson, *Poems by Two Brothers* (Thomas Y. Crowell & Co., 1900). Despite its title, the book also includes poems by a third brother, Frederick.
24 Alfred and Charles Tennyson, *Poems by Two Brothers*, p. 39.
25 Alfred and Charles Tennyson, *Poems by Two Brothers*, p. 91.
26 Alfred and Charles Tennyson, *Poems by Two Brothers*, p. 167.

sense of what constitutes belonging at this stage of his life. In 'The Kraken', the boundaries are between the world above and its breaching, and the world below and its strange intactness: when that intactness is broken, the end is upon us. Those who have been shipwrecked are liberated only by the apocalypse. The (under)sea becomes *all*-place (for that is the nature of tribulation and revelation).

I am further convinced in this by Batchelor's citation of Tennyson's fascinating early version (published so much later in an extended three-part version) of the poem 'The Lover's Tale'. As Batchelor notes, 'Camilla and Julian are looking at a painting of a ship and then find themselves within the painting itself',[27] and lines such as the following persuade me of the very tactile relationship between the imagined and the real:

> That painted vessel, as with inner life,
> Began to heave upon that painted sea;

and:

> ... the storm dropt to windless calm, and I
> Down weltered through the dark ever and ever.

The overtones of Coleridge's 'Rime of the Ancient Mariner' aside, this sense of fusion[28] and fluidity between/across the imagined/creative and the tactile/'real' was essential to Tennyson's realisation of place and presence within the 'aesthetic'. Interestingly, one of the Google Maps sea images taken from Mablethorpe,[29] facing out across the beach into a distant tidal sea with *lowering* grey clouds overhead, looks Turneresque, and as photo encapsulates the visual drive (over many decades of English arts-making) towards 'capturing' the tension between beauty and threat in the English coastline. The rendering of sublimity into artifice was a modus operandi for Tennyson's covering of his tracks, never deleting them. 'Place' is a permanence in all his work (including his later *in situ* investigations for the *Idylls*), even as it manifests as a displacement of the reader's focus.[30]

27　Batchelor, *Tennyson*, p. 54.

28　In his landmark review of Tennyson's *Poems, Chiefly Lyrical* (1830), Arthur Hallam noted of Tennyson's poetry, 'Thirdly, his vivid, picturesque delineation of objects, and the peculiar skill with which he holds all of them fused, to borrow a metaphor from science, in a medium of strong emotion' ('On Some of the Characteristics of Modern Poetry, and On the Lyrical Poems of Alfred Tennyson', *Englishman's Magazine*, August 1831). Hallam's comment might be seen as a prototypical psycho-polysituatedness in its orientation, if not application.

29　Also the 'setting' of the great poem written in the long shadow of Arthur Hallam's death, 'Break, break, break', which carries the deepest resonances and template of place as transitional space of the living and the dead – a nexus. As the late 'Crossing the Bar' would set a (different) literal place within the transitional space/nexus (different from the so-called *liminal*) of belonging, departure and the spiritual-imagined.

30　It is worth considering these lines from the verse in the Delphi *Complete Works of Alfred, Lord Tennyson*:

As an example of Tennysonian polysituatedness, we can see here in an extract from Hallam Tennyson's memoir of his father the interweaving of place 'reality' with place 'imagined':

In his youth he sang of the brook flowing through his upland valley, of the 'ridged wolds' that rose above his home, of the mountain-glen and snowy summits of his early dreams, and of the beings, heroes and fairies, with which his imaginary world was peopled. Then was heard the 'croak of the raven', the harsh voice of those who were unsympathetic –

> The light retreated,
> The landskip darken'd,
> The melody deaden'd,
> The Master whisper'd
> 'Follow the Gleam.'

Still the inward voice told him not to be faint-hearted but to follow his ideal. And by the delight in his own romantic fancy, and by the harmonies of nature, 'the warble of water', and 'cataract music of falling torrents', the inspiration of the poet was renewed. His Eclogues and English Idylls followed, when he sang the songs of country life and the joys and griefs of country folk, which he knew through and through.[31]

Tennyson's imperialistic reaching-out is a case of manipulation through language (verse) to impose place-controls, to occupy other spaces. Even Tennyson's greatest poem (to my mind), that which he requested should end all his future books, 'Crossing the Bar', fuses past, present and future; and as a poem of deliverance and faith, of afterlife, of redemption after or beyond the (metaphoric but historically literal) wreckage caused by a difficult tide-action of the sandshoal/bar, it is, in the reversal of the Pilot's action (moving out to the Pilot), a poem of occupation rather than return. Moving out to sea/death, the protagonist's contact with the Pilot is a dynamic of (a quasi-Christian) deliverance, not to have been guided as an incoming vessel (boat or human) to port (as has been noted by many) but *out* (the protagonist on the verge of death): 'When I put out to sea' – he is being guided out to safety/heaven rather than into safety/his earthly home/dwelling. There's a sense of incipient *conquest* in this, maybe:

Within the summer-house of which I spoke,
Hung round with paintings of the sea, and one
A vessel in mid ocean...

The matrix of internal and external spaces – the painting, the sea itself, the vessel – all interweave and there is no absolute separation of 'nature' from artifice (rather, they are interactive aesthetic and 'real' qualities). Place is polysemous and polysituated.

31 From Baron Hallam Tennyson Tennyson, *Alfred Lord Tennyson: A Memoir by His Son* (New York, Macmillan, 1897), Vol. 1, Preface, pp. xii–xiii.

> For tho' from out our bourne of Time and Place
>> The flood may bear me far,
> I hope to see my Pilot face to face
>> When I have crost the bar.[32]

Strangely, I always think of the irony of Depeche Mode's 1989 song (said to come out of Priscilla Presley's memoir of Elvis Presley) 'Personal Jesus' in the fetish of comfort and familiarity in the here and now, *vis-à-vis* one's eventual journey to the afterlife. One might argue that colonialism is a polysituated desire for paradise (that inevitably breaks down, though it too often maintains a grotesque and equally invasive momentum). An imperialist urge is as implicit in the yoking of fairies and landscape and a heroic enculturation – and it is not hard to decipher why Tennyson has an anxiety about the mystical combativeness of the Celts/Irish in the context of his adulation of empire and the monarch (and the Queen's consort – Albert was Tennyson's fan and powerful backer). In the memoir, Hallam cites Tennyson saying of the Irish (among other things), absurdly,

> For one thing the English do not understand their innate love of fighting, words and blows ... She [Ireland] has absolute freedom now, and more than full share in the government of one of the mightiest empires in the world. Whatever she may say, she is not only feudal, but oriental, and loves those in authority over her to have the iron hand in a silken gloves.[33]

The Irish poet Patrick Kavanagh, apologist for the English language (no doubt because of his lack of visceral connection to the Irish language) even in the

---

32 Roberts (ed.), *Tennyson*, p. 478.
33 Tennyson, *Memoir*, Vol. 2, p. 338. In his biography, John Batchelor cites Emily, Tennyson's wife, as writing in 1861 to Mrs Margaret Gatty on receiving the gift of a book: 'An enthusiastic acquaintance of the Tennyson's, Mrs Margaret Gatty, sent as a gift an advance copy of her book about a holiday in Ireland; she must have been taken aback by Emily's reaction: 'Do you know I love not the Irish [.] I think them a nest of traitors with some honourable exceptions [.] ... patriotism I love [,] nationality I love not. I wish conquered nations could take gracefully the married state upon them' (Batchelor, *Tennyson*, p. 272). One might read into this not only Emily's deep conservatism, but also her frustration with being her husband's literary dogsbody (their son Hallam would become that later)! But lest we think that this attitude was hers alone, one need only think of Tennyson's myopic (literal and figurative) visit to famine-struck Ireland. Consider this observation from Melissa Fegan, in *Literature and the Irish Famine, 1845–1919* (Oxford, Oxford University Press, 2002), p. 99: 'Perhaps it was Alfred Tennyson's shortsightedness which protected him from despair on his tour – or perhaps a more determined self-imposed myopia. The poet spent three months at Aubrey De Vere's Curragh Chase estate in County Limerick in early 1848; his conditions for accepting the invitation were that he should not be expected downstairs for breakfast, he should be able to smoke in the house, he must have half the day alone for writing – and there was to be no mention of Irish distress. De Vere remembered that Tennyson was fond of reading poetry aloud to the family after dinner: "on one occasion after finishing 'A Sorrowful Tale' by Crabbe, [he] glanced round reproachfully and said, 'I do not see that any of you are weeping!'" Only Tennyson could have expected a family who were confronted daily with scenes of destitution and death to weep at a poem.'

context of his troubled Catholic apologism, resented, suspected and was likely jealous of Yeats because of undercurrents of style and prosodic entrapment in the 'Anglo' part of the Anglo-Irish equation. In West Cork where the English hippie culture of the 1970s still has a firm footing, this tension is still present, not only in a suspicion of colonial residues but within the communities themselves, about the nature of connection, belonging and rejection. A sense of 'linking' with pre-Celt is as present as Celt, and an awareness of the 'Others' is part of this melding with place, a kind of circumventing of colonial/plantation history.

Tennyson notes his (admittedly beautiful) poem, 'The Voyage of Maeldune', as being '[f]ounded on an Irish legend A.D. 700', though it in fact owes very little to the original, which is found in the 'Book of the Dun Cow' (the twelfth-century manuscript *Lebor na hUidre*, which disturbingly is said to be inscribed – or what fragments remain of it – on the 'hide of a dun cow') as 'The Voyage of Máel Dúin's Boat' (*Immram curaig Maíle Dúin* – a poem of which I did a 'version' in mid-2015, using Whitley Stokes's translation as a template).

This navigation poem (an 'Imrama' – in this case, 'Three years and seven months was it wandering in the ocean', trans. Stokes), with its tangents to Brendan the Navigator (and other voyagers) who was represented with his boat as the logo of our son Tim's school in Schull, West Cork, and whose statue stands boldly ready to discover the world from Bantry Harbour,[34] becomes an imperial/ conquest/colonial representation in its Tennysonian subtext. The original poem is one of a vengeance quest, with trials and tribulations arising from a violation of the Druid's instruction to Máel Dúin (who seeks the murderer of his father, who himself raped Máel Dúin's mother, a nun!) to only take seventeen companions on his voyage. The tension between a Christian God (providence) and a persistent pagan *real-world* (they are tested in many ways, including on islands of boat-eating ants, men who lament and infect others with their lamentations, a woman who attacks them with nuts and so on) brings knowledge through loss and conflict, so an original crime is forgiven in the end, as it is in Tennyson's version.

The subtext in the Tennyson take on this eighth-century story retold in the twelfth century creates an anxiety over acceptance of that 'iron fist in a silk glove' version of enslavement, a version of More's Utopian *some would rather be slaves in Utopia than…* starving in their homes (and the Irish ended up starved, too – it's all contemporaneous). Forgiveness, rather than vengeance,

---

34 Is it ironic that the statue of a prototypical 'explorer'-missionary was funded by a petroleum company that represents the coloniser and an exploiter of the natural world? Further, in a town that witnessed the oil disaster at Whiddy Island a decade later (50 people died), it disturbs in its embracing of the unknown, its faith in 'discovery'. The West Cork People website on its sculpture trail pages notes: 'The bronze sculpture by Imogen Stuart sits on a limestone plinth. It depicts St. Brendan with arms dramatically outstretched, accompanied by two companions. The prow of the boat carries an interesting combination of sea waves and Celtic interleafing. A plaque at the base states that it was erected to commemorate the opening of Whiddy Island Oil Terminal in Bantry Bay in 1969. It was unveiled in May 1969 by Taoiseach Jack Lynch. It was funded by the oil company British Petroleum.' http://www.westcorkpeople. ie/features/a-west-cork-sculpture-trail-part-seven/ (accessed 4 July 2016).

is something I believe in and admire, and is part of the creation of the very text of this book as much as any citing of a secondary or primary textual source outside my own agency, but Tennyson's poem is essentially a self-apologia for the voyages of exploration and colonialism, merging accident and fate (departing was an accident and knowledge and awareness came through a form of divine decree and witness) with destiny – we are our enemy, and we are bound together in our being. It ends:

> And we came to the Isle we were blown from, and there on the shore was he,
> That man that had slain my father. I saw him and let him be.
> O weary was I of the travel, the trouble, the strife and the sin,
> When I landed again, with a tithe of my men, on the Isle of Finn.

The letting-be is a moral lesson to the Irish, not to the British conquerors. In Whitley Stokes's translation, we read the end thus:

> At nightfall they sight land like the land of Ireland. They row towards it. They find a small island and it was from this very island that the wind had borne them into the ocean when the first went to sea.
> Then they put their prow on shore, and they went toward the fortress that was in the island, and they were listening, and the inhabitants of the fortress were then dining. They heard some of them saying: "It is well for us if we should not see Mael Duin."
> "That Mael Duin has been drowned," saith another man of them.
> "Mayhap it is he who will wake you out of your sleep," saith another man.
> "If he should come now," saith another, "what should we do?"
> "That were not hard (to say)," saith the chief of the house: "great welcome to him if he should come, for he hath been for a long space in much tribulation."
> Thereat Mael Duin strikes the clapper against the door valve. "Who is there?" saith the doorkeeper.
> "Mael Duin is here," saith he himself. "Then open!" saith the chief, "welcome is thy coming."
> So they entered the house, and great welcome is made to them, and new garments are given them. Then they, declare all the marvels which God had revealed to them according to the word of the sacred poet who saith *Haec olim meminisse iuuabit.* Mael Duin (then) went to his own district, and Diuran the Rhymer took the five half-ounces (of silver) which [he] brought from the net, and laid them on the altar of Armagh in triumph and in exultation at the miracles and great marvel which God had wrought for them. And they declared their adventures from beginning to end, and all the dangers and perils they had found on sea and land. Now Aed the Fair, chief sage of Ireland, arranged this story as it standeth here; and he did (so), for delighting the mind and for the folks of Ireland after him.[35]

The paradoxical nature of Tennyson's 'relationship' with Ireland, the Irish and Irish literature, and the fabric of empire that underpins the world of his recognition, as affirmation against uncertainty (family disruption, fear of madness

---

35 Whitley Stokes, *Revue Celtique* 9 & 10, http://sejh.pagespersoorange.fr/keltia/immrama/maeldun_en.html (accessed 2 May 2015).

and aberrant sexuality, of grotesque aspirations to nobility while enacting a parvenu-like rise himself using his son as his excuse), is embodied in a comment in Hallam's *Memoir*:

> My father continues: 'The oldest form of "Maeldue" is the *Book of the Dun Cow* (1160). I read the legend in Joyce's *Celtic Legends*, but most of the details are mine.'
>
> By this story he intended to represent in his own original way the Celtic genius, and he wrote the poem with a genuine love of the peculiar exuberance of the Irish imagination.[36]

Interestingly, Hallam Tennyson, not long after publishing his *Memoir*, became Governor of South Australia (1899–1902) and even acting Governor-General (1902) then Governor-General (for a year – 1903–04; he was in conflict with Prime Minister Deakin) in the early years of the Australian Commonwealth. Hallam notes in his memoir of his father, 'He explained the "Pilot" as that "Divine and Unseen Who is always guiding us".'[37] The unseen was always part of his polysituated self, anchored as it was in Lincolnshire (and later the Pyrenees, Isle of Wight, Farringford etc.). Of Lincolnshire idiomatics, Hallam wrote, 'The Lincolnshire dialect poems are so true in dialect and feeling, that when they were first read in that county a farmer's daughter exclaimed: "That's Lincoln's labourer's talk, and I thought Mr Tennyson was a gentleman."'[38] It strikes me that the Tennysonian (father & son) publicity machine was as honed as the tweet-soundbite-Instagram image is today!

14. In creating paracosms of place, we template place. Take this piece I wrote on 16 April 2015 and typed into this Word document from its typewriter draft:

Jam Tree Gully Paracosm

for Tracy, who knows about paracosms

1. Location

North of east, south of west,
you'll find us *in situ*, local
in tableaux, locale, but not
property anathema to appease
presence of taking where else
we ask we say genuinely up
the crescent not thrown horse-
shoe, up from the silent wheatbin, almost opposite the elevated
wandoo – the highest point.
In the semi 'down here which

---

36 Tennyson, *Memoir*, Vol. 2, p. 255.
37 Tennyson, *Memoir*, Vol. 2, p. 366.
38 Tennyson, *Memoir*, Vol. 2, p. 10.

is still well above the plain north,
we coexist with York gum
and acacias, partially thrive
a pocket against much weathering,
encouraging and gathering some,
pocket microclimatic sac inside
sheep zone where in come
the *baaaas* but not from where
we huddle amidst *surroundsound*
and speak back nothing from them.

2. In the eye

Dirt in the eye in the eye of
being here and being rated
citizens of the shire, shire
fantastical to ward off
the poisoners of verges
the potions and tipples,
match-winning days
where a local inflection
is a translation of clubs
and drinking compadrés
shout and stomp and alley-oop /
alley-oop! to funnel down valley
all the way, all the way
down the road and railway
to the sandy plain, to the city.

3. Venturing out & about

Stepping off into woodsmoke
and contradiction of crisp cool
sunlight, wisped warm strains
dance an isobar jig, stepping
out to realise landscape is bent
to shape to vent our form
by testosterone and oxytocin,
that dirt and sticks and rocks
and flesh are at the mercy
of the soup of life.

15. The indigenous Australian poet, Jack Davis, wrote his early poems on lunch papers way out from the homestead and buildings of the stations he worked in the Gascoyne. Those poems were lost but were later remade and collected in his first book. They were in his memory, and they connected with the memories of other indigenous people and peoples he encountered at the time, during his life – their trails, their namings, their stories, their ways of seeing and

hearing, of reading country, overlaid the Western mannerisms and gestures of versification he made use of.

What he wrote 'out there' may have pertained to other places (Yarloop, the Moore River Native Settlement, Perth, Brookton, Carnarvon), but they were mediated through the place/s in which they formulated, came into being, gestated and became realised. A polysituated poem has many lines of overlay and connection and polyvalent communication – it might be from a rocky outcrop to a pool below (intrinsic to each other but also 'separate'), or it might be across hundreds even thousands of kilometres or strides or footsteps. *In situ* poems are built in the here-and-now as a memory to come. They are a repository for all time and were always going to be made and stored.

Jack Davis: A Life Story[39] is a work based on Jack Davis's 'taped conversations' with Keith Chesson who 'fuses' his own 'writing into that of the narrative'. We read:

> In my own way, I was a member of that company of 'eccentrics'. One literally inclined stockman nicknamed me the 'Black Banjo', for the habit of writing had become ingrained. Throughout my stay in the Gascoyne, I was consistently composing poetry. There was a constant flow of inspiration, and with the stub of a pencil I continued to scribble verses on lunch-wrappings and other scraps of paper. At the age of twenty, I submitted a poem to the *Northern Times*, and received a letter of acceptance from the editor. I can still remember that poem:
>
> > I built a boat of dreams
> > I set it sailing on a calm, blue sea
> > With silver sails
> > The fabric of my schemes
> > Floating on a sea of unreality.
> >
> > The storms clouds gather fast ahead
> > Too late to care
> > My silver sails are torn to shreds
> > I am left standing forlorn and in despair.
> >
> > I cannot build a boat again
> > My eyes are dim with age of old
> > Far too soon I have reached my mount of pain
> > My eyes grow dim, my flesh grows cold.
>
> For some reason the poem was not printed and I assumed that this was because Aboriginal people were not expected to write poetry. I saw discrimination in the off-handed way I had been treated and didn't attempt to publish again for many years. But I went on writing for my own amusement. A lot of the poems that I wrote were lost, as old lunchpapers are apt to be; but I have been able to recall many of them, and they form the bulk of my published poetry.[40]

39 Keith Chesson, *Jack Davis: A Life Story* (Melbourne, Dent, 1988).
40 Chesson, *Jack Davis: A Life Story*, pp. 111–12.

So, for Davis, poetry became an act of retrieval and this is not unconnected with his growing respect for and understanding of traditions of Aboriginal education and learning in which retention and passing on are intimately tied to the storyteller's personality as well as to community in the corroboree and singing around the night fires. As we read, when Davis was working stations as a drover and fence-rider in the Gascoyne during the late 1930s, he built on the knowledge and awareness of 'his people' that he acquired through his nine months at the Moore River Native Settlement when he was fifteen. The text reads, 'At Williambury my respect for my Aboriginal origins became firmly established.' It continues:

> Many of the older people were well educated, in every sense of the word. Most could speak three or four languages, and some even more. They could memorize about seven hundred sets of human footprints and read every movement of men and animals from the records left in the sand. Very little escaped their notice. Some of their song-cycles consisted of more than two-hundred verses, and these were memorized and passed from group to group.[41]

In his act of retrieval, when he later started to rewrite his poems from memory, or to create new ones for the manuscript that would become *The First-Born and Other Poems*,[42] Davis created an intense juxtaposition between being 'brought up in European culture', insofar as his life and schooling in the wood-milling town of Yarloop south of Perth was just that, while his family stories and knowledges tapped into the indigenous heritages of both his mother and father, children of the stolen generation – his father had a Sikh father and his mother a white father (their mothers being their lifeline and connection to country). Davis's engagement with his indigenous heritage was intense and also orientated by the places he felt close to, especially the Noongar land he grew up on (his parents were born in the Northern Pilbara region, but he himself was born in Perth), focussed through the knowledge of his stepfather (his mother's second partner, following her moving the family to Brookton to be with relatives, after struggling on her husband's death and having to take government native rations, which she'd never done before). Jack Davis's stepfather was an elder with profound knowledge of his people and country in the region around Brookton. This energetic boy who loved to study the dictionary as a child, whose ('illiterate') mother harboured hopes of him becoming a writer, produced a vital and new poetics in the sense of how and why a poetry text is created, working alongside the reconfigurings of English verse in Kath Walker (later Oodgeroo) who preceded him to book publication by some years, and changed the scape of Australian poetry forever.

In collecting Jack Davis's poetry,[43] I did not include his first 'accepted' poem (see above: 'Boat of Dreams', accepted for newspaper publication though

---

41 Chesson, *Jack Davis: A Life Story*, p. 101.
42 Jack Davis, *The First-born and Other Poems* (Sydney, Angus and Robertson, 1970).
43 John Kinsella (ed.), *The Poems of Jack Davis: A Retrospective* (Broome, forthcoming).

never actually published) in the body of this collection but rather an as appendix, though a different version of it appeared in *Black Life*.[44] It bears the motifs of hope and ambition, of the redemptive nature of metaphor and its failure, the harsh jolt of an unsympathetic reality. It was a symbolist poem perhaps without Davis having read the symbolists (we assume), but the later 'reversioning' (construction from memory) is even more symbolist when we can assume he had fully absorbed and processed symbolism as literary trope and translation of experience. Where age and the body and seeing the elderly Yamatjis around him on the station underpin his youth in the first version, by the second, 'place' is *also* rendered as 'literary motif'.[45] On the mulga plains, herding sheep, fixing fences, experiencing lightning strike and seeing death, the sea becomes an *idée fixe*, a motif of difference. Davis loved the land he was on, so it's not escape in the literal sense, but it is aspiration for something ineffable with which he is coming into contact through the dispossessed peoples of the place and wider implications of belonging and connection.

One is reminded of Davis being told of approaching storms by Aboriginal people with whom he was working on the stations, and one also can imagine that though he felt connected and engaged with country, there was a disturbed sense of self in place that was driving him to search further, and to keep searching. In this early piece reconfigured twice in two different contexts (in 1988 in *Jack Davis: A Life Story* and 1992 in *Black Life: Poems*) we see the activist, the poet, the playwright, the memoirist and the searcher/wanderer all at work. It's not one of his finest poems, but it is an important reference point in understanding the complexity of even the most straightforward image or motif in Davis's work. He was an indigenous artist with European awareness – the paradox allows him to crack open so much colonial injustice, and to touch on country and people with love, compassion and respect.

Jack Davis told his life story in many and various ways over the years – as part of recorded tapes transcribed, in his work *A Boy's Life*,[46] in his introduction to his first volume of poetry, *The First-born and Other Poems*, and in his plays and later volumes of poetry. He was always recounting, holding himself to account, and opening connections between his own experience and that of other Aboriginal people. The slippages between tellings are illuminating – in many ways ambiguities and uncertainties are the materials of poetry: constant refocusings on the same material, which we know of course is never really the same, and constantly altering in the recollection, telling and hearing. In his introduction to *The First-born*, Davis writes:

Life in the North-west was very different to life in Yarloop. But I loved the North. One time, as a matter of fact, I lived on an out-camp for two years on my

44 See Jack Davis, *Black Life: Poems* (Brisbane, University of Queensland Press, 1992).
45 The 'Catch 22' of witness and experience becoming poetry and the crisis for any activist poet. The tension between text and event is implicit in all such poetics and poems.
46 Jack Davis, *A Boy's Life* (Broome, 1991).

own. I saw the Boss in that two years about eight or nine times ... It was the country I liked.

This place where I was, was break-away country, the valley floor was down about three to four-hundred feet; and the hills, which were sheer, were all around me. It was really beautiful country, stark, the green of spinifex; and when it did rain, which was seldom, the grass would green up very quickly, flowers would come out, live perhaps three or four days and then die. I used to feel that that particular piece of country was my own and there was many and many a piece of verse which I wrote and which I unfortunately lost or destroyed myself.[47]

The telling of the loss of these poems in different ways under slightly different circumstances (including the choice of destruction rather than abandonment or losing them) reiterates the paradox of pain and compulsion (the generative drive) this period had for Davis as a writer. It is significant that he calls the country his 'own', especially when set against his commitment to writing and acknowledging whose traditional country it was and is.

This layering of belonging and connection, of being resident and passing through, and the dynamic of spatiality and locale this engenders, is at the core of Davis's poetry, which is reconciliatory, open-ended and inclusive. He never takes a back step from resisting the colonial project, dispossession by white expansionism and greed, nor from the spiritual and material rights of Aboriginal peoples over *their* land. But Davis's claim to connection does not disenfranchise or deny other 'ownerships' – his connection does not delete other presences or their claims. Rather, they are co-determinate, co-exist and share place on numerous overlapping levels while acknowledging other levels that are private, reserved, privileged and outside general access. To me, this is the epitome of polysituatedness. The poems Davis created in this place matter because they fuse a found sense of connection that also sends out axons received by the dendrites of other peoples with whom he shares much even though of a different skin and country. The poems are the speaking and the reaching out. Davis continues:

Don't forget, I wasn't always on my own. When I was on that out-camp, sometimes the tribes came through. At one time there was about four hundred and fifty camped there on their annual pingai – that's their walkabout – about seven miles from me...

I stayed with them that night and all next day until it got cool and then I went home. But I had a really wonderful time with these people. They broke up into little groups that night and one group started singing and I can still see the scene, the pool down the bottom of the hill with the gum-trees around it, their moving around in the moonlight, the windmill behind them where they could get water if they wanted it, although they had the creek, small fires dotted over the hill itself – a small hillside where they camped – you could hear them talking in their own language and now and then there'd be a burst of laughter.[48]

47 Davis, *First-born*, p. xiii.
48 Davis, *First-born*, pp. xiii–xiv.

This is no romantic rendition of the way Davis would like it to be, but a genuine admiration, respect and sense of privilege in connecting with country and people. He returns 'home' because home is where he is, where he needs to be, and where the tribal people clearly allow him to be. An understanding of connection through place, rather than a conflict over that place, drives Davis's language of warmth and engagement. He suggests a kinship of sorts, yet respects the distance and difference. He searches out and honours points of contact that change who he is and help him grow into place. Culture and place are mutually dependent.

It is disturbing to note that Davis believed his father (Bill Bung Singh who later changed his name to William/Bill Davis), who was taken from his Aboriginal mother in the far north and sent to work at a young age in the region, had himself possibly participated in the extermination of tribal people on the station where he was working as a young man. Davis was very close to his father, whose tragic accidental death when Davis was fifteen was to mark the family in such dramatic ways. Bill Davis had worked at the woodmill in Yarloop for many years, and even during the Depression managed to support his family, sustaining them with his wage (work hours diminished as the Depression bit) and with bush tucker. Davis's father was, as Davis himself would become, an efficient and skilled bushman.

Davis almost expresses this knowledge and possibility in terms of the inevitable outcomes of being *stolen*, being forced into servitude to white mores and to the whole colonial machine/edifice. Davis's 'encounter' with a local tribe at his outcamp (as quoted above) would have created anxieties as well, and we should never underestimate how any white heritage or even connection instils a paranoia (extending Hodge and Mishra)[49] when encountering one's perceived legacy, be it people of your own skin or not. In A *Boy's Life* Davis writes of his father:

> He worked as a stockman from the age of eight. He remembers holding his boss's horse outside the Roebourne police station while his boss went to obtain a permit which gave him permission to shoot troublesome blacks on his property. The cost of the permit was one shilling.
>
> Father was reticent about his early life and it was only by occasional snatches of conversation between him and mother was I ever able to glean much. As father lived with, and was reared by whites and his growing up was in the frontier days of the Pilbara and the Kimberley, I suspect he would have been a part of any action to curb blacks in those days.[50]

Davis goes on to describe an incident when his father placed a saddle under a blanket to make it appear as if he were asleep under the blanket, and hid

---

49 Robert Ian Vere Hodge and Vijay Mishra, *Dark Side of the Dream: Australian Literature and the Postcolonial Mind* (Sydney, Allen & Unwin, 1991).
50 Davis, *A Boy's Life*, p. 2.

elsewhere overnight; the next morning he found a spear embedded in the saddle. The angst in Davis's recounting of the story is palpable here, but also in his joyous relating of the encounter at 'his place' which was not truly *his* place. Anxiety, and there's no avoiding it anywhere. The mere mention of frontier is an effort to compartmentalise what is reactivated and made to live over and over in the poems, as it always will be. All the traces of place and incident are in the words, around them, everywhere.

In a poem from *The First Born*, 'The Artist', Davis uses the artist's totem, 'the eagle-hawk', as a timeless point of reference for country and belonging that goes well beyond any European notion of poetic conceit. The hawk's totemic relationship with the Aboriginal artist cannot be replicated by the artist on the stone the artist is painting:

> For they were flesh and feather, bone of bone,
> And this was the law and not to be defiled.[51]

but is embodied in all he does and is. The representational nature of art as expression of cultural belonging is monadic *and* dyadic, of the individual's skin and kin and personal relationship to place. The mobility of a cultural aesthetic and an extra-Western notion of trade and exchange is built into the artist 'walked a hundred miles to trade' his 'wilgy', which a note tells the unfamiliar reader is 'the paint or ochre (red, white or blue) used by Aborigines in 'corroborees' and initiation ceremonies'.[52] The artist as artisan and practitioner, and as cultural-spiritual medium for place within the law of his people and the place, is emphasised, but so is his personal agency (and not the collective generic of 'Aboriginal art'):

> Time goes by, he sits back satisfied,
> His work alone,
> The emu in full flight,
> Stark and clear, outlined in wilgy white
> Against the black and brown and reddened weatherbeaten stone.[53]

Davis is emphatic in his poetry generally speaking, and especially so here. The image is 'stark and clear', and its place on the stone and within the network of belonging is assured. But the place of the artist himself tragically is not. With ruthless irony, we see how place is mediated by dispossession and occupation. But vitally, not deleted. The artwork is present, its meaning intact, and the totem hawk – though at a loss because part of him, part of country itself

---

51 Davis, *First-born*, p. 23.
52 In Len Collard, Sandra Harben and Rosemary Van Den Berg, *Nidja Beeliar Boodjar Noonookurt Nyininy: A Nyungar Interpretive History of the Use of Boodjar (Country) in the Vicinity of Murdoch University* (Murdoch University, 2004), we read of '"Willagee, the place of red ochre" (p. 39), and Bates (cited in Vinnicombe 1989, p. 18) records that Goonininup is a key camping place on a major trade route used by Nyungar travelling from other areas to Perth in order to trade for the highly demanded wilgi (red ochre)' (pp. 40–1). Both the naming and the trade are of relevance here.
53 Davis, *First-born*, p. 23.

has 'vanished' – is there. The 'passing through' of the tourists is of the most ephemeral form – a been-there-seen-that sentiment which Davis intimates is the most degenerating and offensive form of encounter with place. Nothing is given back, nothing exchanged and little growth seems possible. Such poems of loss are at the very heart of Davis's politics, poetics and conviction of resti-tutional activism. The hawk glares, is angry, and there's also a challenge to the type of visitation – relatively privileged, stylised and simpatico in their desecra-tion of everything the artist believed in and stood for: they are 'blue-rinsed' (as a marker of class and not age), with 'clicking cameras', 'parlour coach', and 'gleaming bright'. What's more, where the artist walked for 'a hundred miles to trade', these tourists have only walked 'a hundred yards' from the coach on the bitumen road.[54] The tracks have been replaced by conduits of occupation, insensitivity and ongoing 'passing through'.

'Belonging', in such cases, becomes arbitrary and temporal, and the 'non-place' becomes a Möbius strip in which makers, surveyors, those who rely on it in the traffic of their daily lives, and those who make momentary use of it to see something of the world, become inextricably bound up with the history, pres-ence and fate of what was fixed and in motion along those lines *before*.[55] The final stanza reads:

> There's a gleaming handrail around the ledge today.
> The hawk whistles vainly for his vanished brother.

54 In *Beeliar Boodjar: An Introduction to Aboriginal history of the City of Cockburn based on existing literature* (Spearwood, City of Cockburn, 2011), we read: 'The Cockburn area was a well-established place of trade activity amongst *Nyungar* groups. Dr Richard Walley is a traditional owner of the *Pindjarup* region. His family has a long association with the Cockburn area. He spoke of trade: *Nyungar* have always been engaged in trade, right back well before settlement … Our people, the *Nyungar*, went as far as Uluru and the centre of Australia and those people, the Aboriginal people from there, came back here to *Nyungar* country as well … The different groups would bring stones and ochres and all sorts of different things from their country that didn't exist in *Nyungar* country and that is a form of "paying their way" when they visited *Nyungar* country. So trade in *Nyungar* country is very, very old. Thousands of years old.
   Non-Aboriginal author J.E. Hammmond observed that many items produced by *Nyungar* in areas around Cockburn were traded to areas far north of Perth. While in the Gascoyne, in 1873–74, I found evidence of exchange with the Southwest … [They] had blackboy gum and red tail feathers and white tail feathers of the cockatoo, which I had never seen or heard of north of Perth … We also saw several *koilies* of the South-West on the Gascoyne, and this left us with no doubt that some sort of exchange was carried on … I much inclined to think that the blackboy gum we saw in the Gascoyne was also taken north from the South West with the spears, *koilies* and feathers. *Koilie* is a *Nyungar* term for "boomerang" and the gum that Hammond refers to is an adhesive produced using the resin of the *Balga* or Grass Tree (Xanthorrhoea preisii)' (pp. 19–20, footnoted with: 'Polglaze, R., 1986, *The Aboriginal Significance of Coolbellup/Walliabup Wetlands (North Lake and Bibra Lake)*, Unpublished, Perth; Harben, S., & Collard, L., 2008, *Recording Traditional Knowledge.* also Booklet of the Avon Catchment Region, Wheatbelt Natural Resource Management, Northam, p. 65, Hammond J. E., 1933, *Winjan's People: The Story of the South-West Australian Aborigines*, Hesperian, Perth, p. 24. Ibid pp. 36–38.)
55 Or 'prior' to colonisation.

> He glares at blue-rinsed tourists clicking cameras at each other
> And skitters aloft, an angry flight,
> From the parlour-coach, all gleaming bright,
> On the bitumen road a hundred yards away.[56]

Marc Augé, working out of Michel de Certeau, writes,

> Space, as frequentation of places rather than a place, stems in effect from a double
> movement: the traveller's movement, of course, but also a parallel movement of the
> landscapes which he catches only in partial glimpses, a series of 'snapshots' piled
> hurriedly into memory and, literally, recomposed in the account he gives of them,
> the sequencing of slides in the commentary he imposes on his entourage when he
> returns. Travel (something the ethnologist mistrusts to the point of 'hatred') con-
> structs a fictional relationship between gaze and landscape.[57]

I am bemused how such statements get made! Maybe it's the difference between being a poet practitioner and…? Davis captures the 'visit' and the movement is implied, and he certainly shows the loss of respect and appreciation between slippage of encounter and the history of belonging indicated in the 'artist' figure's interaction with his painting and surface. But to call the 'relationship between gaze and landscape' fictional is to deny the deadly agency of indifference and consumerism. The temporary/fleeting relationship, as vague and unfocused as it might be, is *part* of place, as is all space (they are not parallel non-converging concepts!), and is real and destructive.[58] Augé is a part of the very subjectivity he locates and critiques in his explorations of ethnography and anthropology, whereas Davis sees direct cause and effect in encounter – the polysituated is not arbitrary and its impacts are real. If the visitor expected something other than what they actually encounter because of false tourist advertising, this does not make the encounter or passing-through any less real or actual. No 'non-place' is created by its becoming a conduit; rather, a hyperreal encounter with place that is devastating in its apparent indifference, a cumulative damage to locale and to the self who encounters with ignorance, and might even grow in the polysituated self and compile greater comparative models of subjectivity, but denigrates the place briefly visited itself. There is no linear narrative of encounter, intervention, removal, residue and waste (the litter, for example, left behind).

One also thinks of Augé's consideration of a traveller like Chateaubriand in the nineteenth century seeing 'the disappointed shards of crumbling monu-ments … but it was the journey's movement itself that seduced him and drew him on. A movement whose only end was itself, unless it was the writing that fixed and reiterated its image.'[59] In the Davis poem we have Davis himself as

---

56 Davis, *First-born*, p. 23.
57 Marc Augé, *Non-Places: An Introduction to Supermodernity*, trans. John Howe (London and New York, Verso, 2008), pp. 69–70.
58 Temporary or fleeting interactions – 'snapshots' – have real impact on 'place' as well as on the traveller. Denial of this is a fetishisation of authenticity and prevents effective consideration of the impacts (and, in some cases, positive outcomes), of *temporary* contact.
59 Augé, *Non-Places*, p. 71.

traveller who stays (for work) and develops a set of complex relations to place, who extrapolates to make poems (be it 'The Artist' or other poems), who is on a journey of life in which he wrestles with self and community, contact and isolation, intactness and dispersal, that is relieved through depicting the clear (neo-colonial) wrong of the visitation by the 'blue-rinsed'. There is deflection in this.

One of the most devastating poems Jack Davis wrote was 'John Pat' which carries the following epigraph:

> John Pat was a 16-year-old Aboriginal boy who died of head injuries alleged to have been caused in a disturbance between police and Aborigines in Roebourne, WA, in 1983. Four police were charged with manslaughter over the incident. They were acquitted.[60]

Davis's poem makes a seemingly matter-of-fact, flat but horrifying and inherently traumatic refrain of 'concrete floor' and 'cell' in its beyond-Foucault model of prison where there's no panopticon for watching because the prisoner is to be killed. A death watch is death, and all that is the person's past – his people, his country, his spirituality – are subsumed by the killing machine of the Roebourne police lock-up:

> Write of life
> the pious said
> forget the past
> the past is dead.
> But all I see
> in front of me
> is a concrete floor
> a cell door
> and John Pat.

After John Pat's death there is an eternal presence (of the 'author', of the witnesses who are there in spirit and obligation) of witness, of confronting the killing over and over. To have been there and been able to stop it – the inability and lack are an agony lived by all those related, connected, and who care. It is a death of humanity and it is a death of art, writing, of text itself. This is no *superconductive*[61] highway, no network or hub of interaction, but the collapse of a neural network into brain death. Place:

> and a place to dwell
> like Roebourne's hell
> of a concrete floor
> a cell door
> and John Pat.

60   Jack Davis, *John Pat and Other Poems* (Melbourne, Dent, 1988), p. 2.
61   The portmanteau seems justified here – theories of networks, conductivity and Augé's own deadpan 'Supermodernity' are all ironised in the face of real trauma that this poem is depicting. It happened. It still happens.

John Pat is an eternal active presence. His deletion by the machine of the state will fail, and place be reclaimed, reconstituted outside the cell, the haunting 'silhouette/ of a concrete floor'. Each of the four, thin stanzas ends with,

> a concrete floor
> a cell door
> and John Pat.

All of them are absolute facts of that place now and eternally. 'Place' cannot be retrieved from this without resolution, acknowledgement, restitution. The poem is as much about allowing a spirit to rest as about confronting the crime committed against John Pat and the consequences that must ensue. The sixteen-year-old is a child with ways of looking indirectly, behaving, that would confront the racist, white adult police – Davis sets 'play' traumatically against consequences, normalcy against murder. As the poem 'concludes':

> He's there – where?
> there in their minds now
> deep within,
> there to prance
> a sidelong glance
> a silly grin
> to remind them all
> of a Guddia wall
> a concrete floor
> a cell door
> and John Pat.

(Davis includes this note, 'Guddia: Kimberley term for white man'.)

In 'John Pat', a polysituatedness reaches a nadir, a point of absolute overdetermination in which all spatial and place(ment) experience falls into a vacuum. The cell is created as an enemy zone, as a place of deprivation not only of liberty but all human rights, all cultural identity, and ultimately, a killing field of concrete.

In this poem is a *raison d'etre* for refusing both de Certeau's and Augé's definitions of 'non-place'; or rather than definitions, their identification and claim to the existence of 'non-place'. If in future people take tours of the Roebourne lock-up, or maybe the site of its structure long removed and replaced by a marker sign, as we see all through Australia where an old school house or town hall stood, we are making contact with polysituated place with all the implications of witness or participation that such visitation brings. Davis's poem is active in the penumbra surrounding John Pat's death; it is a decisive intervention in which authorial 'participation' is as a conduit to witness, as an indictment of the colonial machine that murders, and all of us for standing by as these things happen. The situation has been declared; stay silent if you will!

If, as in Fremantle Gaol, you visit (I never have, and never will) and hear of the suffering that went on there, even though the bodies are long gone, you are culpable in a variety of ways – a vicarious participation in suffering but also the inflicting of suffering. The words used to show how the machine operated in its time – right from 'gaol' to 'Moondyne's cell', or any other displays of words standing for real events and real suffering, don't become unreal; they ARE real, it IS real. For that matter, when we see 'Tahiti' on a sign in the airport, it is equally real, and especially a place. The place is not the word; the word is literally the sign of place. You can't unwrite this – to do so is to give excuse to distance via news reports and disasters, to feel the impact less and less; Augé's observation set as fact, dispassionate declaration of the empty signifier that is capitalist-fetishised 'place' as shangri-la (but not, and never, Tennyson's place-invested 'Timbuctoo'! his prize-winning poem of interior exteriority). Matter-of-fact awareness is not enough for me. Augé writes:

> Certain places exist only through the words that evoke them, and in this sense they are non-places, or rather, imaginary places: banal utopias, clichés. They are the opposite of Michel de Certeau's non-place. Here the word does not create a gap between everyday functionality and lost myth: it creates the image, produces the myth and at the same stroke makes it work (TV viewers watch the programme every week, Albanians camp in Italy dreaming of America, tourism expands).[62]

Out of this accurate glibness, I think of the indigenous poet Robert Walker, killed by guards in Fremantle Gaol in 1984. Born in Port Augusta, he died a long way from his country, but Kevin Gilbert in his note on the poet in *Inside Black Australia*[63] tells us that Walker's sister, Charlotte Szekely, wrote, 'Robert's spirit isn't really here – not in the grave here in Adelaide. It's over *there*. In Fremantle Prison in the pool of blood. Aboriginal culture, the spirit can't rest until evil is stopped.' Gilbert earlier writes of Walker's death:

> Isolated, subject to fear and hatred made even more intolerable by the claustro-phobic walls of the prison cell, Robert Walker cut his wrists and began playing his guitar. He didn't intend to die, his wrist slashes weren't that critical. His personal-ity unerringly dictated that he protest his treatment, that he force someone to take notice.
>
> Someone did. At about 4 a.m. on Tuesday, August 28th, 1984, prison officers removed him from his cell. Emerging from the cell to the landing he noticed the officers and began screaming with mortal fear. In a grassed area within the prison confines and within full view of a large number of prisoner-occupied cells, Robert Walker was held by the officers and beaten with fists, boots and truncheons.[64]

Robert Walker's murder, for that's what it was, goes beyond any abstractions of definitions of place and what constitutes its co-ordinates, but is still an act of

62   Augé, *Non-Places*, p. 77.
63   Kevin Gilbert (ed.), *Inside Black Australia, An Anthology of Aboriginal Poetry* (Melbourne, Penguin, 1988)
64   Gilbert (ed.), *Inside Black Australia*, pp. 125–6.

place, *in* place. It is blood on the ground and it is indelible. And space is place to its bitter, unresolved and unjust end. Walker had written in his poem 'Solitary Confinement':

> Have you ever had a door slammed
> Locking you out of the world,
> Propelling you into timeless space –
> To the emptiness of silence?[65]

This is not a timeless space of presence, but rather a timeless space of oblivion in which place is hijacked and denuded of signs to ensure the habitus of the colonial and its ongoing 'progress'.

I have witnessed police brutality in lock-ups and have experienced it myself. I have seen an old white man beaten; I have watched a young Noongar man be beaten until he was literally as limp as a rag and tossed around a circle of uniformed police, and I have been kicked in the head by a policeman and thrown around by others. Which is not to say I haven't met reasonable police, because I have (and one also saved my life once). As Davis met *reasonable* police as well, but one would be wilfully blind to deny the murderous intent that has driven black deaths in custody. Davis himself had experienced prison and had no desire to return to it again if he could avoid it. His imprisonments were arbitrary and outrageous misuses of white man's law. The imprisonment of indigenous people, and their relocation away from their people and country, have had and continue to have dire and tragic consequences.

This is not a case of a white man's version of place and events, but direct interaction and witnessing of consequences. When a relative of mine was in prison, he got through the ordeal by identifying with his Aboriginal cell-mate's sense of country. He went from a working-class white man's ignorance of 'blacks' to a confessional bonding in letters he wrote me. I understood. My father remarried in Roebourne at the court house; I have visited the town with my younger brother. The place and circumstances of John Pat's death, which happened when I was twenty and either in Perth or looking after the farm for a few months, are also part of who I am as a 'Western Australian', former 'young' male and as progeny of colonisers. The culpability and responsibility are shared. The cell where he died was no mere Western fetishised 'non-place' of trendy theory, inculcated with a critique of social mobility through motion and capitalist underpinnings in which personal rights coalesce with corporate desire, but rather a zero place of unconscionable deletion of country. Even country itself, which outlives all and denies all the remodelling 'outsiders' might impose on it, is closed off and denied any form of presence, as with a sensory deprivation tank. Lines of connection are severed and the totemic utterly destroyed. This is not a 'non-place' but a denial of place, a deletion!

When Jack Davis writes of Rottnest Island (popular Western Australian destination for tourists and local mainlanders alike), a sacred place where spirits

---

65   Gilbert (ed.), *Inside Black Australia*, p. 128.

go after death, being turned into a prison for indigenous men, where many met their deaths – a concentration camp in which the machine of extermination worked in its nineteenth-century colonial fashion – the conflict between this deletion and the totality of spiritual presence creates an irreconcilable tension in this poet of reconciliation:

> No flight of soul for them
> But chained they waited
> for their lot's conclusion
> to be forever part of
> the island of the dead[66]

15 (b) At a read-through of Davis's poetic oeuvre, a number of factors stand out. First, the overwhelming aim not only to draw attention to the 'plight' of Aboriginal people in Australia in the face of ongoing colonisation, but also to affirm uniqueness, tradition, ritual, tenacity, knowledge and spirituality. Davis's work is that of a non-violent freedom fighter, a call to action. Yet his work is also an engagement with song, dance and art, and also an autobiographical progression towards self-analysis and knowledge, and deep connection with creation and origin spirituality.[67]

Across the twenty-five years of his poetry publishing, we see recurrent themes and rewriting of specific approaches to social and cultural issues in Davis's poetry. But in there are also his wonderful Yarloop childhood, his contact with traditional Aboriginal people at Moore River, his life as a stockman (and with many other skills) in the North-west. There is a growing knowledge of the space a writer lives in and how it does or doesn't overlap with his material, and a consideration of black rights issues across the world.

Davis was an expert at the conversational lyric – the poem intentionally forced into a straitjacket of Western versifying to enhance the often anti-Western point being made. In his lyrical insights into country, into the flora and fauna of the world he grew up and lived in, in the tension between urban and rural, he allows voices he has encountered in a wide variety of situations and 'settings' to come into play. We always hear Davis – sad, angry and joyful – speaking with the world, especially to those with whom he shares so much, whom he considers 'his people'. This great poet of reconciliation pulls no punches in saying what's what, and in pointing to those who have committed

---

66 Davis, 'Rottnest', in *Black Life: Poems*, p. 37.
67 In *Wheatbelt Noongah: Recording Traditional Knowledges* (Literature Review for Avon Basin Noongar Heritage and Cultural Significance of Natural Resources by Murdoch Project Team, Principal Researcher Sandra Harben, Cultural Consultant Leonard Collard, Kura, Yeye, Benang, Kalykool *Past, Present, Tomorrow, Forever Ngulla Budjar Our Country*), Whadjuck Ballardong elder Len Collard is quoted as saying, 'Author and poet the late Dr Jack Davis, a northwest Aboriginal man who spent most of his life in Noongar budjar, wrote the play *Kullark* (1982). The audience could hear Dr Davis's version of the local Whadjuck boordier Yagan's ceremonial chant which could be heard loud and strong as he pays tribute to the Warrgul [sic] for creating the Noongar universe. (Snell 1988, p. 16).'

and continue to commit crimes of injury, murder, rape and dispossession. These aren't just metaphors; they're reality.

He talks of forgiveness that goes unappreciated, unanswered. He talks of greed and rapacity. He takes on mining companies and loggers. He expertly and deftly moves between the apparent contradictions of being a hunter and loving animals – some of his most moving apostrophes to animals come from a hunt where there's respect for the creature's escape. His deployment of birds as totemic/spiritual entities and as symbols is tempered with a very real sense of the bird as an intact spiritual entity and physical being in itself. The poem 'Red Robin' is a superb example of this, which finishes with the nurture of the Aboriginal spirituality that understands a totemism that is complex and as diverse as there are individuals within community. Davis can be the hunter and the protector at once in his poems. And towards the red robin he feels a protector against the hunters, the butcher bird and the chooditj:

> Now butcher bird with cruel beak
> and butcher bird is his name
> him and chooditj are alike
> they have a diet the same
> So hide your home my little one
> where prickle bushes grow
> and you can keep a watch above
> and I'll watch from below[68]

Embedded in the prosody of this poem are also biblical language cadences, and an artificial, consciously poetic syntax and diction that has 'a diet the same' rather than more conversational 'same diet' but juxtaposed and interleaved with a familiar address – 'chit-chat' between human and animal where they are both equals of the same creation forces, which elevates the whole to an apostrophe, or almost holy (if very earthed) address.

Animals and the human conversation with them, predatory or friendly, are often the source of humour in Davis's work – he laughs at them, with them, and hears their laughter at him. Selecting Davis's poems for the retrospective I collated, I chose a few poignant examples of this – he wrote many others. For Davis, a sense of humour is a vital part of survival, but it in no way lessens his anger and determination regarding battling injustices for his people, as well as inequalities and social abuse in any context. Poverty is something he feels we should have abolished long ago. He highlights disjunctions and the gap between the haves and have-nots. He shows a child starving while the middle class who care are saving a stranded whale – he doesn't mean that the whale shouldn't be saved, but rather that those who are capable of lamenting the whale's plight put human suffering in the too-hard basket all too often. What is visible and invisible is salient to Davis – or maybe, where we choose to see and where we don't.

Davis was always aware of the ironies of human existence, especially at

---

68 Davis, *Black Life: Poems*, p. 86.

points of contact between cultures, and contact between the human and natural worlds in their many configurations. Modernity brought much damage, and only the tools of communication with which to challenge its own untrammelled belligerence. Though he grew up in a sawmilling town, the realisation of what his father's work and family's survival rested on was a paradox he didn't shy away from. In *A Boy's Life*, he wrote of when he went by train (he was later to become a train driver) with thirty other schoolkids up to the hills to see the great jarrah trees being chopped down:

> For some undefined reason within me, I felt sad. But being merely twelve years old, I could not explain in words the hurtful finality of what I was about to witness. The saw seemed to sing as it bit into the tree. Spurts of sawdust flew out from either side of the ever deepening cut. The fallers did not pause. This was their work. Honed to perfection, they were experts at their trade. Imperceptibly the forest giant began to bow her head. The fallers with one accord stopped, removed the saw and stepped back.
>
> For long seconds she began her inevitable return to earth. Then with a headlong rush she passed the point of balance and with a mighty woosh of sound, crashed to earth, sending dust and scattered undergrowth into the air. Then when the dust and branches had settled, the children ran to the fallen giant to examine her more closely. But there was a sadness in me. Somehow I felt the tree had been killed and I knew it was gone forever.[69]

This is more than anthropomorphism,[70] it is the knowledge of interconnectedness and wholeness of the biosphere. It is the butterfly flapping its wings on a monumental scale, and such witnessing resonates through all life. I myself come from a 'timber' family (my grandfather Claude Kinsella was one of the original State Foresters), and have spent my life actively campaigning against old-growth logging. As a child I also went out (on a camp) and saw trees felled and then taken to the mill. Davis's morphing of animal and tree, making the blood of the tree the blood of the land itself, is a conceit for the brutal condition of reliance on such acts to live, and the imposition of the condition through colonialism in the first place. There's a short-circuiting of Boodjar that he can only reconcile through poetry. In 'Death of a Tree', from *Jagardoo*, we see him textualise this crisis as the tree falls:

> I walked away and left her,
> saddened,
> aware of my loss.
> Yet – still,
> part of the gain.[71]

The tree's loss of its own life is implicit. But the loss is also his, and country's. And he acknowledges he will 'benefit' from the tree's loss, but it doesn't mean

---

69 Davis, *A Boy's Life*, p. 98.
70 Another convenient 'Western' modernism that actually separates animals and humans in theoretical rather than (necessarily) actual ways.
71 Jack Davis, *Jagardoo: Poems from Aboriginal Australia* (Sydney, Methuen, 1978), p. 3.

he desires or is comfortable with that gain. This is the key to understanding Davis's poetry – witness in which part of us all, at least, is implicated. In the poem 'Forest Giant', in the later book *Black Life*, we read of a tree that 'missed/ the faller's axe and saw/ But they destroyed the others/ down the slope…' and the aloneness of the tree is one that Davis feels himself. Davis was a complex man with ties to Noongar country with which he identified, to his north-western skin, to Aboriginal people throughout Australia, and also to his own journey of discovery in the world as a whole. The poem finishes:

> Now you and I
> bleed in sorrow and in silence
> for what once had been
> while the rapists still
> stride across
> and desecrate the land[72]

This poem is as abrupt and severe as the act itself. As Oodgeroo notes in her short introduction to *Black Life*, such conservation poems are 'hard hitting'. Davis is not trying to appease anyone. The same can be said of his anti-mining poems, with one of the most poetically powerful being 'Yellowcake' in *John Pat and Other Poems* – alongside it sits the poem 'Nuclear', leaving us in no doubt about cause and effect. In the chanting nursery rhyme calls of 'Yellowcake', 'innocence' is dressed up as a potent and malignant force: the land is sacred, but it is dangerous and needs to be interacted with in highly ritualised and knowledgeable ways, and traditional law also embodies geology, sociology, genetics, biology, astronomy, physics and chemistry. It is interdisciplinary. As the child's (Western) game-chant goes, 'pat-a-cake, pat-a-cake', Davis begins the first of the four quatrains (loosely rhyming – there are a couple of effective non-rhymes):

> Yellowcake yellowcake
> Where have you been?
> I've been asleep in the ground
> Not part of the scene[73]

Yellowcake delights in being woken so it can enjoy inflicting harm and death, finishing in an ante-natal death chant that undoes the childhood innocence played with in the poem's opening. From law to game, greed (mining) alters the balance of life and death:

> I can shatter the earth
> I can leap to the sun
> And cut off your birth
> Before – it's begun.

---

72 Davis, 'Forest Giant', in *Black Life: Poems*, p. 63.
73 Davis, 'Yellowcake', in *John Pat and Other Poems*, p. 22.

This 'elsewhere'[74] we might determine is necessary to our 'here' is not a component of polysituatedness, because here and elsewhere are the same and different points at once; but vitally a centre is its own periphery and vice versa. As children are taught that 'stone age' is a point in human development, a mode of pedagogy designed to show 'progress' and usually advances in consumerism twinned with advances in human welfare (medicine, food 'production' etc.), it is rarely taken into consideration that technological development may have been eschewed early on, that bush medicine and a technology that relies on the natural environment and is entirely renewable may be preferable to mining, tree-felling and land-clearing to make the best standard of life possible.

'Stone age' may in fact be the most techno-philosophically advanced state of existence. Agency, decisions made collectively, may ignore technological discoveries (the mining and casting of metals, for example) as causing more damage than good. Choices to retain direction within one tribal or social group might well rest on the initiative of an individual or a small group within the larger group, but what is interesting is that across, say, Australia, Aboriginal people consistently chose to remain within the technologies that had worked over millennia, and not to indulge in a more ecologically rapacious 'progress'. The relationship of the individual and 'tribe' seems vital here, and it is interesting that Jack Davis, while acting with the agency of the 'author', of the creative self-determinant, was always working in his activist and publishing life to align himself with 'his people', in all their language and tribal differences, by editing (and publishing) the literary journal *Identity*, and being foundational in organising Aboriginal publishing, the Aboriginal Centre in East Perth:

> Between 1967 and 1974, the Aboriginal Centre was a continual bustle of activity. Organizations such as the Aboriginal Legal Service, the Aboriginal Medical Service and the National Aboriginal Conference had not yet emerged, and the AAC was the hub of most welfare activities. It was also a referral-point to which newspapers could turn for information and Aboriginal opinion, a forum through which Aborigines could freely develop and express independent opinions, and a springboard from which they could initiate programmes and services within their neglected community[75]

There is a negotiation to be made in considering the earlier and later periods of life of someone such as Davis (and many other contemporaries from Aboriginal families and communities that were barely recognised as being part of modern Australia), where the 'full blood' was lionised as 'pure' but entirely disrespected and robbed of his/her space, and the 'urban fringe-dweller' was treated as belonging nowhere, as a mistake. Davis had grown up in Yarloop *without* any overt sense of 'otherness'; he had not to his own mind been

---

74 Augé writes, 'Certainly the European, Western "here" assumes its full meaning in relation to the distant elsewhere – formerly "colonial", now "underdeveloped" – favoured in the past by British and French anthropology' (*Non-Places*, p. 9).
75 Chesson, *Davis: A Life Story*, p. 141.

separated off or treated differently for being a non-white, and was part of a community made up of various ethnographies, 'contrasted' with his deep discovering of his Aboriginality at Moore River through its repressions and awakenings (encounters with other Aboriginal people).

In his 'introduction' to *The First-Born*, which is entitled 'Introducing the Author' and noted as being 'From the transcript of a tape-recording made by Jack Davis with Richard Beilby' who was the person we learn from *Jack Davis: A Life* who encouraged Davis to publish and who submitted his work to a publisher, Davis discusses his experiences at Moore River. This is a truncated and somewhat 'glossed' version compared to the far more harrowing 'expansion' we are offered in *Jack Davis: A Life* (or even the version in *A Boy's Life*). All the same, there are a couple of paragraphs important to quote in their entirety, both as a glimpse into the circumstances of his going to Moore River, but also in his creation of the all-important character of Warru, who resonates through Davis's work. I say 'character' because in some ways he was a composite (as has been acknowledged) but also a very real individual – an elder, a traditional man who had great knowledge but who would later suffer and become entrapped in the city unable to remember much of the past (or Davis). The poem 'Warru' opens:

> Fast asleep on the wooden bench,
> Arms bent under the weary head,
> There in the dusk and the back-street stench
> He lay with the look of the dead.[76]

In the transcript opening the book we read:

> In the poem about the hunting trip, I first met this old chap who I wrote of, called Warru, when I first went to Moore River Native Settlement when I had left school. This was a plan which my dad had to learn me and another brother who was about two years older than me to learn the rudiments of farming and to get us on to some land eventually. The few months I spent in Moore River Settlement was the first time I had met up with my own kind. Warru fascinated me. Although I was only fourteen years of age and he was a man of at least forty-five, he came from the North-west, the same area where my dad came from and he was of the same tribe. I used to spend many hours talking to him: he used to sing aboriginal songs and I used to write down the aboriginal words, and of course, the first chance I got to go hunting with him I was happy.[77]

In the dramatic narrative of the (lyrical) poem, Davis plays with time and what he knows of Warru to make a symbolic as well as literal figure of 'Warru':

> I looked at him, then back through the years,
> Then knew what I had to remember –
> A young man, straight as wattle spears,
> And a kangaroo hunt in September.[78]

---

76 Davis, 'Warru', in *First-born*, pp. 19–20.
77 Davis, *First-born*, p. xi.
78 Davis, *First-born*, pp. 19–20.

Idyllicising the memory is necessary as affirmation and as restorative, and the act of memory reclamation is also an act of eternal, symbolic memory, of the desired 'timeless' land that has been created out of confrontation with the chronologically and property-based materialism of an invader. Time is what marks off loss. Timelessness is outside the thief's reach, as well as being an inherent part of a creation story and land-place spirituality.

Returning to the transcript, it is worth noting Davis's recording of words. The transcription refers to his transcribing. At the end of *The First-Born* Davis has a small dictionary of Noongar words he has collated, and words were always vital to him. In recording the words of his own skin, he was regaining obscured identity. He was recreating himself. He continues:

> He was a remarkable man. He could track things which I couldn't see. He could also throw a spear forty or fifty feet, deadly accurate, and even a stone thrown at a bird, seven times out of ten he would bring the bird down. He had a beautiful voice and to hear him sing in his own language was something which I am afraid is lost because he has been dead for many years. His songs were something for Australian culture to remember.[79]

This is nothing short of an apotheosis and an epiphany. Warru is the heroic embodiment of what is threatened and possibly lost: he is an ideal, an archetype, who has been made mythological. But he's also *real*. He is also an embodiment of positive values and a way forward for Davis and, to Davis's mind, his people. The description is tactile and swerves through and past biblical cadences; this palimpsesting is something Davis will strip back further and further over the ensuing twenty years to get to the core of colonial invasiveness, language appropriation and its deceptions.

The composite 'nature' of Warru is emphasised in this stanza:

> We camped that night on a bed of reeds
> With a million stars a-gleaming.
> He told me tales of Noong-ah deeds
> When the world first woke from dreaming.[80]

Warru, we have learnt, was a north-western and not south-western man. His knowledge and songs were of the north. Being at Moore River, he would have heard local tales, but Moore River aimed to destroy identity through displacement and confusion of language and identity. Davis's poem is doing a number of things in processing and reclaiming identity: reterritorialising in a post-Deleuze and Guattarian sense. The concluding stanza shows Davis's purpose: to refuse any further deletion and invasion of identity. In the composite we have an act of humanity and intactness and belonging to all time:

---

79 Davis, *First-born*, p. xi.
80 Davis, *First-born*, pp. 19–20.

> I will let you dream – dream on, old friend –
> Of a boy and a man in September,
> Of hills and stars and the river's bend –
> Alas, that is all to remember.[81]

This is Davis working the conventions of the poem, of Western prosody and Romantic convention. His subjectivity is at question, as old Warru doesn't recall. Davis always questioned his own role, his own position in the telling. Colin Johnson (Mudrooroo) mentions Worru's[82] influence on Davis in his introduction to *John Pat and Other Poems*: 'A further strand in his development as a writer came from his early association with an old man Worru … It was a knotting of the severed ties of community, and Worru in a sense replaced Jack's father.'[83] But that was later, in the remaking of Warru as universal symbol of loss and what needs to be restored, reclaimed, remembered. Davis's father died after Davis returned from Moore River, but the reach of Warru was through Davis's life (as well). Johnson/Mudrooroo: 'his play *The Dreamers* may be described as an epitaph to the man. In it he lovingly describes the approaching death of Worru and his ascent into "the Dreaming". It is his most moving play, and it is noteworthy that he himself played the part of Worru in the stage production.'[84] Worru was Davis and Davis was Worru, but they are also separate and unique (Davis becoming Worru) – there is an ongoing conversation of belonging, knowledge and sharing. It was an idealised but essential process and enactment of becoming in a polysituated place: the north-west of skin, the south-west of connection with country, the traditional world of law and the modernity of Western life and literature, it was a fusion of language which in Davis is what becomes the specific and universal at once – the paradox his art is driven by.

Activists such as Davis formed a bridge across which a new awareness of autonomy within 'Western' structures was possible; a reclaiming of identity would bring with it pride and cultural strength. When Davis was involved in setting up the tent protest outside Parliament House in Perth in 1972,[85] he

---

81 Davis, *First-born*, pp. 19–20.
82 'Warru' in *The First-born and Other Poems* and 'Worru' here are the same person. In Davis's play *The Dreamers* it is 'Worru'.
83 Davis, *John Pat and Other Poems*, p. xi.
84 Davis, *John Pat and Other Poems*, p. xii.
85 Murrumu's actions in Australia are vital to the embodiment of polysituated rights: rights within rights (as with my earlier notion of an 'umbrella anarchism' (see my *Activist Poetics: Anarchy in the Avon Valley*, ed. Niall Lucy [Liverpool, Liverpool University Press, 2010], pp. 148, 203–4). Further, his use of United Nations covenants in the context of his people's rights and laws, and in the context of (oppressive) Australian laws of 'state', is a polysituated act and an international regional act.

In the *Guardian* newspaper of 27 May 2015, we read: 'Murrumu, who was formerly known as Jeremy Geia, has renounced his Australian citizenship, declared his intent to live only under Yidindji tribal law and is behind the establishment of an infant sovereign Yidindji government near Cairns. He is now the nation's "foreign affairs and trade minister" and says he has referred the matter to his "attorney general for further investigation"' (http://www.theguardian.com/

attempted to make a physical connection between dispossession and identity, between traditional law and the law of the state. One of the markers in Davis's life was the ability to own his own house – to own property in a land where the 'property' of the land's 'first-born' – country itself – had been stolen and the relationship interrupted. For him it wasn't a case of accumulation of goods, but the claim of rights to food, housing, health and land. On being asked how long he'd be camping outside Parliament House, Davis replied, 'We have no intention of leaving until sufficient funds are set aside for Aboriginal housing.'[86]

Davis's least effective poetry is often concerned with urban social issues, because of the desire to report and to use for purely social commentary, rather than morphing activist social commentary with a deeply felt sense of place. But this is not to deny the fact that urban has as much quiddity as 'place' – of course – but further, it is literally overlaid 'country' (even if it entails such obfuscating 'overlays', the land is still *there*): it is as traditional as anywhere else (the park on Beaufort Street is still an historic and essential Noongar meeting place); only to note that the weighting of traces of place in the poems is sometimes less fused with the language of identity and belonging (for example, his poem 'Streetwalker'). Davis was outraged by the double displacing of urban Aboriginal people, dispossessed of land and identity by governments and public who saw them as less 'Aboriginal' (a perverse bending of truth and reality to impose an 'other' on the 'other'). The poem 'Urban Aboriginal', from the collection *Jagardoo: Poems from Aboriginal Australia* (1978), includes a note, 'This

---

australia-news/2015/may/27/murrumu-charged-after-driving-with-licence-issued-by-his-indigenous-nation). This example of non-violent resistance to assert identity and rights is a temporary rendering of the polysituated into the artificial construct of the 'monosituated' in order to, in fact, enhance agency and polysituatedness. Murrumu and others wish to create a state in order to negotiate a treaty with the oppressor state in order to gain rights within that oppressor state (Australia) while reclaiming and enhancing cultural sovereignty. In some ways, it's a simulacrum act, as one is always polysituated through the circumstances of lived and absorbed (family stories, reading, tribal connections etc.) experience – be it within a 'nation', a region, the broader world, or even one outcrop as opposed to another a day's walk away. We further read: 'The Yidindji wished to ultimately participate in the Australian state once a treaty had been agreed, he said, but not until then.'

Jack Davis in his camping outside state parliament in Western Australia made the monosituated moment (his tent) an embodiment of his polysituatedness in order to make claim and demand for action on the lack of housing and rights for indigenous people (dispossessed from the very lands the buildings of the state existed on – which serves as a further example of the contradictions of Heideggerian 'dwelling', the most Western of constructs despite its consciousness of 'the Western'). Polysituatedness might be deployed as an activist tactic of contracting and expanding articulation of presence – an awareness of how place is strategically manipulated by the state to retain control over large swathes of area and cultural difference (to iron it out and assimilate). Finally, from the same *Guardian* article: 'On the risk of spending time in custody as a result of living under Yidindji law to the exclusion of Australian law, Gaan-Yarra said: "You've got that inconvenience of a few days, could be a few years [in custody], you don't know how it's going to play out but Mandela did 25 years."' All hail Murrumu! All hail liberty! All hail equality! And all hail indigenous rights!

86 Chesson, *Davis: A Life Story*, p. 157.

poem was written in reply to a statement made by a Minister for Aboriginal Affairs that urban Aboriginals are not true Aborigines'; we go from the first stanza:

> She was born with sand in her mouth,
> The whisper of wind in her hair;
> They washed her clean in warm wood ash
> And wrapped her in loving care.

through to the fourth and last stanza, when the brutalities of the colonising city machine have failed to take away identity, failed in trying to wipe out Aboriginal pride, culture and skin:

> With murder, with rape, you marred their skin,
> But you cannot whiten their mind;
> They will remain my children forever,
> The black and the beautiful kind.[87]

Jagardoo, Davis's second collection of poetry, was published eight years after Davis's *The First-born* which had opened with:

> Where are my first-born, said the brown land, sighing;
> They came out of my womb long, long ago.
> They were formed of my dust – why, why are they crying
> And the light of their being barely aglow?[88]

It is the same 'brown land' speaking in the 'Urban Aboriginal' poem as speaks to all its people. It 'owns' them and they 'own' it, to use an inexact 'translationese'. To take any discussion outside the discourse of Aboriginal community is to render it but a skeleton of its complexity and depth. But in essence, who one is can't be defeated by anything thrown at you by the colonisers and their tools of torture. This sounds extreme, but it *is* extreme. Davis doesn't take a step backwards; he has created a poetry of immense power, legitimacy and justice that helps us reassess place right down to the components of rural and urban, open and 'closed' spaces.

Though Davis was an auteur, he knew he didn't operate alone; though the influence of preaching, Mary Jones and the Brookton Aboriginal Church may have honed his public rhetorical skills and moral convictions, it was only one link in a social network. Augé writes, 'the problematic character of all established order would perhaps never manifest itself as such – through wars, revolts, conflicts, tensions – without the triggering flick of an individual initiative'.[89]

On the war against Aboriginal peoples in Australia, and a colonial war it

---

87 Davis, *Jagardoo*, p. 19.
88 Davis, 'The First-Born', in *First-born*, p. 1.
89 Augé, *Non-Places*, p. 19.

has been, Davis is extra-tribal, belonging and not belonging, and individually resolved to sublimate himself into a range of tribal connections from Noongar to the skin of his father. He becomes a spokesperson for indigenous Australia. Augé continues, 'Neither the culture located in time and space, nor the individuals in which it is embodied, define a base level of identity above which otherness would become unthinkable.'[90]

Recently we (re)visited Brookton, and walked around Davis's old church, found the Aboriginal reserve land where his mother lived and where he stayed, on the outskirts of town, not far from the cemetery and wheatbins, and noted that 'Bennell Street' bore the name of his stepfather.[91] In and around Brookton, Davis gained a lot of his bush knowledge and made important connections between country and story, spirituality and the cosmos. Further tracing his journey, we had earlier gone out to Mugumber, a place full of the spirits of those who died at Moore River Native Settlement. The experience so profoundly affected me that the only way I could deal with it was in a poem.

Mogumber

There's a disturbance in the air,
the clouds thickened and stretched,
raining intermittently over sandplain.
In this place of the Yued people,
many other tribal affiliations
separated from their country
and family – they rest here
in the sand of Mogumber, their
names on the wall. Down a trail, a sign
says to stay clear of Christmas trees
because those buried at their base pause
in the canopy before moving on. The
tale of a black hand holding the white hand
of a fencer to stay the picket from piercing
the burial place. The body wishes
to rest. I am there with Tim and Tracy
trying to track the journey of Jack Davis,
poet and playwright, whose politics
of freedom were formed in this place
where girls were exploited and old people

---

90 Augé, *Non-Places*, p. 19.
91 In *The First-born* there is a poem entitled 'Aboriginal Reserve' (p. 34) which contains the lament for loss of access in so many ways. The second stanza reads:

They stir a fire that is dying,
The sparks fly upward blending
With night and a people crying.
O where, O where is the ending?

died in torment away from their country,
children taken from their mothers,
the families. As Jack says, so many
unwanted babies of white men and boys
of white families where the girls
were sent to provide *service*, buried
away in the pines, *in the pines*
where the sun don't ever shine.
Why does this traditional American
folk song play over in my head?
Why do I reach for a correlative
to make sense of what I can't cope with?
Long from this highpoint, sweeping
the horizons, so decisive, contour
drawings, the distant hills hemming
in the anguish. I lack the tools
to express grief. I delight in birds
breaking the language barriers and giving
us stories in common. I want to speak
in my silence. We all walk in circles, dazed.
The Aboriginal Wheatbelt Corporation
runs the place now – this 'stolen
generation site', this 'place in the heart'.
Tracks down to the long pool of the river
are closed off with dieback warning signs,
and the gate to the farm has Keep Out.
On the other side of the road, vast
stripped tableaux, place of agriculture
and emptiness, all small birds darting
towards the cemetery, to the burial place
inside the tall fence to harvest nectar
from the brilliant and overwhelming
candles of banksia in full bloom. Banksia,
the irony of a name undoes our presence
and at first I ask Tracy to photograph
and then delete, knowing images
will carry none of the truth.
How can I have written these
wheat-growing regions for so long?
Jack Davis went to learn farming skills
and spent his days digging stumps
and splitting zamia palms, the grist
to Neville's and Neal's mill. Our visiting
Northam to do the shopping; replay
his *No Sugar* over and over, the transfer
of people from Ballardong land to land
of the Yued. The silos, the machinery,
the flour laced with strychnine. All
I have alluded to, all whispering

through full crops in their mono-
cultural glory. Subtext to all I write.
But today, where Moore River
Native Settlement once was
and always will be, I carried away
the cost of my words, of *l'écriture pastorale*,
the colonial rebound I put in its place,
the words I write hollow as wind rushing
over bare ground but as audible and entangled
as it meeting the shrubs and woodland, touching
even the spiny-tailed skink whose name
I dare not utter, stuck in my taxonomy
of intrusion, what belonging I have
clings to jam tree and York gum country
not so far away. The weight cannot
be lifted. I cannot write it out.

We need to rethink the individual and culture in the context, as Davis was offering a means rather than an end, even in his poetry, in which he acts as conduit not only for stories and observation, but for his own interactions with the natural world. Davis's trips during the 1970s with other black Australians to the United States, and later Nigeria, had a profound effect on his sense of a black world, but one which seems to have ultimately strengthened his commitment to reconciliation rather than conflict, and also to regional purpose. An experience at a Black Panther workshop in the United States convinced him that violence was no answer in combating violence.[92]

Though he spoke across tribes and communities, he also spoke with them. He never wished to universalise a polemic of self-determination, but rather to make self-determination exactly that – determined by 'his' people, for his people. This is why his brief contacts with Native American culture so appealed to him. At the core of his belief was, 'The land has been ours since the creation, *kundum*: the land and the Aborigines belong to each other.'[93] This is where the individual, the group, culture and country merge into a picture outside anything Augé can determine,[94] or maybe I should say that Augé detects in the governance of place (signs, instructions to observe or see in a particular way travelling a highway etc.) – the act of being in country supersedes any semiotic discourse about its fetishisation by corporate-military-state-governance. It is specific and can't be used as a comparative case because it is *this* land, not *that* land.

The origin of Davis's first book is a complex one, going back to his fascination with the dictionary during his schooldays at Yarloop. It reaches a form of

---

92 Chesson, *Davis: A Life Story*.
93 Chesson, *Davis: A Life Story*, p. 149.
94 And I am not confusing the author with the 'I' of the story – rather that whatever critical distance a theorist proffers, participation is implicit in the making of the text – it's a case of the satirist being part of what is satirised.

resolution within the narrative Davis created of his life with a relatively brief intrusion into his account of activism and advocacy, and the general movements of his life journey:

> Throughout this period I was composing poetry at night. Writing had become an ingrained habit, and the calm after midnight was the most productive time for me to write. At home I was surrounded by a large healthy family capable of generating plenty of noise, and it was seldom earlier than ten or eleven that I could settle down behind a pen. Once there, I was able to withdraw into a world so real that I could virtually converse with the vivid images my mind created. This capacity to imagine characters talking to each other, as if I were standing amongst them, has been of immense benefit to my playwriting.
>
> My writing desk has generally been a table in my bedroom, but I still prefer to spread my papers on the bed and write there. Many a time I have written through the night, dropping off to sleep at five in the morning. Working at the Centre, I had to be a little more careful of my energy. Sometimes a poem takes weeks, even months, of struggling and wrestling before it emerges. My most successful poem, 'The First-born', was written spontaneously, in a few hours, and took very little alteration.
>
> The second week in July has been set aside as a week in which to celebrate Aborigines in Australia. In 1970, as part of the festivities, the AAC held an exhibition of Aboriginal arts and artefacts. Since my disappointment with the *Northern Times* I had not thought to attempt to publish my poems, but on this occasion I pinned some of them up on a board outside my office. One visitor, Dick Beilby, was quite taken with a number of them and advised me to send them to a publishing house. (Later he was to use 'First-born' as an epigraph to his book *Brown Land Crying*.)
>
> 'All right, Dick,' I said. 'If you want to you can post them away.' And he did. The result was my first book of poetry, entitled *The First-born and Other Poems* and published in 1970.[95]

I have included this long quote because it shows something of the public–private nature of Davis the activist and Davis the poet. Though driven by individual conviction, in the public story it takes someone else to declare the poems' publishability, and to take the action of sending them off. This is in the context of Davis's early disappointment with the *Northern Times*, but it also reflects on the position of an individual working for Aboriginal causes, speaking in his poems to and for Aboriginal people, as well as his Aboriginal self, and a sense that grandstanding is going to be, presumably, readily perceived. How much one works with the occupying forces is always a question in the striving for liberty, and we shouldn't doubt that this is part of the humility. It has to be.

In talking over Davis's work in his author introduction in *Inside Black Australia*,[96] Kevin Gilbert praises Davis for his activism: 'Jack firmly established himself as an Aboriginal poet shouting, sobbing, demanding that his song, the Aboriginal song against injustice, be heard. The opening cry was one of outrage

---

95 Chesson, *Davis: A Life Story*, pp. 144–5.
96 Gilbert (ed.), *An Anthology of Aboriginal Poetry*, pp. 53–4.

and lament from which the title of the book emerged: "Where are my first born, said the brown land, sighing."'[97] But further on in the entry, Gilbert says, 'In 1977, much to Aboriginal disgust, Jack was awarded the British Empire Medal for services to literature and the Aboriginal people. Aboriginals collectively believe no "honour" can come from one as dishonourable as the thieving British Empire, believing instead that our, "Good on you, Bunji" or "Youai Moodjarng" is the greatest accolade we, the sovereign sons and daughters of this country, can bestow on one another.'[98] Gilbert mitigates this with approval of Davis's later plays *Kullark* and *The Dreamers* in depicting 'events as they were'.

All acts of the individuated writer speaking on behalf of community, peoples across the landmass and country are going to be scrutinised carefully regarding the causal links between what they write and how they act. Writing is an embodiment of more than personal subjectivity, and always more than entertainment when written out of conditions of injustice. Somehow, clockwork Augé just lacks conviction and experiential knowledge when he glibly notes, 'and finally there is the individual, defined by all ritual systems as a composite steeped in otherness, a figure who is literally unthinkable...'[99]

16. It may not be self-evident that there is a connection between polysituatedness and the way we treat animals. What follows is an attempt to draw a different kind of discussion into the orbit of this book.

Socrates: Cock Crow and Swans. Place is what we have read and will read. It's where we read and how we apply our reading. I walk around the house at Jam Tree Gully memorising from books. In recent times I have been thinking of Socrates and animal rights. Of ancient Greek theatre, poetry and philosophy and place and animal rights. As I walk and read and think and look up and listen – walking familiar ground, I still need to flick from page to ground in case an insect happens by; my focal length is challenged constantly – I de-map and reconstitute the place of which I am part, with which I am familiar. Polysituatedness is about reconfiguring place without denying its autonomy and agency – it's always a dialogue, even an exchange. I walk and I hear a cock-crow in the distance – it is mid-morning and sunrise is long gone. It is a still day, and the cock-crow carries and carries. It could have come from 'miles away'. I can't locate its origin in the mental map I have of sounds and animal husbandry in the district. And then I am thinking of the swans of the waters – inlets, bays, tidal rivers, rivers coming down from the mountains, of West Cork. White Swans. And that takes me to the colony of white swans at Northam, introduced in the early twentieth century by a town mayor.[100] A dislocated line of descent. White swans among the local black swans. But the white swans, after generations, are

97 Gilbert (ed.), *An Anthology of Aboriginal Poetry*, p. 53.
98 Gilbert (ed.), *An Anthology of Aboriginal Poetry*, p. 54.
99 Augé, *Non-Places*, p. 19.
100 For more information one can go to this 'populist' website: http://www.westaustralianvista.com/white-swans-of-northam.html, but I have reservations about some of its subtexts.

local, too. They don't exclude the black swans nor the black swans exclude the white swans. We often walk as a family around the Avon River in Northam and see both kinds sailing near each other.

Avon River Mute Swan Scholia

'But because they are sacred to Apollo and have the gift of prophecy and anticipate the good things of another world, therefore they sing and rejoice in that day more than they ever did before.'[101]
  Plato

 'scriptible'
  Roland Barthes

Not swans known for a deathsong – as lament or celebration
of joyous departure – the mute swans of the Avon colony
have had reason to sing out when one of theirs is struck down by a car
or killed by a swift kick. Emblem of businesses, product placement,
they have fixed on survival amongst black swans and teals,
grebes and yellow-billed spoonbills, sidestep the machinations
of a regional town making claims – they rarely take wing,
as if observing a law in their social contract.

Tracking back to the nineteenth-century tall-mast migrations,
brought upriver, up over the scarp, from Perth by a Russian migrant –
town mayor – just before the First World War – the markers of *history*
in the old world of their extrication, they have tested mythological
affiliations with over a century of loyal demography.

But there's system failure: recently, cygnets have been injured
and killed in 'suspicious circumstances', despite the 'swan watch'
of local enthusiasts; and an ageing cob struck by a car, taxidermied
by the Museum just in time to pose gleaming for a composer
excitedly melding traditional instruments with computers.

Mute swans hiss and grunt but those hit by cars send blasts
out of their lungs – no need for that modification, the tracheal loop,
to make a song and dance about being deleted.

You'd be surprised how much is invested in an emblem's
transmigration from its living, ruffled body into a pristine, dead one.
In Ireland, I saw only a single flock of whooper swans, bellowing
on the banks of the Lee just outside Cork City, opposite
an ornate and defunct Eglinton asylum.

There are more whoopers during a West Cork summer.

---

101 Plato, *Phaedo, The Last Hours Of Socrates*, trans. Benjamin Jowett, Release Date: 29 October 2008 [EBook #1658] Last Updated: 15 January 2013, http://www.gutenberg.org/files/1658/1658-h/1658-h.htm (accessed 1 May 2016).

But winter encounters with mute swans in loughs and bays,
inlets and rivers, bring an awareness with silence –
their weight of presence – as you are embraced,
sailed up to and swept in with elastic, curving wings.

Journal entries lift intimacy from its setting, a grammar
of body and love against red sandstone – not swans known
for a deathsong – as lament or celebration of joyous departure –
they swim close by famine pits, elicit photos as art, living proof.

Since infancy I have walked near the white swans of the Avon
at Northam – gene pool to unsettle weir-held waters,
trained and broken river, hotspot of blue damsel flies darting –
fast wings chanting – below the suspension bridge, shadow water-
weed reach up to the light of where white and black swans dip.

De-oxygenated water – algal blooms – floodwater levels,
meeting-places on banks and within the sound shell, steel horse
culture at a trot through greenspace, the town's focal point, fenced
nesting area for white swans to lead their silent on-the-brink lives.

I am reminded of Socrates waiting for the urn of hemlock,
and his faith in the *daimonion* with whom he talked things over,
no aporia on his deathbed, just clarity and an open ear,
hearing the deathsong of an absent bird.

Not swans known for a deathsong – as lament or celebration
of joyous departure – the mute swans of the Avon colony *must* have
reason to sing out when one of them is taken to Melbourne Zoo
to make new white swans of Australian derivation.
Spreading the love. Bound together for life. Resisting
temptation to extract the numinous language
fabricated around their broken presences.

Without prophecy, giftless, I note their long memories,
sidelong glances at the dysphoria of aging – stages
we visit, length of a life. I spoke to *that one* in elegy
almost twenty years ago when the summer was cooler.

What's left to nurture or erode in this swan-geography –
this topical treatment of souls? A narrowing gap
between childhood and now, a swansong,
those arias of collective memory.[102]

Socrates' last words according to Plato in *Phaedo*:

and said—they were his last words—he said: Crito, I owe a cock to Asclepius; will
you remember to pay the debt? The debt shall be paid, said Crito; is there anything
else? There was no answer to this question; but in a minute or two a movement

---

102 John Kinsella, unpublished poem.

was heard, and the attendants uncovered him; his eyes were set, and Crito closed his eyes and mouth.[103]

Socrates had overturned the divinities in favour of a more elemental belief system (air, aether, clouds etc.) and much has been debated about his seemingly strange retraction at the end – like a Catholic who has left the fold taking last rites. And there's the perennial question about the actual meaning of these words, but that's not where I am going with this. What captures my attention is the sacrifice to the god of health, the costs of human medicine at the expense of animals. Be it symbolic or literal, the semantics of exploitation exist therein. All humans have benefited from the medical research exploitation of animals, vegans included, whether they are aware of it or not, and yet we work hard to avoid it being so. The development of vaccines is a concrete example, especially when it comes to methods of mass production (cows are great sufferers in this factory processing). But a few points of fact: Crito comes before dawn, before cock-crow, and light is to be Socrates' death (the following day – the ship returning from Delos and the month of no executions (for religious purity reasons) come to its end – 'and therefore tomorrow, Socrates, will be the last day of your life').[104] And Socrates resists the arguments for escape by saying that to break one law of Athens would be to break all its laws, to invalidate his 'social contract'. This has consequences for his health in the afterlife.

There are no symbols without correlatives in what we perceive as the 'real world'. The symbolic cock is always a literal cock. Socrates values reason and justice above all other things (though he has been done an injustice in being condemned) – the justice of his acceptance of the law and refusal to escape doesn't of course bring justice to the cock whose life will be taken in the giving. The failure of all human justice has resided in its failure to be extended to other animal life. So many humans grow up within the laws of animal consumption: that it is just, that it is the 'social contract' under which they're raised. Socrates quotes Athenian law (personified – note!) as saying, 'But he who has experience of the

103 Plato, *Phaedo, The Last Hours Of Socrates*, trans. Benjamin Jowett, http://www.gutenberg. org/files/1658/1658-h/1658-h.htm (accessed 1 May 2016).

104 Plato, *Crito*, trans. Benjamin Jowett, from *Dialogues of Plato* (New York, P.F. Collier & Son, 1900), http://caae.phil.cmu.edu/Cavalier/80250/part2/Crito.html (this text is in the public domain, released August 1993) (accessed 4 July 2016). Jowett would spend Christmas with Alfred and Emily Tennyson at Farringford on the Isle of Wight. Upstairs, in Tennyson's attic study, choked with tobacco smoke, might Socrates' fate have been discussed? As a complete aside, I think of John Batchelor's comment in his biography of Tennyson, regarding *In Memoriam*: 'In lyric LXXXIX "some Platonic dream" was changed to "Socratic dream" (presumably because "Platonic" in itself could signify homosexual). He would have been sensitive to the anxiety that Arthur's father felt about what he saw as the excessive tenderness towards another man expressed in Shakespeare's sonnets (which his dead son had so loved and admired)' (Batchelor, *Tennyson*, p. 181). Arguments about sexuality and Tennyson's masterpiece aside, this dissembling is strangely useful in tangentially illustrating the *polysexual* vectors of polysituatedness. Anxiety is always a key to bringing a reader/writer into the vicinity of a 'location', if not its absolute co-ordinates!

manner in which we order justice and administer the State, and still remains, has entered into an implied contract that he will do as we command him.'[105] It is worth contemplating the dynamics of the cost to Asclepius in the light of Socrates being celebrated as (an apparent) 'vegetarian'. There is no direct evidence he was. One vegetarian site constructs (through selective editing) a false 'dialogue' from *The Republic* in an effort to prove Socrates' vegetarianism (never mind that it is actually Plato we're dealing with!) that has spread like a virus through the internet to the point that philosophy students on US academic discussion forums cite it as literal text extracted direct from Plato's work. Such claims do the cause of animal rights no favours. The sacrifice of the cock is not the act of an animal rights vegetarian or vegan! To import the ethics of another time and cultural spatiality is clutching at straws. One might even question what is actually being said and why in 372e of *The Republic* regarding 'the healthy state' [it's not proof!].

The choices given to abdicate from a relationship with Athenian law are those of the empowered, and don't speak for the vast 'masses' of humanity. Choice to abdicate from laws is a privilege democracy has always strained to protect for the few – the majority protect the rights of these few in the hopes they will become one of the few. So humans are the few to all animals. The law in *Crito* does say, via Socrates:

> 'There is clear proof,' they will say, 'Socrates, that we and the city were not displeasing to you. Of all Athenians you have been the most constant resident in the city, which, as you never leave, you may be supposed to love.'[106]

Maybe the acceptance of fate lies in acceptance? Even tacit acceptance? Do we need to evidence our disapproval? Refuse to attend school? To accept the slaughterhouses? To vote (in Australia – compulsory, though I do not vote)? Logic here is specious. Not 'some logic fails and is specious' – logic is specious, a tool of privilege to obfuscate rights. In closing off all defences of escape, Socrates back himself into a position of acceptance, or rather refusal to contradict the sentence he receives: 'But you pretended that you preferred death to exile, and that you were not grieved at death.'

He has made his own bed – he has had so many ways to deny, object to, refute the laws, but has benefited, lived by and barely challenged them (though historically, during the naval trial, he had). This defence of the state is Plato's of course, but even so it is taking the ship down with the captain, rather than captain going down with the ship. The cocks will be slaughtered because they haven't shown any resistance to those who laws they live (and suffer) under. Socrates shows great ignorance of his own enslaved position, of the cock's enslaved position, regarding the 'inevitability' of both their executions. Socrates resolves it in the ultimate defence of the state, poor pawn that he has become:

105 Plato, *Crito*, trans. Benjamin Jowett, http://caae.phil.cmu.edu/Cavalier/80250/part2/Crito.html (accessed 4 July 2016).
106 Plato, *Crito*, trans. Benjamin Jowett, http://caae.phil.cmu.edu/Cavalier/80250/part2/Crito.html (accessed 4 July 2016).

Then will they not say: 'You, Socrates, are breaking the covenants and agreements which you made with us at your leisure, not in any haste or under any compulsion or deception, but having had seventy years to think of them, during which time you were at liberty to leave the city, if we were not to your mind, or if our covenants appeared to you to be unfair. You had your choice, and might have gone either to Lacedaemon or Crete, which you often praise for their good government, or to some other Hellenic or foreign State. Whereas you, above all other Athenians, seemed to be so fond of the State, or, in other words, of us her laws (for who would like a State that has no laws?), that you never stirred out of her: the halt, the blind, the maimed, were not more stationary in her than you were. And now you run away and forsake your agreements. Not so, Socrates, if you will take our advice; do not make yourself ridiculous by escaping out of the city.'[107]

Socrates, bound into apostasy and a crisis of religious doctrine, also indicts us all (animals and humans) to the greater will, the law of 'god', of existence: 'Then let me follow the intimations of the will of God.'[108] In conversation with his *daimonion*, Socrates personalised the godhead and threatened its embodiment in human law, in the state, in Athens. He was in a position to step aside from the strictures of his own pleasure and participation in the state – just because one benefits (as one should) doesn't mean one should acquiesce in all the state's impositions. The state fears its dissolution through even a minor digression – it offers security and maybe even leisure, but it controls life. Animal rights embodied in the state allow for the contradiction of benefiting from the state while rejecting the premise of its existence to serve those who have voices within its (restrictive) structures.

The argument of almost all human laws/societies is along these lines: to stop eating animals, to become their advocate, is unreasonable, unjust. It makes a case that a society's (human) members have benefited from animal exploitation (directly or indirectly) and should thus follow its (society's) laws even when an injustice is evident (two wrongs don't make a right?) It's a web of self-hatred, a suicide as well as a death cult. Thanatos is enmeshed in animal sacrifice. The nuclear holocaust scenario is the sacrificial blade at the world's throat – deliverance through following the war-laws humanity has lived under – it overarches and possess (almost) all cultural, geographical, social and political difference.

In being seemingly a-political, Socrates was the most political of (non) citizens. In not 'avoiding' his own death, he makes of himself a 'benign' form of (self) sacrifice. Animals are cast as self-sacrificing in the human search for the greater human good. Agency is actually granted to appease the guilt over agency being denied in the flesh. The elemental secular belief system of existence becomes a vehicle of choice over obligation (gods requiring sacrifice – no choice, or if a choice not to do so is made, punishment is meted out). Thus Socrates' last words

107 Plato, *Crito*, trans. Benjamin Jowett, http://caae.phil.cmu.edu/Cavalier/80250/part2/Crito. html (accessed 4 July 2016).
108 Plato, *Crito*, trans. Benjamin Jowett, http://caae.phil.cmu.edu/cavalier/80250/part2/Crito. html (accessed 6 July 2016).

become a symbol of control and not reversion/conversion, because they both deny apostasy (the religious scientist) and are pragmatic (the atheist scientist).

And then there's 'payment' – the vivisector's paradox – to supposedly make (human) life, they take life and inevitably profit either financially or socially or in terms of their own sense of purpose.

Metaphorically, the cock crowing at daybreak heralds the day of death – imbibing from the urn of hemlock, and the awakening in the witnesses of what their loss will mean. When the cock is killed as sacrifice, human desire, vulnerability and need are awakened as the animal's life gives way to open a path. Catharsis blinds empathy and sympathy with other living things, and repetition wears down any childhood feeling of 'pet care' and identification with the subaltern position of child and animal.

Three events come to mind on a personal level. First, having seen many animals slaughtered as a child, I was taken aback by one incident as a chicken was slaughtered and 'ran around headless', when a girl I had grown up with sat on a fence (literally) and laughed watching it. I had been raised with the gun, but had never laughed at what I'd killed. It bemused me. Second, also as a child, I watched roosters fighting in a chicken pen and using their spurs to destroy each other, and wondered if I should intervene. I figured they were under constraint by human hands and human intervention might be appropriate – I can't recall how I resolved it. Finally, just this morning, I heard '*Dad!*' from the dining-room area, and then Tim and Tracy were at the library door telling me they'd just seen a peregrine falcon (could have been a brown hawk) outside under the shade-cloth where it had flown, a rabbit in its claws. Startled by Tim calling '*Dad!*', it had released the baby rabbit in shock at there being other creatures nearby (since we had been away for long periods, it had probably used the place on previous occasions to consume its 'kill'). The rabbit had bounded away, the falcon flown up and out. I said to Tim that it was an omen, and would have been in the ancient world. A life-affirming omen. Then I was reading Plato's record of Socrates' last line and thinking of dawn cock-crows across the valley, and the fate of those sentinel creatures.

Fate? A polyvalent subjective co-ordinate? Consider the search for an effective Ebola vaccine: its absolute necessity *and* the costs to animals. The originating case of this outbreak was a single child, his corpse touched at the funeral by hundreds of people, who consequently died. The 'bushmeat' vectors, the bats as reservoirs (these words…!), the movement of virus from non-human animal to human animal. The implied divisions, and as I wrote in a poem ('of') thirty years ago, referring to an Arthur Boyd painting:

> of Julius Civilus with a Dead Cock
> arrogantly accepting what is
> over and over, back and forth.[109]

---

109 John Kinsella, *Poems 1980–1994* (Newcastle upon Tyne, Bloodaxe Books, 1998), p. 231.

The fact that Ebola remains for up to three months[110] or considerably longer in a man's semen, and that recovered people are asked (appropriately) to refrain from sex for that period, is at a 'tangent' to the sacrifice that is disease transferred from animals to humans. The cock is the literal cock. Avian flu is another example. Again, the cock. Health and the cock, the god of healing, the sacrifice. There's repugnance in the keeping of death-records, the counting of victims stripped of identity, exposed in front of the (essential) biohazard suits (scarce in West Africa because of a run on them in the US), that speaks of how animals suffer. Gorillas have been wiped out by poachers, habitat loss and Ebola. They know. I feel that in order to help sufferers we need to create a broader empathy with all living things – to understand what alienation and isolation and death arise from the failure to empathise with all life, especially animal life with which we are so closely connected. We can cure without cruelty or abuse. Even in the case of the antibody-boosting ZMapp and its harvesting from tobacco plants, there has been (or was) discussion of taking it over to the existing, quicker, larger production facilities utilising animal hosts, because the industry is already there.

Some years ago when doing a reading tour, I asked for my fees to be donated to the non-animal-exploiting humane medical research of the Dr Hadwen Trust – I am not sure if any of the venues honoured this request, but they were asked and I received no money (except one cheque, despite my request, which I never cashed). Maybe Socrates' final words were ironic – how they play out in the theatre of Plato is a different matter. But Socrates had been a hero-soldier, and death was the cushioning beneath his unsandalled feet. The blood of cocks, sacrificed or eaten, was not unfamiliar to him. And if he was lamenting the sick world he was leaving and welcoming the 'ease' of death, as many critics have suggested, then we understand that Plato missed the supreme poetry of his age (unsurprisingly) – living is a metaphor, and cocks die because we are unable to appraise reality and the costs of our actions. Awareness of death is awareness of consequences. We exist inside the figurative and our sense of reality is dictated by the constant need to reconcile strained and contradictory impressions into our desire for the 'real'. The blood of the cock is sold as divinity when it *is* a reality.

Socrates' final statement is both the aporia of his entire life's non-work, and a cut-and-dried statement of irrefutable fact, because nothing is more certain than that a cock will die somewhere. Whose cock is it? I would answer that the cock is the cock's, and no one else's. Its death is theft, and a payment based on a false premise. Socrates' last statement is the embodiment of the poem – it is a statement

---

110 A recent case in Liberia of possible transfer of Ebola in a 'cured' patient to his partner, who had no other known vector of exposure, has led to a reassessment of the nature of retention of Ebola entire or in genetic fragments in the testes of men due to their being outside the defences of the immune system. Present advice is that it is a permanent state until proven otherwise, and that survivors should practise safe sex until told it's safe by medical officials/researchers. Ebola is also thought to survive in the placenta, which is also 'outside' the immune system's attacks against foreign bodies, and a recent case in the United States has revealed the virus persisting inside the eye.

of fact, and an enigma. It induces contextual bewilderment, and yet fits. But if we wrest it from its performative gesture and see it as our reality, it is a clear statement that human life comes at the cost of animal life. There's no approval in it, just an acknowledgement. Poems should make things happen. If Walt Whitman's flippant embracing of self-contradiction underpins his cumulative welding of all into his own and making it a clarion for democracy, so might we take Socrates' *elenchus* as an acknowledgement of fallibility, an ultimate error in making the cock take the weight of the inability of the human body to comply with the ills of the world.

We can't make people pay for what they suffer; neither should we make animals pay. Underneath so much poetry is this distress, so rarely offering ways out. Maybe poetry can't do so?

Let's follow Cebes speaking with Socrates before his death in Plato's *Phaedo*:

> What natures do you mean, Socrates?
> I mean to say that men who have followed after gluttony, and wantonness, and drunkenness, and have had no thought of avoiding them, would pass into asses and animals of that sort. What do you think?
>
> I think that exceedingly probable.
> And those who have chosen the portion of injustice, and tyranny, and violence, will pass into wolves, or into hawks and kites; whither else can we suppose them to go?
>
> Yes, said Cebes; that is doubtless the place of natures such as theirs. And there is no difficulty, he said, in assigning to all of them places answering to their several natures and propensities?
>
> There is not, he said.
> Even among them some are happier than others; and the happiest both in themselves and their place of abode are those who have practised the civil and social virtues which are called temperance and justice, and are acquired by habit and attention without philosophy and mind.
>
> Why are they the happiest?
> Because they may be expected to pass into some gentle, social nature which is like their own, such as that of bees or ants, or even back again into the form of man, and just and moderate men spring from them.
>
> That is not impossible.
> But he who is a philosopher or lover of learning, and is entirely pure at departing, is alone permitted to reach the gods. And this is the reason, Simmias and Cebes, why the true votaries of philosophy abstain from all fleshly lusts, and endure and refuse to give themselves up to them – not because they fear poverty or the ruin of their families, like the lovers of money, and the world in general; nor like the lovers of power and honor, because they dread the dishonor or disgrace of evil deeds.[111]

Aside from the purity of the philosopher and his *ascension*, animals embody the human, finding their correlation. Animals embody place and humans embody

111 Plato, *Phaedo, The Last Hours Of Socrates*, trans. Benjamin Jowett, http://www.gutenberg. org/files/1658/1658-h/1658-h.htm (accessed 1 May 2016).

animals embodying place. In death they leave a residue in a place – last breaths, ashes, bones, decaying flesh. Or the memories others have of the dead having died there, of having been there. As people consume animals they make of the place of consumption an engagement between Thanatos and belonging: a declaration of being there. The airport 'non-place', the service station off the highway and all the other locales of Augéan non-place are places of absolute dedication and resolution of Thanatos as people eat their animal burgers, the numbered subtexts (traces of animals) in their sweets and savouries. Though they can't see the animals, they are still eating them. Though they can't see all the components of place (or 'non-place') they're at/in/around, they exist nonetheless. Erasure of people, of animals, of truth, has always been the way of imperialists and those who fear the 'other'. The industry that kills and eats animals is an industry of erasure.

However humans view animals in religious systems that perceive a link between the human and animal soul, the movement between the corporeality of one and the other, the animal is a convenience for the human in its movement. Dressed in variant theologies, animals are too often denied rights in their allotted role-play. Transmigration of souls is one-way traffic – even the greatest respect for the animal because it is a repository in the journey of the soul (denomination ultimately human) is not valuing the animal as separate entity with its own spirituality. This rigidity denies agency outside the human at any level.

Socrates says of his end that swans sing not as a lament that they are dying (the propaganda of man) but rather as an outburst of joy, full of prophecy as the birds of Apollo, for the afterlife:

> But because they are sacred to Apollo and have the gift of prophecy and anticipate the good things of another world, therefore they sing and rejoice in that day more than they ever did before. And I, too, believing myself to be the consecrated servant of the same God, and the fellow servant of the swans, and thinking that I have received from my master gifts of prophecy which are not inferior to theirs, would not go out of life less merrily than the swans.[112]

This identification with the animal, in particular with one species of (majestic-looking) bird, connects him with myth and fact, blurs the symbolic and real, the figurative and reality; he becomes animal, and is animal, and also rejects animal as unique and pure entity. The cock is sacrificed with a pained squawk while the swan sings empowered, wise and sure. Animals can be what we want to make them – we speak animal and yet we allow them no voice in their own governance. We take them from place, we eat them in place, we invest images of them in place, we define place through their presence or absence and our relationships with these variables. Polysituatedness is all living things and an awareness of the consequences of our human interaction with other life and what part we play in their stories as much as they play in ours. If we don't consider all these conditions, we risk erasure. We risk loss.

112 Plato, *Phaedo, The Last Hours Of Socrates*, trans. Benjamin Jowett, http://www.gutenberg.org/files/1658/1658-h/1658-h.htm (accessed 1 May 2016).

PART III

Displaced acts of writing

DISPLACED ACTS OF WRITING

The embodiment of polysituatedness is a material fact for me. I wake to fog in the valley and Jam Tree Gully, as we have named 'our' place, is part of a tamped-together whole in a low cloud of specificity and yet occlusion. Tracy is teaching Tim about the relationship between people and land in indigenous Australia. The text that they are using (among others) says that wars over 'territory' were probably 'non-existent'[1] (though fights over 'people' were not uncommon). We are in a textual landscape. And in country itself we dialogue out of (against) the colonial. We might deduce that the spiritual relationship to country was so strong that to take someone else's spiritual place and leave one's own was unthinkable. The identification of particular places with particular spirits, of creation figures and their stories, makes the sacred both a highly locatable and site-specific 'thing' and also some*thing* that accords comparative understanding when 'applied' to reading another's place. The dynamic equivalence of different creation stories means different stories overlap in terms of belief (of how one relates to country).[2]

This sense of a binding presence is a core of the polysituated. Even the forcible removal of children from 'native' parents (mainly Aboriginal mothers who had children by white fathers) could not delete belonging, though it destroyed families and lives in an indelible way (and stands as one of the major human rights crimes of the twentieth century). The polysituated necessitates a sense of connection, even when disconnected. Voluntary migrants who leave one place for another because they see better opportunities elsewhere, or want to connect with family who have already migrated, or even to escape

1 Robert Darlington and John Hospodaryk, *History Alive 7 for the Australian Curriculum* (Milton, Qld, John Wiley, 2012), p. 75.
2 This is not a 'factual' analysis of social and territorial interactions between indigenous communities/tribes in pre-colonial Australia, but a comment on the essential awareness of a polyvalent understanding of presence, and how that understanding is (or isn't) augmented by daily experience.

'bad memories', take with them the place of their birth and the stories of belonging or alienation that connect with that place.

Once, privileged to hear a talk and performance by Trevor Jamieson at a wheatbelt literary festival in Northam, I heard him discuss the 'four points' of Noongar belonging. I had heard the same from a number of Noongar elders over the years, and wrote a poem[3] in response (dedicated to Jamieson and also

3 The Sands of Djarlgarro Beelier

for Trevor Jamieson and Noel Nannup

1. Conception

We don't like to ask, but I'd guess it was
in the house bought for the purpose. Bateman
Road, just up from Bateman's Farm – a colonising
space. A bike-ride from the paperbarks, the thin white
riverbeach, the grey jetties, seagulls cormorants pelicans.
Sharks were seen that far up. Sharks in the *Canning*,
as I first heard it named – in the womb, listening.
Speedboats would come and introduce me to irony,
the violence of the outdoors, waves wearing
away at the river's walls. The city starting
to close in around, the plentiful made sparse –
river prawns netted at night, lights singing
tanned waters, then gone. There were masses
of blue manna crabs and mulloway and the river
thronged with fertility. I was conceived
with limestone foundations between flesh
and black sand. Edging to grey, white
by the river's edge lit up by the close moon.
When the seed bit the egg and I cried out.
The river's business. It's the river we ask.

2. Birth

I was born in the South Perth Hospital
not far from where Djarlgarro and Derbarl Yerrigan
diverge. I became where the rivers branch.
I was taken home to the banks of the 'tributary'.
The water flowed down from the hills, down from forests
and farmlands. I was taken up to the watershed
before I could talk or walk – early, it was my in-between
place. As soon as I was old enough, I was carried
up to the wheat. Up through jarrah into wandoo.
I went up from water and sand to stone and clay,
up from pelicans and bream to parrots and echidnas.
But I was born *near* the fork of those rivers, where black sand
meets white sand, where blind snakes and sandgropers
burrow their way and water rats range across meeting-places
and bloodworms work the mud, the summer sun glinting.

Noongar elder Noel Nannup). Noongars see the place of conception, the place of birth, the place where the umbilical cord is left and the place where first steps are taken as elements of belonging. Conceived, born and first walking by the Swan and Canning rivers, I naturally identify strongly with that as home, but also inland beyond York where I started to visit and be as a baby. The use of indigenous naming is a contestable and sensitive matter, and I respect the rights of indigenous peoples to allow usage (or not) accordingly, though mostly such names are appropriated by colonists and those who follow without any awareness of origins. The names of the rivers are Derbarl Yerrigan and Djarlgarro in Whadjuk Noongar. I carry these places everywhere I go. They have been with

---

3. Umbilical Cord

I imagine my cord was stolen not far
from where the 'Canning' and 'Swan' rivers diverge, branch.
Taken to the incinerator. My first cremation, my ash,
my mother's ash, floating high into the atmosphere
then drifting down on riverfoam, on lawns
of half-dead buffalo grass, on Bristile clay roofing tiles,
on black sand, on yellow sand, on the white sand
of riverbeaches edged by paperbarks with blisters
ready to burst with watery sap, with goodness.

4. First Steps

I lifted and stepped quickly before falling
a few blocks from Djarlgarro, a measure of houses
where tracks had waved through banksias and marris,
a short walk from where the river bends to continue up to the hills,
a moment from where a spur leads off to a cul-de-sac,
a semi-dead-end, where a creek feeds Djarlgarro through reeds.
The snakes were there. That's where they moor boats
away from the weather and build houses to the water.
Bamboo. Bateman's Farm. The history it enforces.
Up on my feet, I walked the Axminster carpet,
then out onto lawn, then into the black sand
which covered my steps. I observed
the ant lion, and later the lacewing,
plentiful about the river – down through banksias,
marris, onto the white sand, into the salty water,
onto the mud flats, the fresh creek water running over,
mingling, diluting. The reeds hid clutches of duck eggs.
The sand hid me. I planned where I'd go. Where
the sea water joined the hill's water, the creek water.
Where salt and fresh waters meet. Where salt water
would meet salt water when I was older.
And I was sad for all that my birthing hid.

Robert Drewe and John Kinsella, *Sand* (North Fremantle, Fremantle Press, 2010), pp. 133–5.

me in planes, in cars, in trains, deep underground in Victoria. The imprint is indelible. The Swan River is the Avon River of where I live now. Often dry in summer, the Swan is fed by the sea in summer and retains its body of water.

In an essay entitled 'Netdeath'[4] I talked about the loss of data being a form of dying. To extend this further, the web is not a tool of polysituatedness but a simulacrum of place, a form of death of belonging. Of course, it can inform the polysituated, as any experience of reading, seeing or hearing does, but of more effect is where (not as a notion of position as per GPS coordinates but as experientially 'trackable' interactive presence!) one 'logs on' and sees and reads and hears. People sitting on laptops or tablets or phones might 'tune out' their surroundings (the ubiquitous almost-being-run-over-while-phone-checking scenario writ large), but those surroundings necessarily inform and mediate how one absorbs information. The fact we can now access broadband (slow, but nonetheless) in the bush where we are – a recent phenomenon for us – has only increased distance by creating a surreal sense of connection. It's not a case of 'non-places', but real imagining of place. On Streetview we can walk through a Romanian village we've never seen before; we can visit places we are familiar with and see seasons bound together in a single image as recorded at different times. We can see the radar domes of Schull blurred out; we can see a moment that is not the moment we remember. Our own place shows skulls on the gate, a horror to us – it evoked my series of 'Sleepy Hollow' poems, which is what this place (i.e. 'Jam Tree Gully') was called by its previous 'owner'. And that's eight years ago. So the Streetview of the entry is 'out of date', but a true encounter within the moment it was taken. This is life in death, but an entombing as well. The skulls have long been removed, but the 'technology' creates a false reality of 'this place'. However, even a 'live' webcam would give a false reading of place as the distance (literally and conceptually) between the viewer and the viewed means such a mediated version of 'here' that it is both unreliable and displacing.

The polysituated cannot deny the life in all experiences, even the horrific – they exist as long as the memory functions of the brain exist. They are electro-chemical. They are biological. Netdeath isn't just a loss of data and the 'reality' they purported to contain, but also a death-as-limbo for the data retained as it loses the moment and becomes a form of stasis of the perpetual moment. There is software (and server memory) called Time Machine that captures a moment and retains it against deletion. It is of its time, a photo of data. But a photo taken of where you *weren't* evokes not you but what you are not or weren't at the time. It becomes part of you through denial of agency. And in this negatively geared way, the web becomes an informant of the polysituated self. It strikes me that augmented reality games such as Pokemon Go and its predecessors, in their framing of place through camera and screen (and satellite), desensitise the player to place itself, reducing 'surroundings' to virtual markers. I have seen flora and fauna in a nature reserve on the coast of Western Australia being

4 John Kinsella, *Disclosed Poetics* (Manchester, Manchester University Press, 2007), p. 119.

stomped down as players forged their way to their goals, only partially tuned in to the 'elementalism' of the place they are playing in. If we have 'netdeath' we also have 'placedeath' through play.

*

So I read an article in the *Guardian* online this morning on the enclosure of a 'pygmy' from the Congo in a New York Zoo in 1906.[5] The article traces the history of the man's life from capture to suicide. It is a horrific imperialist story of racism, cruelty and the ironies of science and 'civilisation'. It is the sick side of spectacle, and incriminates right down to the level of reportage.

The article attempts to critique all conditions of production, but is ultimately, of course, a form of spectacle itself, as the unfortunate comments section of the paper illustrates. In those comments are refusals to accept that what happened in this context in 1906 can be called 'racism'; damnations of white imperialism; sadness at the human 'species' as a whole'; some overtly racist comments that got past the moderator; and inevitable comments that 'though cruel and exploitative' (etc.) the imperialism of King Leopold of Belgium also brought good railways and towns!

But most disturbing is the link given by a commenter to another article[6] in which the eating of 'pygmies' by fighters in the Congo region (with the eating of sexual organs supposedly increasing prowess and making 'invincible' etc.) carries with it the intimation that the ethical evils of the zoological pornography of the 1906 New York Zoo scenario might be linked to Africa as a trope. In fact, Ota Benga had been called a 'cannibal' by his captor, so the ploy of linking the

5 See   http://www.theguardian.com/world/2015/jun/03/the-man-who-was-caged-in-a-zoo published as 'The man who was caged in a zoo' with the lead, 'In 1904, Ota Benga was kidnapped from Congo and taken to the US, where he was exhibited with monkeys. His appalling story reveals the roots of a racial prejudice that still haunts us.' The piece is 'adapted' from a work by Pamela Newkirk, *Spectacle: The Astonishing Life of Ota Benga*, (New York and London, HarperCollins, 2015). The article begins: 'The black clergymen who had been summoned to Harlem's Mount Olivet Baptist Church for an emergency meeting on the morning of Monday 10 September 1906, arrived in a state of outrage. A day earlier, the *New York Times* had reported that a young African man – a so-called "pygmy" – had been put on display in the monkey house of the city's largest zoo. Under the headline "Bushman Shares a Cage With Bronx Park Apes", the paper reported that crowds of up to 500 people at a time had gathered around the cage to gawk at the diminutive Ota Benga – just under 5ft tall, weighing 103lb – while he preoccupied himself with a pet parrot, deftly shot his bow and arrow, or wove a mat and hammock from bundles of twine placed in the cage. Children giggled and hooted with delight while adults laughed, many uneasily, at the sight.'
6 See http://www.theguardian.com/world/2003/jan/09/congo.jamesastill. The article headline reads: 'Congo rebels are eating pygmies, UN says' and the byline reads 'James Astill in Nairobi'. The article begins: 'Marauding rebels are massacring and eating pygmies in the dense forests of north-east Congo, according to UN officials who are investigating allegations of cannibalism in Ituri province, where fighting between several rebel groups has displaced about 150,000 people in the past month. Many of the displaced tell of rebel fighters capturing and butchering pygmies, Manoddje Mounoubai, spokesman for the UN ceasefire monitoring mission in Congo, said yesterday.'

oppressed to the oppressor in linking these pieces becomes a use of the horrific act of cannibalism as a control vector in targeting culpability and levels of wrong. It's an attempt to displace responsibility and agency for the cruelty meted out to Ota Benga by a mere *link* – the claim doesn't have to be made, just the unmediated linking to a psychogeography of 'presence'. The 'pygmies' suffer in both cases, but the cannibal oppressors are worse. It's difficult to highlight the ironies in such debased conditions. It's not said, but the 'linking' does the work. Netdeath par excellence – the chain of command to moral decision-making is decided not by the context of the moment of encounter, but by the encounter constructed outside its timeline. The first article is 2015; the linked article is 2003. The subtexts are Congo and pygmy – the tags become the signs, the markers of connectivity and belonging.

I am informed by the articles. I reflect on the horrors in the light of imperialism in Australia. Further, I read another article on uranium contamination of a lake in Malawi.[7] This article takes me to my own 'backyard'. It's an Australian company that is responsible. I campaign against nuclear power in Australia, have done for thirty years. I worked with radioactive substances, including enriched yellowcake when I was a teenager (at Associated Laboratories near Geraldton, alongside two enormous mineral-sands plants). Uranium mines are opening up in Western Australia. Prospecting is aggressive and claims have been made in the wheatbelt. When it comes to the networking of the industry, the indifferent-to-borders radiation, the shared international pain, no region is separate or isolated from another. *This* article adds to my dossier of information on another – a dominant – thanatos scenario. And yet netdeath has its way – so many servers and computers are powered by nuclear energy. So much of our lives and non-lives are entangled in this industry that colonises the air, the earth, everywhere. It is part of our polysituated selves even if we deny it. Across the planet, since atmospheric detonations, but also through mining and underground tests, from reactors and their extensions, we live with more and more radiation. Even the capitalist imperialists are being colonised by their own exploitations.

Which brings me to why the pieces in this section are relevant to the core concerns of this book. All I have as a polysituated argument, really, is myself. I am responsible. Whatever I have written, creatively or critically (and often both at once), feeds my sense of presence, my sense of connection and disconnection.

My displaced self searches for a 'place' that can't exist for me in my postcondition of awareness. What I read as a child (and those books I have held on to against the odds), what I write now, what I rediscover and back-engineer in

7 See http://www.theguardian.com/global-development/2015/jun/03/lake-malawi-activists-uranium-fears-paladin. The article, 'On the shores of Malawi's lake of stars, activists raise uranium fears', has the standfirst: 'When dead fish were washed ashore in northern Malawi, activists and residents looked to a nearby uranium mine for answers – the latest battle in a protracted conflict with Paladin, the mine's Australian owners', and it was written by 'Santorri Chamley in Kayelekera' (the location is all-important within the dynamic of polysituatedness).

an effort to discover what I have 'lost', that I won't accept as a kind of death. My novel *Morpheus*[8] (and its strange textual history) is a refusal to allow a 'netdeath' of memory and the human brain, of my own embodiment of all I have experienced and done, of where I have been and what I have been told.

This extends to how and why a text is written. The prosody is a template of intent – to guide a reader, even if we refuse readerly outcomes. The text is recreated with every reading, but we are also constrained by the techniques used in that text's creation. We need to break away from them, to break the lyric in order better to use the lyric as a vehicle of liberation, to read against the ownership of a fiction when there can be no ownership but only our sense of it being ours as we create it.

The time of 'owning' a text is brief. So what is the writer left with? Probably very little, but the reader is constantly re-embodying him/herself – creating new co-ordinates out of new reading, or even more pertinently, re-seeing through rereading: shifts in the temporal and spatial bring changes, obviously, but it is the registering of the same experience as different experience ('I was too young to understand that fully', or 'having visited Haworth I see the poetry of the Brontës in an entirely different way', or 'having lived in Ireland, I...' and so on). And the transcendental signifier becomes a gesture of the poem as hope and activist tool as much as a belief (or hope) in something outside the powerlessness of self, especially in the face of damage done. The polysituated is the 'breath of the snake' (I hear Tracy in another room reading to Tim from a [home] school text)[9] which to someone unaware, to an outsider taking what knowledge they have, what experience they see as 'confirmed' to an unfamiliar place, is the wind through a pass in what the colonisers called the Olgas in central Australia – Kata Tjuta to its people. It is the sense of reverence one gets entering an ancient building that's a place of worship even when one is a non-believer. 'Feelings' – the impositions (they are!) of the sublime – are the fifth element of polysituatedness.

Everything I read, everything I hear, everything I see – in fact, it runs the gamut of all the senses – everything I receive has to undergo translation. Translation is a literal cornerstone of international regionalism, and even where I don't speak or read a language, I try to translate using the experience of translation I already have. I have done this with the Chinese of Ouyang Yu's poetry, creating texts out of shape and inference and a basic knowledge of context. Inevitably, something so new is created that many would doubt it could be called 'translation'. I myself deploy descriptors such as 'versions', 'distraction', 'extrapolations' and so on, but in the end, it's always an attempt to recreate in order to create some grounds for understanding.

Translation is the tool with which I commune with animals and plants, with the geology of the earth itself. It's an old concept, but for me a truism. I barely

---

8 John Kinsella, *Morpheus: A Bildungsroman* (Buffalo, Blazevox, 2013).
9 Darlington and Hospodaryk, *History Alive 7 for the Australian Curriculum*, p. 77.

speak 'John', never mind any other language of sharing and presence. As a poet I work with the natural world (I think here of Les Murray's *Translations from the Natural World* but Murray's ethics of interaction with place are fundamentally different from my own), but not as a translator in a superior position of knowledge and language, but as one struggling to understand and respect, offering imperfect calques of what I see and hear. I have to interpret and then write and then reinterpret what I have written, constantly critiquing my own privileged position as consumer and 'coloniser' of place.

To work with another poet, as I have with Iranian-Australian Ali Alizadeh, translating poetry from a culture I have largely been 'outside', is a liberating experience that co-polysituates both parties, and the texts being translated (though maybe not the poets ... however, we had some feedback that suggested a sense of sharing that may have been *polysituated* for them, too). Further on in this section, I explore this collaboration and also look at translating work from a different period and culture, but also from a place I have become familiar with, at least on a superficial level, and if only on a temporary basis. What I implant of my places into the place/s of Lacaussade might not literally be addressed but is always there as a subtext, as the occupation of Noongar lands, of their boodjar, 'quietly' (but loudly in inference!) overwhelms my earlier work of poetry *The Silo: A Pastoral Symphony*.[10]

This exercise in placement is constantly displacing. It cannot do otherwise. I polysituate through my engagement with the work of Kathy Acker and especially McKenzie Wark (as I do in the earlier piece on Moondyne Joe, written in the context of a collaborative book with Niall Lucy, who delved deeply into representations of the Western Australian escapologist and bushranger, and remade what he could become in an age of historical-colonial fetishisation of the 'outlaw'). Speaking across time zones and geographies after an encounter in Australia, Acker and Wark are caught in the desire-loss of polysituatedness, and their interaction becomes a netdeath relationship. So encountered and so imminent and yet so distant. I wish to register the polarities of desire in the international, the regional, and the polyvalent.

10 John Kinsella, *The Silo: A Pastoral Symphony* (South Fremantle, Fremantle Arts Centre Press, 1995).

ANTI-'CRAFT' IN THE CONTEXT OF WESTERN CAPITALIST CULTURES

There's a major issue around notions and terms such as 'craft'. I am concerned with the way 'craft' in present discourse is a mode and articulation of reaction-ary constraint, and fear of innovation, and embodies a pro-aesthetics control (I am anti 'aesthetics') over how we see and experience. It mediates experience, gives it a setting and validates it through rule-compliance to fit a world order that has long suppressed liberty and fairness.

'Craft' is used by the *retro-'lyrical'* and 'clarity of meaning' poets as a sign for permanence and validation of text as '(the) object'. Now, that statement wouldn't be 'feeling' enough, but in the end it's what happens when so-called 'craft' (often limited and narrow in its actuality) is used as a tool of measure-ment (and competition!) It is curatorial and reductive process/procedure, and it's about fetishised production values. It purports to be about the unique handmade object, but is actually about marketing and controlling the market in such objects. It's more *production line* than they'd like to think. Their problem: how to get around the mass production of books (even if they are small print runs for poetry), and to have the privileged legitimised object created for the 'art' of it. This is compounded by that neo-romantic sense of being discovered, of not putting it out there but still letting everyone know of one's 'genius' … these are the dissemblings of the *craft/ers*. They want the attention but deny they look for attention. Politics stumps them because the point of a politics is to articulate a position re something. The 'craft'/ing affirms the power of the guild, and operates as a sinecure: the makers of 'craft' as criteria for judging the worth of a poem approve of craft in others and give it the official stamp of approval, or deny that stamp, but always the ones who cite craft position themselves as authorities and interpreters of the past. They use the past to validate and valor-ise the present, and to concentrate power in (their own) hands.

The idea that language, which constantly changes, should be constrained by a set of rules of good behaviour and a straitjacket of form and function I entirely reject – that's why I wrote the book *Shades of the Sublime*, as a refutation of 'aesthetics', 'craft' and the encultured rules of prosody. What bothers me is that a wide group of Australian poets still hold a cringe regarding 'craft' – that they can only prove their mettle and prowess through subscribing to the rules of English-language cultural precedent. If they choose to do that, fine, but notice how 'they' wish to impose their 'model' on all else. *They* wish to teach it, judge it and ensure its permanence to the exclusion of whatever threatens (they allow a little innovation around the edges, but only, in the end, if the primacy of their activities is publicly and even privately acknowledged ... it's a paranoid reaction while in denial of paranoid readings that reveal the theft, bankruptcy and disrespect in so much non-indigenous culturising in Australia that they are sourcing). Sure, they inflect their 'craft' with the 'local' (at best, it's a kind of new wave Jindyworobakism that's in denial), but in the end they are about chronologies of belonging, a community of heritage and projected (future) values. *Values* ... a disturbing and deeply conservative notion. They. *They*. 'They'.

I think all poetry is an extension of memory, and recalling memory *is* 'craft'. However, the application of that recall is where I'd depart from those I feel are too conservative – to deploy an extra article is not 'sloppiness', but a choice about speech and its implications. Repetition isn't an accident, but a form of refrain (not a replacement, but a diversion, a tangent in the sense I mean it – too many 'students' over-edit their work and basically destroy anything challenging it had to say formally and/or thematically ... the university creative writing 'craft workshop' has brought sameness, a lack of political purpose (it has to comply with the university/institution in the end), and merely highlights their teachers as exemplary models ... disturbing).

Obviously, one is always calling on precedent and the (pre-)existing rules of prosody and certainly literary texts when creating a poem – that's the 'template' (I use early writing not to extend but to undo ... some seem to think this is disrespectful, but most of the texts I use had already done this to other texts in their time, directly or indirectly!) – but the template alters as it is tested by language and the socio-political conditions under which it's existing. There's a worrying cultural purity at work in this 'craft'-emphasis that also bothers me – rather, *all* 'crafts' from *all* cultural spaces should be acknowledged (I am not saying appropriated, but I am saying that an awareness of them should feed into the 'language' of locality and experience one is part of by choice or default). Comparative literature came about not through a desire for more entertainment, but as a way of finding how common ground does or doesn't work, and how we might translate the universal experience into the localities of 'history', place and language without disrespect (or, at least, attempting to minimise disrespect).

I would use Lorenz's summation of chaos in a different way from the 'craftsmen' and 'craftswomen', I'd imagine. First, I'd take on the gendering and its implications. Then I'd break the constraint of rhythm which I don't recognise as a given, a universal. I think the bending, substitution and slippage (and downright wrecking) of rhythm is a vital 'tool' (ha! craft?) in dismantling the status quo of aesthetics and enslavement to a hierarchising of existence (as soon as I see 'good' and 'bad' I am distressed). Chaos rather becomes a way of ensuring a future can't be approximated through 'craft' because, so far, 'craft' has underpinned the destruction of the biosphere. Further, 'craft' has underpinned war, imperialism and police states. 'Craft' gives the artisan an excuse to ply his/her trade in destructive causes. Craft creates degrees of separation. And then there's the quantum leap from 'craft' to 'lyric'.[1]

I am sometimes portrayed as the 'enemy' of the lyric. I am not, but I *am* a resister of the poetics of the unified self and of the so-called lyrical I. No secret there – I've been saying it for decades. But it's not just for the hell of it. It's because I see that poetics as the vehicle through which the poet becomes the mouthpiece for the status quo, for the concentration of power and its dire consequences for liberty and the actual 'self' (individual *and* communal). It's one of the reasons I find artistic collaboration so generative – it affirms and denies subjectivity at once, and though it can generate its own compliances and even impositions re power, it at least suggests that the unified self is questionable, if only by the act alone. But even that's challengeable, as the voice of the work as construct so easily becomes a tool of the language and ecology of place it works in. I *like* singing, I like hearing song, I even like writing poems as songs. But I will not sing along with the faux-lyricists who see it as a mode of linking 'real' *feelings* with undifficult 'musicality' (while denying 'ideas' – the craft movement in Australian poetry is anti-intellectual in so many ways), with the damned beautiful rhythms of life (producing what I hear as a kind of muzak!) That's not about what's inside people, it's about advertising what one is given permission to show as being inside oneself. The lyric so easily falls into step with the status quo when it doesn't have to. That's what conventional rhythmics does. It subscribes.

'Craft' in the poem, however, is a layering of place as absence in the poem. Received forms developed in other spaces, in (and for) other cultural/ritualistic discourses, in 'different' places, come into dialogue with the raw 'draft' forms of where the poem is created (the location of conception then writing), and in doing so, polysituate. But to critique any politics of presence an awareness of the impact of constraint is necessary. Craft that follows the rules rather than undoes them potentially becomes a colonising device. Craft can 'infect' liberty with control. Craft doesn't need quarantine, but it does need leavening – to open itself, flip its lid like a eucalypt fruit. Craft growing through anti-craft.

---

1 I am not speaking of 'craft' as it functions in *culture* here, but in the context of Western capitalist fetishisation of the art object. 'Craft' – as is well attested – indicates very different values, imprints and outcomes in different cultural spatialities.

A BRIEF LOOK AT THE AVANT-GARDE
AND 'WESTERN' SPIRITUALITY

I've often been asked how many 'religious' poems are experimental. My answer is that most experimental poems are at least concerned with the question of existence and/or are ontological in nature. First and foremost, the primacy of language is questioned; second, the space in which language is being presented comes up for scrutiny. The relationship between words and people, between language as thought and language as written, is highlighted. A binary is developed which invites questioning, wonder and a desire to break (it) open – a transcendence. And, ultimately, a pantheistic interface with all life.

These are issues of spiritual presence, for me at least. For students, I always use John Donne and George Herbert, Emily Dickinson and Gerard Manley Hopkins as examples of 'historical' poets whose concern was both language and spirituality. In the case of Herbert it may be argued that as language was purely a gift from God the question of innovation as a 'thing-in-itself' was entirely redundant. Still, I think of the altar, I think of the use of conceit and many other metaphysical devices in general, and I'm left feeling at least suspicious that on occasions the inherent wonder and beauty of words, on their own, got the better of him!

So, into the twentieth century – the presence or absence of not only a Godhead but a space for at least the possibility of faith has been at the core of poetry. The question of presence and absence is central to modernism. The colonising forces of modernity (that the enemies of Baudelaire so often touted) aside, it was the historic drive towards the mechanisation of cultural spaces that obsessed the popular imagination. When I read Apollinaire's 'Zone' I read a poem of 'religious' wonder – the signifiers have shifted from icons of the church to icons of modernity but the process is the same. When I read Eliot's 'The Wasteland' or 'The Hollow Men' I read of the despair that the shifting signifiers of faith have brought with them. War, war on a massive scale, is only relative. The desolation of the Napoleonic Wars, of the Punic Wars, of the Persian Wars in the Eurocentric world just for starters, was on a massive scale given the parameters of an individual's or indeed an empire's frontiers during these times.

When faced with apocalypse, poetry that seeks to become more than merely a 'lyrical I' rendition (and indeed repetition) of what is comfortably absorbed by a complacent society makes of language a device for self-examination, self-questioning and deliverance. That's why innovative verse may always ask, at the very least, spiritual questions. The avant-garde acts as a warning, much in the same way as it acted as the vanguard, the shock troops of the Napoleonic army.[1] Irony aside, the mixed metaphors of religion and the military have much to do with the power of language. Language is the gift from God. Prayer is our gift back to the Godhead. Poetry is a type of prayer, a type of prayer that works individually and collectively.

The renaming, the recoding and the reinvention of spiritual signifiers in language arise out of the need to stay one step ahead of the state, capitalism or any other (commercially or spiritually) profit-orientated system of control. The most nihilistic works of the Dadaists are in fact playing with the potential absence of God. And the stronger such a belief is, the more a process of self-questioning, of considering the 'isness' (as Veronica Brady calls it) of existence, is stimulated. The avant-garde and spirituality are never far apart. The *spiritual* polysituates through the poem (whether we like it or not), as the material world (the words, the 'form' of the poem) coexists with ontology (the intimations of the poem). 'Being' and 'existence' are in dialogue with the machine of the poem: dialogue between body and soul.

Recently I heard that a colleague of mine was being treated in Paris for a serious illness. I knew him only slightly as a man of broad tastes with a strong wit and wry sense of humour. I wasn't sure of his religious beliefs but felt the need to write a spiritual poem for him – a poem that reflected a faith in an existence beyond the immediate and physical, a poem with a sense of a Godhead, and ultimately a poem of hope. But I couldn't bring myself to do this in a prescriptive way as faith for me is only valid in that it is qualified by doubt, and one's certainty should constantly be questioned. The avant-garde is always an interesting combination of enthusiasm and rebarbativeness. The fact that poetry is a vehicle for prayer and a vehicle for questioning makes it the perfect medium for a 'gift' to the vulnerable.

The chapel (here) at Churchill College, Cambridge, is interesting in that its architecture (by Sheppard) is overtly 'modern' and is in a style that might be termed 'inverted gothic'. It encourages us to aspire to the God within, rather than to a-spire (vertically). It also has an unusual history, having been built on land leased by the college for a peppercorn payment to a trust formed by a committee of Churchill Fellows and others. This came about from the opposition of Francis Crick (of DNA fame) to the presence of a chapel in the college. The Master at the time, Sir John Cockcroft (a religious man who had much to do

---

1 And/or maybe out of Thomas Malory's *Le Morte d'Arthur* (1485) in terms of its defunct military usage.

with the nuclear bomb!), was a supporter of the chapel project. Its simple lines but complex use of light make it a calm and contemplative space.

Given its unusual position of being both inside and outside the college community, its interesting blend of the modern and traditionally 'contemplative', and its non-denominational status (the avant-garde as belonging to no camp?), it seemed to me the perfect vehicle for a poem that explored the ontological potential of language in itself, how form might or might not limit spiritual expression, and a 'place' from which a figurative gift might configure itself, be configured, exchanged, or sent. The 'kneeling' referred to is an evocation of an exact moment in time – saying a prayer in an otherwise empty chapel for someone suffering, transposed to the occasion of writing. The prayer and the poem become interconnected, universal and interactive in terms of subject and object:

Kneeling

It's a sultry afternoon and the inverted gothic
of the chapel draws all to its ecumenical centre,
as if prayer might help reduce your troubles,
or take you far away, or make you cooler –
air-conditioning for the soul – a guilty conscience
like an attack of Legionnaire's disease.
So the hazy reddish light is doubly altered
through the coloured glass and you tell yourself
nothing is to be trusted. And yet here you are –
tacky icon from the bedroom wall – kneeling
as if the air's so heavy you can barely hold
it up, as if the tricks of the light are too much,
as if you're being watched and won't look up.

Of course, it's a wry and ironic poem. But a dark humour and spiritual questioning go hand in hand for me. I do and don't believe in the Godhead in the same way as I do and don't believe in the potential of the avant-garde to liberate. Believing and unbelieving are present in me, are in dialogue, as I imagine they are in many others. The polyvalent spiritual, the conversation between soul and *self* in perpetuity. The processes of the avant-garde are like those of religion – they are a framework for collective self-realisation. But ultimately one has to separate oneself off and ask the question: do or don't I believe? In giving a 'linguistically innovative' poem as a gift, the imagined exclusiveness of the experimental is undermined. The process of receiving it, especially if the receiver is not familiar with the codes of the avant-garde, demystifies and renders it 'sacred'. Spirituality is a floating signifier. In a sense one can only really interact with it in a progressive way – that is, in a language that is capable of growth and acceptance. Spiritual language, like the 'experimental', must be flexible and fluid. If this is not the case we find ourselves worshipping objects, converting prayer into the icons through which prayer is normally focussed.

And icons – or chapels – are like form in poetry: they are only points of focus for meanings whose terms of reference are infinite and constantly open to interpretation. What we are left with is a belief in process.

A magnificently simple innovative poem, 'Psalm', by George Oppen (1908–84) captures something of the exchange between language and the dynamic of spiritual certainty and uncertainty. It begins:

> *Veritas sequitur…*
>
> In the small beauty of the forest
> The wild deer bedding down–
> That they are there!

and ends:

> The small nouns
> Crying faith
> In this in which the wild deer
> Startle, and stare out.[2]

In this poem there is place as forest, there is place as 'strange woods', place of 'Their paths/ Nibbled thru the fields'. There is the place of 'shade' and 'distances/ Of sun', of language and the notion of faith and where it is situated – regarding the deer, from the deer, out of the ecology of the poem, the idea of the psalm ('sacred song') within its human spiritual and ritualistic context. The polyphony and polysemy of (the language/words of) place, spirituality and the shaped poem itself.

---

2 George Oppen, *The Collected Poems of George Oppen* (New York, New Directions, 1976), p. 78.

REREADING

At the age of fifty, I am rereading books I first read when I was in my mid-to-late teens. These are the books I was reading when I wrote my novel *Morpheus* which, after thirty years and various acts of reconstruction to cover the lacunae of lost chunks of manuscript, is about to be published.[1] The books formed the matrix out of which at least part of my own textual spatiality came – in terms of language and formal issues, but also in their hyperspatiality, their accrual of place registers.

Reading was the most essential referent in the creation of *Morpheus*, a 400-page 'text', and, in going through copy-edits and then proofs, I thought it would be a self-enlightening process to revisit the works that 'informed' my late-teenage writing process. Of course, there were many books, and I certainly don't have time to revisit them all, but a handful of salient works have been with me over recent weeks.

First, I went back to Beckett and Joyce, but they've never been far away anyway. Then I went to Flann O'Brien's *The Third Policeman*. Strangely, and quite tangentially, I've also gone to Anthony Burgess's 'sweeping' and 'parodic' novel (problematical in so many ways) of the twentieth century, *Earthly Powers*.

Earthly Powers has particularly surprised me with both its desire to mock-shock (there's a coinage!) and the deep conservatism that lurks at its essence. I am fascinated by 'lurking' in texts, and this book lurks in ways it doesn't seem to know it's lurking, while making much mileage out of a lurking in the 'seamy side'. Which 'side' *is* Burgess on? Are we supposed to ask this? Well, it's not hard to work out (*then* as a eighteen-year-old and now as a fifty-year-old!) Though his protagonist in this fictional memoir is homosexual, and the bigotries of the literary and religious world are tracked through him, one can't help but feel the protagonist-narrator is made use of for a lurking moral superiority

---

1 *Morpheus: A Bildungsroman – A Partially Back-Engineered and Reconstructed Novel* (Buffalo, Blazevox, 2013).

(actually, it's homophobic and racist) – I get the same feeling from Burgess's *A Clockwork Orange*, which I also read in my late teens.[2]

Reading books thirty years later is likely to bring a change in attitude. But surely the same philosophy and process should apply to reading one's own writings thirty years later? Surely this is the point where better judgement should come into play and the work be left to its time, as manuscript? Well, I've never thought that way. When I read *Morpheus*, I feel as if I am reading a past self, someone vaguely connected with myself, but connected nonetheless. I am the sum of my past, but I am also separate. I can read the work as by someone else, almost, but here I have been reconstructing lost bits from memory. So they become of the now, with the place I write of sublimated into the text. When I first wrote the novel, I did so in the suburb of Victoria Park, Perth, in Geraldton (where my mother and brother still lived), and Wheatlands Farm (20 km northeast of York), and later in a flat in Cottesloe overlooking the Indian Ocean. The revisitations that were part of 'back-engineering' and 'reconstruction' (of lost segments) involved revisitings of Nedlands, Busselton, York and Geraldton. So Perth and the wheatbelt remained constants, and Jam Tree Gully became a later vector, while back in the late 1990s there were injections of text from Cambridge.

I did these reconstructions between 2007 and 2010, at the behest of the original publisher and editor who retrieved the manuscripts from the National Library in Canberra. In the process, the self of that era meets a self with much wider life experience and reading experience, fixing the missing bits to the best of a memory growing ever more distant. Does this make it a newer, fresher work (for me)? Whatever the case, I find the work interesting enough to want others to read it. That's the bottom line. And its intertexts and homages to Joyce and Beckett, the influence of Flann O'Brien, have an urgency and enthusiasm that a later, jaded self would never tackle. Not that it isn't a 'jaded' novel … it is, but really (also) an unrestrained hallucinatory explosion of words and experience. The smallest experience becomes a growth of words, and recalling that it was a time when I was just coming into contact with the *nouveau roman*, I see how a dust mote can grow and become a subject in itself.

I have long been interested in the interstices between short fiction and poetry, where they do and don't touch, and have never been one for genre barriers. *Morpheus* was my declaration of this, seventeen years before I wrote the novel *Genre*, or numerous essays on the hierarchies and negatives of genre (border) control. It's a 100,000-word *ars poetica*, where plot is secondary (though it does exist), and the main character, Thomas, is struggling to write a new kind of poetry (without really declaring it as such). He hangs around with a bunch of friends (Old Henry, Therese – his 'sort-of' girlfriend – his grandma, Mr and Mrs Hubbel – middle-class debauchees – a unicorn, a chimney sweep, and the odd lascivious mentoring male). At the bottom of all his interactions

2 And as I proofread this, I am (re)reading via Somerset Maugham's short stories!

is a desire to make literature. To read and write. As I've said, this is a novel of reading, a novel in which a late teenager is attempting to digest experience through the lens of reading.

I've always felt text is political, and at the bottom of this novel dwell Kropotkin, Bakunin and Marx. But there's also John Locke and others who (we might say) come from the other side of the political fence. And there are conversations in ways of seeing that I would never envisage now. I find this liberating in so many ways.

As part of my rereading 'adventure', I have also engaged with political texts I have spent decades using but not reread from *cover to cover* since I was in my teens. *Das Kapital* would be the ur-example. I read it (yes, the first volume and Engels's edited second and third volumes) when I was fifteen. I have sampled, used, written essays and quoted from chunks for thirty-five years, but not reread from beginning to end (and of the latter two volumes, I bear in mind how many manuscripts Engels had to work with!) I have just started reading it again. Every word will be part of what I write in the future, as it was part of writing *Morpheus*, no matter how tangential.

As an anarchist (vegan pacifist), I often profoundly disagree with Marx (and Hegel), but there's so much to admire (I feel the same way when I read Freud – I bought the complete new Penguin translation a few years ago[3] and read my way through, and no matter how ridiculous I felt they got at times, I always admired the writing as writing – and that matters too).

What am I tackling next? Durrell's *The Alexandria Quartet*, Irving's *The World According to Garp* and Dostoevsky (though I have reread all works many times over the years). *Morpheus* was not made out of literary classics, but all kinds of readings (as was my *Genre* later: from Descartes to porn magazines in European-language captions). All kinds of reading, good or bad, high or low, or whatever categories one might wish to impose (I don't) constitute the dramatic curve of novel-length fiction to me. I am not interested in (much) plot – but am interested in crisis points, epiphanies and prompts towards change, as a character (or characters or just a weird abstracted narratorial voice) confronts 'ideas' and issues in the world around him/her. Reading does this: a diegesis of textuality is desirable and frightening; it's a smokescreen and an addiction. Once again, good or bad, it's the writing and reading of texts as indissoluble parts of each other (we write *to* writing), that fascinate me, along with the codes of place embedded in the text – the places of writing. It is not my task to retrieve those places from *Morpheus* – it does that itself – but to highlight the inseparability of the 'story' (whatever it is 'about') and its places of writing.

---

3 Sigmund Freud, new Penguin Classics series commissioned by editor Adam Phillips in fifteen volumes (2003).

THE ETERNAL WORK-IN-PROGRESS

Writing *Morpheus* in my late teens went hand-in-hand with my fascination for long, cumulative works of poetry. In *Morpheus*, through the character of Thomas, I was subtextually mapping possible approaches to creating the work-in-progress, with its echoes of Joyce's *Finnegans Wake*. Also, though I despised him politically, like many of the 'left' I felt intrigued and compelled by Ezra Pound's unfinishable life-work, *The Cantos*. I have a strong scepticism of Pound these days, but he convinced me, along with Olson's *Maximus Poems* and Zukofsky's 'A', that anything we write is inevitably part of what we will write in the future. The interconnectedness of literary writing became an obsession for me. (This was the case for me even with Emily Dickinson's *Poems*, which in their editing, and the fights over their publication or presentation, gave the sense of a collection of smaller self-contained poems yet also of one long, growing body of work that might be read as a single poem in many parts.)

In the same way that I can revitalise a thirty-year-old novel for publication, so I can continue to build on a poem 'sequence' I began in the mid-1990s. *Graphology* is an ever-growing body of interconnected, though not necessarily sequential, poems. But it is a sequence of sorts, depending on your definition. I have defined sequences in a variety of ways to include non-linear (or partially non-linear: it is very linear at times and hopefully actually suggests different kinds of linearity), and in the spirit of this, I would term *Graphology* an open cumulative sequence come out of landscapes of language. In my critical book, *Disclosed Poetics*, I offered the following 'definitions' of poetry sequences:

> Three general sequential types: (1) narrative, where sections work like chapters in a book; (2) lyrical/cumulative, where an overall picture is built by adding parts that share linguistic qualities and may offer different angles on the same subject matter, but don't tell a story (amplify, augment); (3) the conversational sequence, in which the disparate parts speak to each other 'dialogically'. One might also add another possibility – (4) the sequence of fragmentation in which the parts may seem to operate totally independently from each other, and may be broken down not only

on the level of the line but on the level of the word itself. Narrative and lyrical/cumulative types can comfortably fit within the lyrical-I tradition though you could have non-lyrical variations on this. Third and fourth types lend themselves very much to the non-lyrical-I approach. Fragmentary sequence undoes narrative as much as creates a sense of movement. Parts of the whole don't necessarily add up.[1]

In *Morpheus*, the character Thomas tries to create a number of sequential poems with a variety of 'stylistic' approaches. They are relatively short sequences, written in short, 'impressionistic' sections. As I was writing the novel, I was reading Lattimore's translation of the *Iliad* and Albert Cooke's translation of the *Odyssey*: the book is imbued with these texts, as much as with Joyce's *Ulysses*. But I was also reading Pound's *Cantos*, and 'Canto 1' echoes throughout *Morpheus*:

> And then went down to the ship,
> Set keel to breakers, forth on the godly sea, and
> We set up mast and sail on that swart ship,
> Bore sheep aboard her, and our bodies also
> Heavy with weeping, and winds from sternward
> Bore us out onward with bellying canvas,
> Circe's this craft, the trim-coifed goddess.[2]

These words, and events of my own life (of course), fed into the writing. Looking after Wheatlands farm for my uncle and auntie during the summer (the sheep!), dealing with drug and alcohol issues, sailing on the Swan River with a friend, and relationships of the time that I can't even quite define after thirty years' distancing. These experiences, and the experience of reading, were focussed through my (very fictional) character, Thomas, who wanted to write a *new* poetry. And what Thomas began, I continued. What's clear from 'now' is how the novel was an attempt to create a polysemous text of place – of landscape and language and the paradoxes, contradictions and tautologies of presence, belonging, reading and experience.

My first *Graphology* poems were published by Equipage in 1997, but their antecedents go back to my first encounters with the poetry of J. H. Prynne (to whom the 1997 chapbook was dedicated), and further back still to the pastoral and radical concerns of my character Thomas, and the multi-phased rural-urban collider that was my youth.

I have written a number of articles on the poetics and content of *Graphology*, and its grounding in the 'pseudo-science' of graphology: the reading of individuals' characters through their handwriting. My first (submerged) forays into graphology actually predate *Morpheus*, where it is a shadowy presence. I read books my mother had acquired when I was about fifteen, and often mixed typewritten text with handwritten text when I wrote early poems.

1 John Kinsella, *Disclosed Poetics* (Manchester, Manchester University Press, 2007), p. 133.
2 Ezra Pound, *The Cantos of Ezra Pound* (New York, New Directions, 1996), p. 3.

Handwriting had a tonality that was like a pianist's touch on the keys. Notes are just not enough. Graphology was very much a subtext in my 1995 collection *Erratum/Frame(d)*, and I see that as the 'true' beginning of the process of writing *Graphology*.

Sans *Erratum/Frame(d)*, the 'sequence' now runs at over 800 pages. It was not composed in consistent numerical order (though it has numerical patterning). In fact, it jumps about, and there are many lacunae in the numbering, but its threads and linguistic concerns create a different kind of numerical correspondence that is spatial as well as temporal. The 'section' I am engaged with at the moment is 'Graphology Heuristics', which links the act of reading writing as well as the process of discovering for oneself. *Graphology* is a poetry of reading and experiencing, of witnessing and reacting: its open form allows all that interests me to gather to its magnetic centre, establishing its own co-ordinates of categorising and arranging figurative and factual 'information'. There is, for me, something of the plotless novel in this, but one in which the fiction is conscious of the compromised position all writers are in through mediating 'experience' with language that seeks to frame and cross-reference that experience.

Graphology has been going for twenty years. At times I have declared it 'ended' (it can and could never be 'finished' – it is 'open'); that I would write no more. But I always find myself coming back to its central premise and also its certainties: it is a solid body of work to add to, grow out of, experiment and take risks with. It's not a journal, not even an artist's workbook: it is a structured poetic work that plays with time and space as artefacts that need iconoclastic (un)treatment, but it shares qualities with diaries/journals/daybooks. At other times, it becomes so over-polished that I recognise none of the experience that went into the original draft of a piece. The work-in-progress is there to encourage, entice, mock, reject, answer back, unsettle and comfort. There are lyrics, prose poems, concrete poems, list poems, scribbles, squibs and sonnets (sometimes one and the same); there are literally drawings and long sequences (within the overall 'endless' sequence) and texts written in the dirt of firebreaks, shaped with sticks.

The word itself, *GRAPHOLOGY*, is an echo far from its cause, its origins, throughout the years, the many pages. My handwriting has always been difficult to read, I am told. Thomas, the protagonist of *Morpheus*, might have been working towards his own *Graphology*, but then again he seems to have gone in a very different direction. His explorations brought different paths and different 'ends'.

Here are two of the most recent:

Graphology Heuristics 34

Fires have been raging all over the last few days.

We see the columns of smoke at all points, as if we're the centre, biding our time.

Near the detention centre someone lit-up ten or eleven times.
Two years ago women with 'bomb the boats' t-shirts
leapt up and down, chanting, in front of t.v. cameras.
No one is suggesting a direct link, but.

On Wave Rock a BMX thrill-seeker rides the erosion
and has a whale of a time. The photos are accessed
across the planet. The shire is wary
though a businesswoman is stoked.
Soon, it will be a tidal wave
wrecking inland.

Some would mix metaphors above,
but they're separate issues.

Bright sparks drive
firebugs and vandals
and their apologists.

And bringing this to light
makes the personal pronoun
a killjoy.

Don't worry, it'll all wash over.
Time covers up the dirty work,
the detonations.

Graphology Heuristics 35

Funny how a single word can trigger
a dictionary.

Others want to get in on the act.
Why not? United we fall,

divided we stand. This sequence
of words. This operational

*If I say; If I say so; If I say
so myself.* The lower leaves

on the tree outside the window
dying to boost the canopy.

I'LL TELL YOU A STORY

I possess two items from my childhood. Both are books. Somehow I have held on to these through the upheavals of my life, including having twice sold vast collections of books to support my various needs (and long-past addictions) twenty and more years ago. When I did my last big 'sell-off' in the early 1990s, I managed to hang on to my early J. H. Prynne *Poems*[1] and a few signed collections of poetry, but that's about it. I occasionally run into people who remark that they own books containing dedications from writers to me. But that's the way of it, and though I enjoy having books around me, I am not stuck on owning things and have little regard for material possessions. I do not believe in property. Property is *not* place. But one of the problems with 'place' is the apparent indivisibility of 'place' and 'property' – the acquiring and imposition of 'rights of ownership'.

Yet I do have those two books from childhood. One is *Bedtime Nursery Rhymes*, which was given to me on my second birthday by my maternal great-grandmother Coupar. She wrote in the front in her very formal, aged hand: 'To dear little John, on his 2nd birthday from his Great-Grandma S. G. Coupar 1965'. This intrigued me through my childhood, because it became my only memory of this Goldfields woman, and I long mused over the formality and affection working together in the capitals for Great-Grandma, the initials in her name, counterpointed by the 'dear little'. Should they have been in caps as well, I wondered? This seemed to me as much poetry as the wonderful rhymes inside which I still know by heart and recited to my son Tim when he was still in his cot.

But what's more interesting, I think, is that the rhymes in that book are 'Tales Retold for Younger Readers'. The nursery rhyme being given the recognition as adult text it should be accorded? Some of them are terrifying, even in their simplified and versified forms (some derived from fairy stories, others from Mother Goose and so on). 'Solomon Grundy' was the complete horror narrative.

---

1 J. H. Prynne, *Poems* (Edinburgh and London, Agneau 2, 1982).

Which brings me to the theme of this interlude: how much plot it does or doesn't take to tell a story. As I have said many times regarding *Morpheus*, plot has never greatly interested me. And the material I am tracking here is integral to the writing of *Morpheus*, as it is to other fictions and certainly poetry. The retelling of a tale is not just condensation, bowdlerising and censorship. It's also reconfiguring for an audience in the expectation that will find alternative points of entry. My nursery-rhyme book, mass-produced on cheap paper, printed in the Eastern bloc ('Printed in Czechoslovakia by PZ Bratislava') becomes a perverse détente at the height of the Cold War: the publisher, based in London, was the ubiquitously and fetishistically named Golden Pleasure Books Limited (purveyors of folk wisdom to children). As a child, I shared its 'versions' with thousands of other English-reading children around the world.

But getting back to the 'point': these tales-in-rhyme are partial, incomplete or 'lacking' in some way, yet for me they were entirely adequate and told enough of a story for me to envisage 'the rest' or more. And this became the principle of my writing life (though I don't always observe my own precepts! for me, really, anything goes in text): to show glimpses, not complete pictures. To let part of the tune be heard, not the whole thing. To have an incomplete music, rather than the full score. And for the painting to suggest rather than illustrate (all of the illustrations in my nursery-rhyme book are in blue: that was partial enough insight for me!)

When I discovered science fiction at the age of nine, my life changed. I devoured four or five books a week and this went on for years and years. I started with John Wyndham's *The Chrysalids* and *The Day of the Triffids*, and though they have plot aplenty, it was more the glimpses into fear and inevitability, cause and effect, that compelled me. I would read large plot-driven Silverbergs or Frank Herberts or Asimovs, but it was the atmosphere of, say, *Dune* or the great Library of Trantor that lured me. And my reading of imperialistic, totalitarian, militaristic urges was done at the same time as reading Marx and Kropotkin (I was in my teens by this stage), and rather than enforce a reactionary politics, it illuminated the history I was so forensically interested in by giving it imaginary status and manifestations as well. Analogies, parables, fables … tales … have all interested me. All of this took me to *One Thousand and One Nights*; it took me to the theorists Propp and Todorov. Reading against my political grain was illuminating.

But I digress again. Tangents. That's what drives a narrative for me. Plot is digression, is movement: it just doesn't have to be event-driven to be causal. Back to Great-Grandma's precious gift. One of my favourite limerick-squibs is this:

> I'll tell you a story
> About Jack a Nory,
> And now my story's begun;
> I'll tell you another
> Of Jack and his brother,
> And now my story is done.

This is a piece of metatextual wonder, pure theory. It is completion/closure, *and* eternally open. It is the paradox that entices me to narrative and to reject plot (almost). The rhyme analyses its own condition of telling, opens doors and tells you everything (there is to know) while telling you nothing. This is the glimpse into eternal possibilities: you fill in the gap/s. It is also concision, craft and philosophy. To me, it seemed supremely logical. I liked logic. And I liked tangents. Poetry. Short fiction. The two have always seemed to me so closely related. In the Katherine Mansfield stories, 'The Doll's House' and 'The Woman at the Store', we engage with narrative poetry at its very best. Prose poetry: open-form, run-on, succinct, evocative through telling no more than is needed. When I first read 'I seen the little lamp', I knew all I needed to know. That was the poem in the story, and the story was no story without the poem.

When I was a child, I ran a small magazine: I printed it on a silk-screen printer (as a vegan, I wouldn't use silk now) and distributed to friends, family and neighbours. I filled most editorial, writing and production roles myself, like most kids who do such things. I wrote poems and stories. A magazine should have both. They were two sides of the same coin. The difference? Poems had shorter lines and needed to 'tell' less. The stories had 'run-on' lines and told something, but not too much. An alien encounter, a kid riding his bike towards a corner where a truck had ignored a stop sign. Stop. No more information necessary. The cliff-hanger, but with no follow-up. No part two, no satisfaction. Poetry and stories had to bother, had to irritate, never seem complete. And novels … novels could do that too.

I mentioned two books from my childhood. The other was the classic, *Charley, Charlotte and the Golden Canary* by Charles Keeping, published by OUP. It's an illustrated book of political, social, ethical and imaginative genius. Its ink-smudged illustrations (within bold, sketched lines) no doubt started a revolution in the illustration of children's literature. I have wondered how much Keeping drew on the early advertising work (especially for women's shoes) by Andy Warhol. I could Google it, but I can't be bothered: I don't want to find out *that* way. It's just a personal impression for a book I wish to remain personal, and yet to share. In this book, I see that social contradiction at the core of anarchism: mutual aid. This story of urban development, class (struggle), high-rise and the old city, friendship, loneliness, alienation, redemption, fate, hope and freedom, is brief, to the point, poetic. Not a *lot* happens, but enough happens to make it seem epic. Here are some of my favourite lines:

> Paradise Street was slowly turning into a muddle of bricks, rubble and ruins. Soon only the bird-stall remained. Charley became so lonely that he decided that if he could not have Charlotte's friendship he would have to have the next best thing – the golden canary.

But this isn't enough. What mattered to me was the way the 'prose' seemed like non-end-stopped lines of poetry (sure, I wouldn't have thought of it in such a way, but I did like the lines as they were arranged): the precise way it appeared on the page, above an illustration, mattered. It was in large print and was actually laid out like this:

> Paradise Street was slowly turning into a muddle of bricks, rubble and ruins. Soon only the bird-stall remained. Charley became so lonely that he decided that if he could not have Charlotte's friendship he would have to have the next best thing – the golden canary.

And that, for me, was a short way from the layout of the texts in my nursery-rhyme book. Maybe this, with a ragged edge instead, would convince the sceptical reader that it functions as a poem as much as prose:

> Paradise Street was slowly turning into a
> muddle of bricks, rubble and ruins. Soon only
> the bird-stall remained. Charley became so
> lonely that he decided that if he could not have
> Charlotte's friendship he would have to have
> the next best thing – the golden canary.

And I already knew there was more than rhyme to poetry – my mother, a poet, had told me that!

I won't connect the dots – reader, you can do that. I've just told you a story, as I said I would. It's my story, but it's probably someone else's as well. Maybe quite a few people's. One last thing though: I should say that *Charley, Charlotte and the Golden Canary* carries a inscription from my maternal grandmother (daughter of Great-Grandma Coupar) and grandfather. It says and is laid out thus:

> To dear John with lots of love
> on your 5th Birthday
> From Nanna and Pa.Pa. xx
> ... 1968

USES OF KNOWLEDGE/DATA/DETAIL
IN WRITING AND READING

I've always loved 'data', though I am sceptical of how it is sourced and utilised. My re-engineered novel, *Morpheus*, is a book stuffed with data, yet aims to be a challenge to the 'empirical'; the data of 'learning' – from school, the first year or two of university, private reading and even (scientific) researching. While writing *Morpheus*, I was studying and occasionally working in my own home lab, complete with Mettler balance, Bunsen burners, titration equipment and micro ground-jointed organic glassware, including Liebig condensers and even a Friedrichs condenser, and an old cathode ray oscilloscope: a Cro, which worked well with all the 'crows' in my poems, and also informed my sense of poetic rhythms.

But the home lab was becoming a thing of the past and, leaving the country for the city to attend university, I still worked on and off in a commercial laboratory, preparing mineral sands for analysis and supervising the loading of (mineral sands) ships. Simultaneously, my politics of protest (eventually against the very work I was doing) were simmering and manifesting. I was obtaining knowledge through praxis, knowledge that would be used against its sources.

And 'data' are subjective in their derivations and applications. Maybe this is why 'pseudo-science' fascinates me, with its purported facts (I would argue plenty of facts arising from the 'hard sciences' are purported or dubious as well, especially given I am not satisfied with any 'proofs' of existence in the first place). I have mentioned my poetry of 'graphology', which has its origins in the materials that would constitute the novel *Morpheus* in my late teens, but I haven't alluded to my interest in alchemy. I no longer have it, outside readings of Faust, but it's omnipresent in *Morpheus* and was probably one of the factors that enticed Paul Hardacre to offer to publish the manuscript with Papertiger back in 2007 (after a journey from there, it has been looked after by Geoffrey Gatza at Blazevox – thanks to both for assisting in its passage). Paul's knowledge of esoterica and alchemy is second to none, and it informs his poetry as well as his critical practice. Of his book *liber xix: differentia liber*[1] I wrote:

1 Paul Hardacre, *liber xix: differentia liber* (Sydney, Puncher and Wattman, 2011).

liber xix is a remarkable if not unique book of poetry. To quote an alchemical expression from a quote cited by Hardacre, it's a book in which language 'dissolves and combines'. But for a work so specific in its prosody, the key to unlocking its mysteries actually locates itself in spiritual essence derived from a mixture of the animal, vegetable, mineral, and quintessential. This is a book about the meeting of differences, about the alchemical reactions that arise from these meetings, these mixings. The poem is always more than the sum of its parts, and change is always part of the discourse the poems engender within themselves, between each other, and in the context of the quotes that accompany them. These glimpses into chaos and formation are also mini-epics, condensed 'vedas' and 'sagas' reaching across belief systems and geographies to find a 'universal' way of viewing being. Across the ampersands the components of the poem speak, and accumulate towards a maxim-like 'unconclusion' – the 'noble' is reached only nominally, and the 'lesser' (base) elements of the poem retain their properties. Alchemically speaking, though deeply desiring and even believing a closure is possible, no ultimate 'coniunctio' is reached; maybe it is even studiously avoided in a playback Gertrude Stein would possibly have found enticing (if she had written them). But it's overall this work really comes into its own – it is a narrative, a journey from heaven to hell, from God to the faces of evil. Evil is named. Strands of mystical histories of humanity twist around each other, mingle fluids. This is a beautifully terrifying work. Hardacre is one of the finest poetical transmuters out there. He is to be venerated and feared at once. He is going places few contemporary poets have risked acknowledging, never mind visiting. Like all great innovators, he reaches as far back as knowledge.[2]

Alchemy has an essential space in the evolution of scientific research and can't just be dismissed as turning-lead-into-gold fantasies and a willingness to sell one's soul to gain power. Articulating the body, the soul, of a human's relationship to nature and 'existence' adds up to much more than 'magic' and greed. Reading Paracelsus and Meister Eckhart was part of the protagonist of *Morpheus*, Thomas's, *raison d'être* as much as it was my own. How did this come about? Well, I lost 'religion' when I was sixteen or seventeen and walked out of a Christmas service during which the minister had compared the bounties of Christ's birth to a cash register. Looking back, I'd like to think he was being ironic, critiquing the spendfest that is Christmas, but I doubt it. I was reading Aldous Huxley's *The Perennial Philosophy*, I was reading the *Bhagavad-Gita*, I was reading the Koran and I was reading the Bible. I had been baptised and confirmed; I'd always thought Christ was okay but the trappings of Church were like the trappings of the state: about control, and little caring for anything outside their own existences. Thomas in *Morpheus* struggles with all this.

But what remained from my comparative readings was my own sense of what constituted 'spirit' and 'spiritual', and a lot of *information*. I continue to process that information through my writing, be it poetry, essays or fictions. I am interested in applying it 'correctly', but also 'incorrectly'. I find errors generative, creative and 'honest'. I find the slippage between fact and error enticing.

2 John Kinsella on back cover of Paul Hardacre, *liber xix: differentia liber*.

Why data? Actually, for an event to be staged in a narrative, for an event to provide the co-ordinates for a poem in which the 'ineffable' is framed with an eye to quiddity finding its own voice (metaphor in overdrive), one doesn't need a lot of data. Just enough: let the language do the work.

Or is this undervaluing data? In the same way that the adage 'show don't tell' is the death sentence to innovation and expansion of possibilities (being told doesn't mean you have to 'listen': you can rearrange in your own head), so data can enliven our reading of an event. Superfluous, extraneous, even false (excessive) data lose points of reference, become detached from the causal event. But that tells us something about how such events can't exist in vacuums, that they interconnect on the most obtuse levels. An example: I write about a tree limb being blown down in a storm and falling very near us (my partner and myself). If we hadn't moved from where we were sitting a few minutes previously, the limb would have fallen on us and possibly killed us. The poem is in *that* slippage, surely. So why stuff the poem with detail about the state of the road, a death a century ago and so on? Because it interconnects and paints a wider picture. We are small points in the pointillist whole (which is more of a hole and never complete).

And taking it further, what is the relation between 'data' and 'detail': is 'extraneous' description the same as precise detailed observation, and is detailed observation at least part of the material of 'data'? Detail is not simply an accumulation of adjectives, an eruption of 'purple prose' (though that can be interesting in itself), but the precise deployment of specific information relating to an object/event/scenario. In addition, there's the provision of 'extra' (and additional) information within and outside the frame which enhances our reading of the core subject, the focal point. Fine detail might give us a more 'realistic' or maybe 'vivid' picture of something, and thus encourage a depth of appreciation, but it can also distract from the supposed main object of focus. Yet it's in this diffusion that I find expansion: tangents and alternative avenues for rereading/misreading and reconstructing. No *knowledges* are unrelated.

The misuse of data is equally interesting. Using 'facts' doesn't mean you have to use 'facts' correctly. And facts are never *correct*. To observe a series of high temperatures precisely, and say that it was colder than expected, opens all sorts of possibilities: metaphorically and factually. I believe in the figurative strength of tautology: from the vaguely tautological 'boiling hot' to the more explicit 'frozen ice'. One might translate, say, a series of readings of seismic activity into verbal and numerical tautologies. Therein is a poem.

And the 'misuse' of nomenclature, terminologies and 'information' often tells us more about a condition of being than stoical belief in any 'right' and 'wrong'. Deploying a word like 'algorithm' as metaphor doesn't mean you don't know what an algorithm is. It amazes me how upset people get with what they see as the casual deployment of 'scientific terms'. As a slightly (though not particularly) relevant aside, I was making and programming computers in the mid 1970s. I have no admiration for them now (for non-violent neo-Luddite reasons), but gee, I know how to use them (and, once upon a time, to make them). Maybe if a word is separated from its root meaning, or its acquired practice-application/s, the reader needs to ask *why*, and do some work beyond literal definitions. Facts are distractions as much as confirmations.

Knowledge is implicit in how and why we communicate. Writing is a processing of knowledge. It's also a constant process of recategorising and reformatting knowledge. Those who control knowledge are about not liberty but deprivation. The net is supposed to be a knowledge revolution, but too often it's a zone of mutual policing. The correction of Wikipedia entries is an interesting case in point. Yes, I like to be certain the information I am reading is verifiable, and effectively expressed in terms of conveying these *verifiable facts*, but I also know that facts change and that sometimes an incorrect detail can import more of a 'truth' (behind the scenes) than cold, hard detail. We know we witness events differently, even if outcomes can be 'agreed' upon. But the reading and hearing of many different witnessings make a picture more absorbable. For me, that's what writing is, and why writing can never be limited to a few classics, but must be an ongoing process of creativity: good/bad, right/wrong, 'stylish'/'sloppy', factual/sketchy … whatever binaries one creates, it's all and much more.

Morpheus is a book stuffed full of 'data' (from chemical equations to details from Herodotus, that questionable and often hyperbolic 'father of history' who so stretched truth, but likely with great integrity: those wonderful contradictions). Data morph into the phantasm, the fact becomes the error, and that ambitious but shrewd Athenian, Themistocles, drinks too much. If we suddenly lost the ability mentally to file the facts we learn, what emerges when we try to affirm a 'truth' might well be poetry *and* a 'fiction'. And I feel that 'fiction' is just truth and reality in a decategorised form. Its liberties are in its formal controls, in its 'writerly' concerns of composition and reading.

I notice that books on sports are often foisted on young readers: lots of facts about how a game is played, mixed with aspiration, disappointment and whatever moral message the writer feels obliged to push. Not surprising, really: arranging the figurative with the factual. A little older, and maybe it'll be historical fictions. Combines a notion of 'learning' (historical facts) and socio-cultural application: scenarios and correlations we might draw with our own lives, our own behaviours. A model is made. I'd rather an historical novel with all the facts wrong, but giving the impression they are correct, than one that really only gives me a story trapped in a timeline, and period-appropriate details about clothing. In the slippage, the model collapses, and literature is made. Literature, in whatever form, is about change, and changing how we perceive 'facts' is a vital part of this.

WHERE I SIT IN THE PROCESS: WORKING WITH ALI ALIZADEH TO PRODUCE AN ANTHOLOGY OF PERSIAN POETRY

In the creation of a world configured by 'spaces', sediment of place, conceptual zones of crossover and dialogue, I always come to the collaborative act. The polysituated is emblazoned, highlights made and markers laid, nodal points set and illuminated, through acts of collaboration. Cultural spatiality is enhanced, enriched and grown through working beyond the 'monolingual' *self*, as we reach for an even more complex model of interweaving polysituatedness. To collaborate is to make of one's self a polyglot of place and language. The conversations that have gone on between Ali Alizadeh and myself over how best to render Persian poetry, selected from over a thousand years of writing, into English-language poems run to many hundreds of pages.[1] After three years of swapping emails and versions of poems, we felt ready to offer a relatively slender volume to readers.[2] Though it is slender, we feel it is by no means a narrow selection. We have tried to step outside the usual safety zones of Persian-into-English poetry, and, in doing so, to challenge the status quo of the industry of making Persian poetry digestible for capitalist Western audiences, who might look for solace and spiritual affirmation through often ecstatic and mystical poems that seem to offer an alternative to the materialism and apparent meaninglessness of modern existence.

This is the first of many deceptions we wish to expose. There has been exploitation, and misrepresentation, in saccharine and overly lush renderings of, for example, Rumi, into modern Englishes, to placate the desire for a spiritual heal-all at one's bedside, yet still to enjoy the pleasures of Western materialism (the 'having one's cake and eating it too' school). True, Rumi is big enough to

---

1 The polysituatedness of language is in constant evidence as it morphs, changes, feeds into other languages, and also colonises, hybridises, rejects, deletes, is reconstituted, adapts, 'evolves', is manipulated through political and social control, resists oppression, meets needs, reclaims, creates an aesthetics, maps and unmaps land, is made by land.
2 *Six Vowels and Twenty-three Consonants: An Anthology of Persian Poetry from Rudaki to Langroodi*, ed. and trans. Ali Alizadeh and John Kinsella (Todmorden, Arc Publications, 2012).

stand on his own two feet, and translation is about taking liberties, making a text relevant to the time and space it is to be read in. But such wilful construction of a medieval master to suit all tastes in consumer society, as a way of offsetting that society's spiritual deprivation, is disingenuous to say the least.

Such translations increase in times of imperialist capitalism. The mid-to-late nineteenth century was one such boom, coming out of Victorian Britain's empire-building and resolving of ancient cultures into museum fodder to entertain the steadily rising middle class, and to 'amaze' the threatening working class into reverence for the captors, collectors and collators of such materials. Another surge was post- the Iranian Revolution, which for obvious reasons American translators took as a stimulus to the 'real' spiritual and poetic integrity of Persian civilisation. In essence, the spikes in Persian translation, or Iranian works, old and new, coincide with creating an alternative to the Islamic state version that holds sway. While these kinds of usages are inevitable and deplorable, one can also state that present-day Iran is no easy place for a poet to practise, and state oppression there is absolute.

This is not to speak on behalf of the contemporary Iranian poets included within the volume, as they negotiate their own paths within the state, and each will have their own views on this, but to declare an outsider's view of isolation and enclosure, while noting that the tyranny is not only internal but also applied by countries outside Iran. Essentially, in collating such an anthology, one is laid open to the charges of either being supportive of a pariah state, or opposing it. In my case, I see all states as oppressive, all nations as contradictions of freedom and liberty. Iran's oppressions may be more overt than others, but all states share such qualities.

Six Vowels and Twenty-three Consonants, from my point of view, is a book about the dynamics of poets working in their own space, against social, political, spiritual and environmental backdrops. It is not about me (or Ali) stating a political position *per se*, but, nonetheless, we are aware that we occupy and make such a position through the act of participation. This makes translation more than a conversion of words, an approximation, a version, or a departure. It makes it an act of codification and code-breaking, and if we are to steer clear of the militaristic associations of these words, which is our express desire, then every word and every line translated has to be done in an informed way. We attempted to keep the translations as close to the original as possible. We selected pieces that don't push nationalist bandwagons, though at the same time they reflect nationalist issues and cultural identity in the context of the individual poet's identity. National myths of origin and status cannot be ignored, but they can be accorded a less prominent place. Suffering is a given, and poets never escape it. There is suffering among the poets and expressed in the poems under various regimes. If poets can't speak, then the darkness is overwhelming and hope is lost.

One of the major issues for two poets in translating dozens of poets of both genders and across a thousand-year period is the risk of making all in the same tone – that is, imposing the translators' tone. While this can never be entirely avoided, I hope we have managed to avoid this to some extent. Both Ali and

I have gone for an understated 'exactness' rather than a mystical liberation of often already-liberated texts. It is poetry of one language, and poetry with a cultural familiarity regardless of the era or gender. Issues are different, the body has its own rules, but there is a conversation between poets and poems across the ages.

In the twentieth-century Persian poets, we find an awareness of their same-language predecessors and traditions, but also a growing awareness and interaction with, say, other modernist poets. As we move through the modern period, discourse with the greater poetic world increases, unsurprisingly. Isolated, Iranian poets have created a language of simultaneous connection and disconnection, and seem to speak among themselves, most importantly, before speaking outwards. Diaspora poets often write of their own isolation outside Iran, and their acts of textual resistances take on complicated roles in affirming their own liberties while lamenting the lack for those in their 'home' country. This is a fraught issue, as an apologia for Western capitalist exploitation as 'better' than the obvious abuses of religious fundamentalism becomes a binary opposition, and one that doesn't work. Unless the Diaspora poet is critiquing his or her own privilege, the act of liberation through text becomes compromised. In the end, the few pieces by Diaspora poets we included were chosen because they seem to *not* fall into this trap, by our estimation.

Translation processes differ for me depending on context and familiarity with a specific language. Latin-script languages are far easier for me to work with: I have translated a lot from the French, but also from other European languages. I do not have Farsi, and find it hard to follow, and though I am learning as I go, and seeking to gain an understanding of the language, I am largely relying on Ali Alizadeh's literal English versions. But it's not simply a case of 'converting' this to an 'English-language' poem. There's clearly a process of collaboration: I ask Ali to send me the literal rendering, together with a commentary on the poem itself, on the poet, and any technical/prosodic peculiarities. Ali is a fine poet and an acute reader of poetry, and passionate about Persian/Iranian poetry – as I have become myself – it is one of the great world poetries. I also ask him to send me a copy of the original: I like not only to see the shape of the poem on the page, but to do my best with the script, and with understanding how it is working. It is also important for me to get historical and cultural contexts for the poem, whether of the past or contemporary. As my familiarity with the language has grown, so has my ability to make use of the originals.

In the end, though, it is an inherent 'sense' of the poem that makes it work – some poems I cannot translate, others really find their mark with me. Once I have done my first version, I send it back to Ali for comment. I usually have a few points to query regarding possible meanings of words – variations, subtleties and so on – and broader technical questions. Ali sends back comments and reactions with possible alternative interpretations. I have found he does this more frequently when I am reworking 'classical' or medieval Persian poetry, than when it is contemporary Farsi poetry – I naturally feel more kinship with the latter and tend to 'get' the poetry and poetics more readily. I enjoy working, though, and as someone with a bit of a 'history' background, I like to explore eras and contexts.

A few of the technical questions that confronted me, in making choices from Ali's roughs, concerned whether to retain rhyme, the connected issue of refrains, whether to preserve basic word order or rearrange, and whether to maintain certain characterising prosodic elements, especial of the ghazal. Interestingly, these issues changed with time, and towards the latter stages of the process I tended towards maintaining as many of the original impositions (or rules) as possible. Consistent concerns revolved around retaining the *qaafiyaa* and *radif* or not, along with the more easily achieved usage of the poet's name (*takhallus*) in the last couplet (*bayt*) of the poem. Various experiments were conducted with metre, but metre is most often what I varied to equate with more open-form English-language poetics. Certainly, in the modern poems, the phrase became as much the standard as the line, and the residue of earlier techniques (especially out of the couplet, heroic couplet, quatrain and the ghazal itself) is played against free verse and more open forms.

Particularly with classical poems, I found myself taking slight liberties that could seem great liberties to some. For example, one of my comments back to Ali regarding a Nezami translation went:

> Taken some liberties with this. I have gone for 'the word' (Russian formalism!) and have utilised 'knowledge' (Sufi?!) etc... and changed some of the singular/plurals

Or, wrestling with the great Attar:

> This was real tough, Ali. I have provided some options/queries in the right margin. Regarding 'animated' – I see it more as illumined from what I get of Sufism, but I might be entirely wrong. Go back to that if it's closer. Once again, great liberties. I went for 'wander' because of the spiritual and literary associations it carries, and because it takes a bit of the agency away. Probably wrong!

This doesn't mean we stuck with these decisions, but it's the kind of conversation that took place. And here's a reply from Ali regarding a Rudaki translation:

> maybe 'touch' would actually be better than 'hold' in the last line. The Persian word *gereftan* (roughly: to get) is very flexible; but I think hold might be too strong, although I do like its association with 'hand' through alliteration. I guess the thing with touch is that it could be accidental – perhaps? – and I think the 'getting' of the beloved's sleeve here is quite deliberate. I'm thinking maybe something like 'caress', or 'stroke', even 'feel'? catch? I love 'of yours' rhyme. Perfect.

And so the exchanges would flow until we both reached a version that satisfied us. Sometimes this could take many exchanges; sometimes it was much quicker. Issues of alliteration and rhyme (I wanted to understand exactly how the rhymes for '*qays*' worked, for example, even if I chose not to go down that path), and especially metrics, were constantly raised. Maybe, however, the most significant issues of discussion were to do with cultural register. I think respect is the most important attribute in a translator when representing a language's poetry, a process that seemingly homogenises great difference when one should in fact be scrupulous in avoiding such generics – respect keeps this at the forefront of thought.

Here's a message/query from me to Ali that touches on such issues:

> is religion the same as faith in this context – I guessed the comparison was one between status quo 'religion' and a faith/spirituality that transcended this (Sufi)? Also, do the internal commas work within the dynamic of the original (i.e. the hiatus) – I got the impression from earlier quatrains by other 'early' poets that this might be a problem – if not, great … it expands the syntactical possibilities. One of the reasons I have not done completed reinterpretations (more versions) and recastings is to try and retain the basic movement of the originals. If we can be more interpretive then it expands horizons – but then, overall, that might create problems of 'trust' re readers and this kind of anthology?

And, in the end, the anthology rests on issues of trust – from the poets, from the readers and between ourselves. For me, Persian poetry helps give reason for existence. For me, the sense of who I am, the sense of coexisting and dialoguing places that inform identity, is complemented and enabled through anthologising. And further, I feel that this polysituatedness can make for more informed and respectful interpretations and, where relevant, 'decisions' regarding belonging, place and cultural issues.

AUGUSTE LACAUSSADE

Le Réunion has become a significant point in my lived geography (and that of my family). It is an island of diverse cultures and heritages, and in all discourse and life on the island the spectre and reality of its history of slavery is present. The affirmation of identity of those people with slave heritage and the crimes committed in the name of the French state (and financial gain in itself) make of the island a memorial place, a place of warning of the evils of colonial displacement and profiteering, as well as an affirmation of the strength of individuals and communities to overcome such traumatic origins. This remarkable (geologically young) island with its semi-tropical volcanic and mountainous habitats, its isolated cirques, its vibrant Creole language, its religious and ethnic diversity, and its pluralism 'wrestling' with the notion (and reality) of the French state, makes for a remarkable history of polysituatedness in poetry and literature in general.

Two nineteenth-century Réunionese poets have fascinated me, both of them writing in French, and I have translated these poets in a concerted, committed fashion. There is the remarkable Leconte de Lisle, but also the equally remarkable Auguste Lacaussade.

There is not a great deal of information on the life of the poet Auguste Lacaussade, though unsurprisingly there is considerably more of it in French than in English. However, one of the most substantial pieces written on the poet appeared in English in a journal in 1941.[1] This article, written by Mercer Cook, suffers less from limitations in that era's critical and social 'whiteout' of language than one might (sadly) expect, despite the othering of his model; he concludes the biographical segment of his article: 'The greatest of France's Negro poets died in 1897, however, before his work was completed.'[2]

Despite its limitations, I use Cook's article heavily in what follows, as well as drawing on a number of French biographical sources. Fundamentally, though,

1 Mercer Cook, 'Auguste Lacaussade', *Phylon* 2.3 (1941), pp. 260–74.
2 Cook, 'Auguste Lacaussade', p. 265.

it's time spent on La Réunion that informs my 'angle' on Lacaussade and his work, and also his relationship with the other great Creole French-language Reunionese poet of the nineteenth century, Leconte de Lisle. It was originally an interest in de Lisle and translating his work that drew me to La Réunion, where I first spent a month in 2013 with my family and with which I retain an ongoing connection.

La Réunion is now a place of syncretism and great cultural diversity, of Christianity, Islam, Hinduism and beliefs that often combine elements of these and also a range of African spiritualities, of French and Creole languages and poetries, social unease and intense pride in belonging are intrinsically tied in with physical isolation in the Indian Ocean, a vicious history of slavery, conversations between different religions, cultures and ethnicities, sublimity that encounters soaring mountains and hard-to-access cirques, deep oceans, cyclones, and a volcano that is one of the most active in the world. Roadside shrines to St Expédit, the prevalence of great white sharks, the mainland-French tourist industry (white mainlanders are known as 'zoreilles'), high unemployment, unique flora and fauna, rocks tumbling from cliffs on to roads, the sugar industry, membership of the EU, proximity and identification with the rest of Africa … it's not an easy portrait. It is complex, rich and generative; it is troubled and yet totally possessing of those who call it home. The roots go deep. It was on La Réunion itself that I discovered the work of Lacaussade; he is mentioned in its guidebooks and known as one of the great 'local' writers who also influenced the literature of the colonial power, France.

Mercer Cook's admiration for Auguste Lacaussade as poet and person is strong and convincing, and Cook plays an important part in the (highly) inter-mittent reception in English of this master poet, whose works in a variety of ways bridge cultures, reinvent the romantic and fuse a search for liberty with affirmation of being receptive to place, to nature itself. In some respects, there's a fusing of activism and lyricism that is truly radical in being both a part of mainstream French literature and at a 'tangent', or something, rather, unique in itself.

Long considered an 'exotic' poet in France, he was both an intense writer of place (whose 'displacement' to France in some ways focussed his literary and social gaze on his absent home) largely formed through memory of early life in the island-colony, and also an intensely erudite and well-read poet with multi-ple literary interests – like Leconte de Lisle (Lacaussade's friend up to a point, though the former resented de Lisle's status and absorption into the French literary mainstream which he rightfully perceived as the result of what amounts to racism, given they both suffered bigotry for being Creole; there were degrees of access – Lacaussade had 'mixed-race' heritage and de Lisle was 'white'). As Cook says:

> Seventy-nine years later, in his *Histoire de la litterature coloniale* en France, Roland Lebel agrees with M. Foucque, present-day native of Reunion, 'that Lacaussade, by the accuracy and variety of his descriptions, deserves to be

considered as the first in date of the great creole poets and as the creator of exotic poetry. It may be said that without Lacaussade, Leconte de Lisle, as a creole poet, would never have existed.'[3]

And *degrees* were the subtext of life on La Réunion. As a result of slavery and slave-ownership, and even after slavery's abolition, there was still the deep stratification of island society (the houses of the Big Whites ruled all) that persists to the present day. Truly multicultural, colonised without displacing an indigenous people since it had no indigenes, this is a volcanic island of soaring mountain peaks in which escaped slaves hid and set up their own communities away from the guns of 'governance' and the sugar industry; a place where the history of slavery and crimes against the slaves dominate island identity.

A very fine recent novel written in French (rather than Creole) to come out of La Réunion is Jean-François Samlong's *Une Guillotine dans un train de nuit* about Sitarane (1858–1911); it is a fictionalised history of an indentured labourer (a post-slavery thread in La Réunion's oppressions), a Mozambican arrival whose anger manifested in extreme criminal violence and murder, and who to this day has a cult following linked to violence. Violence makes violence. Some (misguided) people may attempt to make Sitarane a hero for the cause of the island's oppressed, but though he clearly came out of undeniably oppressive circumstances, he was not about human rights activism in any way.

Because of the complex nature of the island's history, there arise many models of 'liberation' that combine to form a greater picture of liberty. By contrast to Sitarane, Lacaussade, though marginalised as a 'non-white' in island society, was nonetheless 'respectable' and relatively privileged in education and had white-French heritage on his father's side. But as Cook implies, even with his 1940s limitations in perception of cause and effect, one has to be wary of making Lacaussade a figure of the full and equitable championing of human rights, someone definitively anti-racist (it's worth remembering that he wanted to succeed in white France as a writer), though he was a vigorous and committed opponent of slavery:

> So consistently does Lacaussade sympathize with the slave that the reader is surprised to hear him refer in one of his poems to 'our blacks.' In this connection it should be noted that many free mulattoes in the French colonies held slaves, and that the usual colonial distinction between the man of color and the black existed on Bourbon Island. It is therefore understandable that Lacaussade did not consider himself a Negro.[4]

Lacaussade was born on the French Indian Ocean 'possession' of Bourbon, later Ile de la Réunion, in 1817, to a non-white mother who was a freed slave and a white father who was a lawyer and whose family were from Bordeaux;

---

3 Cook, 'Auguste Lacaussade', p. 265.
4 Cook, 'Auguste Lacaussade', p. 267.

they were not able to marry due to 'the island's ban on mixed marriages'.[5] La Réunion was still a slave colony (slavery wasn't abolished until 1848) when Lacaussade grew up there, in an environment in which non-whites, regardless of their social status, were demeaned and watched by the white authorities with suspicion. Cook conjectures, 'The latter's poems tell us that his was in the main a happy childhood, most of which he seems to have spent – much to his mother's uneasiness – rambling through the woods with a younger brother and sister who were destined to die at an early age.'[6]

Refused entry into Royal College/Bourbon College because of his illegitimacy, Lacaussade was sent to school in Nantes, France, from 1827 through to 1834 when he returned to his island home at the request of his mother who wished him to be a notary, only to return to France in 1836 to study medicine in Paris (his mother refused to support his desire to be a poet). He lasted in these studies till 1839, then 'dropping out' to focus on writing poetry. Somewhere on the way he picked up English, which would later serve him as a translator of English-language texts into French (and, indeed, towards the end of his life he translated from the Italian of Leopardi; he also spoke/read Greek, Latin and Polish). From his youth, Lacaussade clearly envisaged himself as connected to the threads of mainland French literary culture, even if he was to adapt these threads to the geography and social issues of his home island. Cook notes:

> Though Victor Hugo was still his hero, he had also made the acquaintance of other young poets of promise, like Sainte-Beuve, in whose *Consolations* he had found inspiration, and Brizeux, whose poem *Marie* had been one of his first purchases on disembarking at Marseille in 1836.[7]

It is worth indulging our reading of Cook's article yet again:

> These literary associations probably inspired Lacaussade to publish his first volume of poems in 1839. He named this thin collection of verse *Les Salaziennes*, after one of the island's mountains, and dedicated it to Victor Hugo, thereby combining his appreciation for the homeland's natural beauties with his admiration for one of the fatherland's most prominent young authors. *Les Salaziennes* attracted so little attention that thirteen years later Lacaussade could republish several of the same poems in a volume for which the French Academy awarded him a prize.[8]

Les Salaziennes was followed by *Poèmes et paysages* in 1852 and *Les Épaves* in 1861.

Lacacaussade became Saint-Beuve's secretary (at times), joined the editorial board of *Democratie pacifique* in 1846, became political editor (in Brittany) of *la Concorde* in 1848, and eventually, in 1859, director of *Revue européenne*. For a

5 Cook, 'Auguste Lacaussade', p. 260.
6 Cook, 'Auguste Lacaussade', p. 260.
7 Cook, 'Auguste Lacaussade', p. 262.
8 Cook, 'Auguste Lacaussade', p. 262.

non-white 'islander' to get such a foothold and then much more in French literary society was revolutionary in itself. Cook notes:

> This journalistic activity was characterized chiefly by noble humanitarian motives.
> With what Mme Desbordes-Valmore termed 'his feverish nature', he campaigned
> ardently for liberty: liberty for the masses and freedom for the slaves.[9]

However, it seems Lacaussade grew somewhat more 'resigned' to the circumstances with time, staying in France under Napoleon III and the Second
Empire, and receiving accolades from the French Academy (though, much to
his chagrin, he was never made a member which, given the level of his 'accom-
plishment' within the French literary-state machine, reflects on the bigotries
of the time and system more than anything else) and from the French state in
general, and eventually settling into a sinecure working for the Senate library
from 1872 until his death in 1897:

> But instead of following Hugo, Schoelcher [a leader of the abolitionists of whom
> Lacaussade was one – JK] and others into exile, as his emotional nature would have
> led us to expect, he heeded Sainte-Beuve's counsels of moderation and resigned
> himself to the new regime. For this he was rewarded in 1860 by election to mem-
> bership in the Legion d'Honneur.[10]

Knowing poets as I do, this does not surprise me. He was not arrested on the
island as a resister, but affiliated with 'mainstream' literary culture in France,
and (admittedly against the odds) enjoyed the recognition of literary 'authorities'. Which is not to say his resistance from afar wasn't effective; nor that he
was not fully committed. And the praise that came from La Réunion itself has
to be contextualised within the white power structures that remain in place in a
variety of ways to the present day:

> Impressed by all these honors, the Ile de la Reunion voted a pension for the
> illustrious but impecunious mulatto son to whom it had not so long ago refused
> an education. An article dated January, 1859, in the Album de la Reunion quotes
> 'the beautiful verses of our beloved poet, Auguste Lacaussade', and glories in 'the
> poet's sentiments of filial love and tender respect for the land which gave him birth
> and which proudly counts him today among its most noble sons.'[11]

Furthermore, as Cook is at pains to show, Lacaussade remained committed to a
writing of liberty under the regime of the Second Empire:

> Unable to continue his fight for democracy by direct attack, in his *Revue euro-
> péenne* and in *Les Epaves* he published poems like 'Un Symbole' to show

9   Cook, 'Auguste Lacaussade', p. 263.
10 Cook, 'Auguste Lacaussade', p. 264.
11 Cook, 'Auguste Lacaussade', p. 264.

how 'the voice of the true poet remains mute when an abject Tiberius (Caesar) reigns.'[12]

I believe these translations (and others I have done and am doing) mark one of the rare times Auguste Lacaussade has been translated into English, and for me it's become a commitment to deal with his entire (diverse) oeuvre. Lacaussade is a major poet of place (of absence as much as belonging, of reminiscence as much as engagement): in his poetry about the island, there's an intimacy and reflective distance. And if there's nostalgia in the configurings of remembered experience as if they were *plein air* compositions, there's nonetheless also a sophisticated politics underpinning the expression and sensibilities – Lacaussade has his own kind of 'sublime' at work.

Lacaussade's remains were disinterred from Montparnasse in 2007, and reburied in Hell-Bourg in La Réunion. We have done the dreaded 'switchback', twisting drive up the mountain to that town and can say there are few prospects like it in the world. From there, he can hide or be lost in the woods and mountains as he chooses, the sea never far away. There is a street and a few schools named after Lacaussade on the island, and the 'memory' of him is strong, and even growing.

Le Papillon (The Butterfly)

Your gilded wings, young and stylish butterfly,
Reflect the azured colours of the sky,
You who compete with the breeze's kiss for flowers
As you pass through the air like a sparkling
Breath, and when dying day's light is fading,
Sleep upon their fragrant calyxes.

If you see my love, don't pay tribute to her
Rosy lips as you might the open flower;
Your infatuated eye is permitted this fault;
But I shall be jealous of your supreme happiness:
I alone want to draw from the mouth I idolize
The scents of sensual delight.[13]

---

12 Cook, 'Auguste Lacaussade', p. 268.
13 Auguste Lacaussade, *Les Salaziennes*:

Le Papillon

Jeune et beau papillon, dont les ailes dorées
Réfléchissent du ciel les couleurs azurées,
Qui passes dans les airs comme un souffle animé,
Qui disputes les fleurs aux baisers du zéphyre
Et quand du jour mourant le crépuscule expire,
Dors sur leur calice embaumé;

Orage à Salazie (Storm in Salazie)[14]

'The sky is changed!'
BYRON

How the sky changes! And shadowy night
Has amplified darkness over the pinnacles;
The firmament's flickering light
Veiled beneath its more sombre veil.
In the distance the storm advances:
On all sides reigns a mournful silence;
And it appears as if nature, dumb with terror,
Is listening to the dull sound
Of the coming storm across the clouds,
And contemplates night in its sublime horror.

The air weighs heavily. A fetid heat
From the heart of the ground spreads
Into the air; and occasionally a livid light
From the horizon crisscrosses the wilds.
Oh! What a night! the sky in its wrath
Is going to make a spectacle of itself before the earth!
And, tearing its mysterious veils,
In its intoxication and its reckless high spirits,
Will reveal to my astonished spirit
Something great, imposing and dreadful!

Si tu vois mes amours, comme à la fleur éclose,
N'offre pas ton hommage à ses lèvres de rose;
Cette erreur est permise à ton oeil enchanté;
Mais je serais jaloux de ton bonheur suprême:
Je veux seul respirer sur la bouche que j'aime
Les parfums de la volupté.

14   Auguste Lacaussade, *Les Salaziennes*:

Orage à Salazie

The sky is changed!
BYRON

Mais le ciel change! et la nuit de ses ombres
A sur les monts grandi l'obscurité;
Du firmament sous ses voiles plus sombres
Elle a voilé la tremblante clarté.
Dans le lointain la tempête s'avance:
De tous côtés règne un morne silence;
Et l'on dirait, muette en sa terreur,
Que la nature, à travers les nuages,
Entend venir le bruit sourd des orages,
Et contemple la nuit dans sa sublime horreur.

In his fury, a mortal man takes umbrage,
Bending his head in silence and darkness,
Falls dumb with frenzy and rage:
Lightning ignites and flashes from his eyes,
His fixed stare sparks with light,
And all his features reflect his spirit.
Behind his eyelids one sees no tears,
But his eye has shone with vengeance;
And suddenly, emerging from his silence,
In words of flame he pours out his anger.

Night is like that too. Dark and glorious night,
You were not destined for repose!
In its ecstasy my impudent spirit
Wants to merge with your vast chaos.
The rain has not yet spent its torrent;
Thunder approaches these heights
And rumbles and rolls in the sky with splendour;
Its great voice like a mountain crumbling,
Or like the sea on its shores unfurling,
Fills the immensity with a deep clamour.

L'air est pesant. Une chaleur fétide
Du sein du sol se répand dans les airs;
Et par moments une clarté livide
De l'horizon sillonne les déserts.
Oh! quelle nuit! le ciel dans sa colère
Va se donner en spectacle à la terre!
Et, déchirant ses voiles ténébreux,
Dans son ivresse et sa fougue effrénée,
Va révéler à mon âme étonnée
Quelque chose de grand, d'imposant et d'affreux!

Dans son courroux, le mortel qu'on outrage,
Courbant un front sombre et silencieux,
Reste muet de délire et de rage:
L'éclair s'allume et jaillit de ses yeux,
Son regard fixe étincelle de flamme,
Et tous ses traits ont réfléchi son âme.
Sous sa paupière on ne voit pas les pleurs,
Mais sa prunelle a brillé de vengeance;
Et, tout à coup, sortant de son silence,
En paroles de flamme il répand ses fureurs.

Telle est la nuit. Nuit sombre et glorieuse,
Tu ne fus pas destinée au repos!
Dans ses transports mon âme audacieuse
Veut se mêler à ton vaste chaos.
La pluie encor n'a pas versé son onde;
Vers ces pitons la foudre approche et gronde

But let us listen! The tempest's voice
Rises, increases and grows in the air;
Overhead the firmament ignites
From the vigorous bolts of blood-red fire;
The sky is roused, the north wind howls,

Et dans les cieux roule avec majesté;
Sa grande voix comme un mont qui s'écroule,
Ou sur ses bords la mer qui se déroule,
D'une clameur profonde emplit l'immensité.

Mais écoutons! La voix de la tempête
Monte et s'accroît et grandit dans les airs;
Le firmament s'enflamme sur ma tête
Aux feux sanglants des rapides éclairs;
Le ciel s'émeut, les aquilons mugissent,
D'un bruit affreux les échos retentissent,
Sur les rochers, dans le sein des forêts,
Brille et s'éteint une flamme écarlate;
Et le tonnerre avec fracas éclate,
Et bondit en grondant de sommets en sommets.

C'est à ton tour! réveille-toi, terre,
Sors des langueurs d'un auguste sommeil!
De ton repos, profanant le mystère,
La foudre vient de hâter ton réveil.
Réveille-toi! De tes superbes cimes,
De tes forêts, de tes profonds abîmes,
Fais résonner les échos les plus forts;
Réponds ta voix à la voix des nuages;
Aux mille éclats des vents et des orages
A leurs transports tonnants réponds par tes transports!

Et le tonnerre, avec un bruit horrible,
Ouvre la nue et vomit ses fureurs;
Et des rochers la voix forte et terrible
Semble lutter de désordre et d'horreurs.
O vents d'orage, ô foudres, ô tempêtes,
Emportez- moi dans les lieux où vous êtes,
Entourez-moi de votre majesté!
Et, sur mon front déchaînant vos ravages,
De vos plaisirs et de vos jeux sauvages
Laissez-moi partager la mâle volupté!

Oh! que ne puis-je ainsi que le tonnerre,
Dans mon délire étonner les mortels!
Que n'ai-je aussi les cent voix de la terre
Pour révéler mes pensers solennels!
Mais sous mes doigts, de ma lyre impuissante
Je presse en vain la corde obéissante;
Ma voix est frêle et mes sons languissants.
Terre, cieux, nuit, foudre aux ailes de flamme,
Oh! prêtez-moi, pour exhaler mon âme,
Prêtez-moi votre voix! prêtez-moi vos accents!

Echoes resound with a dreadful noise,
Upon the rocks, in the forest's heart,
A scarlet flame shines and extinguishes,
And the thunder bursts and roars,
And leaps rumbling from summit to summit.

Wake up, earth, it is yours to try!
Come forth from the languor of a noble slumber!
From your rest, profaning the mystery,
Lightning has just pressed you to stir.
Wake up! From your glorious heights,
From your forests, from your deep abysses,
Let sound your strongest echoes;
Make your voice answer the cloud's voice;
To the thousand rushes of wind and tempest
To their thunderous ecstasies reply with your ecstasies!

And the thunder, sounding so hideous,
Opens the cloud and vomits its fury;
And the rocks' loud, fearsome voice
Seems to struggle in horror and disarray.
O lightning, O tempests, O gales,
Transport me to the places where you dwell,
Surround me with your glory!
And, unleashing your chaos upon my head,
Let me share the voluptuous mood
Of your manly pleasures and wild play.

Oh! If only I could, as thunder does,
In my delirium astonish mortals!
If only I too possessed earth's hundred voices
To reveal my solemn principles!
But beneath my fingers, I vainly press
My impotent lyre's responding notes;
My voice is frail and my sounds listless.
Lightning with wings of fire, earth, skies, night,
O, lend to me, so I can breathe out my spirit,
Lend me your voice! Lend me your accents!

1839

ON THE TRACK OF DESIRING AND ABSENCE: A LETTER TO MCKENZIE WARK ON HIS EMAIL CORRESPONDENCE WITH KATHY ACKER[1]

McKenzie Wark begins his preface to his book *Virtual Geography* with:

> We live every day in a familiar terrain: the place where we sleep, the place where we work, the place where we hang out when not working or sleeping. From these places we acquire a geography of experience.
>
> We live every day also in another terrain, equally familiar: the terrain created by television, the telephone, the telecommunications networks crisscrossing the globe. These 'vectors' produce in us a new kind of experience, the experience of telesthesia – perception at a distance. This is our 'virtual geography', the experience of which doubles, troubles, and generally promotes our experience of the space we experience firsthand.[2]

So, another layering of the polysituated self. And in this spirit, I contextualise the virtual letter to 'K' – 'McKenzie Wark' – by way of interacting at a tangent with his life and work,[3] and at a tangent with my experience of reading the fictions of Kathy Acker. Where I write from (in this case, Churchill College, Cambridge) becomes a tangent to the vicariousness of their 'shared' experience, and 'crisscrosses' out of time (and outside the vectors of the original conversation) with communiqués from Australia and America. My reading of their experience augments that experience, as do all other readings (by others). The sediments of awareness are also receptors to new experience: we add to our own experience by sharing in the experience, in the conversations, of others. In Gérard Genette's *Narrative Discourse* we read that:

1 To be with each other in one place, with one party 'disorientated' with jetlag and the unfamiliar (but finding the familiar in this), then being separated by oceans and timezones, displaces physical and conceptual *belongings*.
2 McKenzie Wark, *Virtual Geography: Living With Global Media Events* (Bloomington and Indianapolis, Indiana University Press, 1994), p. vii.
3 I would call Ken something of a 'polysituationist'!

completing analepses, or 'returns,' comprises the retrospective sections that fill in, after the event, an earlier gap in the narrative (the narrative is thus organised by temporary omissions and more or less belated reparations, according to a narrative logic that is partially independent of passing time). These earlier gaps can be ellipses pure and simple, that is, breaks in the temporal continuity.[4]

Genette goes on to denote a second kind of 'gap', which would also suit here, but I mention the first to show how placing a piece of writing in a narrative discourse allows us to use the layerings of the polysituated storytelling of our lives. We are always editing and backfilling, commenting on and expanding our personal narratives. In this way, what follows here is a polysituated encounter with the events of others' lives in which my various points of contact with the text help inform broader narratives of living in/and place.[5]

*

Hi, K[6]

Rereading I came across this from Acker: 'I'm sorry, Ken; do be my friend.' I understand this. I am pretty sure I know what she means outside of the platitudinous. That is, she really does want a friend. Not friends, she has them, but a particular friend. Maybe she has many particular friends, but not this particular one. Is this the key to unlock your exchange? Your almost-love letters of cultural

4 Gérard Genette, *Narrative Discourse: An Essay in Method*, trans. Jane E. Lewin (Ithaca, NY, Cornell University Press, 1983), p. 51.
5 And in the parlance of 'now' – 'digital natives', 'thought leaders', 'infopreneurs', augmented reality gamers – the 'virtual' is actually deleting 'real' geographies and unmaking 'place', signing over belonging to capitalist leisure security and capitalist self-gain in communities of material aquisition. For an astounding piece of capitalist enticement and propaganda, see www.thoughtleaders.com.au and their mission statement that challenging at least one form of 'status quo' means financial reward: 'We help experts become thought leaders – transforming people with knowledge and expertise into highly influential agents of change. We help clever people become commercially smart. For over twenty years we have been developing strategies to enable people to more effectively capture, package and deliver ideas that make a difference' (accessed 10 October 2016).
6 The original 'letter' began with the following paragraph as it was in the context of writing an introduction (that turned out to be an afterword) for a book of the email exchange between Wark and Acker after their brief 'affair'/interaction when she was visiting Australia:

> I have abandoned my somewhat academic introduction to the letters volume, and have decided an email (Acker: 'this isn't a very academic email') that can be used as an intro or an afterword (if you wish) will serve better, and be more honest to the presentation or maybe even manifestation of the *e*-pistolary exchange between you and Kathy Acker. Below, you will find many convention-breakers, including a wild use of parenthesis, and the address (to you?) will be unstable (how else can it be … so?) but how does Acker put it? 'My parentheses have gone to hell.' … *remember*, that was from riding her motorbike for hundreds of miles, and mine are because I've been wandering around in the bush under the wheatbelt sun!

slippage and affirmation? A deep desire to connect: aerially, rhizomically, physically, textually.

I know you reasonably well (or did) in some ways, and in other ways, not at all. I recall, when I first met you, saying, 'I'm not much of a blokey bloke', and you understood. Do you recall? Then later we interviewed each other about space, wastage, masculinity, travel, and non-belonging. I never met Kathy Acker in the flesh, but felt I knew her (as you'll see in what's to come I feel there's a knowing through text: dangerous as that is!), but was really (really) into her work during the '80s. People used to introduce themselves with, Hey, I heard you are into Acker, so am I. Then it faded from view for me, until I re-engaged with it via *Pussy, King of the Pirates* and *In Memoriam to Identity*. And that has faded a little, though my first encounters never truly will: *Blood and Guts* and *Kathy Goes to Haiti*: I wrote a poem about that and wanted to send it to her but had no idea how. I was young then, very young. Now, as you remind me, we've done the watershed fifty-thing (me only just, you a couple of years ago) and Acker is long dead. After she died, you wrote a piece for me at my request (for a journal I was editing). I quote it here:

> Escape from the functionaries of language – that is how she understood the litera-
> ture of the avant garde. One day she will be recognised as a marvellous addition to
> the escape routes it pioneered. Her writing didn't owe much to Woolf or Stein, but
> like them, she wrote as a woman, inventing what that might be as she went along.
>
> Being Kathy Acker was, I suspect, not an easy thing. Like Burroughs, she dis-
> covered that when you set writing free, you become even more aware of every little
> subtle fascism at work in the world. Like Burroughs, she was a visionary writer.
> Her early books describe the nightmare to come. But they also chart the routes out
> of the nightmare.[7]

And I remember her writing about her illness for the *Guardian*, though Tracy remembers it better. Which brings me to memory, which is what this is all about in so many ways. And because the emails pile up on each other in a way that snailmail letter-writing really couldn't, unless servants or confidants were running messages between great houses back and forth, back and forth, sneaking them into palms behind backs, or leaving them carelessly in the foyer for others to steam open and read. Yes, memory, because your few days with Kathy (if I may – seems ungainly in a non-constructive and disempowering way to say 'Acker'; especially given that as reader we're offered the intimacy of the 'strange attractor' mode of email) resonate immediately afterwards on so many temporal levels. Time means loss in so many ways. And in recalling memories of intimacy is the almost desperate desire to gain knowledge of the 'other', to get to know them. You say to her: 'I want to know you' and she replies, 'I'm very into you.' They are not one and the same thing, but parallel lines bend and touch here and there and confound any science. But you also affirm that you're very into

---

7 'The Sailor Turned into the Sea' by McKenzie Wark, private email correspondence, and later *Salt* online magazine, 2008.

her, and that struggle – it is a struggle – is the anxiety below this almost manic exchange. Though Kathy isn't in a relationship at the time of this exchange, you are, and both of you have to configure a language and nomenclature to embody what it is you're 'doing' with each other. You will come to say to her: 'I think the problem was me talking about various emotional ties I have with certain people in the absence of talking about my emotional ties to you. I was deferring something until I found the words … but one never finds the words.'

But memory is a lie and you 'find' this, or always knew it. Playing along as it got more and more real, in the getting to know, ceasing to become the mnemonic extension we all play, the calling out the drag-self (okay, it is the best way of demasking so often), you go through the dramatic curve of a fiction. It's very Henry James. It covers all the categories of Northrop Frye. And your denouement? Well, I won't give away the final line, but almost there, you will say: 'Memory is redundant: it repeats signs so that the city can begin to exist.' And this exchange is about being or becoming or unbecoming 'boy and girl', and about emotions replacing other emotions and priorities, and who occupies what space and how that space is defined, and the grand problem of time: duration and Genettean narratology. Kathy will write, 'The second thing you said: regarding you're always discussing your emotions about your girlfriends, but not about me – that being a problem. You see – I'm awful at paraphrasing you. Your words. Well, sweetie, I'm probably worse than you. And telephones – I can't handle those things at all. I wish we could spend some days together. Perhaps in the future. Time is so weird … emailing now, I feel like the time between your email and this is usual email time: time elapsed. Five days never happened.'

There is a critique of the politics of confrontation with one's own definings outside those imposed by a reactionary social order. To hold oneself to task, to scrutinise the obsession to self-label, self-differentiate, to contest the internal and external man. You both 'struggle' with this. Both take affirmative self-action. Self-discussion comes with its baggage, though, and Kathy fears (and constantly refers to) her narcissism while embracing it. Like an apologia but only because she is not quite certain enough of you yet: one feels she will become so, and that term/'definition' (category error) will become an in-joke. She is no more and no less than we are expected to be (by ourselves, by media, by all mirrors):

> I prefer disavowal of being man. Or of man. Cause drag as perfection of the feminine makes me hate the feminine even more … I don't want that. But then … sometimes … I fetishise the masculine … spreading legs and drinking beer and grunting … and sweating and being stupid and rubbing your crotch … it turns me on. Must be sort of a mirror … (Am I being clear?) I've got to get over my fears around the feminine … oh all this shitty past … the sexist society past.

Yes, 'struggle'. It seems pivotal in this new epistolary confrontation, affirmation and declaration of love and empathy. There's a dialectic of gender and sexuality, of the American and the non-American, the former stating hers is a country of war and the latter declaring the generic love his social co-ordinates direct towards it in all its manifestly perverse destiny. Each undoes the codes, but at times each misreads the signals. Funny, in some ways maybe I know you better and always will: the lust for irony to contradict oneself, to be the media plaything while unpicking its rhizomes. I've moved away in recent years, gone down the dreaded Derridean path – though I might add that he shadows your exchange with Kathy in so many ways. The 'struggle' – yes, for 'tops and bottoms', for 'butch and femme', for the real man and the aggressive über-fem woman who is a 'ball-breaker'. But as Kathy says, she's not interested in such power games outside the bed. She says: 'Regarding het shit. These games. To me, top/bottom is just stuff that happens in bed. Who fistfucks who. Outside the bed, I do my work and you do yours. I fucking hate power games outside the bed and have no interest in playing them. I'm being too blunt, but I'm drunk.'

Really, power is an indescribable monster you both spent your time unpicking in its pain and damage, and differentiating forms of pain and damage. Acker wrote to you: 'Community as communion: that's what Bataille and Blanchot can't stand and so they're trying to find the ground for another way of going about, of even "thinking" community.'

Both in your struggle with the sacred, the new sacred of Elvis's death and the simulacra of money in Warhol (yes, why so neglected?), the acts of believing and for you, Ken, very specifically unbelieving or de-believing. But it was the sacred re-embodied in the media, transmuted via Nietzsche (you and Kathy do always go back to him!) Media was Kathy's angst and plaything; it was her instrument as it was yours, wanting to be the fool rather than the pundit, the accepted critic. To be inside and watch the government's cabinet members grapple with desire and how in fact they could get it to work. Media. I have no social democrat in me; you do. I only have the anarchist, that bit of you that gnaws away. You write, amidst all your necessary and desired contradictions: 'Media is my obsession, see, and it's an ongoing aesthetic experiment. I'm an artist and my chosen materials are the media. So there's a politics and an aesthetics. And a fascination. I'm trying to get beyond Debord and Baudrillard … I'm a leftwing columnist (a fifth columnist!) in a Murdoch paper…'

You wanted America and you're in America now. Of America, looking back to Australia. You say, 'I can't possibly explain the "America question" in Australian culture, only there might be something in the idea of an essay on it that comes at it the other way around – the Australia problem in American culture. I mean, we never get any attention! We love from afar.' Irony of course; but wait, there's more.

Later in this exchange (late, what has passed to this point? a week or just over, since you were first together?! – you will at one stage say 'It's been so strange, not writing to you for, what? 72 hours?'), you are able to say, out of your 'wonderment' for what America is, 'There definitely is a certain kind of stupidity that American culture has raised to a fine art. It's not an essence, but it is a phenomenon. Baudrillard again: leave irony to the Europeans; American art is best when it's like the desert or like crystal.' As for Kathy, riding free without a helmet on her motorbike, 'That's the decent side of the American nightmare', that horror centre of what she calls the Aryan Nation, while affirming there are, fortunately, many different cultures. It's a complex picture she's part of, though needing the distance London gave her (a Bloomsbury crisis?) And of Australia? Well, at first: 'why Australia? I've never thought about Australia beyond having the usual friends who got drunk and ate steak and eggs at five in the morning … (my first intro. to your countrymen)…'

Kathy visited Australia and you toured the bookshops together, spent three nights of which one was sexual discovery. Revelations, that's the compulsion. Kathy will say, a few days later in an email (was she drunk? – she is often drunk or wanting to eat breakfast: the time difference is the true essence of the temporal in this exchange … and then there's the long shadow of jetlag): 'I'm a total Romantic when let loose. And don't actually sleep around that much.' This is a Homeric catalogue of ships, tracking what might become of a relationship by noting what has come before and what will sail to Troy to seize (no rescue, I'm afraid) Helen back, to liberate the fetishised cunt (and still 'enjoy' the fetish), the working-through of what significant others have made of you, in you, of what you might be to each other. In it there are differing degrees of disclosure and intimacy, and always watch for that pirate's dagger in the back (antic-i-pation?)

In queering the turf, we look for liberation, for 'permanent liberation'. I was genuinely touched by your having to curl away, separate, to go to sleep, then in your sleep reaching across and making contact, and the bewilderment that it brings to Kathy. Those mixed signals. Those signals. Negotiations sleeping and awaking. Intimacy, and how much we can have of it and make of it, is at the core of this conversation, this exchange. The need for things to be outside conventions of gender and rage against PC formulations, to be the gays you both are and are not, but contest the bi as in-between. Mid-90s and I knew, as many others knew (growing to accommodate our desires and politics of un-hetero: our queering into relationship), and so many of us wanted not to be anything but what we knew was the undoing of a dangerous 'man' politics.

But Kathy has the throbbing 'man motorbikes' between her legs, and transfers like that. She doesn't deny, just displaces, and you do in your way. The fistfuck is not Pat Califia but Kathy Acker busting through the limits to the body's elasticity. You say Grace (your gender bête noire?) wouldn't stretch to it (though she dreams about it), but not for want of trying. Though there's a supreme affirmation of sex (Kathy: 'One can't argue solely from the rational, one has to account for experience, ESPECIALLY in the realm of the body. That's where sex so amazes me: what delights me is so often what I never suspected. And it may not again.'), surprisingly, so much of this isn't about sex *per se*, but just about love, and how friends who have just become friends position themselves for love. And sexuality here is a broad 'church' (playing with the sacred playing with itself), and the phallus is wondered-over, contested and as Ken (sorry, K, I am slipping into the infomercial mode: my epistle to you has become an analysis of 'you': Ken and Kathy) notes, 'I'm not often very dick-centred these days when I get horny.' There are many acts of curiosity, liberation and rejection in the affirming of a 'sexuality' and sexual practice.

But then you had a knowledge of Kathy long before, through her texts, and that's its own kind of intimacy. You already love or loathe or are indifferent to or curious about or maybe lust after the Acker of the page. In a vulnerable way, she'd expect it, surely. Your early letters have to work through this. Okay, you open a book of hers randomly and the opening is consolidated. I'll do the same:

> Finally, Pussycat and I were able to have sex.
> I talked to her for hours because I was shy. Then she put an arm around me, my back to her. We were sitting together on a crumbled wall by a duck pond. Dead ducks. I turned around and kissed her, I think because I have been waiting to for a long time and because I believed that I was supposed to and because I wanted her.

I find so much of this in your exchange. Supposed to and wanting to: negotiating the matrix of formative relationships. As you know, the book from which this is quoted was published in 1996. Its formulation is concurrent with you. With recording. With the Mekons. With San Francisco. With teaching and travelling and friendships coming in and out of focus.

And she read your *Virtual Geography* on the plane back, and dipped in here and there and in a slightly intimidated way, wondering whom she had slept with. She liked the risk, but felt the pain of uncertainty. A shift in the masochist need and 'repeller' (those strange attractors again). I love the stripping away, the gradual unmasking as you both work out how to go about it. Sometimes you're just blunt or matter-of-fact in the way you state things (yes, the medium, the medium: I love its prompts to terseness) and she takes it as rejection: she doesn't need all that information about previous 'rivals', but she ultimately craves it because it's a spatial process as well as temporal. All that distance between you, then you'll be in San Francisco, but only long enough to get over jetlag because the tickets were booked before you met and she's on to the case, and you are too. I open my own signed copy semi-randomly. That's because I have three markers in there from the last time I was reading the book. I go for the second marker and open to page 194, and read the last paragraph which begins, 'This space of calculation is what Alain Lipietz, following Marx, calls the "enchanted world." It is the world of "prices proposed, profits anticipated and wages demanded."' This zeroes in (binary) on one of my joys in the exchange: the negotiations of space. Kathy says 'I don't fit in', working through her space, but you both create a space in which a very different 'enchantment' works against and concurrently with the economic. You depart from Lipietz in your struggle with the cartoon nature of language's translation of the body into script. You make good, ironically, with your strange but almost 'classical' narratology in the exchange: the revelation of character, the right amount of background detail, the conflicts and possible resolutions, the edginess (what will alcohol bring out!) Okay, I am stretching it here and shifting fact to metaphor, but remember the Philip K. Dick story 'Human Is', where the replaced husband is so much better than the original, and parasitic colonisation is chosen by the wife because she is treated better. I get that both of you are wanting to be treated 'better' in all of this. Not necessarily in friendships or relationships, but in the way you negotiate your own private spaces, especially vis-à-vis public manifestations. You both stick your necks out and the chopper always, *always* comes down. There are good side-effects, but you don't know how or even if you want to hold on to them.

So when real friendship takes hold it becomes 'chatting'? That's more than gossip, but a close relative. It's exchange without overt fear of consequences. One can slip up a little and it will be absorbed. And this all in a few days, really. But time will tell. This short email of Kathy's (though she refers to them at 'letters' at one point, and at others that you have the San Franciscan tendency towards rapid and tireless emailing) captures this for me: 'This is almost like chatting. I certainly don't expect to hear from you re Matias; it's just my habit of saying where I am cause I tour so much if I don't do that I'm sort of nowhere. I'll have to introduce you to motorcycles … one of the last myths left. Actually I think they're coming back. Perhaps what you're referring to as the sacred. /Cool re your comfort with books. I have thousands.'

There's a poetics at work. A group poetics – you and Kathy and whatever else comes into orbit (for Kathy, American wrestling as performance art) – but also your unique poetics of private–public space. In writing her songs for the Mekons, Kathy reached into lyricism and wished for fiction (though she was the most poetic-lyrical weaver and assembler!) You, Ken, have always been a poet in the way Warhol was a poet: making the media lyrical outside itself. Borg-like: of the collective, but also something new and deeply persuasive. Yet not violent and invasive like the Borg – though that buys into issues of the communal, communism (as imagined by *Star Trek* scriptwriters). What would Kathy have known of that – she didn't watch much television and was still wrestling with the idea of *The Simpsons* which you were consuming as TV dinner. Your lyrical insights and interludes, existing as response and as utterances of separation (briefly? you're doing it your way) from the collective you're inside, analysing: 'So it's not that male bodies have to die, but to some extent male bodies are a good basis for the ritual sacrifice of Man. It's one of the things drag sometimes aspires to. It's a refusal that draw attention to what it refuses.' And it's not just a matter of 'doing it', but being it! Lyricism is a song's negotiation of space, the utterance looking for its co-ordinates, where it will and won't reach, those private spaces (from cunts, anuses and eyes of penises to mouth and ears; in those spaces inside the building and those nooks and crannies without) it might settle. I say this in response to your declaration to Kathy: 'I'm not really equipped as a writer to do stupid. But I can do lyricism – the flattening out of the surface of the prose to a simple emotion. Hide all the rest in the architecture.'

How much of this is wrestling with addictions: addictions of communication, exchange and touch? Kathy is a sleep junkie as you are a news and media junkie. I was a *junkie* junkie (that most masturbatory of repetitions). That's my personal needle in the haystack, a kind of sideline that compels a narcissistic reading. Kathy would never be that sort of junkie she says, though her close friend is (good reason not to be). Sex as addiction? I don't think so, not really here, strangely. At times it's forensic. Kathy and privilege, Ken and the great emptiness of the failed sacred that needs to be filled remorselessly to keep away the fear, the shadow of the failed and absent god, the simulacrum (to embrace it). There are some issues over 'identity'. The need to 'misbehave' and discuss such compulsions? Of status and icons, Kathy notes re the *New York Review of Books*, 'I rant against this and *The Nation* but I read them religiously. Perverse.'

In the end, mostly what I love about this exchange are the questioning and the non-understandings. Of all the ability you share to bridge divides, you still struggle with the 'boy'/'girl' binary, no matter how much you queer the turf, or are queered, or stand outside the queer. You are yourselves struggling with embodiment, exhibition, closure, privacy, ambition, disillusionment, thirst for knowledge, thirstlessness, desire for obliteration and deeply felt cautions (whether admitted or not or admitted while not). And how much more are we (we boys, girls, non-boys and non-girls and boy-girls and de-boys and de-girls and all others equally as well), how much more are we to get, to understand. Kathy here: 'This is precisely what Blanchot is arguing against – he's saying that immanence is as belief a ground for totalitarianism. Why the fuck do men want to be "the king who doesn't die" (the false sign that hides the reality of the king-murder, the basis of society, according to Bataille)? This is what I don't get?' We might go with Kathy's thinking into the (discrete and ironic?) contradictions regarding power and hierarchies in Foucault's 'Rule of immanence': 'One must not suppose that there exists a certain sphere of sexuality that would be the legitimate concern of a free and disinterested scientific inquiry were it not the object of mechanisms of prohibition brought to bear by the economic or ideo-logical requirements of power.'[8]

This is called a 'correspondence', and I have used the term exchange. But there is a Baudelairean correspondence at work in the sensual co-ordinates of what has now become (through publication) an active but ultimately curatorial space: an artwork, of sorts. But as we near the end of the interaction as captured in the participants' own words, we have a return to the unconfigured anomalies of the beginning: the brief physical interaction that stimulated the exchange. Kathy and Ken (that's *you*, Ken: or Ken as *he* was, you were, back *then*) talk on the phone and we're without access to the words (and do we, anyway, really have access to all their written words during the timeframe of this correspond-ence?) Ken says, 'It was strange talking to you on the phone cause we've never done it, but it was really good to hear your voice again.' Again. And there's the connection: the viscerality of words, of the voice, of bodies, of embodiment in different spaces. Ken ultimately wants 'a little more of that intimacy, and the *possibility* of sex'. That also describes the act of reading for me, in so many ways.

Best,
JK[9]

8 Michel Foucault, *The History of Sexuality, Vol. 1*, trans. Robert Hurley (London, Penguin, 2008), p. 98.
9 This 'letter' has since been included as an 'afterword' to Kathy Acker and McKenzie Wark, *I'm Very Into You: Correspondence 1995–1996* (Los Angeles, Semiotext(e), 2015).

PART IV

Sublimated displacements in read texts

ON SUBLIMATED DISPLACEMENTS IN READ TEXTS (INCLUDING A GESTURE TOWARDS A THREAD IN THE DEFINITION OF 'DISPLACEMENT')

I read a text and a text 'reads' me in a polysituated dynamic of experience and awareness – I take to the text my experience, and I am aware interaction (or creation of) with that text is likely to alter or change me in some way. It will certainly become part of me, and if I am rereading, then in a different and certainly cumulative way. When asked to introduce authors, review them, or launch their books, I tend first to consider how they 'place' – where they work within their own 'mapped' co-ordinates (inside *and* outside the frame), and where they do or don't overlap with what I already know about this space and spatiality. Most often, a hybrid language of connection comes about, and a tangential belonging, in which I situate myself in order to read, translate, understand and convey, is constituted.

What follows in this section are a number of readings of writers who engage with place in a way that I feel illustrates the polyvalent urge to construct place through not only what is observed directly of that place, but what the writer takes to it. In the case of Charles Walker, we are confronted by conjecture and the absence of a complete text (as alluded to), and are left to reconstruct our own idea of who he was and what he wrote. We have a poem of place written in anger at the theft of a text that might or might not have been of that place, but that is all. We have a connection by name and roughly the same period to 'another' Charles Walker, which creates a polysituated 'Charles Walker' that is both simulacrum and very real in its 'component' parts.

Henry Lawson wrote of his place-experiences, but became increasingly bound up in a broader sense of nation-making in which constituent parts/ stories/characters feed a sense of connectedness and even oneness. It breaks down, of course, but nation bothers away at its localities and localism. Peter Carey's masterpiece, *The True History of the Kelly Gang*,[1] plays national myth-making against the postmodern, book-making, narrativising of a historical

1 Peter Carey, *True History of the Kelly Gang* (London, Faber and Faber, 2000).

story that has been translated into 'character' and 'identity' of 'Australia'. His living and writing out of New York City make for an interesting internationalist subtext.

John Mateer, with his movements between South Africa and Australia, and 'elsewhere' in the world, embodies at least some of the modus operandi of the polysituating artist, while Barbara Temperton, a very 'local' and Western Australian poet, sources local histories and stories to stratify her sense of belonging (and also the alienations this can include) as well as a relationship to the stories of others (including the tragic) through spatial and conceptual proximity. Consideration of a recent anthology of 'Asian-Australian' poetry examines 'region' vs. 'heritage',[2] and I hope readers would conclude of their own volition that such editorial acts are necessarily polyvalent and at the essence of the polysituated in terms of concurrent urges, threads and interpretations of presence and belonging in (sometimes recent, sometimes established over generations) 'place'. It is essential to remember, as subtext, that *all* Australians without indigenous heritage are migrants, whether with the First Fleet or arriving last week. Australia in essence has always been multicultural and only dominating (militaristically) cultural forces have constructed it otherwise. The whiteness of Australia is an 'eternal' myth, but has certainly long been an official (government-military and by extension the cultures arising from these) state of mind.

But as an entry into this section of the book, I want briefly to consider Chinese-Australian poet Ouyang Yu's most recent volume of poetry, *Fainting with Freedom*.[3] *Fainting with Freedom* is Ouyang Yu's most unusual book – it shimmers with language-play and his characteristic wrestling with absurdity, the quotidian and the pain of history; it also has a distinctly different take on what constitutes 'the self'. The slippages between English and Chinese language are enacted in so many ways – misunderstanding becomes a clarity because between the languages a different and maybe more illuminating existential truth arises, yet there's also a tone of lament in this for the persona forever traversing difference. China's and Australia's censorship might manifest differently in terms of available information, but if we lack the interest to find

---

2 John Mateer spends much time in Asia and has an entire body of work he identifies as coming out of his Asian interactions, presences and experiences. See *Emptiness: Asian Poems 1998–2012* (North Fremantle, Fremantle Press, 2012). In an email in 2008, I wrote of Mateer's poetry and future work he was proposing: 'Mateer's poems, though, are ultimately poems of investigation – of culture, place, people, and the self. He is notable for his range of approaches to language-usage, his demonstrated ability to write "across" cultural spaces, and his acute sensitivity to describing not only the natural world but the interactions between people and the world they live in/create for themselves … Its range is exciting, and might well reflect on the nature of not only what it is to be, say, "Australian", but on the nature of exploration and colonisation, of the self versus the public interest, of compulsion, obsession, and obligation, of duty and ambition, and configuring history to make it relevant to the living, as it needs to be.' As someone who came to Australia from South Africa (and its polyvalent identifications), his articulation of occupations, presences, deletions, conjoinings, blendings, blurrings, affirmations 0and refusals is deeply rhizomed in shift, change and the 'comparative'.

3 Ouyang Yu, *Fainting with Freedom* (Melbourne, Five Islands Press, 2015).

it in the first place, what does it mean about how we live and, indeed, where we live?

There's also a lament in this work for the failure of so-called 'Western' philosophy to 'provide' proof of existence and reason for being outside the functionality of day-to-day life, the trivial, survival. But then 'Eastern' philosophy is also challenged in so many scenarios, where people 'met' become the poem, or are met in the poem, their voices becoming answers to our own discomforts, the discomfort of the ironically eyed poet. And then the forces of history with which Ouyang Yu plays – not fitting inside the historically allotted spot (nineteenth-century Victorian goldfields), he illustrates his position as migrant within a country of many and mainly migrants.

What we see and experience, how we present and tell it to others – this concern has long driven Ouyang Yu's work, but in *Fainting with Freedom* he worries that with all the tools of communication at hand, all the dynamic equivalences we use in exchanges with friends, families, colleagues, people in general, something misses. This is a book of the liminal, of the border that can never be fully crossed. Freedom is unobtainable anywhere the persona goes, from wherever s/he speaks. Irony is his tool, but it's a defensive one as well.

Strangely, Ouyang Yu is at his most vulnerable in this work, and I think that takes it to a special 'level'. I know more of who he is as a poet from this work than from any other. He is offering himself up for the reader to join with him, criticise, share joy, laugh, and also become sceptical and even bitter. There's no simple position of viewing in the writing, the painting, the telling.

Ultimately, though, this is a work about truth. What constitutes fact and what makes fiction? Ouyang Yu often seems to answer these questions, but on reconsidering, we find he doesn't. He is questioning *us*, injustice, stupidities of systems, and also himself. 'When the rain decides to fall it is self-publishing' is almost an epigraph to his refusal to be controlled, to be managed by a literary machine, and also a lament that the point has to be made at all.

It is an exquisite piece of wry-caustic writing that actually makes us feel ashamed at our pretensions of good order and 'quality control'. To write is freedom, but it's also freedom to point out that none of us is free at all. It's a paradox that eats its way from tyranny to so-called democracy. The poet is inside and outside these poems. They are 'proems' and dialogues, they are glimpses and compilations, they are words stretched taut and strung out, they are openings rushing towards closure, they are closure that can't happen, they are history and dehistoricising, they are geography and imaginary landscapes. Between China and Australia, in history and ethics, in poetry and society, Ouyang Yu and his poetry *polysituate*. The poems are the dream and its loss and its costs. They are sound and sight, orality and semantics.

I am unsure about the poem 'The Boat' because its irony is so multifaceted that I wonder if white Australian anti-asylum-seeker bigots might actually misunderstand and see its irony as being in their favour when it's so clearly mocking them and the fetishisation of 'Asian Art' as consumable product for middle-class Oz audiences. But that's part of this book as well: the irony that eats itself. The book that consumes itself and the reader. Watch out! 'The pressure is always there/ To delete you from yourself…' The private made public actually increases the privacy – so revealing of 'the poet' as he is, he remains discreet, cautious, if not 'hidden'.

Is there any other way for the poet? There is no confessional, never was. Just tension between experience and fiction … reporting and what people want to know or not as fact. But 'You look like someone who hasn't given up…' and Ouyang Yu never will! I call him 'brother' because of this activism. He is one of the most persuasive and potent of the modern poets because he will not relent, and makes language something vocational as well as conceptual. He speaks it, uses it, teaches it, writes it. There are no limits to his poetics and his skill as a poet because he is open to all knowledges, is constantly 'experiencing', witnessing and recording; takes personal history into the contexts of broader histories, and acts as witness for those who have been silenced, dispossessed and disempowered across times and cultures. His is a multi-dimensional internationalism, and his regionalism is a consciousness of the communities he co-inhabits. This is the essence of polysituatedness.

In writing or reading texts, no time is lost for 'being' in a place. These acts are co-determinate with presence, and do not necessarily displace that presence. Rather, they can augment it. But what is displaced is so because of external forces that are internalised – social and cultural pressures, consumer and market pressures, spiritual pressures and ennui – and external forces that interrupt and damage (process, the body, the ecology). Displacement is what is imposed upon a place and those within it by forces wishing to colonise, occupy or simply profit from it in some way. To read and write, even out of desperation, can be the most affirming of responses to this, as it can also be a 'forced' response to coercion. When we occupy a text through reading, we displace the writer and the culture of that writer. This is incidental and selective at once. It's the paradox of textual encounter. In remaking ourselves through the process of textuality, we oust many others. But we also open doors of perception and can create inclusiveness and connection. This is the faux desire of the internet, that child of the military. In the end, even at its most altruistic, somewhere someone pays, through the energy required to run it, malicious code that might ride on a message of hope, or just exploitation. It is the pyrrhic victory of a capitalism that will consume itself with viruses of its own making that it doesn't recognise and can't treat. The virus is itself, much more than those sent by militant hackers wishing to undo it for their own (often private and tangential) pleasure, satisfaction or triumph.

A RAGE FOR VERSE: THE CASE FOR CHARLES WALKER AS THE AUTHOR OF THE FIRST VOLUME OF VERSE PUBLISHED IN WESTERN AUSTRALIA (1856)

In doing research for the Western Australian Poetry Anthology[1] that Tracy and I are editing, I have come across some bizarre and quite sad material. John Hay's 1981 essay 'Literature and Society'[2] draws heavily on Beverley Smith's UWA thesis on early Western Australian writing written in the early 1960s, and makes interesting if very brief points of reference worth following up. This is one that interested me in particular because as I have written elsewhere, Henry Clay's *Two and Two*[3] is often considered the first volume of poetry by a single author published in the colony.[4]

Yet as Hay notes, 'In February [?] 1856, the convict Charles Walker seems to have published a small volume entitled *Lyrical Poems*, the first book of verse to be published in Perth. No copies are extant.'[5] One might guess that the claim (not Hay's claim but asserted in various places) for Clay's being the first book of its type published in Perth is due to the 'No copies extant.' There is no evidence outside newspaper advertisements that Walker's book existed at all. Naturally, this has got me intrigued, especially as, through drawing on colonial and later sources, I have made the same claim for Clay's book myself.

So what do we know of Walker? Almost nothing. In the Western Australian newspaper *The Inquirer and Commercial News* (1855–1901), Walker published almost weekly advertisements from 19 December 1855 through to late March 1856, relating to a work entitled *Lyrical Poems*. The advertisements up until that

---

1 John Kinsella and Tracy Ryan (eds), *Western Australian Poetry Anthology* (South Fremantle, Fremantle Press, forthcoming 2017)

2 John Hay, 'Literature and Society', in C. T. Stannage (ed.), *A New History of Western Australia* (Perth, University of Western Australia Press, 1981).

3 Henry Clay, *Two and Two: A Story of the Australian Forest by H. E. C., with Minor Poems of Colonial Interest* (Perth, 1873).

4 Concurrently, the Fenian convict and escapee from the colony, John Boyle O'Reilly, published his collection of poetry, *Songs From the Southern Seas*, in Boston, USA, 1873, which contains a number of poems relating to Western Australia.

5 Hay, 'Literature and Society', p. 607.

of 6 February 1856 are worded '"Lyrical and Other Poems", By Charles Walker. Persons requiring a copy will please to forward their wishes to the author, at Mr G Marfleet's, Perth; which will meet with due attention.' Then they change to this: 'Just Published LYRICAL POEMS by Charles Walker Copies can be had at the Stores of Mr G. Marfleet, Perth. PRICE – Half-a-crown.'

So, we might assume the book was printed and published, and might we conjecture that it was done through Marfleet's booksellers? In itself it's thin evidence, though it would be strange to pay for advertising so consistently if there was nothing intended and ultimately nothing to show.

But it gets stranger. Searching the newspapers of the period, there is no evidence of Walker publishing poems in them – the usual method of dissemination of the time. Being a colonial poet prior to the boom of 'Manly poetry' (as A. G. Stephens, editor of the *Bulletin*, would call the outburst of goldfields' versifying that began in the 1890s, starring poets such as 'Crosscut', 'Bluebush' and 'Dryblower') was no easy thing outside whimsical versifying, either praising or mocking (complaining of) colonial life and administration. As Hay quotes Henry Ebenezer Clay writing in his introduction to *Immortelles, The goal of life and other poems* (which, according to Hay, was serialised in the *Church of England Magazine* in 1872, and then published in book form in Perth in 1890), 'The pioneers of local literature in a small community should prepare to encounter special difficulties and a probable harvest of loss. Without assumption, they should have sufficient self-reliance to hold their ground against the saucy badinage of amused spectators and the practical indifference of friends.'[6]

Or is there perhaps evidence of Walker publishing in the papers? Well, there's one poem in the same paper where he promoted his book. It's a poem with a twist – a threat poem, an investigative poem, a sleuthing poem. As a mirror of the convict system that saw him (as we will discover) working under the 'care' of Mr G. Marfleet, presumably as a ticket-of-leave man. This poem-advertisement is nothing less than a hunting poem. But it carries above it an epigrammatic (separate) advertisement giving his reasons and what he wants in transparent prose (is the poem transparent in its call?) This is what we read:

> [Advertisement.]
> WHEREAS a manuscript book, containing about one hundred pages, was taken away from me about eighteen months ago, and, from circumstances which have come to my knowledge, believing it to be in the possession of some person well acquainted with its contents, I hereby offer a reward of Two Pounds for the recovery of the same. CHARLES WALKER. Perth, April 24, 1856.
>
> NOTICE.
>
> WHEREAS a man, some five feet ten,
> (No matter whether *Charles* or Ben)

---

6 Hay, 'Literature and Society', p. 608.

Has took it in his empty head,
The equal empty tale to spread,
That all the dreamings of my muse
Are of the ladies' charms profuse,
But scarcely ever condescend
His vocal talent to commend;
He wonders why *his* foolish tales
So little on your mind prevails:
And why the slander he has sown –
I find it has been all his own –
Has never been received as truth,
By any mind of common growth.
This is to let that tall chap know.
That he may find a 'bar' or so,
To mar the quiet of his path,
Should he presume to tempt my wrath.
AUTHOR OF 'LYRICAL POEMS.'[7]

What is plain from this is that either this manuscript is a new work, or maybe it's the old work and it never actually appeared. Conjecture. Who is to know? Is the offender Mr G. Marfleet, or is even supposing so a smear? A little more evidence comes our way shortly. But in the meantime, the poem itself is telling – clearly his verses (likely *Lyrical Poems* given the lack of newspaper and journal evidence of other publication – though some may yet surface) had attracted negative attention. The slighting of his work as effeminate had brought the phallic response – 'he may find a "bar" or so,/ To mar the quiet of his path.'

There is bitterness and zeal in this poem. I hesitate to call it doggerel because it is too convinced, too passionate, too driven. Its awkward syntax and odd parsing don't invalidate its desperate anger. Politeness is only formal – this is a poetry wanting to burst out of its constraints. A 'self-promoter', that ludicrous accusation pointed at the poet who feels passionate about being heard, about speaking out…? As he accuses, the offender is all bluster and 'talent' and no substance because it is 'he' that is the fraud. But sadly, Walker undoes it all with the threat – a moment of vulnerability, weakness and brutality. But really, it's about his own feeling of inadequacy more than any other, any 'five feet ten' swell, be he Charles or Ben or whatever. I think Charles Walker was the most modern of colonial poets.

But our poet sadly didn't have to pay to promote his work or threaten others for taking his creativity and manuscript away. On 6 August 1856 – such a short time later – he is discussed as 'news' in the 'Local and Domestic Intelligence' columns of the paper. We read, with shock:

A few days since a reconvicted man committed suicide in the establishment by cutting his throat with a razor. His name was Charles Walker, formerly in the

7 'Advertising', *The Inquirer and Commercial News*, 30 April 1856, p. 2, http://nla.gov.au/nla. news-article66005007 (accessed 27 March 2015).

employ of Mr Marfleet of this town, from whose service he absconded a few months ago. It was for this offence and for being out of his district without a pass that he was returned to the Establishment for twelve months. While in the employ of Mr Marfleet his general character was good, but his manner was flighty, and there was no doubt a tendency to insanity. He was a somewhat conspicuous character in consequence of his rage for verse making, which found vent in the advertising columns of this journal, and in a small volume entitled 'Lyrical Poems,' published some six months since.[8]

The account of this tragedy appears to give us a third-party confirmation of the existence of a book of poetry written by Charles Walker – *Lyrical Poems*. It doesn't confirm the book was printed in Perth, but it would seem likely given Walker's convict status, and what we might assume were limited means. But then, he could pay for the advertisements, and he did offer a (sizeable) two-pound reward.

Did his book sell well enough at half-a-crown to yield him a windfall? Did being 'the first' add a mystique and appeal to the collection or was he crushed by his critics before he began?

The conservatism of reading environments as well as the tendency to self-help (see Hay regarding the later Mechanics Institutes) publications – how to be a more effective settler – probably counted against this convict. John Boyle O'Reilly was said to have scratched poems on prison walls wherever he was incarcerated (see H. Drake-Brockman in *The West Australian*, 19 July 1952: 'Perhaps at Fremantle gaol some poem may still lurk under whitewash. O'Reilly wrote poems with nails on his prison walls in Ireland and England. After his escape, he declared that he would like to revisit old cells and find his scratchings. This never happened.'), and Henry Clay would battle on against negative attitudes regardless, but outside newspaper opinion versifying, little poetry was actually printed (in pamphlets, books etc.).

Charles Walker's 'rage for verse making' fits. His self-inflicted death (if that's actually what it was) and the reference to his employer the bookseller (or storekeeper) who clearly reported him for going AWOL fit the profile. What became of his missing verses, his published book? Creativity in the colony was impractical in so many ways. My great-great-grandfather was a labourer, a farmer and later a schoolteacher – the first full-time schoolteacher in the first Catholic school in the Vasse (Busselton). No doubt he ranged from the practical to the creative – he certainly propelled himself forward and self-taught himself to another 'level' of colonial society, no easy thing for a just-post-Famine migrant with a huge family. Charles Walker's poetry was a direct conduit between his inner self and reality as he perceived it. We see that in his one remaining poem, his self-promoting advertising verse-threat.

There's no biographical data readily available on Charles Walker outside what I've presented here. He was a 're-offender'. The establishment took him

8 *The Inquirer and Commercial News*, 6 August 1856, p. 2, http://nla.gov.au/nla.news-article66005540 (accessed 27 March 2015).

back. Convict Establishment – Fremantle Gaol – consumed those used to create it. This self-eating in the new Eden was the paradox of the colonial, but of the state in all its manifestations. It needs what it can destroy. Charles Walker wanted to be heard – was desperate to be heard – and he was punished for it. Was he paranoid, did he carry out his verse threats, was he hard-done-by?

There's a history and embodiment of poetry in this, and none would know this better than the indigenous singers, storytellers and poets of early colonisation in Western Australia, and what has followed. We have reports of the threats of Yagan and what colonists did to him, but nothing of the poetry of his people, of himself. In *Jack Davis: A Life Story* we read, 'Yagan had made every effort to bring some sense to the worsening situation. In March 1833 he had arranged corroborees to bring about a cultural exchange with the settlers.'[9] Of course, Yagan's head was cut off and smoked. This is the brutality at the foundation of the Swan River Colony. Convicts were controversially brought into the colony in 1850 (until 1866) and the cruelty and degradation meted out to them are never to be forgotten, and come as a direct extension of the treatment of Yagan and his people. Charles Walker wrote in this environment, and wrote out of it. Isolated, keen to speak out, he advertised his condition as celebration but with passion. He raged until the very end. We can get this much from what we have.

Without going into the content of the newspaper the same day Charles Walker published his reward and poem-advertisement, take one item in the same column:

> POWDER MAGAZINE. PERSONS having Powder deposited in the Magazine at Fremantle are requested, in demanding the same from the Commissariat, to state, –
> The marks on the package
> The size, whether whole, half or quarter barrels
> The contents, giving the description as well as the quantity of powder.
> And no demand will be noticed unless this notice is complied with. The Magazine will be open for the delivery of powder between one and two p.m. on Mondays, Wednesdays, and Fridays.
> Commissariat, Fremantle, April, 26, 1855.

This is the material of the frontier.

Whether or not Walker's poems were over-delicate and fey versifying as we might assume it had been said, he certainly had decided on a verse that was confronting, aggressive and of the place and conditions he was part of. His violent death was of this, too. The poetry and his condition of being, his manifestation within the colonial body-without-organs, within the city of Perth, and the gaol itself, as a form of textual projection. As Derrida gesticulated (waving his arms), 'Everything is a text; this is a text'[10] and so we have the first

9 Keith Chesson, *Jack Davis: A Life Story* (Melbourne, Dent, 1988), p. 193.
10 John Rawlings, Stanford Presidential Lectures in the Arts and Humanities, 'Jacques Derrida', Stanford University, 1999 (https://prelectur.stanford.edu/lecturers/derrida/).

book of Western Australian poetry by a single author. The advertisements, the poem-advertisement, the plea and accusation and the mediating figure of the 'bookseller', the report of his death ... accusations of loss of control to the (illogical?) forces of poetry ... this is a full book. It is there for us to read. You don't judge a book by the number of pages it has, or even by its format. It is text, poetry is text, and it is here with us now. It is the truth of the lyrical urge. It is *Lyrical Poems* by Charles Walker, 1856.

FURTHER RECONSTRUCTION: CODA OR PROLOGUE?

The plot thickens or maybe gains a little more clarity when it comes to Charles Walker and the first published volume of poetry published in Western Australia/Perth. I have got hold of pages from Beverley Smith's 1961 MA thesis 'Early Western Australian Literature: A Guide to Colonial Life and Goldfields Life'[1] in which she writes, 'On the 6th August 1856 the following item appeared under "Local and Domestic Intelligence" in the *Perth Gazette*',[2] and there follows the item I quoted earlier about Charles Walker's death and 'rage for verse making'. Smith then goes on to say, 'Walker's volume was the first book of verse published in Perth, but apart from this reference there is no trace of *Lyrical Poems*.'[3] Smith footnotes this sentence with, 'A search of advertising columns of the *Perth Gazette* for the period failed to disclose evidence of Walker's verse-making.'

The tongue-in-cheek reference to 'verse-making' aside – maybe a tone of mockery we can forgive, given the broader context Smith is attempting to create, and the possibility that, like us, she is offended by the mockery of the press or persons who clearly demeaned Walker's obsession as poet (as poets should be!) – clearly Smith made an error in attributing this piece to the *Perth Gazette*. In fact, as I've shown, it appeared in *The Inquirer and Commercial News*, and that is also where the alluded-to advertisements appeared.

But Smith does furnish us with some further, vital information. She continues,

> Its author arrived in Western Australia in 1852 on the *William Jardine*. The offence for which he was transported is not known, but existing records describe him as a baker by trade, twenty-six years of age and married.[4]

1 Beverly Smith, 'Early Western Australian Literature: A Guide to Colonial Life and Goldfields Life' (MA thesis, Department of History, University of Western Australia, 1961).
2 Smith, 'Early Western Australian Literature', p. 66.
3 Smith, 'Early Western Australian Literature', p. 66.
4 Smith, 'Early Western Australian Literature', p. 66.

Smith references the 'Register and Shipping Lists, Battye Library A/128' regarding her source.

What helps fill out our narrative of the book in this is the fact that Walker was a baker. I return to the premises from which Walker was to sell and apparently did sell his *Lyrical Poems* – Mr. G. [George] Marfleet's store/s. Further newspaper investigation reveals to us that Marfleet was a prominent Perth citizen of the period, being both a baker and a confectioner and a purveyor of other goods. Some seventeen years after Walker's death, we read of items other than baked goods and confectionery evidently being sold in (certainly stolen from!) his store/s:

> SHOPLIFTING.– Three men, named John Gallagher, a shoemaker, Delap, and Melville were committed for trial at the Perth Police Court last week for stealing a chest of tea and a bag of sugar from the shop of Mr. Marfleet, in William Street. The property was found secreted in the prisoners' lodgings.[5]

Now, it's possible (likely?) that as his business developed, Marfleet (our 'bookseller') increased the range and nature of his wares; all the same we might equally assume he wasn't averse to selling other items in his shop – maybe Walker's book.

Or was Walker just using it as a point of contact? The book was not on display, but available by writing or dropping in, and it would come out of the back rooms where Walker, with floury hands, would hand it across, Marfleet taking a small cut from the half-a-crown?

When Marfleet died, *The Inquirer* ran his obituary, clearly sympathetic to the good citizen with his 'liberal' religious belief, and fêting his life as a model for the young. This was the same newspaper in which Walker had advertised, maybe with the support of Marfleet, or maybe taking advantage of a connection through his place of work/labour (depending on the conditions of his post-convict status until being reclaimed by the Establishment). Here is Marfleet's obituary:

> Death of Mr. Marfleet. – A mournful duty devolves upon us to record the death of an old, highly-esteemed and worthy citizen, Mr. George Marfleet. Arriving in the colony when quite a young man, in the year 1851, he soon afterwards entered upon the business of his calling as a baker and confectioner, in the establishment at that time conducted by the late Mr. Henry Devenish, in Hay and William Streets, and of which some time afterwards he became the proprietor, continuing the direction of its affairs until within the last fortnight, when rapidly declining strength prevented his taking an active part in his business. He was a staunch and liberal Churchman, and as a citizen and tradesman he has left behind him an example of patient industry and well-doing worthy of emulation by all young men entering upon the duties of life. He leaves a wife and four children, one of whom is married,

5 'TO THE EDITOR', *The Perth Gazette and West Australian Times*, 2 May 1873, p. 3, http://nla.gov.au/nla.news-article3752307 (accessed 29 March 2015).

and the others, we believe, are tolerably well provided for. The funeral took place on Monday afternoon, and was attended by a large number of the deceased's personal friends and other citizens, the brethren of the City of Perth Lodge of Oddfellows, of which he was one of the oldest members; besides several of the brethren of the New Swan Lodge, M.U.I.O.O.F., 4406, Fremantle. The offices for the dead were read by the Dean of Perth. Br. DeLuey, of the Fremantle Lodge, at the close of the Church Services, read the exhortation as set forth in the ritual of Oddfellowship; the brethren meanwhile standing around the grave, holding in their hands the usual emblem – a sprig of acacia – which they deposited on the coffin in the manner enjoined by the Order.[6]

'Establishment' resonates here – a life of propriety and religious conviction that brings business and a foundational certainty, against Walker's rage for verse making and his death in the penal Establishment, as contrast. A tale of at least two Perths. But Marfleet was acknowledged as one of 'liberal' (as in 'reason' and 'tolerance' within churchmanship – that is 'broad church') views, so we *might* suppose he at least supported Walker's poeticising, even if with some trepidation or wariness. Maybe he's a reason the book came into being at all, rather than the one who thwarted it or abandoned Walker to his 'fate'. Maybe Marfleet enabled Walker to pursue the one who stole his manuscript, or stood against his material and metaphysical interests? The spiritual baker and the poet baker; the capitalist-bourgeois baker and the convict baker.

I search further for evidence of Charles Walker's poetic life in Britain. He was only twenty-six in 1852 and thirty when he died. Did he publish in England before being transported? He was a tradesman probably outside the usual publishing avenues in London/Britain, and yet a book by a Charles Walker did appear in 1853 in Mayfair, London, published by Saunders & Otley of Conduit Street, entitled *Irene. A Tale. In Two Cantos. And Other Poems.* A search of the book doesn't reveal anything of bakers, baking, crimes committed or the prospect of Western Australia, but it does begin with a 'Dedicatory Sonnet to my Mother' which carries the lines:

This little tribute then may raise a tear –
Remind of me if I am still not here –
Or speak in gentle whispers of a time
    Then long gone by and never to return

Now, it's ludicrous to suggest that the year after he was transported our Charles Walker (the insidiousness of taking possession of the dead to paint a picture in the narratives of our own textual lives) published this book, or that these were the works of his youth, but it can't be *entirely* dismissed. By this, I don't even mean to suggest they are one and the same poet – our advertisement-threat poet

---

6 *The Inquirer and Commercial News*, 15 June 1881, p. 2, http://nla.gov.au/nla.news-article65958465 (accessed 29 March 2015).

is rougher and readier in his delivery by the evidence we have, and one might doubt he would then go on to say:

> When I might from a Mother's bosom learn
> Sweet lessons of the Great and the Sublime.

But we are playing class politics here and forgetting the stress of his circumstances. His marriage. His likely separation. His loss. In this book the title poem roils through orientalist-Greek-mythological-heroic-Christian-romantic-Bible-Koran-Sultan-Turk-Vizier-despot-love-loss-goat-swoon-royalbed-Irene that finishes:

> Howe'er in low disguise he came alone,
> To see the fun'ral he himself allow'd,
> And shed a feeling tear upon her winding shroud.

The 'Miscellaneous poems' section of the book includes a version of Lamartine and many poems reflecting on and inflecting death, travel (Cologne), family, the seasons, vistas/views, Nature, a chestnut tree, and carries a list of 129 subscribers (of which there is no mention of a Marfleet).

This is not our Charles Walker, of course! Of course it's not. I am sure a trip to the British Library would yield a bold (if hard to find) declaration of a very different life lived in a very different way. For example, there are a lot of John Kinsellas out there, and I know that over the centuries a few others among them have written poetry. I don't know them (though I did correspond briefly with one John Kinsella who is a Canadian artist and who dabbles in poetry – I have seen some of his paintings online but not read his verse). And there's a John Kinsella who is a monk-poet, I believe, who wrote some kind of dedicatory chapbook of verse thirty or more years ago. I haven't read his or any of the other John Kinsellas' works, but strangely, I feel connected with them even if they have had dramatically different poetry, politics, ethics, life experiences from my own. We share the body of a name and an interest, and especially when the durations of our lives cross, we share the body-without-organs that we fill with life experience and textuality.

Maybe the same can be said of Charles Walker? The London-published Charles Walker had an exiled, exported, fetishised Antipodean Charles Walker contemporaneous 'double' who became part of the crime-as-profit modus operandi of the colony of Western Australia. This consequence of a 'rage for verse making' echoes like rings in Narcissus's pool. Narcissus wasn't all bad – he knew in himself there was a truth, he knew the 'other' was a truth, and if he didn't know the mirror, the mirror knew him. The conceptual, even 'virtual', polysituate.

Our Charles Walker was the Doppelgänger, the twin, the shadow, the mirror image in a construct of a world that had a centre – London – and its colonies. It's North and it's South, it's opposition, it's inversion, it's less-than – *Terra Australis*… it's Antipodean. An English-speaking baker-convict who wrote and read Greek? This dialogic of text and poets, this obsession to versify our being in even the most adverse conditions.

Is the connection between *Irene* and *Lyrical Poems* any more absurd than the travesty that is the so-called 'Internet of Things' and its triumphalist consumerism? Is there any real difference between the reality we have constructed, in which Charles Walker can be 'our' example, our guide to the journey through the Underworld, at half-a-crown supported by the upright if bewildered Marfleet, and the relationship between your jogging heartbeat and your acquisition of goods from Adidas?

No. The evidence might take us away from this first book in its context, but in the end that distance will only enhance and confirm the connection. Though I have become less (and less) convinced by Deleuze and Guattari's notion of 'rhizome' as outlined/configured in *A Thousand Plateaus: Capitalism and Schizophrenia*, I take this on notice:

> There is no longer a tripartite division between a field of reality (the world) and a field of representation (the book) and a field of subjectivity (the author). Rather, an assemblage establishes connections between certain multiplicities drawn from each of these orders, so that a book has no sequel nor the world as its object nor one of several authors as its subject. In short, we think that one cannot write sufficiently in the name of an outside. The outside has no image, no signification, no subjectivity. The book as assemblage with the outside, against the book as image of the world. A rhizome-book, not a dichotomous, pivotal, or fascicular book.[7]

No longer? Thus it ever was, if at all. The Charles Walkers – ours and the *other* – are the world the book the author. This text is the assemblage of the 'missing' and 'existent' texts of poet/s Charles Walker. The periphery, the centre, the city, the colony. I remember reading a doctor's report once that described someone – was it me? – as being delirious and 'quoting poetries and philosophies' as if these were evidence of instability and a need to be 'calmed'. This is my personal investment in a place I live in, and often feel exiled within and from. 'Embattled', some have said. Charles Walker, I have been illuminated by your work, even where I do and should disagree with it.

---

7 Gilles Deleuze and Félix Guattari, *A Thousand Plateaus: Capitalism and Schizophrenia* (Minneapolis, University of Minnesota, 1987), p. 23.

HENRY LAWSON: NATIONAL DISPLACEMENTS[1]

Henry Lawson's stories and poetry form part of the Australian national psyche. At least, they are constructed as part of a perhaps imagined national psyche. A bit like the way that 'Come on, Aussie, come on' was absorbed by a generation of television watchers as a national statement, when in fact it was part of an advertising campaign for privatised sport – World Series Cricket.

I would argue that we need to let go of the nation-making (so central to Lawson's belief and identity, and much of his writing) to get to the core, to the literary heart of what Lawson achieved. At his best he transcends even the very bush, the very outback, the very up-country, the very pub or selector's hut he conveys with such brevity and yet so acutely: he makes specific places universal. Lawson speaks a language that can travel everywhere and remain loyal to its region, its place of origin. It is not surprising that distance allowed Lawson to write some of his greatest stories. The bush recreated in London. And the stories told to those who weren't of the place he came from on the goldfields, around the scrubby outcrops of New South Wales.

There is (somewhat ironically) something of the international regionalist about Lawson. Something that draws the locales of his stories into dialogue with other locales in terms of characters' relationship to place. Despite Lawson's jingoism, a stronger jingoism among some of his readers has obfuscated the 'universal' in his work. The layering of spatialities of upbringing, local conditions and locally acquired knowledge, isolation, 'hardship', camaraderie and mateship meant that Lawson created extramural spaces in his stories (and poems), and we need to consider the generative and interactive qualities of these. In a work I take to task for its failing to comprehend 'ecological thinking' in my most recent work on space and place, *The Production of Space*, Henri Lefebvre writes:

---

[1] This section on Henry Lawson originally formed the introduction to the *The Penguin Henry Lawson Stories* (Ringwood, Penguin, 2009). Substantial additions/amendments have been made.

Any 'social existence' aspiring or claiming to be 'real', but failing to produce its own space, would be a strange entity, a very peculiar kind of abstraction unable to escape from the ideological or even 'cultural' realm. It would fall to the level of folklore and sooner or later disappear altogether, thereby immediately losing its identity, its denomination and its feeble degree of reality.[2]

Lawson's stories do produce their own 'space' but not the one/s we might think. They are faux realities – they represent and simulate at once. They append to national culturalisations which seek the 'authentic', but they are also generative, energetic and 'convincing'. Lawson is both a committed reader of place and a generalisor and projector of a desired reality on to the screen of national (literary) identity.

Lawson would have to be the most written and talked about Australian writer. There are so many different versions, so many different takes on the man and his work. Manning Clark's *Henry Lawson: The Man and the Legend* is one of the better known ones – although it's a ridiculously digressive book. I think Manning Clark gets his readings of Lawson's stories quite wrong at times. He states that Lawson doesn't see the bush itself, that is, its flora and fauna, with a close eye; but there are numerous descriptions in Lawson that to my mind contradict this. It is a mistake to see Lawson's descriptions as generic; rather, they capture the bushperson's interaction with place, producing a different kind of description.

It is easy to admire Lawson's acute sensitivity to 'mateship', his sense that even swagmen up-country, seemingly wandering without purpose, can find moments of deep connection through anecdote, humour or recollection. However, Lawson's vision is ultimately a negative one, in which as he writes more of the country, a loss and lack of purpose overwhelm. Manning Clark is good at recognising this. Still, a figure like the character Joe Wilson, with his poetic spirit and grim determination, is always going to be admirable. To one like me who has a shearer for a brother, the anecdotes of the bush that Lawson creates, almost as refrains, are entirely recognisable and transferable from generation to generation.

My brother says that humour in the shearing shed works as the escape valve on the pressure cooker. For Lawson, for whom humour was so definitive in characterising the ordinary Australian bushperson, it was more than a release, it was an entire worldview, an acceptance that grimness and hardship ultimately could not be overcome. They had to be cherished because they were the actuality.

Lawson feared that the old ways of the bush would give way to technology, but more often than not they remain strangely constant, including the inherited bigotries of the invader/settler culture. Lawson's parents, the feminist and publisher Louisa Lawson and the Norwegian sailor-cum-prospector Niels (Peter) Larsen (Lawson), had a notoriously difficult marriage that eventually resulted in their separation, and a kind of split view of the world in their son. The mother's moral

2 Henri Lefebvre, *The Production of Space*, trans. Donald Nicholson-Smith (London, Blackwell Publishing, 1991), p. 53.

rigour and desire to escape the limitations of the 'bush', and the father's choice to inhabit the 'bush' world, really do create a tension and a fusion in Lawson.

His portrait of bushwomen (of *white* 'settler' stock) has been increasingly underrated by critics over the years, but I think it is phenomenal in its admiration and respect. Lawson also gives an insight into how this portraiture does and doesn't segue with the blokesy world of the bush. Lawson's earlier portraits of women often fuse elements of the masculine and feminine, and it's really in his depiction of sexual relations between men and women that the distance is created. Without consciousness of sexual difference, it is easy for a child of either gender to embody characteristics of both and not create a hierarchy.

Two of Lawson's great character creations invite close analysis here: Jack Mitchell, the garrulous, witty and even wise swagman, whose recounting of tales from his past supplies Lawson with one of his most effective narrative devices; and Joe Wilson, the sensitive selector who is still a mate and a man's man, the vehicle for Lawson's greatest series of stories, the four interconnected Wilson tales included herein and arranged by editor John Barnes in order of composition rather than in original order of publication. I use the words 'devices' and 'vehicle' cautiously. Indeed, any reader who finds in Lawson what so many Australian readers have found – an affirmation of settler identity through 'bush' characters so digestible and recognisable, encompassing traits we are often sold as being 'Australian values' – would find such terminologies reprehensible, and think of them as getting away from the integrity of Lawson's bush vision. But I think in the end Mitchell and Wilson are vehicles that carry a set of views as much as they are characters in themselves, or combinations of people Lawson specifically knew, or, in the case of Joe Wilson, Lawson's view of himself.

In a Lawson story, a word seems to trigger a yarn, a sketch, a telling. The Mitchell story 'Our Pipes' will seem surreal in the age of cancer and death by passive smoking; smoking, like drinking, is a bonding tool in Lawson; smoking, though, becomes a timing device, a way of pacing narrative – drinking is often destructive and a tool of crisis or a cause for assessment and narrative shift. At the story's beginning, we read: 'The moon rose away out on the edge of a smoky plain...' The 'smoky plain' starts the sequence of associations that takes us to pipes and tobacco, to where 'conversation drifted lazily round various subjects and ended in that of smoking'. There's an associative knitting of words and ideas here that leads to Mitchell starting his tale – the story is framed '"How I came to start smoking?" said Mitchell...'

Lawson wrote of the bush in so many ways, re-covering the same territory so often, that he needed framing devices to carry his message in interconnected but differing ways. Mitchell doesn't evolve as a character; he remains constant, and his epiphanies are epiphanies provided by the expectations of the sketches themselves. A trigger-narrator (Jack Mitchell and *me* ...) sets up the conversational 'other' for Mitchell to tell, to yarn to. Joe Wilson is different, and in many ways the collection of Wilson stories gives a sense of the novel that Lawson wanted to write but never did, or maybe never succeeded in doing. I can honestly say that I have known Mitchells and Wilsons, and in my younger days have worked with them, hay-carting on farms, in a fertiliser factory, and even in market gardens.

For many years I lived an itinerant life. Carrying a drinking problem and looking for occasional work, there was something of the swagman, and at times the sundowner, about me. I can relate to the people Lawson is talking about, though my experience was almost a century later. But as a writer I can also see how an idea stuck and he got stuck in it. When Lawson went to Brisbane in 1891 to work for the *Boomerang*, he was hired to write the 'Country Crumbs' column. After a period of time he began writing the column in rhyming paragraphs. Lawson started, after all, as a poet, not as a writer of short fiction. His short fiction comes out of his ballads, his social verse – his work on the socialist *The Republican* and the feminist *Dawn* (founded by his mother) – in many ways drives his prose.

What Lawson himself called his sketches – generally low on narrative action and detail, and sharp in mood and occasion – have the sense of the poem-fragment about them. And as with sequences of poems, or poems collated in book form, a reading of them is cumulative. Much has been written about Lawson's original reading of Robinson Crusoe, Dickens, Marryat, Bret Harte, Mark Twain and even Edgar Allan Poe, and though clearly all of these had an influence on him and his writing, it might be just as true to say that his work developed independently from his reading. Is this possible? A heresy to suggest? Lawson himself acknowledged his influences. But it was life itself near the diggings, on the small selections, and his lonely childhood around Pipeclay, Eurunderee and Mudgee, and maybe the tensions between the idioms of his parents, that etched his creative vision.

Deaf in one ear from childhood, he paid special attention to the stories of people around him and the relationship between these people and the rebarbative land. A love–hate relationship with place evolved. His little formal schooling (he was nicknamed 'Barmy Harry'), his work for his father (helping build a schoolhouse early on, no less), the tough conditions on the selection, right down to a goldrush in the neighbouring 'Log Paddock', which resulted in the mining and working of the Lawson's own selection by prospectors, as well as his mother's spiritualism, rejection of her domestic 'slavery' and her aspirations as a poet – all these made language for him.

He was never grammatically sound and couldn't spell. After his family split up (the final story in this collection is often seen as being a map, at least in part, of that failure, of two people who were profoundly mismatched), Lawson went to Sydney with his mother and siblings, and while working as a coach-painter attended night school. He failed twice to graduate. He was criticised for his failure to write correctly. A. G. Stephens, in many ways Lawson's bête noire, would constantly persecute him (to Lawson's mind) on these pedantic issues. Much of Lawson's work was copy-edited into shape. Even whole poems and prose pieces were rearranged by editors, especially the founding editor of the *Bulletin*, his mentor in many ways, J. F. Archibald (Archibald had a Lawson poem framed on his *Bulletin* office wall), and David McKee Wright, who disturbingly altered and 'corrected' text. It might be argued that this failure of correct English made Lawson's work what it was. I am considering writing an essay on the use of the 'dash' in Lawson's stories. Its timing and intensity might be seen as similar to those of the dash in Dickinson's poetry. Sounds extreme, but I think a reassessment of Lawson's syntax is essential.

In 1902, after Lawson returned from a two-year stint in Britain – a place he'd damned so often but where he went to make a literary reputation, where a number of his books were published, and where some of his best stories were written – he finally succumbed to drink entirely. He lost his marriage to Berthe, attempted suicide and spent years in and out of prison for failing to pay maintenance, with spells in the mental hospital, cadging drinks off 'mates' in local pubs, while still churning out poems, sketches and journalism, all offset against his early (also drink-fuelled, in large part) years of creativity.

The updated Penguin edition of Lawson's stories that I refer to ends chronologically with those final great stories written in London ('A Child in the Dark, and a Foreign Father' was begun in London and completed in Australia), but I would argue that he continued to write brilliantly, at times, even after his return to Australia, and that his bigotries, wrought out of bitterness, increased and overwhelmed his ability to recognise the 'common' universal moment in swells and swagmen alike. I don't think it's because he exhausted his reservoir of stories – repetition is not necessarily a problem if those repetitions show different views of the same thing. Lawson's life took over his writing in so many ways, and alcoholism can never be separated from his 'decline' as a writer.

I really struggle with Lawson's racism, for which there is no excuse. There are occasions when his very brief portraits of non-whites show some empathy, sympathy or recognition of something outside subalternity; but largely this is not the case. I don't really know how in the end one can respect even the most astute writing of place as any more than a surface gesture where racism is part of the picture. Especially given that he's writing about an Australia constructed out of the destruction and dispossession of the traditional owners of the land.

The strange thing about Lawson's racism was that he basically thought that in mateship all are made equal.[3] In 1890 Lawson wrote an article on trade unions entitled 'The New Religion'. He wrote:

> Trade unionism is a new and grand religion; it recognises no creed, sect, language or nationality; it is a universal religion ... open to all and will include all – the Atheist, the Christian, the Agnostic, the Unitarian, the Socialist, the Conservative, the Royalist, the black and the white, and a time will come when all the 'ists', and 'isms', etc., will be merged and lost in one great 'ism' – the unionism of labour.

---

3 And this is where Lawson's thinking (in general) runs the risk of failing to allow his works to create their own space and to dwindle as a consequence – to simply reproduce or mimic racist tropes and social markers, to 'extend' but not simultaneously critique their/his own bigotry.

And yet Lawson's most dependable biographer, Colin Roderick, has written of this:

> There was one flaw in his theory of universal brotherhood. He disposed of the 'lesser breeds' by elimination: 'The American Indian, the African and South Sea savage, and the aboriginals of Australia will soon become extinct, and so relieve the preachers of universal brotherhood of all anxiety on their account.'

It has been pointed out that Lawson's bigotry was to do with how peoples fitted into this picture of universal brotherhood, and indeed the notion of Australia itself. If 'others' were willing to join the mateship, then they were generally accepted. This vision of anxiety, this reaction to fear of being an outsider in the place one is born into, permeates Lawson's fiction. The iconic story 'The Drover's Wife' is a distinctive illustration of this vision of anxiety struggling with a desire for resilience. The character of the drover's wife epitomises this resilience, despite her vulnerability in having a husband frequently absent and having to fend for herself and her children in a physically difficult and often threatening space. The men in Lawson's stories are often absent from their womenfolk, as was characteristic of a time when work in the bush meant travelling far – the selector struggled and even the large landowning squatters had their own survival issues.

In 'The Drover's Wife' there is the anxiety of the threat of the primal, the indigenous, the bush. And this is carried over into the male world as well, where role-play blurs in a story like 'Brighten's Sister-In-Law', in which a child in the bush with his father is close to death, and only removal to even a rough shack and the intervention of a woman ensures his survival. Gender roles can shift, but the ground becomes shaky, and they are most often restored. In 'The Drover's Wife', the snake itself is not only the snake of paradise, tempting; it is the land, it is the spirit of the dispossessed. The subtextual crisis of the story is one of belonging and identity, that bonds genders in claiming rights of presence, no matter how forbidding the place: 'Her husband is an Australian, and so is she.' The Aboriginal people who pass through are both 'reassuring' and defamiliarised, even made mildly malevolent, as is the fire she resists on an occasion that 'threatened to burn her out'. It's all bound together in contradiction and crisis. These are not necessarily the stories of national affirmation they are said to be.

Lawson, like Marcus Clarke, readily deploys the 'weird', and the bush is 'weird'. Even born of it, you remain alien to it. The immense humanity in Lawson's work comes despite his views, and despite a lot of the fiction he wrote. In the great stories the land, the people, the narrative of his life itself takes over. He makes the connections between the brief glimpses. His work in many ways is the novel he would never write in the literal sense, a postmodern work, and not a retrograde one.

I read a disturbing comment the other day about how we can't judge Lawson by the 'PC' standards of our time. Well, wrong is wrong. But even a non-PC work that offers insights into the failings as much as the successes of the human condition is to be welcomed. Lawson was a difficult man with many self-negating polysituated place(ments) in his writing and 'self'. His work may sometimes seem easy on the surface – it yarns straight – but it's not. And even when the land wins, as it always does, and its victim – especially female – is 'past carin', the resilience of the universal, extended across all people, is in the brilliance of an echo, of a lifeline such as 'and she said to be sure and water them geraniums'.

Back when I was a drinker I said and did some terrible things. I wouldn't like to be judged by them. Whatever Lawson's sins in action or viewpoint, his great stories speak beyond them. There are many Lawsons – from left-wing to right-wing, from feminist-sympathetic to misogynist, from racist to someone who believed in a humanity without race or creed. And in his stories he is most often *another* Lawson again.

ON PETER CAREY'S *TRUE HISTORY OF THE KELLY GANG*

A key to understanding Peter Carey's *True History of the Kelly Gang* is to realise that this is a book about speech and text, witness, and the question of the reliable or unreliable narrator. It explores the need to explain one's actions, motives and character in the context of possible histories and their receptions by personal and public audiences. The narrative of Ned Kelly is constructed for a private audience, though made public through the machine of research and public interest. Or so Carey directs his reader. As a child, Kelly hears tales of Cuchulainn and Irish mythology, of the legends and terrors of the district, but only spends a limited time at school because of poverty and his father's death. Kelly's great moment of childhood bravery, saving a boy from drowning, is rewarded by the boy's publican father – a sash with Kelly's heroics blazoned across it is awarded in front of the school. Text is the hero here. And though resentment surfaces regarding its value, it's the pride that links his narrative together.

Rhetoric, and the possibility of truth and passion mingling, inform Kelly's whole character here. In a book told as history – a history recreated from an apparent personal journal, a narrative epistle to an unseen daughter – the tale is told and the words are what we receive. The book is structured as 'parcels' of text preserved in a deposit library, and we travel with the 'historian' in the reading and reconstruction of possibilities through the reading of this text. It's one version of history, played off against the official versions. Of course, the 'true history' of the gang is told by Ned Kelly himself, so even within the framework of 'faction', truth is Ned Kelly's truth, and not that of his younger brother Dan, Steve Hart with his chivalrous takes on the Irish Sons of Sieve, or Joe Byrne with his opium addiction and adulation and respect of Ned, the gang's leader. Ellen Kelly, matriarch of the tale, is both understood and misunderstood by her son.

The irony is that Carey has based his novel on the official versions of the Ned Kelly story, and created a verisimilitudinous language for Kelly. Kelly doesn't just speak to us through the author – he narrates, he writes himself. And as we will learn, that writing is closer to thought than speech; it's closer to truth because stories can be told in so many different ways. Ink is blood. He dreams of his mother, then in jail, saying:

> I see Mr Irving finally made you the monitor she smiled. Looking down at myself I seen the ink on my hands & up my arms it were bleeding down my shirt & moleskins.[1]

The sash of heroism then appears:

> I spilled it I said tho I did not remember having done so I were surprised that I must be back at Avenel Common School. You put that sash on she said do you hear me. It were 7 ft. long & fringed with gold I had nothing to be ashamed of Mother and me walked side by side along the catwalk I looked down to the ground floor where there were much smoke and destruction many policemen was lying dead.[2]

The boundary between 'heroism' and murder can be a fine line, and Kelly's guilt over the murders he committed at Stringybark Creek, when he and his gang surprised the police out hunting for them, drives his narrative. Carey plays with the inscription of guilt on the land, the pathetic fallacy of the land reflecting the individual's psyche, of the condition of human events at a particular geographical location. Carey is exploring the conventions of Ozlit, as well as those of American wilderness writing, and more suspiciously, American transcendentalism. This is also debatably a novel about American takes on cultural histories, and if its nationalism can be unpicked, it is through this polysituated array. Carey, the commercial novelist, also knows how many readers in his main market might interpret the text. It will give them exoticism as well as identifiable points of reference.

This is an oedipal book on every level, and one in which guilt is developed to a pathology. At its best Carey's work is an analysis of how such neurosis can be turned into the stuff of myth, how as part of an oppressed people, despite the factionalisms and betrayals, the 'criminal classes' might operate out of an agenda of survival that's not to be judged by the accepted rules of honour and justice. Questions of fairness and justice are at the core of the work:

> Her baby is taken from her I said and they did not answer. And here is the thing about them men they was Australians they knew full well the terror of the unyielding law the historic memory of UNFAIRNESS were in their blood and a man might be a bank clerk or an overseer he might never have been lagged for nothing but still he knew in his heart what it were to be forced to wear the white hood in prison he knew what it were to be lashed for looking a warder in the eye and even a posh fellow like the Moth had breathed that air so the knowledge of unfairness were deep in his bone and marrow. In the hut at Faithfull's Creek I seen proof that if a man could tell his true history to Australians he might be believed it is the clearest sight I ever seen and soon Joe seen it too.[3]

1 Peter Carey, *True History of the Kelly Gang* (London, Faber and Faber, 2000), p. 335.
2 Carey, *True History*, p. 335.
3 Carey, *True History*, p. 299.

Carey's verisimilitude expects a willing suspension of disbelief, and is flawed. There are sentences where the register changes, and though this is also a feature of Kelly's real texts such as the Jerilderie Letter, the changes in Carey's text sometimes seem more like authorial intrusions – regardless of potential interpolation or hybridising within the pseudo-narrative, the juxtapositions don't often work.

The novel is full of wonderful vignettes though, and it's the stories within the stories that Carey does so well. Be it the boxing match staged in the Commissioner's mansion after he is arrested as a teenager and taken to Melbourne, or the tale of Whitty selling his soul and his clever wife getting it back for him, the asides make for wonderful digressions that richly inform the main narrative. There's no doubt Carey is, above and beyond all else, a storyteller.

Yet the more I let Peter Carey's novel *True History of the Kelly Gang* sink in, the more uncomfortable I feel. This fictionalisation of the life of Ned Kelly participates in the creation and continuation of so many national myths that I begin to comprehend why it is that right-wing groups in Australia connect with Australian literary identities like Henry Lawson and Banjo Patterson. Carey has 'factionalised', and cleverly at that, not only the story of Kelly, and to some extent the members of his gang, but tropes in Australian history. This is done with critical awareness, and his own textual procedures are under review throughout the work, but in the end it is hijacking and rendering saleable a mythology that has, as we regularly hear, had Mick Jagger play the bushranger and been a source for much contemporary literature – from poetry to novels.

One of the websites dedicated to Ned Kelly, tied up in the kind of Australian republicanism too often intertwined with xenophobia, carries a warning that people must not read Carey's book as fact. The site decries the book's elements of transvestism, Ned Kelly having a child and so on. Details, it claims, that don't match the 'true history'! On one level this is missing the point, but on another it is also a rebuttal of the hype that goes behind such a work. The novel is a work of pure advertising. It interweaves the language of Kelly as dictated to Byrne in the Jerilderie Letter – Australia's manifesto of the oppressed Irishman, declaration of independence and map to the individual–community dichotomies of Australian mateship – and the two other extant letters spoken by Kelly, in addition to newspaper reports and other archival information, rendering them into a fictionalised account that preserves language and yet plays with the idea of literary production.

It is a book that deals with the issues of Australian Irishness, but more of a secular than a religious variety. Irish Catholicism is there, but this is not the real basis of the tale, though superstition is strongly represented in the form of rat plagues, Banshees, marks on horses' foreheads and so on. A connection might be drawn between the appearance of the Banshee at a time of death and the mystery of war machines like the Spencer rifle, carried by police, inducing fear in the Kelly gang. It is a symbol of power, but as with the armour designed to make them immortal, it too lacks the power of the transported beliefs from the mother country.

The history of Ned Kelly, Australia's archetypal bushranger, is known by most Australians of British or Irish descent, and probably by many others. That in 1880 he was hanged apparently uttering the words 'Such is Life' – as noted at the end of the Carey story – or, as some prefer, 'Ah well, I suppose it has come to this', is legendary.[4] Whether or not he is known by the Chinese communities, given his extreme racism towards any but those of Irish heritage, is questionable. Or Aboriginal people. Carey doesn't shrink from showing this side of Kelly, and he is conscious of the narrow take on the cultural politics of then and now that comes with working with such a mythology. Yet he still participates in and indulges that mythology, in a way that might be seen as perpetuating some of the deepest problems of Australian nationalism. The Irish are no longer an oppressed people in Australia, and as Kelly himself was a currency lad – that is, born of the colonies rather than in Ireland – his reception of Irish nationalism and its drive to throw off the British oppressors was mediated through stories and memory. Which is not to downplay the obvious oppression and extreme brutality of the British judiciary and its often Irish supporters and 'traps', but to contextualise it.

When Kelly is designing his armour, with interesting subtexts and transvestite connections to dressmaking, he is inspired by the monitors of the American civil war. One of his retreats in the bush has walls lined with out-of-date newspaper articles of the civil war. The connections with things American occur through individual characters and the texts of history. Words become armour.

This is a fascinating and telling quote as much about Carey's narratology as about the character of his Kelly creation:

> I read a lot about you Mr Kelly but I never heard you was a scholar. Let me remind you how LORNA DOONE sets out. Then the strange little cove balanced himself on his crippled crooked legs and held his book of Shakespeare across his heart and closed his eyes and from his great head he dragged out the following words of R.D. Blackmore. AND THEY WHAT LIGHT upon this book should bear in mind not only that I write to clear our parish from ill fame but also that I am nothing more than a plain unlettered man not read in foreign languages as a gentleman might be nor gifted with long words save what I have won from the Bible or master William Shakespeare whom in the face of common opinion I do value highly.
>
> Curnow opened his eyes and smiled at me.
>
> IN SHORT he quoted I am an ignoramus but pretty well for a yeoman.[5]

The character Kelly recognises the condescension, but understands the power behind knowledge. Shakespeare can make us bleed.[6]

---

4 See http://www.abc.net.au/local/stories/2014/11/14/4128818.htm for a contestation of this claim. Whether we believe he said this, or 'Oh well, it's come to this at last', or nothing discernible, the act of Kelly making 'final words' has become iconic.

5 Carey, *True History*, p. 337.

6 There is also the sublimated polysituatedness of learning, of what is said but also left unsaid. And the sense that Shakespeare 'knew' and the Bible 'knows' (all?). And that knowing is experienced in innumerable direct and vicarious ways.

In the way that landscape is evoked in a context of a discourse of Australianness, so is literature. A landscape reference for all Australian writing post the nineteenth century has been Marcus Clarke's famous 'weird melancholy' introduction to a volume of Adam Lindsay Gordon's poems. Extracted from a longer piece written on Australian art, it defines both the terror and the soul of an artistic cultural view of Australian identity via the bush. It is not surprising that we find a Mount Desolation mentioned in Carey's book – this is the stuff of such cultural icono-mythologies. Carey does ironise to create distance at every opportunity, and he certainly captures elements of Kelly's known sarcasm.

Kelly is also a tamer and destroyer of the bush, and is unable to get truly to its soul. In the same way that Clarke avoids indigenous presence, just sensing something is there, so does Kelly. It is 'his' country and he is determined it will work for him. It's a battle with what Clarke noted in a different context as 'weird melancholy'.[7]

It is interesting to see that within Carey's narrative the vehicle for the Kelly gang's downfall is a schoolteacher. Kelly's last entrustment of script epitomises his love–hate relationship with learning, with this rendering of knowledge into 'fact'. The teacher will betray him and take his words in a locked chest away with him. He will be the fading hero who condemns Kelly to capture, who will question why Kelly's fame increases, why it's all based on bloodshed – at the same time as preserving the texts and even, we learn, making emendations in pencil. The teacher plays this ambivalent sort of role in other Australian literature too. Consider the teacher in *The Chant of Jimmie Blacksmith*. The teacher symbolises both liberation and tyranny – often the more repugnant because he or she should know better than the law.

To reinvent the story of the Kelly Gang as emotively as Carey has done, many generations later, is to use the facts for a different kind of mythology. To highlight what makes the Australian experience different. It is the tool that allows Kelly Country to become a sacred place, more sacred to the European-Australian nationalist than the indigenous histories that lie 'beneath' and exist concurrently and independently. And there is often a denial by such nationalists of their own polysituating presence and its *affect*. This is disturbing. Carey is an intelligent storyteller who sees these problems clearly, and attempts to defuse the potency of national myth-making through Steve Hart and later Dan Kelly donning dresses, which we later find formed part of an attempt to connect with campaigns of terror enacted by the oppressed Irish back home.

As someone with an Irish background, I've heard many of these stories

---

7 Which – along with the unfamiliar and what we might now configure as the 'uncanny', and a sense of disconnection on the part of the 'settler' – is informed by trauma created through the invasiveness of the many strands of the 'colonial', through the appropriation of indigenous narratives and coordinates, and through the displacing of belonging by 'claims' from those living *outside* ('back home') the surveillance of their own traumatising, vicarious colonial presence. Complicating the 'picture' is the mass of contradictory variables arising from the tensions between the 'settlers' and the 'penal' (sometimes inseparable).

of British tyranny in Ireland, and in the colonies – not so much through my family, but from other Irish-Australians who feel I should participate in these memories. My partner also has this background, and recalls her father ringing her from Victoria, full of emotion, talking about being in Kelly Country. For those with Irish families it's as powerful a national myth as that of the Eureka Stockade. In fact, Carey literally plays with this comparison and has Ned tell us that more power is invested in his campaign. That the same mistakes won't be made. Kelly is portrayed as a compassionate man; we are always on his side. That is not surprising, given that the text is constructed out of journals Ned has written for his daughter to read when she comes of an age. They are his 'truth', so the 'true history' will be told, rather than the lies of the official press. Inherent in this is the rebellion Carey is trying to stage – the stuff of manifestos and constitutions, which is where empowerment lives. It is a paean to the value of literature, to the primacy of the word in culture. National identity comes through its arts. The pen is mightier than the sword, but it also goes hand in hand with it. Carey's Kelly knows that to be heard, to be read in print is to enter the bodies of the reader. The song, the written word, stories told around fires – these are what gives power. These are where identity is located.

Carey's book is a work of inscription – it is a writing of the body as landscape, as repository of inherited wrongs. Kelly entrusts his words to the printer's wife when the gang raids Jerilderie and the printer runs away, and his words are then handed over to the police. He walks into town with the words strapped to his body, his blood running with the ink. Kelly as a child waited till all others had had a go at being ink monitor; he went last because of his Irishness. The ink became a symbol of empowerment. He wanted to do it better than anyone else does. This inscription of the body has a political significance within the nation, but also in terms of the body.

There is a fatalism steadily eroding away at the myth of the individual and community that is intended to have the reader ironise the circumstances of a crime, to question whether or not, finding ourselves in Ned's position, we would have done the same things. Ned asks this question himself when he takes people hostage while staging a robbery, or when addressing someone he feels has wronged him. Vengeance is tempered by reason.

This is a Greek tragedy with the rules rewritten to accommodate that big extra player, the Australian landscape. An entity that doesn't fit the rules of European tragedy. A total affirmation of its independence. What is this landscape in the Carey novel? The locations shift from Kelly's boyhood home before the death of his father, to his relations' place, to his mother's selection, to bush boltholes devised by the master of his youth – his mother had apprenticed him for 15 pounds – the bushranger Harry Power, and so on.

We have a very geographical picture of where Kelly lived, the landscape he identified with. Power, he remembers, told him that if he knew the country he would be a wild colonial boy forever. Carey's Kelly knows the untruth of this, but still wishes it to be so. He respects the power of the bush, and knows that it will win out if not accorded due respect. When he is working his mother's selection, he talks constantly of how many trees he can fell, and the language is that of a war being waged. This is a book of many wars, of many revolutions and fights. In the end, they fall into a pattern deployed by the real narrator, the novelist, to create something for Australians at the turn of the millennium to hang their restless hats on. It is also a book written to market a saleable view of Australia to the outside world. Who can forget those stockmen riding nauseatingly around during that grotesque fund-fair called the Olympics opening ceremony – something, I'm glad to say, I only saw in retrospective snatches.

This is a book about narrative, and Bank Teller Lyving's narrative is a wonderfully staged account of the techniques Carey has used in composition across the work. The retelling of a story via archival material and creative possibility is rendered to bold text, to living faction. We hear the voice of Kelly commenting on a text he is using as an account of his actions in place of his own writing. Why rewrite what's already there – but to make truth he adds the annotations. A book of marginalia and commentary on narrative, this extract epitomises the forces at work behind the creation of the simulacrum, the tautologically false faction:

Kelly also told Devine that he intended shooting him and Richards,

I would never kill them but it were essential they obey

but Mrs Devine begged them off. Ned Kelly said that if Devine had not left the force in a month he would return and shoot him.
    On Sunday night Edward Kelly again rode up to Davidson's Hotel where he had a great many drinks,

If 2 be a great number then he does not lie

and entered freely into conversation with the barmaid.[8]

One of the subtexts of this novel is that of masculinity. Apart from the obvious bonds of male mateship and the subtext of homosexuality in the 'gang', and all that word entails – between Steve and Dan, Ned's brother, are major threads, in the 'web' of text, that allude to the connections between male and female bodies – of flesh, spirit, knowledge, etc. A cultural body is provided, a Deleuze and Guattarian Body Without Organs, filled by a narrative told by a man verging on a literacy that is empowerment, to a child born out of sight, and, indeed, in San Francisco after his 'wife' Mary has abandoned him. His non-literacy engenders something more powerful than canonical literature. And for those who have read Kelly's original words, this might seem to be a 'truth'.

The male with a nurturing heart, birth, offspring, the blood of the parrots that is the blood of the land feeding the body, are interwoven. Fate and survival are written against fear. 'The baby's silence was as valuable as life itself.' This is the son of Ned's stepfather, born to the woman who will bear his own child in turn.

8 Carey, *True History*, p. 310.

Family extends; filial ties are complex and inscribed as responsibility. In the almost beautiful scene when Ned cools the feverish body of Mary's baby, everything connects. It is one of the main vignettes, or more accurately, emotional and spiritual nodal points of the imagery. Even here things are written in flesh: 'The baby's eyes was sunk his protest against the icy water were as weak & thin as paper.' Words make for different lives, but death ignores them. His greatest faiths, beliefs and passions are vulnerable.

> I woke in bed next morning to discover Mary sitting over me the baby in her arms. It were still too early for any birds except a solitary robin in the scrub beside the hut. You must leave me here she whispered I replied there were no choice we all of us had to keep on moving.
>
> His fever is too high he cannot travel.
>
> I did not speak roughly but in the leaden light I firmly removed baby George from her arms carrying him out of the hut down under the twisted black ti tree past the wet dresses which Dan or Steve must of washed in the middle of the night the garments was spread like catfish skins upon the river bank.
>
> What are you doing?
>
> We are going to cool him.
>
> At my command she got down in the freezing water then I unwrapped the steaming baby from his shawl it were a shocking vision he had always been a hefty wombat but now his ribs was prominent his skin the colour of lamb fat in the river water.
>
> O the poor darling she wailed as I baptised him holding him under his arms in the mountain water O dear Jesus it is a cruel thing to have a baby in this country.[9]

A question of abjection, of relationship to the mothering body, is examined over and over. It is partly updated Freudian. The relationship between Ned and his mother – her giving birth, his fear that people will talk of him having seen his mother's bottom, the accusations that he is both a mother's boy and her boyfriend, his punishment of the men who leave her, the liminality in the selector's hut where the mother has no freedom to even fart in peace – is played out constantly. When he sleeps with Mary the first time he remarks on wondering whose milk he is stealing while sucking her breast; he then discovers the child. That child is the child of George King, Ned's mother's new husband. The lines of connection, of incest and kinship, are blurred and interwoven. This is the nature of an oppressed people, the outcome of a criminalised ethnicity.

Connections between text and the body are also prevalent. This notion of inscribing the body in terms of identity is a strong signature of feminist theory. Carey has claimed part of this for the male. He is trying to revolutionise the rough Australian male as being something entirely apposite to the female experience. He has created a hybrid body and spirit. This is a particular clever political ploy given the anti-PC reaction to the sensitive New Age guy in Australian

---

9 Carey, *True History*, p. 280.

(and American and British etc.) society. It does, of course, have problematic overtones.

True History of the Kelly Gang is bound to become a popular classic, but in essence does nothing new. It is a great read; the imitation of the language of Irish 'letters home' of the nineteenth century in Australia is basically well-handled, and the use of Ned Kelly's Jerilderie voice is effective, but the stock-epithet repetition of Kellyisms also, ironically, imprisons the narrative. What worries me is the ends a book like this may be put to. It doesn't create anything new, doesn't adequately address the problem of racism outside the Irish-British condition and doesn't really challenge the notions of narrative that inform it. It will shine brightly in the Carey oeuvre, but it is not one of his great books. It is, however, a book in which place is infused via a *sub*-diagesis by many external coordinates (though these might not be obvious), such as the author's internationalism, his looking to (re)create an historicised regional Australia, his experience of Australia before and after his move to the United States, and a desire to reconnect with the psychology of 'the nation' and to envisage it anew.

THE COLLAPSE OF SPACE: ON LISA GORTON'S *THE LIFE OF HOUSES*

I think comparisons to other writers are somewhat distracting from a novel's achievement. If there was another novelist who came to mind during my reading of Lisa Gorton's *The Life of Houses* it was actually Virginia Woolf, though this was in a distant modernist way, and echoed my reading of *To the Lighthouse* of almost thirty years ago. [Tracy literally just called out from her study and read a piece to me saying Lisa Gorton affirms/confirms this link to Woolf – I didn't know it when I read the book and thought it.] No, what came to mind was actually the 'tension' between 'technical drawing', representational painting and a late expressionism. My markers were visual, which might be assumed with Anna running a gallery and the subtext of the novel being representations of the actual world as aesthetic, and how much they don't translate. Scott's drawing of Kit is wrong and he knows it, and so does Kit, but in telling a lie about her it also tells her a lie she needs to hear. In that liminal dubious way he interacts with her, giving a snowball effect (in a hot climate) to rumours of impropriety with the teenager Hugh he'd also sketched in school uniform, board shorts and various states of 'naturalism'; though the subjects were dressed, in the sketches the capturing of skin, hair and flesh is more exposing than the naked body – juxtaposed to the 'life drawing' classes and the indifference of the model, and Kit's fascination with the colour of her breasts. Patrick's being something of a forger who taints the family name in odd and abstracted ways is also a disclaimer that affects the way the reader interprets and absorbs the visual in the book.

Though possession of place may seem stable, and there is only one specific reference to the land being stolen (from indigenous people), the fact of a distorted seeing gives a sense that all is in fact far less stable than it seems. Things are described with clarity – description of place is anchored in known co-ordinates that remain firm through memory (Anna's, Treen's by implication) and the here-and-now (Kit's encounter with place configured through absence and expectation, and Anna's re-encountering and finding things more like they were than she was ready for) – and yet are often deceptively ambiguous. The house is stability, but the kitchen has been modernised in a dysfunctional way, and the neighbour (Carol's husband) is eyeing the property off for development (Anna resents the strip of land not having been sold off to fund her art education in London). The co-ordinates of the plane, of the cube, the cuboid, of the parallelogramic qualities of rooms and the plasticity of the house itself, the block it sits in, the sea and paddocks that surround it, the lines of connection that are beaches and roads and railway lines, are offset by the uncertainty – the history of a place and its lives that can't be finished (Audrey haunting the children's presence in the house with her unfinished or even unstarted writings, as much as Patrick's ghost riffling imaginations and acting as sentinel to the real history of the house). In the 'close-up' descriptions, I am interested in repetitions of the generic 'tea-tree' (always a local name for another species, in the case I am assuming a coastal melaleuca), the ubiquitous dune/s which operate/s disturbingly as a singular notion of separation from a sea that is not always seen but is always heard.

Space is inside and outside, and you fill your spaces. Interiors are as important as exteriors, and it is within that the unsettled look for grip – in an object (the black painted table of mourning) or the four-poster bed – but all objects are strangely alienating as well. In terms of pioneering mythology, this work serves as an example of the grotesque, and maybe the 'weird melancholy' located in Adam Lindsay Gordon's work, and the painting that led Clarke to name this characteristic in the first place. What I am interested in is space, which is clearly a major 'theme of the work', not only how it is used and in how it is conveyed or how it is described, but rather in how it is configured and the politics of this. To portray space requires multiple co-ordinates always active, and Gorton takes us across the plane of the page, following a pencil stroke that will not render what we are seeing, or think we are seeing. The angel painted from the 'realistic' feather of a chicken. People seeing our mothers in us when they have never seen the father.

Ancestry is a spatial act of association and the desire for a place in a scheme of assurance – against the state, against other families, against history itself, the tracked and pursued line of inheritance assures us there's substance to the foundations. The Ozymandias Sea House reassures by its past but is also equally assured of its (failed) future. New houses are begun, as much in the utility and middle-class comforts of Anna's city dwelling as in the (inevitably) tacky residential development Treen will become one with, in her becoming town, community, place. This Deleuze and Guattarian becoming echoes throughout the book, as much as the rhizomes of art position cartographically – and for me, all maps are untruths. Anna fears Kit has fallen victim to Scott, Peter wants Kit inspected by a doctor though he knows her not at all, and Kit asserts her independence and resists the twisting of what happened. But she has the evidence of encounter, the drawing – the lake, eye that the sea is not, knows, but the 'white long-legged bird' (again, without species identification – a generic entity of transfiguration that's nonetheless anchored in place) is witness (stilled, figurative, ontological sign) to an inner turmoil.

So space is witness in this work, and not just a geometry. It is a witnessing through configuration. It is a spatial metaphysics in which the low-key plotting – city/country, life/death, suspicion/reality – unfolds in a simulacrum of real time. No more could happen in this novel than happens – no more should. It is enough. It is enough because the body and place, the body and space (it occupies, where it is, how it is seen), are in constant dialogue providing a tangential series of plot-points in which a wonderful curve of connection and disconnection, encounter and refusal is constructed. Constructed. It's a three-dimensional configuration and I could draw a bubble chart showing where events lead to subtexts that branch and branch again. The more specific an observation, the more close-up, the less precise it becomes, the more open to expressionist interpretation, even abstraction:

> Now, seeing them turn their backs, she felt herself to be nowhere. Her hand on the arm of her chair, that freckle on the back of it: she remembered primary school, holding her two hands up to her face. That freckle had meant her right hand. This body, her own, but she was not here: her body, not her, was in the room, with them. Something had happened: somebody had died.[1]

And I offer, as further evidence, that this book of space and place is actually about a tangent to 'reality' (to actuality) this:

> She said, 'We're never anywhere. One is a dream or the other. This is real and then I go home and you're nowhere. You're saying it's simple but that's what we haven't been.'[2]

This comment of Anna's to Peter ripples through Kit's less sophisticated and formative senses of self in her grandparents' house, in her interactions with others in the small town. An act of defiance such as buying a packet of cigarettes, with its visual health warning, and her thoughts of her own body as Patrick is dying and her consciousness of this, is a case of 'this is real and then I go home'. All but her mother and the unseen father – Matt (with his grasping father) – are unreal to her, and she questions the very reality of her mother because it's the only way of defining herself (or, maybe, through not-being-Miranda!) This, if you like, is her first step to her mother's London; it is an awareness that the certainty of catching public transport to school, of looking at photos on her phone, are as certain and uncertain as the ghost of the murdered girl. It is notable how self-tormenting this book is in its understated, steadily paced way.

Again, back to the visualisation of space. Full spaces are empty, narrow dining rooms are (too) full, the light in the painting changes and breaks out of its palette. One is dealing with the harsh, washing light: with the loss of focus and the new clarities. We read of shaded eyes; we read of the sea that 'Only the light has made it vast' and of 'painted over blankness'.[3] The authorial voice travels

---

1 Lisa Gorton, *The Life of Houses* (Sydney, Giramondo, 2015), p. 62.
2 Gorton, *The Life*, p. 75.
3 Gorton, *The Life*, p. 114.

with the indirect discours(ing) of the character – of Anna and here, Kit – they are so different, even at loggerheads (as Audrey and Anna are), but are so much and too much one and the same. Is this learnt behaviour, is this genetic, is this familial programming, is this all of the above and more? Is it the house? Is it the myth of colonial Australia imposing its schools of painting, its revisioning of the European under duress in a defamiliarising place (no matter how much developers 'tame' it)? If there is an *ars poetica* paragraph in the book it is, for me, this one:

> Dirty sand, a smell of oil and seaweed, everything crowded and vacant: this every loose-end hour. She had no place, did not exist in it. The shaver in her bag, the stuff on her face – and after that, what? Her despair extended to everything she looked at: useless, immense, a painted scene.[4]

In her defiance, in her *rite de passage*, Kit must try to geo-locate in order to keep a grip on the real. Yet she is in this strange (and I use the word selectively) familiarised place – she is an an alien in the vaguely familiar, she is left with nothing out of a paradox. She wishes to grow into 'woman' yet clings to 'girl' – okay, we'd expect that. But what surprises is the annihilation of space as part of her existential teenage angst. What would be predictable becomes body-dysphoric. Body has no outline, no sketch, no place. Even a wrong (flattering?) sketch is better than none. The family comes together to fall apart. Send a text to London. Reach for the absent father? And the absent maternal grandfather – the failed and fallen forger and Jesuit priest. Anomalies. '"The house will be yours one day," Patrick said.' Hers? What can this mean? She will occupy a place she feels estranged from, frightened of, that is 'violated' by the Scott 'encroach-ment' in which 'nothing' happens? What is he doing there? (reminds me of the Tom Waits song that has that wonderful refrain, 'But what is he building in there?') Patrick is the liminal male outside lines of inheritance: 'Her grand-father stepped with a sleepwalker's familiarity between the drawing room's small tables.'[5] And that room is full of things: 'Crochet antimacassars on the armchairs; tasselled Persian rugs the size of doormats: the room had a layered indoorness: it absorbed sound.' Indeed, it absorbs history and consequence as well – it seeks to placate but bothers and leaves discomfort. Houses do – they collect. Yet Kit finds her liberations outdoors; Anna finds hers 'closed in' – her prejudices, fears and ways of seeing (the curatorial space of the gallery – right down to 'capturing' a Rover Thomas for her rich father-in-law … exported to London as part of the sell-out that's also the foundations of the house – theft and forgery). We read: 'Closed in her car, she felt recovered enough to call out...' Her past, the spectre of Scott and his 'failure', his coming back from the world neglected and even abandoned, cast as (and becoming?) 'incestuous' within

---

4 Gorton, *The Life*, p. 114.
5 Gorton, *The Life*, p. 127.

the town in a way that we don't quite register with Treen, who has, strangely (again), undergone a similar-different journey.

Where do we go when we occupy someone else's space? This stolen land? Even the hospital where Patrick is dying, where the whole family (sans Matt – the 'other side'! and not of the blood) are closed in together in the unfortunate 'family room' – was once partly a house, a space taken over. The tensions rise. We read: 'The hospital itself – it had been someone's house once.'[6] Then Anna is back at her childhood house with its memories (her tutu performances, her ghost, the sea you can't quite see!), with its embodiment of her body (her betrayals, her lies, her decaying marriage). The body of the house is dying ('Anna could still feel under her finger the crumbling wood, so eaten out it gave way like icing sugar'[7] – Anna can't force Treen to 'draw'/sketch the same conclusion … there is a wilful painting of the now as death of the past) and Anna wishes to disconnect it from life-support. Even good memories are tainted by the body of her life as is, the choices she made and the blames she apportioned. 'Cautiously, like pressing a bruise, she tested what she felt, being back.'

But the house is not just Anna, neither is the place, and '[t]he house was keeping itself back from her'. I found myself as a reader shifting between a female and male gendering of the house, and a neutral alternative. It is a prison of gender and outside gender at once. Like so much of this book, states of being and ideas of presence and (self-) identity are caught in stasis, a paradox and oxymoronic display of language and painting, of speech and internal monopoly, the indirect discourse of being. For me, the most frightening lines of the book, the sheer destructive exploitation of them, the rendering of place as object, the fetishised *coup de grâce* of self, comes with Anna's warped epiphany: 'Following Treen down the hall she had found herself imagining the show she could put together, seeing the objects around her in the gallery's clean clear light.' The clearest lights are not the most truthful lights, any more than wrong sketches are actually wrong. There's no quid pro quo of belonging, alienation, seeing and obfuscation. Anna needs to break the cycle of the house, of generations, of inheritance (though she is bypassed by the house going to Kit, she will still benefit, of course – restitution for the house not paying her back for inhabiting it!)

It seems appropriate that Anna has a further realisation about belonging and alienation in the deadspace of a motel room, a motel built around a car park (car parks are spaces of ontological failure in the book – piazzas without community, overlays without the beauty of art – an art of the real that is confronting and deadly in its aesthetic implications): 'So many other days have gone without a trace … I was right, she thought, all those years never to come back here. Here I can only ever be a child of the house.' And Anna wants to be the child of no one – she longs for a control she can't attain, for a partner who will support but not challenge her (the males in this book work intentionally as 'ciphers',

6 Gorton, *The Life*, p. 179.
7 Gorton, *The Life*, p. 184.

and even Scott, who is shaded and textured, distresses gender embodiments), but she reaches an endgame in a motel room in her old town with a prospective partner who has essentially been neutralised by the imploding vastness of the space that emanates out of and around Sea House (though he has not been there).

Tracy has just emailed me a chunk of an article that was run in the *Sydney Morning Herald*. The first quote says,

> She's [Gorton] not so much interested in telling a straightforward story as in constructing spaces: houses, rooms, places where people search for a self that is not just based on how others see them, and where they shape their lives by a series of actions and reactions that turn out to have consequences. 'I was wanting to work with a prose style that was very mixed up: memory and perception always jumping in and out of what you'd call action in a plot.'[8]

I'd agree with this, but would add that narrative is actually a series of spaces the reader negotiates along with character/s. In some senses, this is a meticulously constructed engagement with narratorial spaces. The house becomes the body becomes the story. Shelter is inseparable from movement: we move from shelter to shelter. We polysituate ourselves with each sheltering, each space of sleeping and contemplation of our situation and condition. Even when we have lost liberty and are forced into spaces of habitation, they become our *points de repère*. This is a novel about abandoned and lost points in life-narratives, and points that are impending or latent (but always active in themselves). The story of Anna and Kit, mother and daughter, is one of reconciling these disparate elements in the spatial narrative: a reconciliation that is like forcing the same polarities of a magnet together. They repel for all the (material) properties, all the embodiedness they share. The constructed spaces collapse and make a vacuum, which is the result of all colonial enterprises. Figuratively speaking, I am reminded of the music of Einstürzende Neubauten ('Collapsing New Buildings') and their wry-beautiful, even strangely disturbing lyric, 'The Garden': 'You'll find me if you want me in the garden/ unless it's pouring down with rain'. I see Patrick looking into the house. I see Kit stepping out of the window of her mother's childhood bedroom into the early morning light before the others are up. To encounter Patrick. To encounter the failure and energy of the past. Room by room.

Further, in another snippet of the *Sydney Morning Herald* article, it says of Lisa Gorton,

> It was during that time [during her postgraduate studies on Donne at Oxford] her fascination with rooms and spaces developed further: 'I love the way Donne plays with space. He has people imagined in rooms set in the cosmos and then he flips

---

8 Jane Sullivan, 'Lisa Gorton: Prize-winning poet writes her first novel', *Sydney Morning Herald*, 18 April 2015.

them inside out.' Donne was writing at a time when the new cosmology was throwing everything into doubt: 'We have these brief astounding lives and it's so overwhelming we have to set up structures for ourselves. Rooms are a way to imagine emotional structures like habits.'

Yes, I can see this in *The Life of Houses*. But the rooms of this book are vulnerable and bothered even in their certainties. The new cosmology is also in the mobile phone and in the fetishisation of art, of God. The house is not the teleology you expect when you first encounter it. It is more blurred than the specificity of the writing admits. In the same way that the most acute descriptions entangle with the haunting generic, so the house is simultaneously vague and specific, realist and abstract, as are the lives that pass through its rooms. When Michael Dransfield wrote of his obsessively necessarily imagined 'Courland Penders: going home':[9] 'The gale outside anthems a dead family', I find the anxieties that tread the halls of this novel. It is a work of archetypes shifting on their foundations, of the animus and the anima struggling to assert themselves with neither able to force itself into the space, into the co-ordinates of what constitutes 'place' and its collapse.

9 *Michael Dransfield: A Retrospective*, selected by John Kinsella (St Lucia, University of Queensland Press, 2002), p. 17.

INEVITABILITY AND SEARCHING IN JOHN MATEER'S *ELSEWHERE*

The persona behind these poems is a wanderer, and is indeed ghostlike, making small witnessings as he goes – even in his home-place – which pass through him, leaving a residue of loss, even pain, though often too degrees of love. The poet's persona is a thing of emptiness that craves to be filled but must always remain bereft. Even poems that celebrate friendship, and celebrate the strength of resistance against imprisonment, oppression and a litany of human wrongdoing, still convey a sense of the loss this process of witnessing must bring.

Poems for Mateer are not cathartic but inevitable. Though his poems express themselves clearly and concisely, noting observations of human behaviour communally and socially, there are also the private individual moments glimpsed and refracted through the wanderer-poet-ghost. For example, a street kid or a prostitute or a white uncle and aunt who inflect the trauma of white colonisation in South Africa, or the tourist held up in a toilet block without surveillance, bitten on the shoulder by someone in 'this land of AIDS'.

The achievement of Mateer's verse is that he has the art of the storyteller but also an intense lyrical interiority that brings us close to both the experience being witnessed and the persona doing the witnessing. That doesn't mean we're necessarily reading Mateer himself, of course, but it does give a sense of great humanity.

As the poet wanders the globe in search of the meaning of the poet's role, and ultimately in search of redemption in humanity, he focuses an acutely local eye on what he sees. By this I mean he is not appropriative of local custom and identity, but rather attempts to become a conduit for witnessing and even experiencing the uniqueness of any given place. Having said this, he can also be bitingly satirical towards those who hold the cultural and political capital, and how these are used to deprive others of their own heritage and rights of place. In a remarkable sequence of poems on the culling of elephants, Mateer manages both an elegy for the loss of elephants themselves and their complex social interactions, and the creation of a non-diminishing analogy for the broader condition of the oppressor and the oppressed.

One of the vibrant and deeply intelligent characteristics of Mateer's verse, even in bleaker moments, is the revitalising nature of words themselves. He comfortably switches between English and languages of location, but this shouldn't necessarily be seen as a celebration of the power of language to redeem; in fact, quite often in the case of Afrikaans the language carries an ominous weight that is almost invasive – as does English itself. Rather, language can ironise its own terms of production and allow us to see the faults in those who use it, including the poet himself.[1]

It should be said, though, that there are also moments of great linguistic beauty, where friendship, place, experience and words themselves light up and almost synaesthetically become one. Mateer has also made himself a master of the line – he paces the line perfectly. He judges exactly when to end a line, when to enjamb, and when to break the stanza. In many ways, he is a formalist using a whole variety of prosodic techniques, but his crossing between language and place inevitably invests the English he primarily uses with a new energy. This energy isn't just for pleasure, but is political. It implores the reader to follow 'him' into these witnessings.

Don't for a moment think that these are travelogue poems – they couldn't be if they tried. The persona behind these poems feels too much of the pain, and even more than that, fears the possibility of ennui. He desires love, though is not always sure of its presence; he celebrates the body and its sexuality but is always hesitant in exploring these. This hesitancy is what brings a trust to the reader of the poems; they are never lascivious.

I should say that there is also a searching spirituality at work here. At times you feel as if some inner peace has been arrived at, but then the doubt overwhelms. In seeing a truth, we find, to quote one poem: 'The translated man I am is becoming numerical: *zero, ok.*'

It would be a mistake to read this persona across *Elsewhere*[2] as consistent and the same traveller-ghost in every poem – he is not. He transforms and transmutes – even though in many ways the external observer, he always absorbs a bit of the place he is in, which alters him. Then there's the haunting intelligence which leads to the inevitable ironising of his own condition. Irony becomes his survival technique, the only way he can get through the trauma of this witnessing.

In the final section of the book we are in the Americas. His harshest insights are there at the centre of empire; 'after the eagle has sprung to the Astroturf', we join the eagle as empire inevitably draws us all to its centre. From America to Mexico, the final poem of the book, which is in the voice of the drug smuggler (as Holy Ghost), the final line is 'Wherever there is commerce I Am There'; the harshest judgement is reserved for the poet-wanderer-ghost-witness himself. This is also part of his persona, as inevitably all witnessings involve vicarious

---

1 This paragraph also appears in John Kinsella, *Spatial Relations, Volume 1*, ed. Gordon Collier (Amsterdam and New York, Rodopi, 2013).
2 John Mateer, *Elsewhere* (Cambridge, Salt, 2007).

participation. He does not depict himself as standing outside the problems. There is no sense of the holier-than-thou in this book, and this is what makes Mateer one of the most genuinely ethical, sincere and visionary of poets.

The title of the book is so telling. Whenever we are not 'at home', we are elsewhere.[3] And yet home for Mateer is one place and many. The book has made me realise how often the concept of elsewhere in so much other writing is an evasion of the responsibilities of respecting each and every place we pass through. The word 'elsewhere' as it is generally and generically used seems so dismissive, but in the context of Mateer's poems is so strongly evocative of the diverse threads that make up all of us, and our responsibilities towards each other. Elsewhere is also a marker of a non-interaction in terms of origins and belonging, a restlessness and angst, and an ongoing examination of what constitutes familiar space/s and where and how we might appropriately (or not) enter those spaces. This movement has not always been straightforward or comfortable for Mateer, and tensions have on occasion resulted from his searching (see Kim Scott's argument with Mateer's work in *Kayang and me* [South Fremantle, Fremantle Press, 2005]). Sometimes our consciousness of our polysituatedness is generative, at other times (self)conflicting, even paradoxical. It's an observational and awareness process/ing, not a methodology.

---

3 We might venture into Augé's *Non-Places* here: 'Certainly the European, Western "here" assumes its full meaning in relation to the distant elsewhere – formerly "colonial", now "underdeveloped" – favoured in the past by British and French anthropology' (Marc Augé, *Non-Places: An Introduction to Supermodernity*, trans. John Howe [London and New York, Verso, 2008], p. 9). Augé's 'defence' of Europe as a site of anthropology is disturbing to me (though his argument is more complex than it may seem), and one might think it would be to Mateer, reading through *Elsewhere*. To my mind, the inside-out status of the colonial subject in a Euro-colonised space necessitates a language of slippage in both recognising the privilege arising for one of colonial heritage in the context of the colonial 'enterprise', and a desire to counteract that through confession and articulation of that privilege. 'Elsewhere' in the decolonising desire of the non-other in Western (post-) colonialist discourse is positioning the self as other-by-proxy, and that is its paradox. Returning (tangentially, again) to Augé, it is useful to hear, 'In Western societies, at least, the individual wants to be a world in himself; he intends to interpret the information delivered to him by himself and for himself' (p. 30). Augé's struggle with what it is (or what he desires) to be a Western subject occludes the fact of the self as the maker of art out of self-accumulated information. This is the poem. And this is what one probably needs to resist – himself, herself, or outside the gender binary!

TALES OF PLACE: BARBARA TEMPERTON'S
SOUTHERN EDGE

Barbara Temperton is interested in where folklore and folktales intersect with fact, reportage and place (and their spatial geographies). She has taken tales come out of specific locations –especially around Albany and the surrounding coastline – and merged the figurative and the narrative. She tells tales in verse, but that is not all she does – she shifts the stories, language and locations of these tales to make them much more than the sum of their parts. In *Folk and Fairy Tales: A Handbook*,[1] D. L. Ashliman looks at why 'we tell stories' under the following headings: 'fantasy wish fulfilment', 'expression of fears and taboos', 'explanation' and 'education'. One might add more than this to the list, certainly in the case of Barbara Temperton's reinvigoration of the form, but in essence these aspects are all present in the three stories told in *Southern Edge*.[2]

Before progressing, it should be noted that 'Southern Edge' refers literally to the coastline that looks down on Antarctica, though we read that land and sea, indeed body and sea (and nature in general) are interconnected and fluid. Each of the characters in the three narratives that make up the book flow in and out of the seascape and landscape to varying degrees. The narrative voices also flow in and out of the stories. In the second story, 'The Gap', which refers to probably the best-known coastal feature in the south-west, the male narrator charts his relationship of addiction in terms of love, obsession, admiration and drug addiction with Julz, a junkie who is also, in essence, a free spirit. It's a perverse freedom, though, as her talismanic and shamanistic exchange with the natural world comes at a great cost – to her and to the young male narrator. Woven through the story are reportages of loss extracted from local newspapers, signs and other sources, that set the tale against a background of fact. In a dreamlike montage of events and moods, the stories of Everyperson are reflected through the love story of Julz and the narrator.

---

1 D. L. Ashliman, *Folk and Fairy Tales: A Handbook* (Westport, CT, Greenwood, 2004).
2 Barbara Temperton, *Southern Edge: three stories in verse* (North Fremantle, Fremantle Press, 2009).

This technique is also at work in the other two narratives, each of which relies on the other in their telling. Julz, whose living and isolation spread across the folkloric space, is a form of natural bridge in one sense, but also the froth and foam of the never-ending crush of the water within the gap. I don't say this lightly – in Temperton's book the oneness of the elements and characters is absolute. And those who are outside this merging are ciphers. Julz is archetypal female renegade free spirit who even affirms the feminine in the male farmer-fisherboy narrator figure. This figure is an unreliable narrator, as we shift outside and around his viewpoint at times, in an eclogic way.

Moving back from the centre to the beginning, 'The Lighthouse Keeper's Wife', we also find a shamanistic figure in the lighthouse keeper, mostly absent from the narrative but omnipresent in the mood of the piece. Reversing the vulnerability of such positions, this is the God-like figure who controls the elements, including his wife. She, in her loneliness of kerosene tins and domestic duties in isolation, reaches out for others. Her need for love is ultimately defined by the sea, though, and indeed, by extension, her husband. Her escapes are illusory.

In fact, each of the tales is tragic in this way – the characters are not able to find the liberation they seek, trapped by their own emotions and by the natural world of which they are part. The lighthouse keeper is the magician who controls the sea but not his wife on one level, but ultimately neither escapes from the 'roles' that the sea has forced on them. Even one of the wife's lovers, Knut, who loves and leaves her, will come back to her in the context of an elemental death: he will remember her as his life flashes past him in the pocket of air in an overturned boat far away. What the lighthouse keeper's wife searches for is unfindable but paradoxically archetypically present.

The final tale in the book takes us to the Kimberley, but ultimately back to the southern edge as we follow the 'traveller' in his escape from himself and the forces of 'nature' embodied in the bird woman. A psychosexual drama of denial, it confronts us with the uncertainty of responsibility for a crime which the traveller might or might not have committed. The tale is montaged through a variety of prosodies and narrative techniques. We are intimately inside the seeing and experiencing of the (male) traveller, his observations of the bird woman, his sexual confusion and frustration and inevitable 'consummation', shifting to witness statement, through to fragments of narrative and imagery driven by journeying south – from the scene of the crime – that implicate elements of the earlier stories, 'The Lighthouse Keeper's Wife' and 'The Gap'. The merging of fluids – sexual fluids, blood, the ocean (the body of the bird woman literally melts into the ocean only held together by a cloak – she is like a bird killed by an environmental disaster – she has been polluted) – blurs the boundaries between cause and effect, between land and sea, between crime and folklore.

We are able to accept even the most horrendous crime as symbol and tale when it recedes into the past and is told and retold through symbol, allusion and archetypes. That's how community absorbs the distressing and the disturbing. These tales are about women, about the isolation, the vulnerabilities and strengths, the archetypal feminine, and the mythologies of the female body and its oneness with the earth, water and air. Temperton is not interested only in critiquing or verifying such mythologies, but in investigating how and why stories like this are told. The work is very sensitive and highly attuned. Its presentations of gender are complex in that male and female are defined so clearly, are counterpointed, and yet they blur in terms of time and the elements.

Barbara Temperton has managed that rare thing, finding a methodology to present stories in verse that are also mosaics of impression and intimate observation of specific places. She has a pinpointing eye for local detail and can actually make her characters seem real although mythological. She manages to finely balance sexual menace and sexual joy – the undercurrent of sexual threat as cautionary tale is at the basis of so many folk stories. Our sense of time is altered and the stories themselves become timeless. And yet the details are so specific to time and place. That's a skill. It might be Bald Head near Albany, or 'an old Morris mounted on blocks' or a detail as clinically specific (for the witness statement) as the 'Northern/Southern Hemispheres Bird Migration Study'. Great care has been paid to lineation – the lines vary from pared-back imagistic glimpses to longer prose-poem-like flowings in which the story is told at a steady pace.

The overwhelming feeling this book left me with was that loss is a trauma we tell stories to overcome. The bird woman was about to leave the traveller as she'd finished her project, and the reader is shocked by what ensues. Either way, the traveller's loss is given focus, not as an excuse but as a vehicle for the way stories might be told. In 'The Gap', the narrator is left stranded between his ideal of Julz and the brute reality of the situation, and the lighthouse keeper's wife tragically never escapes her isolation but her longings remain so intense that she wishes to destroy her singing, her voice, to, in essence, stop 'telling' the tale:

> Kerosene smudges everything
> with its hazy-blue skin,
> is the lighthouse's other tenant,
> always present, never seen,
> a bitter layer on the lips
> after she kissed her husband's hand.
>
> Remembering the children's dog
> barking until its voice was gone,
> she wonders how long she could scream
> before she would not make another sound.[3]

The irony is that each of these tales needs to be told – needs to account for all the tales of pain that could not be told by those who experienced them. This is how story and poetry can become universal.

---

3 From 'The Lighthouse Keeper's Wife', in *Southern Edge*, p. 36.

ON *CONTEMPORARY ASIAN AUSTRALIAN POETS*[1]

This is one of the more vital, relevant and significant anthologies of poetry to appear in Australia, and as such makes its mark in any consideration of conversation around place/s coming *out of* Australia. It has been compiled with a purpose as sophisticated and complex as the arguments for existence that it posits. It is an anthology not so much of 'region' (it's a massive region!) as of the experience of being or having been from Asian heritages in contemporary Australia.

I am not going to consider closely the issues of compiling poetry ethnologies, but I will say that as long as readers insist on rubrics such as 'Australian' through which to focus their desire to read place, identity and culture, then collections of work that challenge the ethnocentricities of such national labelling will be required and inevitable. In the case of an Australia over-identified with Western 'civilising' and subjectivity, to signify Europe in national discussion will necessarily create and get a response from all *others*. That's a given for me. We have to challenge the edifice in as many ways as possible, especially when the edifice claims to represent 'all' but doesn't. Not that many of these poets aren't well-represented elsewhere – they are – but here there is a community of poetry that is comfortable with articulating itself as such.

Contemporary Asian Australian Poets analyses and presents ways of viewing the deeply personal and concomitant social manifestations of 'self' within an idea of place. I say an idea of place because wherever you are physically located is the result of not only your own histories of presence and movement, but also those of many. And the 'many' are not only your 'own people', but those who pre-date you, and those who are there when you arrive. How those arriving respond to their new homes depends on both the welcome they receive (and how supported they are in 'adapting' to their new home) and the damage that's been done in leaving their previous homes.

1 Adam Aitken, Kim Cheng Boey and Michelle Cahill (eds), *Contemporary Asian Australian Poets* (Sydney, Puncher and Wattman, 2013).

As well as the Preface, written as 'we', this anthology carries three short introductions by the editors, Adam Aitken, Kim Cheng Boey and Michelle Cahill. All are concise, assertive and generous. In creating a space for Asian Australian poetry, the editors refuse solely to walk the liminal line between a Eurocentric Australia and the many Asian countries of origin or heritage to, through, and out of which the contributors write. Rather, they show perceived liminalities to be centres in themselves. It is a testament not only to the skill of the editors, but also to the poets included, that few fall into nostalgia or the very debilitating nostalgic 'race memory' one finds in many anthologies that equate nation with ethnicity. Kim Cheng Boey writes of the Perth (!) poet Ee Tiang Hong, 'His poems resist the sentimental backward look; they are an attempt to yoke disparate locations and cultures together in a new mapping of self and place.' Yes, precisely – in many ways, a poet's calling. It's terrific to see a selection of Ee Tiang Hong's poetry here – we don't hear enough of him, with his 'strange' and varied voice.

Of course there *is* often a sense of loss, especially in the work of those driven from their originating spaces by war, oppression and cultural conflict. But any centre's desire for gratitude at 'taking on' the oppressed can be as damaging and debilitating as the cause of those oppressed 'leaving' in the first place. This book is intense with leavings and arrivals, but also with modes of retaining contact and connection. That is the nature of heritage, family and language. Although it's an English-language anthology, there are more than residues in many of its poets' linguistic memories.

In choosing to be part of this anthology, some poets will necessarily be making a statement of collective refusal to be othered in Australia; but maybe more, there's a collective statement of sharing and communalism. After all, one country of heritage isn't another, any more than one religion another, or one province another, and so on. Geography and cultural narratives make for complex arrangements of borders – forever shifting and fluctuating – but whether the precedents and antecedents are Iranian or Filipino, Chinese or Indian, patterns of interaction and familiarity built over long periods of time attest to a collectivity as much as any notions of a West (which I'd argue is actually a military construct as much as any binary East).

Adam Aitken, a brilliant poet and one of the sharpest thinkers on poetry and (post-)colonialism around, 'lightly' observes, 'Embedded in transnational connections, the Asian-Australian is no more certain of self definition than any other kind of Australian.' The anthologist, and indeed the poet and the reader, constantly risks creating bathos out of sincerity, out of a personal need to articulate the difference they think a reader might expect in their work as 'other'. All poets are 'other'. Aitken notes, 'In Nguyen Tiên Hoàng's poems about Vietnam, which he left after the end of the war, Vietnam is not the topos found in popular Australian cookery books and travel shows.' He continues by pointing out 'that the concept of "the Vietnamese" is a contestable category'. Indeed. As is every category of nation and national identity. Belonging is subjective as much as by the demands of family and community.

In a work of such sensitivity to issues of categorising and (mis)representing, it will come as no surprise that the elucidating of power games around positioning the 'migrant' in the new home-space will be extended to women's position as both migrant and often marginalised voice/s. Michelle Cahill's introduction affirms and notes the power of language to bind as much as liberate women within male paradigms, and works out of a crisis of the 'materiality of women's labour and the limitations of patriarchal spaces [which] marginalise women within the body as text' to a generative poetics of great agency.

Singling out poets and poems from this superb volume might seem in some ways counter to the intent behind the work, though the editors list and discuss attributes, similarities and differences of many. But some of my favourite poets have work in here, including the lingua-cultural dialogics of Merlinda Bobis and an investigative Ouyang Yu, the latter with samples of work less acerbic than he often writes (though maybe this is good, because it's too easy to say Ouyang Yu is acerbic – the 'accusation' can be a reductive ploy).

But this is not an acerbic book – it's not an attack on the centre as much as an intelligent and firm but polite contesting and affirmation. There are fine, probing poems of controlled irony, and testings of identity and belonging, such as in Jaya Savige's stunning 'Currency Lad', Shen's almost bitter re- and de-culturalisation 'Noodles', and Misbah Khokhar's matter-of-fact declaration of intactness, anti-violence and sexual agency in 'Veils of Flags'. But at times I wish there was more 'anger' across the book. I was taken by Subash Jaireth's poem 'Meena, the Elephant, in the Kabul Zoo' because of its quiet fury and deconstructive deployment of the cover of Les Murray's *Collected Poems* which finishes:

> As if
> to complete the picture
> a girl as young as the one
> on the cover of Les Murray's book
> walked in the evening.
>
> She fetched
> water from the river
> flowers from the field
> and after taking off
> her Jaipuri-legs
> sat on the ground
> kneeling against the elephant's back.
>
> That is when
> I imagine
> the man with the camera
> decided to shoot.[2]

2 Aitken, Boey and Cahill (eds), *Contemporary Asian Australian Poets*, p. 133.

On the other hand, identifying 'food' as a thing of security and commonality, of heritage and comfort, seems problematical. Indeed, there are many 'food' poems in this book, but all humans identify with eating, and very often with the modes of food preparation and the (especially) familial bonds and patterns around this. To make claim for something extraordinary runs the risk of appeasing 'Australia's' fetishisation of food as identity. But it's a fraught issue, and one I concede has as many fors as againsts.

This anthology apparently started life as a thematic collation before ending up in alphabetical order, which works well because it emphasises connections and disparities without imposing a reading of place that is necessarily artificial and constraining.[3]

---

3 I particularly enjoyed the fortunate juxtaposition of the prose poems of Misbah Khokhar and Bella Li.

ON THE POETRY OF JANET MCADAMS

Janet McAdams's first volume of poetry, *The Island of Lost Luggage,*[1] was a vital, prize-winning book that explored self and identity, social and personal issues, with a honed political lyricism, while the poems in her second volume, *Feral,*[2] were even 'bolder' and more expansive in their tackling of disjunctions (especially of the relationship between humans/self and earth/place).

The tensions between humans and nature, and how close or distant they might be or might have become, resonate through McAdams's work. Her voice is always politically active, but never polemical – language lives for her, and she lets language evoke and stimulate the reader's response to whatever social issue or mythology or observation of place or familial relationships she is considering. She is also a very 'modern' poet, and comfortable with 'popular culture', but never without some irony when juxtaposing it with 'tradition' and 'nature'. She is a poet of many angles.

McAdams is also an accomplished technician. In much of her poetry of the last few years, cumulative fragments and sequential structures are mixed with 'complete' single-section poems that are contained and finely controlled. On a technical level, in building cumulative mini-narratives in her sequences, she is allowing voice to move in and out of metaphor – the work is both figurative and engaged with a questioning unified self or 'voice'. This allows the 'real world' – and a hard political reality it can be – to merge and shift through more timeless mythical narratives. The writing is deftly handled, and quite exciting in its subtle experimentation: in some ways, subtle experimentation is the most radical experimentation. The use of anaphora and other devices of statement and refrain builds a mesmeric and sometimes quietly terrifying picture. This is balanced by a gentle poise – a deeply humane and interested interaction with complex emotional, spiritual and cultural issues. There is great warmth and

---

1 Janet McAdams, *The Island of Lost Luggage* (Tucson, University of Arizona Press, 2000).
2 Janet McAdams, *Feral* (Cambridge, Salt, 2007).

sympathy in her work, regardless of how concerned and confrontational she is over an (always deeply relevant and significant) issue. The intrusion of a dream-like voice frees the poems, and allows transcendence no matter how disturbing imagery and fact might be.

On the level of cultural significance, her poems are remarkable in their generative and 'positive' hybridity – they move between cultures, and while they critique the dominant and colonising culture, they do not imprison the colonised voice in any way. In McAdams, cultures meet and breathe. Her Native American heritage mixed with European ancestral concerns allows her both to participate and to stand outside. Her most recent work relating to her proposed projects is exciting because it explores issues of family and issues of movement of peoples (or a people): the family as still point, as centre, juxtaposed to the journey.

Janet McAdams's new poetry shows significant departures. Though she is still developing investigations of her upbringing in the American South (and her relationship to her new home in the American Midwest), and building on her work of combining glimpses, narrative, snapshots and imagistic distillations of events and experiences, in sequential forms and interconnected poems, she has stepped outside America and begun looking at issues of witness, experience, horror and interrogation as an 'outsider'. The question becomes one of how different sufferings inform each other, how the poet (how we all) have a collective responsibility for noting these wrongs. In a remarkable set of new prose poems, *Seven Boxes for the Country After* (Wick Poetry Series, Kent State University Press, 2016), the self, the 'other', the body, objects, experience, history, witness, sharing and loss, all cross-talk: questions are asked, and asked again. Another's story becomes a means of survival: to tell, to listen … to share and exchange. McAdams has said of this work, 'The poems move between a kind of hyper-awareness of the surveillance state (think Foucault's panopticon) and the possibility of a magically real "country after".'[3] Here's one of the poems from the cumulative whole:

> If white is the color of mischief, then these white walls, this little house of marble we hide behind, willing the man with his notebook to find someone else to follow. We hide, kin to bone, to tuft of fur caught in the chain-link fence, to everything under the snow: tooth, grass, a skunk's belly bloated and facing heaven. If earth, then ground and the body it blanketed. If winter, then salt to eat the rubber from your boots, to sting skin already cracked and weeping. skin, that blue edge between weather and the bodies we used to carry. Didn't we hope something else might rise from the snow and rock us to sleep? rock us long past the dreaming of what we had lost.

---

3 Private email correspondence, 7 October 2016.

a confrontation with the now, and with memory. How we record our loss, how we note the changes imposed. The pressure for answers is remorseless as we struggle to define ourselves, even in the 'country', even in our relationships, even with our 'selves': 'Is this your notebook? Do you take notes? What did you write / down? How many did you influence? Where did you lie? / Where do you sleep?' another of the poems asks. The reader, accompanying the 'we', 'you', 'she' and other modes of identifying, also comes under surveillance through the implication of the breached privacy of the poem read, the making public of what is already known by covert presences. The poems are remarkably unsettling and activist in this. The sequence finishes with the 'declaration': 'They take until we are tender as babies, until we have nothing left to declare.' And thus in our innocent vulnerability, we are eaten by the machine of the state (which can by rural and urban, outdoors and indoors, approving and disapproving of love) in a Swiftian irony that leaves us devastated. It is the 'soft touch' of these taut, compacted prose poems that's so effective.

Can an 'outsider' share, become a conduit for loss and pain? What relationship does the listener's own story have when weighed against this? McAdams's is a poetry in which cultural growth and even forms of reconciliation might take place, in which place and its 'history' do more than become artefacts for Western capitalist delectation.

PART V

Emplacement

CORTHNA, CARRAIGLEA, ANCHOR LODGE – FROM SCHULL JOURNALS

5 October 2013

Back to the Corthna house after a day of preliminary 'exploring' of the Mizen Head, Sheep's Head and the pass into County Kerry. There's a stench of oil fumes through the house. I can taste it in my mouth, it's sharp to the eyes, and is causing severe headaches. It's a disgrace. We're searching for another house. We love the area, though the radar domes (bombed by the IRA in the 1970s) on Mount Gabriel, highest point on the Mizen, cast a shadow over the area. We are 5 km away from them here. They infiltrate one's nights and days. And now toxic slurry is being spread across the fields, flooding the house to conjoin with the oil fumes, penetrating every cell of this house, even saturating the linen. We feel invaded.

Pastoral pointillism. Raddled sheep near pass.
Irish verse form: 4 × 7 syllables. A poem of mine in this register:

Graphology Peninsulas 1 (West Cork): Irish verse forms

The signal towers shone bright
Then fog extinguished their light;
What every signaller dreads,
Between Brow and Mizen Heads.

8 October 2013

Looked at various houses yesterday and today. Only one that appealed – it is perched out on rocks overlooking Roaringwater Bay and on to the west side of Long Island, on the Colla Road just outside Schull. Quite small and 'let go', but unique and magnetic. It's popular with visitors who come back year in year out, but it's not one for long-term living as we are planning. Still, as I sit here in the lounge at Corthna being gassed-out by the oil fume stench, it seems a pretty good option!

Apparently, a 'Booker-shortlisted novel' and a 'couple of PhDs' were written or completed there. It's called Carraiglea, which is appropriate given its rocky foundations. Seals, dolphins, otters and even a whale have been seen from there. Undoubtedly a place of poems … but … something doesn't quite click for me. I am not sure what it is. We'd be compressed into a small space – with a magnificent view (the 'feature' window is massive!) and admittedly the kind of spatial constraint that can be creative … Still not sure.

12 October 2013

In Carraiglea – relief from the poison at Corthna (the house from hell)! Carraiglea has many (functional) problems but is the most beautiful situation you'd ever imagine. On a rocky promontory overlooking the bay. Opposite Long Island and the mouth of Schull harbour, adjacent to Otter Point. Briar, heather, gorse and bracken surround the house, extending along the rugged coast. Paths have been cut in three places on the block down to the sandstone rock-pools. Hedge birds, sea birds and rich aquatic life, especially anemones in the rock-pools. Am reading Gerard Manley Hopkins and John Donne in the evenings because they are the least mouldy books on the shelves.

13 October 2013

Mid-morning. Sun breaking through cloud in patches. Tracy did some rereading and revision work last night and I watched a DVD that was in the drawer – *Mona Lisa* with Bob Hoskins, which I've seen before. Now Tracy is having a shower and Tim is reading his World Countries facts book in the living room. He and I have been memorising poems for our 'on the rocks' readings we plan to do daily. He recited a Langston Hughes poem yesterday and I recited a Blake. We move to Anchor Lodge next Monday. It's expensive but we hope it will be a longer-term solution to the housing issue. Carraiglea is a great bolt-hole for ten days. I want to do a series of poems (more 'Winter Let' poems), on the amateur paintings on the walls here and their unusual history. But I am interested in the paintings *per se* more than their (still fascinating and essential) biographies. One of them I'd like to use as the cover of this book I am writing. From its position at the wall, it looks at us and then out through the triptych of glass that makes up the feature window/s, and across to the beacon on the northern tip of Long Island. Speaking of beacons, we can look across the bay to Baltimore in the distance and see the 'famous' and massive 'white beacon' when the light is right.

In the bracken-thorns-heath-gorse there are so many birds. Skylarks, pied wagtails, meadow pippits, stonechats, goldfinches and reed buntings.

Evening. Went up to Gougane Barra in the mountains. Up through the pass. Also to the Gaeltacht town of Ballingeary. Will go again soon!

14 October 2013

The bay is rippled with a slick-like stillness spread with tidal movement over channels forming coronas around islands and coastline. The play of depth and breeze and tide. Not like the thin expanding oilslick we saw yesterday after a trawler went out. Clearing weather today. Sun out, little chunks of cloud. Tracy teaching Tim maths and German. I had to go to Corthna to find a missing pair of my boots – the house was still enfumed and I have a headache now. Saw Old Pat out front dealing with the bins, which had not been emptied yet. I wrote him the 'Massey-Ferguson Tractor' poem in his honour (a poem of tractors in Cork and tractors of my childhood in Western Australia) – he drives his tractor everywhere (as farmers do here into town to the shops). He said I could have a drive (though I didn't). Might read some of Sinclair Lewis's *Arrowsmith* later (bought it with a bunch of other books from the excellent Whyte Books in Schull).

15 October 2013

Rough weather at Carraiglea.

Gannets.

Small boats doing it rough traversing the bay.

Binoculars (on the ledge before the feature window/s).

Tim will start school on Thursday. Went up to meet the principal yesterday. Tough woman who sized us up.

Wind howling. Nightmares. Probably out of the Famine stories/history. As Tracy says, 'The bones howl here.' Hopkins felt 'exiled' (his complex relationship with Ireland through St Patrick) here but I don't. I feel connected. He wrote in sonnet 44: 'I am in Ireland now; now I am at a third/ Remove.'

Evening. Blowing hard outside. Waves breaking over the rocks – red sandstone, slate slabs angled out from the coast to confront the sea, weathered away to sharp if brittle lines. And water sliding back out into the bay through the polished sluices.

Thinking about Jam Tree Gully and John's 'Guru Reports'. The final Jam Tree Gully volume, JTG4, will be a concrete/concretion, visualised book. I am seeing it from here in my mind's eye and through John's eyes as he looks it over.

16 October 2013

Graphology Peninsulas 2

In some ways it's easier
to know your ancestors
than your living relatives.

Bright sunny morning. Rewriting local myths.

7 pm. Moon full and really close – over the bay, entering Carraiglea. Through the binoculars, it is precise and intense – the pole, impact craters, the complex of landforms. Almost there!

Full Moon Over Long Island Bay

The moon is frighteningly close.
Things are going to be pulled apart.
Tim is watching a DVD about meteor
impacts and is worried about Apophis
but we tell him it has already passed.
This doesn't alleviate the tension.
The moon sucks at the bay
and we can see the water
curl towards impact craters.
I have the binoculars out and give
a running report. The bay will undergo
a name change and people will forget
what it was like before this event.
And I am not the same person
writing this minutes later,
taken away by the eyes,
my old self, already changeling,
welded to glass, the moon, the bay.

17 October 2013

Almost finished sorting the fume house at Corthna. We get sicker every time we enter. Fortunately, because Tim started school today we have managed to get the cleaning etc. done. Tim will be wearing the St Brendan The Navigator emblem on his shirt. All water imagery here!

The boatmen empty and reset their lobster traps every morning out in the bay – including just out from Carraiglea (which gives us trauma). The gulls swarm about them and their boats. We are told that if fishermen don't see a car at Carraiglea they sometimes beach their boats or pull up alongside the rocks and come ashore. The evidence: 'cooked' crustacean shells on the rocks. They picnic in the wake of their efforts.

18 October 2013

Wild weather. Gale-force winds. Rains. Choppy seas.

The visitors' book here includes a list in a number of different hands of the flora and fauna of the place. A poem will come of this, as it must.

Tim's second day at school. Gulls hanging in the high winds.

Those against (or failing to comprehend the politics of) détournement are often ethno-plagiarists. They are happy to talk of 'race' and describe characters in ethno-stereotypical ways but cry foul when 'found' or 'strategically' positioned external text appears in the flow of 'original' writing.

Drafting a short poem on anemones. Thinking about the lobster man who plunders just off Carraiglea...

The Lobster Man

Who daily pulls his pots
from the seafloor just off Otter Point
through to Croagh Bay in the television
of this great feature window –
his bird crew ghosting
his at-peace-with-himself moves –
the quick and the dead,
the golden apples,
the dead cannons,
the faded cartographers
clawed from plumbing the depths.
Sometimes he lands on the rocks
just down from the house
when he thinks we're out,
the silent window a mirror.
He crunches cooked lobsters
from his mid-morning lunchbox,
burlesque in his yellow oilskins,
stretched braces bold as brass,
tossing shells to the ghosts.

19 October 2013

Poem on the Baltimore Beacon. They call it Lot's Wife.
The sun illuminates Lot's wife... or The sun lights up Lot's wife...

20 October 2013

Went out to the wedge tomb at Altar, which is about 10 km from here by road. Looks on to the Mizen and fierce seas. Slabs enlichened and mossed.

We leave here for Anchor Lodge in town tomorrow. Prefer to be here at Carraiglea.

Distressed by the 'state of poetry', especially in Australia. The triumph of the state-ists, the gatekeepers. They need unpicking and the whole edifice of good, proper and 'talented' art brought down. It reinforces the police state and most participants in this can't see it. I will quote at least one non-attributed line of Bill Burroughs in all novels I write. I like to think he'd want it this way. I recall swapping faxes with him in 1994 – he wrote in letters almost as large as the width of fax paper.

21 October 2013

Moving from Carraiglea to Anchor Lodge today. Full of regret at leaving. Will miss the proximity of the sea (we are almost in it), though we'll only be a couple of blocks from the harbour/pier at Anchor Lodge.

Finished *Arrowsmith* yesterday. A morally repugnant book though it does show the selfish self-obsessiveness of 'scientists' and the ultimately anti-humane nature of science, regardless of Lewis's intent. Knowledge does not have to be science. Then again, in some ways, I feel I'm an (anti-)scientist of figurative language – I like data, details, proof (and come out of working in laboratories and working scientifically throughout my teenage years). But in the end I think the unprovable more necessary. Maybe that's where I lapse into a 'nihilistic' metaphysics. I doubt it, though – poetry is built for and out of contradiction. But the activist can never lose sight of the data, the materials of the issue.

23 October 2013

Have settled into Anchor Lodge. It is enormous, characterless (though it could grow on one) but very clean. We miss Carraiglea. Returning there for a stay in January. Tim still loving school. I am planning a version of *The Táin*. I am reading Thomas Kinsella's version and also Ciaran Carson's version.

Evening. Thinking about Shelley vs. The Táin – the MTV version. Or Medb VS Mab!

Compiled a rough version of the *Marine* manuscript – working around Alan Jenkins's poems, injecting my selection around his. Have now sent to him for a working-through. Working on a new Lacaussade translation for *Marine*.

Tracy and Tim working on Tim's Halloween costume for the school dress-up tomorrow.

24 October 2013

Have spent the day indoors – first time in a very long time. Have been reading *The Táin* and developing an idea/structure for a new book. Based on *The Táin*, but more than that – a dialogue, a struggling-with, a departure in the context of Famine exiles/migrants who took it conceptually to Western Australia. My Ludlow ancestors. Maybe it feeds into a fourth verse play – I have the forest trilogy looking at their lives in Australia (with elements of their lives in

Leighlinbridge), but maybe the fourth play reaches into *The Táin*? *The Táin* reconstructed.

30 October 2013

Corvids

Up the church's steps
The hooded birds boldly hop
Towards salvation.

MORE FROM A SCHULL JOURNAL

17 February 2014

Went to Macroom yesterday via the Gearagh, and home via the 'Mouth of the Glen'. Saw an entire forest devastated by the storm and thousands of trees down across the county. Wrote a 'devastation' poem on return. Bereft.

18 February 2014

The Sea-mist Scenario (of Place)
11.18 am Just back from walk to Schull pier. Fog over Colla Road and on hills around Schull harbour, as well as a retreating sea-mist. Clear Island, even Long Island, not visible through the mist/fog. In writing this place I have the *in situ*, but lack the childhood memories and stories for comparison and juxtaposition. Images rely on 'stories' overheard or told to me/us by others (their collective memory). The sea-mist becomes 'separated'/isolated/of-the-moment, though locals have reference points and we can trace a comparative instance back to September. So events out of the ordinary – like the extremity of the recent storms which bring comparisons to events well outside living memory – create their own set of references and become anchors for future comparisons (and being there at the time as witnesses, we become part of that collective experience and consequent memory, especially Tim as a child being brought home from school as the storm closed in). Ancestral memory can be called on by accumulated archival and family anecdote (passed down through generations), but it always contains significant lacunae. The verbal and print record can be filled in (in some ways) via the 'record' in soil, rocks (lichen, moss, erosion, deterioration), vegetation etc., but that requires knowledge and tools for reading (I have some of these but inevitably rely on those with not only more expertise but the physical tools/aids to reading).

How to build a comparative model – which is the basis of metaphor and simile – for figurative constructions of place. So I draw from 'outside', from afar and create possible models. In legal language, it is constructing a scenario out of available evidence – a 'law' of likelihood – the plausible conclusion based in prima facie plus later evidence to build a scenario. Not a case of 'res ipsa loquitur' because the thing-in-itself speaking is not the complete picture – the 'evidence' must factor in other information, other voices, create a cross-referenced model.

However, Tim at eleven is a child building his comparative experiences *in situ* with where he has lived before – for when his adult self builds a sense of 'world' out of comparisons with this childhood (mediated by the factors that restrain them – being under the guidance and restrictions imposed by parents, teachers, society in general). These impressions are affected by a different notion of liberty. The sea-mist to Tim would be formative – a lifelong reference point – a *point de repère* that telescopes through a life.

My own childhood *points de repère* in terms of the sea-mist locate themselves in south-west Australia:

   (i) mist over the Canning and Avon rivers
   (ii) fog over Cockburn Sound
   (iii) mist/fog over the marshy/saline areas of Wheatlands farm
   (iv) mist/fog over the school oval
   (v) mist over forest rivers and creeks – jarrah and karri

My childhood *points de repère* being from another place (not Schull) causes tension in the construction of metaphor – maybe necessary in a disrupted ecology of my childhood places and the disrupted here and now.

The international-regional representation of the biosphere – separate but interconnected parts. Yes, aspects of the so-called deep ecology model (while denying many of its rightist inclinations/applications!) but with a socio-economic and mutually dependent cross-section, marking cause and effect. I think of William Blake's drawing for *Paradise* Canto 10 – the unfinished/incomplete spiral staircase in terms of ascending to Paradise. This spiral can work as a model for the progress/decline of human activity in the biosphere.

12.16 pm Just back from a walk up Ardmanagh Road, then left on to L4410 and down across the Goleen Road and up to Town Park. Passing the cowshed on the corner, I noticed the cows lachrymose and still in the hard shade inside their wintering shed, the sun – so rarely out over recent months – shining like sarcasm just outside their reach.

Just read that the storm last Wednesday is being called 'Storm Darwin', and that it carried with it the largest recorded wave in Irish waters – it was off Kinsale and reached 25 metres.

21 February 2014

Spending the night in Killarney (Cill Airne) after driving over the Shehy Mountains and then into Kerry. Now opposite the Reeks (which are lightly snow-capped). Drove out on to the Dingle Peninsula – through Castlemaine with its Wild Colonial Boy propaganda and its Australian ricochets – then on to Inch, its intense beach with dozens of rows of breakers, and on into Dingle town and up to Connor Pass (An Conair), the highest pass in Ireland at 456 m. Astonishing views to Dingle Bay and north-west to Brandon Bay (over the Paternoster lakes). The wind was literally howling and some fool threw his lunch wrapper from his car window over the edge to catch this gale. But the entire experience was ultimately dominated by the presence of a dead and rotting sheep just over the fence from the car park/lookout, obviously a victim of Storm Darwin, its legs caught under the fence. It was a traumatic sight (even with much experience of seeing such things), and even in the wind the smell of decay filled the air. It will take a long time to process. It's the essence of *The Táin*'s eschatology. The unnaming – the fate of sheep in high places. Then, with this in mind, on to Camp then over the Slieve Mish (Sliabh Mis) mountains back to Inch and on to Killarney.

Elegy for a Kerry Highland Sheep at Connor Pass

Over the edge of the carpark, stretched vista
to Brandon Bay, the wooden-posted ringlock fence
with single barbed-wire strand topping it like pride
of completion, the architectural monument
to enclosure, the compartmented mountainsides;
what emphasises is the lookout, the sightseer
epicentre, the epitome of pass – to the south-east,
Dingle Bay, and to the north-west the Atlantic
having its say against the strands wound out
to take the breakers, bog to sand, a roughneck
rousing of sublimity – postcard to the great
metropolises and their insularity. But what
interests and traumatises me – is – is the corpse
of a Kerry highland sheep clearly taken down
by Storm Darwin, deadliest storm since
the Night of the Big Wind in the early
nineteenth century, a corpse of straggled wool
and clots of flesh, the already eroded head,
skull protruding through, ill-shaped horns
twisted off by some force beyond weather,
legs trapped beneath the fence. Wrapped
on either side by mountains – Mt Brandon
with its teased snow, barely a cap, and Mount
Beenoskee, sending snow back up to steely
cloud, to ignore or pity, this residue of Darwin,
the evolutionary anomaly, battle for adaptation
against the bloody-minded fencing, resistance
to either side when legs slipping through
and breaking make a joke of separation.

The scratching around the unseemly body –
one fool in his people mover, having fed
the vulnerable family, gathered his rubbish
and hurled it over the edge, bypassing
the Kerry highland sheep corpse whose smell
was never lost to the howling, to the winds
too violent to be haunting, as in cars
it gathered, a sinking feeling, a dragging
down the narrow mountain road, the stench
of lowland fetor. But yes, the scratching
around the body tells me that another sheep
tried to prise the trapped sheep free: when
the winds allowed no visitors, when wool
braided and dreadlocked, horns hooking
the wire up without success, a moment
of mutual aid in the face of Lamarckian
bullying, those rubbish-throwers who
adopt his creed as precedent, unholy
howling on the precipice, so level-headed
in the levelled carpark, all falling to worry
beads, or prayers rubbed bare, those paternoster
lakes that catch the spirit which runs
in streams, cascades down the sandstone
jags and across dogged pasture, shapes
itself around the hoofs of sheep determined
to hang out, their slaughter in the eyes
of passers-by, the most enthusiastic
of their admirers, those to whom
'gorgeous' and 'authentic' come fast
to lips yelling into glorious view:
across the corpse or looking
the other way, pinching their noses.

22 February 2014

Went through the incredibly narrow and intense Gap of Dunloe today! Where Charlotte Brontë fell from the pony. Through pincers/jaws of rock – the Old Red Sandstone Devonian mountains aching in the rain. Exhausted tonight but will draft a poem tomorrow. Then on through the Black Valley and up to Moll's Gap.

24 February 2014

Stormy again! Got caught in driving wind and rain on Ardmanagh on the return leg of my walk. Struggling with my longish 'stitches' poem (the opening is all wrong). It will form an essential part of my reversioning of *The Táin*, so I want to get it right. Finished the biography of Dickens and am starting the Patrick Brontë bio.[1]

1 Final draft of the 'Stitches' poem, which is at the core of my reversioning (and, in a sense, 'displacing') of *The Táin*:

Stitches

The tug when stitches
are removed is more
a reminder of mortality
than the excision and stitching
were themselves. That nick nick
as you hold the blue examination
table, half enjoying the sensation
because the middle suture
has become inflamed,
body rejecting it outright,
as it did the sun-growth
burrowing into your back.
To pass the time, quick
as the doctor is, you ask
the nurse assisting
how it went with the cows
on her farm, bulging with milk
after the storm knocked
power out. It's not rural
chit-chat – you are seriously
disturbed by the labour
cows are put to, you deny
the glory of red or blue cows,
the names of passes cut through
red sandstone amounting to victory,
the accumulation of ear tags
in the boggy patina of 'farms'.
Rather, it's an interest in pain,
the ethical underpinning
of our condition. Earlier,
when the lesion was being cut out,
the nurse was telling you
of her worry about the pain
the cows were experiencing,
having missed one milking.
You were finding common
ground in all your difference,
both of you in situations of reliance.
How you respond to the work
she does on your body, part
of her history, as the signature
of stitches plays with the script
of a scar to come. She'd told you
then that they'd luckily bought

a generator at a sale the week before
and were wiring it up that evening
to power the machines that suck
the teats, drain the udders.
You'd heard cows through the district
bellowing after the storm, the pain
of withholding, the memory of calves
long gone but clinging on. Too many
to milk by hand, just a favourite
relieved of her burden, and the confusion
of bulls in their distant *gort*. Cows
held in sheds, in stalls, bellowing
white blood with no heart
to recycle it. Just the drying out
that follows like deliverance.
Not the happy cows of Ireland's
dairy adverts, of its meat industry.
You weave veins and arteries
of ancestral irony, your forebears
clearing great tuart and karri trees,
jarrah and blackbutt, dappled cows
on grass itching on strange soil,
inflamed stitches. So you ask now
how it went, nick nick, and she says
that the generator was a dud,
didn't kick over once, and the cows
bellowed birth and mastitis and death.
But, she added as she stepped back
from the clean dressing, we hooked
up a wreck of a generator,
forty years old, that our neighbour,
an old German who can make
anything work – if it's broke
he can fix it – got going,
the machines relieving
the cows. A battle won.
Briefly, you thought of her,
that nurse, kind woman
with skill in her hands,
as Medb. Why? You'd been
reading *The Táin*, over and over
and searching for a clue in the local,
though set at almost the opposite
side of the country, a rewriting
of geography and patrimony
and hero-violence-epic language
cult, a release from *bondage*
in the southwest, the anglicised
namings, the residues of lingual
resistance, the Schulls, the overlays
of Marys and 'taking the soup'
ultimatums, as memory transcribes

into your Australian southwest
where small farms
under English landlords
buttered American whaling
ships, as you head back down
Ardmanagh, unravel the high place,
look across as the solid, robust convent
house, the religion your great-grandfather
and great-grandmother would fight over,
he taking to the forests with the son
he went to war with,
she staying with the youngest
and remaking them as Protestants.
You don't hear any of the labels.
In your secular isolation you
hear the cows bellow, yelling
across the district, a red bull
as large as the convent
battering its way through
Mount Gabriel, the white cupolas
with their hidden radars smug
in the misty rain, the red bull
with copper-tipped horns
smashing down Ardmanagh Road,
a truck laden with supplies
still trickling in after the great storms –
Christine and Darwin –
and as you throw your hands
up to protect your eyes
from the light, the sharp light,
you feel the deep stitches,
the hidden stitches
that will dissolve
into your body,
tearing away,
and white blood
lymphing its way
onto the dressing,
the milk of your settlement,
the ink of your residency,
you pacifist warrior
and freedom fighter for cows,
wondering at the ingenuity
of the old German, the rain
and the wind, the premonition
of storms from the Atlantic
'conveyor belt', the thin black shirt
lashing against you – no blue cloak,
no gift from your patrons –
and the damp dressing
covering your wound,
Medb heading home to her cows,

25 February 2014

Storms continue.

Thinking about the art of Joan Mitchell and my feeling of colour deprivation through an inability to get hold of vegan art colours. I want to write pages of colour as substitute or to fill pages with grey/graphite – grey for me is alive with the possibility of colour. Grey best catches the storm reality of now.

Back from walk to pier, then to the 80 kmh sign on the way to Ballydehob. Between rain showers, though got caught (as always) in the end. I noticed the standing stone down near the Standing Stone B & B – have long wondered if there was actually (still) a stone there or just a liberty taken with the name. There it was, upright next to the fence near the top of the driveway – I could see it due to the angle of the sun bursting through clouds – so Feb 25th works as its trigger, its calendar moment/sign (rather than the solstice which would not catch it or entirely absorb it). Of course, it could have been moved from its original position, as seems often to happen, and 'time'/spatiality has shifted over the millennia. Not the intention but the circumstances. The presence of the standing stone where we hadn't been able to see it becomes part of a new cartography which takes into consideration a decolonising process.

The harbour was a turgid grey-green – the runoff from the range thundering down into the bay. The mouth of the harbour was angry and the few winter boats were tearing at their moorings.

26 February 2014

The Frequency of Storms in Otherworld – thinking of this as the title for my poems of Southwest Ireland (location in Celtic mythology of the place of the 'others').

I feel, in fact, that my connection is, in many ways, with the pre-Celtic here in Ireland. I feel strongly connected to the standing stones, circles of stone, wedge tombs etc. The stonework of place.

Raining again and little sunlight.

27 February 2014

Tracy picked up a copy of Enright's *Walks of Ballydehob and Schull* today. In there is information regarding the strange cross-hatching in the rock surface of Mount Gabriel – what I have described as a lattice-work, baked effect.

---

the doctor seeing his next patient
without prejudice, without fear
or favour, acclimatised
to carnage and peace.

Apparently, over millennia, winds drive rain into the rock, causing north-east parallel grooves.

Also, we discovered that what we thought was a type of pandanus (a vague reminder of La Réunion!) is actually *Cordyline australis*. Known in New Zealand (to which it is native) as cabbage tree (and probably not the source of what was used for the 'Cabbage Tree Hat' of early colonial Australian repute – I think that was likely woven from the *Civistona australis* plant?) Our error of observation (or, rather, deduction) is of interest to me in terms of local knowledge but also with regard to how we ascribe qualities to something local by applying experience from elsewhere – i.e. what we are previously familiar with. The slippage can be generative. I have adapted a poem I wrote after the St Jude's Day storm that reflects on my experience of pandanus around the world to become a 'pandanus-ti tree synthesis' – seeing one thing as another in order to make sense of the 'up-close' in a broader international context. The politics of belonging are fraught with the *intrusions* (which are actually enrichments!) of outside knowledge – do we invalidate presence of the 'newcomer' through such 'errors', or does it broaden the terms of identification and the characteristics of the place itself? This 'ti tree' mistaken as pandanus becomes an anecdote – 'some people mistake it … but it's really…' This is the *in*exactitude of the figurative, but also its exactitude – a honing of 'fact' by placing (or planting) it in an 'error zone', a place of slippage. In this slippage is the key to my belief that the most 'imprecise' metaphor is in fact the most precise of sciences.

Having been, earlier in 2013, in La Réunion, where pandanus is omnipresent and used to secure unstable and eroding coastline, the leap/mistake of misattribution has implications of desire, connection, continuity and form. Misnaming becomes part of place – errors become truisms in a default setting. Reminds me of the stoat being called a 'weasel' here when it is not, in fact, a weasel. Enright notes this in his walking book.

ON THE TRAUMA OF WRITING 'SEEING' AND THE URGE TO CREATE A POEM AFTER JOURNEYING OUT ON THE MIZEN

28 February 2014

Just back from an excursion to the Mizen area. Searching back-roads, we passed through a small sandstone gap, then were funnelled on to what became a narrow, grassed and pitted road to 'nowhere'. Views of Fastnet and the Atlantic, and unbeknown to us, a slow climb up a mountain named after the people of the otherworld. We had to backtrack when we reached a farm gate and wound our way back to the main road.

Heading back to the coast, we travelled through sandstone, pasture, cows, some plantation silver birch and spruce, tidal flats stretching a long way in from the 'coast'. Amid these was an intense and still egret, 'sleeping' with eyes wide open, absorbing all the waking world into its 'otherness', a conduit for the conscious and the sleeping, the living and the dead. The whole area had an uncomfortable and disturbing, if 'fascinating', feel about it. The moods we impose upon seeing, the gravitas and readings we impose on creatures? The egret taking the weight of our unease as well as being part of it?

Later, home at Anchor Lodge, we discovered that the area is associated with a horrendous, violent crime of decades ago – one that lingers in the region because it remains unsolved and because a 'local' (though not born here) was accused/said to be 'involved' (a 'person of interest'). There is a taboo around discussion of the incident in some circles, and a general anxiety, as well as anger and overt fear. It is unspeakable and I do not want to refer to the details or even consider its specificities.

However, despite the massive discomfort it gives me even to write in this way about it, I will say that any understanding – even a superficial one – of this place necessitates some awareness of that crime's impact and ongoing 'resonance'/ripples/repercussions. Knowing what we now know, for example, means we would never take a rental in that area (we had been looking at a possible house far down the track). Searching Google Earth (the ultimate tool of colonisation and occupation!), then discovering the road's name, we looked for further information about the area and came across details of the crime. The poem I was going to write about passing through that small, jagged gap and seeing the egret was immediately abandoned. Of course, in a sense, this magnifies the need to write these matters in the context of place, though in a different/ aware way. I write poems via 'anchor points' – specific details of up-close observation – but they inevitably contain 'error zones' in which things are not quite clear/resolved because immediate impact isn't informed by all available information. 'Research' comes later and is layered into further drafts. Sometimes I include 'wrong' seeing and extend (say) a sequence to show how that original impression is modified and mediated by accrued information gleaned through research made at a distance, from afar (from the original location of experiencing and seeing – that is, distant from the *in situ* moment of encounter with the materials of the poem). Thomas Bristow has picked up on this dynamic in my work – though, as I've said, the immediacy-and-removal process of writing is not a binary.

Anyway, the 'Egret Below the Gap' poem can't be place-specific without bringing a level of disturbance to the poem (or my future interactions with the poem) that I don't want or won't countenance – evoking the traumatic residues of the crime of which one has become aware (though we don't know the precise location of the crime, we know it must have occurred within a few kilometres' radius of where we were today). The 'irony' in this – as we might read through Hodge and Mishra's process of paranoid reading – is that such crimes are the underlay of all non-indigenous poetry in Australia, and indeed most poetry of place – it seems one can apply this reading to the migrated-from as much as the migrated-to location (and further, the victim of the crime was someone from another European country who had a second home in the area).

Even within contexts of settlement/post-settlement and colonial continuums (some call this 'post-colonial', which I do not believe exists as any intact state of being), violence underpins presence. My poem 'The Silo'[1] is about this very matter. The farmer-colonists (we don't know they are 'white', so why do we automatically get a sense that they are … or why do we assume it, if we do?) incarcerate their child in what amounts to a cycle of punishing their own heritage and posterity, perpetuating the crime of dispossession and occupation through locking up their own genes, their own claim to presence (the child being born in a place is automatically of that place – the American blood and soil equation, for example, relies on the sense of connection in a similar way to Noongar boodjar, even if this is ethically disturbing insofar as American patriotism is an overlay of Native American belonging and this is a form of palimpsesting or, worse and more likely, overt deletion).

When we were kids playing on Wheatlands farm, there was an old house – Sandsprings – we were told to avoid. There was rumoured to be something

---

1 John Kinsella, *The Silo: A Pastoral Symphony* (South Fremantle, Fremantle Arts Centre Press, 1995), p. 58.

sad and tragic associated with the place (what, specifically, I've never truly been able to ascertain, but maybe I just don't want to ask the 'right'/intrusive questions). I wrote this apprehension of going even near the old house into some early poems in a vague, intimating but anxious way. It became a point on a hidden compass of presence, dispossession and deletion I couldn't quite explain.

We have been reading about the mythology of pre-Celtic presence in Ireland, especially as it pertains to West Cork and the peninsulas. First, the Fomorians, then their defeat by the Tuatha Dé Danann, and finally by the Celts. The intermarriage/'mingling' of all three peoples works as a legitimising of presence in the 'here and now'. *The Book of Invasions* maps the exclusion-presence paradox. The Tuatha Dé Danann become 'the others' out of fear and respect (and anxiety), the otherworld a mirror to the guilt of extirpation – the paranoid made concrete, the dispossession that constantly threatens to over-turn, invert 'this world' by intruding and snatching away the living, those in the present, tactile world. Strangely, as mentioned earlier, the hill/mountain near where we went today is named *unto* a spirit of 'the others', of/for a sprite figure (shapeshifting animal-human-figure: *púca*). It's not mine to comment further on this, but it can't help getting under the skin of the poem/s I intended to write out – they were already mentally drafted *in situ* (it's a visual process for me) – and there's no undoing that, even if they/it doesn't find its way on to the page. A poem must project on to the page, but in this case I am not sure in what form. I do know place is about seeing, hearing, knowledge and respect. It's also about giving back, but knowing how that giving can be damaging when it might seem to the writer to be a positive engagement.

I am searching for something positive out of the bleakness. The sun was out today (so rare over the last few months) and the sea was lit silver and blue and the sandstone changed colours as you stared at it. But the knowledge of the crime has been added to the 'picture', overlaying this first draft, inexorably and entirely altering the import of the poem. Out there, my 'echo-locator' was in full drive mode, drawing all on to the page in my head, but now there are contra-dictory and confusing signals. This is the truth of place – there is never clarity. Clarity is only propaganda and the epigraph to invasion and occupation and deletion, both metaphorically and literally. We must resist these slogans and decorations that are not deployed ironically or as a means to prompt us to look anew, that are not deployed to increase our awareness of the constrictions and restraints in our own ways of seeing.

As an aside, the rental house we looked at down by the tidal flats on the inlet, down from the gap in the sandstone, is in a place that suffers from tidal flood-ing. The front 'garden' was actually a coastal bog with a framing of common reeds (terrific, but not a good sign for a home). Numerous small songbirds were darting about, and heather was beginning to flower. It was bristling with life, which makes the knowledge of the crime all the harder to absorb. Such violence is the truth behind *The Táin* with its brutality and killing (as a process of naming and possession!), its mass destruction cowering behind the performance of heroism. There needs to be an anti-*Táin* – an anti-war poem, a pro-cow/animal poem, a pro-ecology poem. And maybe it needs to come from an ancestral 'blowback' or someone who has been away psychologically as well as physically. It can never work in the realm of nostalgia – it must be a declaration of respect for textual and cultural 'origins' but also in opposition. An act of positive resistance. This is what I want to do.

As I process this commentary, buds are starting to appear in trees: one can almost watch them grow in real time. The sodden bogs are coming alive. Saw a long-tailed tit, blue tit, song thrushes, blackbirds, jackdaws, ravens and stonechats dipping across roads between hedges. Animals and birds are, in my experience, highly attuned to trauma (in any form – human or animal or even plant) in the locality of their lives. This is not imposition or pathetic fallacy, but observable dynamics. To deny this is to deny them agency and sensitivity outside the range 'we' allocate to them. To separate them off completely is to protect our own desire for uniqueness, to ward off our own anxiety about the damage we inflict on them and their habitats, and maybe arises from a fear of accepting that they can perceive/see who and what we are.

I am trying to reconfigure ways of seeing and place and articulate a 'displaced' belonging, a 'new spatiality'. I am trying to build a comparative model, to create a practice of participation enacted with respect. Here's the rough draft of a poem as visualised *after* further 'knowledge' interrupted its 'painting' – it probably won't go further than this for reasons outlined above. It's a distillation poem:

Egret Disturbance to Anthropomorphics

A 'late arrival', this egret
has brought about the renaming
of a house and an overloaded
sense of stillness to a rough
tidal inlet. It is *stiller* than swans
and has defined or redefined
poise among people. Its
closeness is alarming, an
endgame to hopes, to meditative
constructions. But it does carry
a weight – the imposed and osmotic –
the trauma all residents live with –
animal and human, the day-
to-day business of nothing said.

FURTHER EXTRACTS FROM A SCHULL JOURNAL

3 March 2014

Just back from my walk up Ardmanagh, down to Toormore-Goleen Road and on to Newman's to talk with John D'Alton about our poem-photos collaboration; then down to the pier, back up into town and down to the 80 kmh sign on the road to Ballydehob, and back. Most of it in sunshine. Strong, gusty breeze, heavy swell in Roaringwater Bay, and plants/shrubs coming into bud.

John and I discussed the 'rules' of our collaboration – its boundaries and range. We are now to work within a triangle (very good – another V – i.e. a gap/ sluice) within and including Mizen Head, Durrus and Baltimore (including sea and islands in this area). Rather than 'just' local gaps – e.g. Barnancleeve – we will consider gaps, channels, passes, furrows, canyons, partings etc., both literal and figurative.

So, as John says, 'channels between islands', 'splits in islands' and other such natural configurations are to be included. He will take me out in his skiff in May and we'll spend time looking at places such as (the) Calf Island(s) (where surf and spray break over the shacks of those few living there!)

I suggested we also include conceptual and metaphoric gaps. To include, say, the 'furrow' of the sun as it sets over the bay (John has a wonderful photo of this, hanging upstairs at Newman's, which gave me the notion). I am now thinking of boustrophedon structures (long a favourite 'verse form' of mine) and subtexts to the whole. John sees his photos as maybe doing their own textual acts (my words) and I always think of my poems as visual entities.

Very distressing to hear the chest-thumping desire among some journalists to see military confrontation with Russia. It's as if Thanatos has them by the balls. The excitement and Cold War echoes/frisson they display is frightening. They start getting the military maps up and gushing over comparisons between military forces (they love their diagrams). They want a Western bully (some have even called for a new Reagan) to 'face up' to the 'Eastern' bully, Putin (who is clearly deluded and mentally ill). Sky Television glamorises war. What's more, any press that is rooted in profit-making is not free! The desire for profit is as controlling and censoring as the controls imposed by governments.

4 March 2014

Walked down to the pier. Very bothered by hay fever at the moment. Saw (and was snuffled by) a small, muscular dog (boxer with bull terrier, maybe), with a very old, grey-whiskered, 'wise' face. After investigating me, it responded to a whistle from its 'master', leapt down the stairs off the pier on to the lower boat jetty, and into a dinghy. The dogs of town are getting to know me – they scan me, sniff me and register me as part of the furniture. This one clearly knows the ropes.

5 March 2014

Tracy wrote a fine poem about Ash Wednesday (and also one about Shrove Tuesday – equally good). What interests me is how one can write culturally about religion in poetry and not 'religiously' about religion. An issue of acquiring distance but also the desire and ability to separate ethics and morality from culturalisation and indoctrination.

Journeyed down to Letter (*Leitir* – 'the wet hillside') – very narrow grassed road into bog, which has been forested with pines and deciduous trees. Looking up to Mount Gabriel, it struck me as being like an 'underpass' rather than overpass or gap. Later, returning from Bantry, the ridges on the lower side (the east side) really stood out ('razor-back' almost).

I've noticed that the fewer native animals a place/region/country has (especially animals of 'size'), the more the people of that place obsess about those few represented in their literature/s. And where 'native' animals have been all but wiped out, domestic animals are given massive allegorical and often magical qualities (comes out of herding etc.) – in inverse proportion to the reality of their condition (usually servitude and slavery, without agency, and de-mystified).

Watched a frisky male goat being pursued by (or leading) a mob of sheep/ewes with lambs in a boggy field below Gabriel today. The sheep were so 'at it' that even when the goat pissed, the sheep tried to nudge and smother it. The goat butted them off, finished its business, then leapt up and gambolled with four or five sheep, and three or so lambs gambolled after them. Like an illustration to Bacchic rites from an ancient Greek or Roman vase.

6 March 2014

Phatic.
A pacifist Sweeney. His bragging ended. The Village Idiot Poems – a version of the Sweeney story.

I am interested in the way Sweeney is the fool (as punishment and/or intrinsically) who is a visionary – 'feeble-minded' but the possessor of 'language', the reader of poems beyond the 'phatic' (in which he fails). Before leaving Jam

Tree Gully, I was thinking of writing a series of 'Village Idiot' poems – in fact, I wrote a few drafts and took notes towards them. This was in reference to the Toodyay neighbour tendency to view/interpret the 'alternative' as village idiocy. George, for example, basically called 'book stuff' the sign of a pathetic fool (and 'wanker'), and children bullied Tim at school for having interests in 'foreign stuff', maps, books and 'statistics'. He was cast as 'quirky' by the teachers in a mock-approving way – their coping mechanism for difference? An effort to be respectful while fearing the madding crowd? – i.e. so as to fit in socially and comply themselves?

And there were/are in Toodyay the cases of 'right-wing' kids (children of right-wing nationalists who hold deeply racist beliefs and speak openly and horrifically of 'solutions' to what they perceive to be the nation's ills), who treated Tim as the village idiot they saw me as (without ever having actually met me), via their parents' interpretation of my/our (left-green) politics. A specific example of this harassment, in which son was linked to father, was over my opposition to the Targa Rally, and a few years back when kids verbally attacked Tim on the school bus for having a 'drunken village idiot father' (I hadn't had a drink for over fifteen years!), because their parents were supporters of the car rally.

So, I think the 'village idiot' is a dynamic figure (maybe I would!) Does this mean that I am attempting to invest myself with some kind of visionary capability – to place myself ironically in a position of wisdom and truth above/over other locals? No. The village idiot is personalised and does act as a mediating gestural figure of witness and observation, but he is equally flawed and lacking in sight/insight. However, one who is accused without being known in any meaningful way, accused only because of wishing to protect/conserve, becomes a liminal figure and a mirror to the xenophobia and violence of community. The outsider is lonely, isolated, but privileged with a form of 'seeing' because of this.

So my Village Idiot is a medium, a symbol and a location in which 'I' interact with many possible 'Is'. Paradoxically, a fragmenting unified self. It is not purely a portrait of self. On the other hand, the 'Sweeney' figure I will use for my sequence of related poems 'set' primarily in Ireland will be quite distant from any 'Is' and will become a figure of mediation and connection, able to identify contradictions and traumas at a distance (through irony, self-questioning and other rhetorical 'flourishes', including understatement). But there will be overlap: they are colonial-blowback paradoxes wrestling with each other and the 'broader community/ies'.

Reading Sweeney via Seamus Heaney's *Sweeney Astray* but going up to University College, Cork, to get hold of O'Keeffe's version of *Buile Suibhne* which Heaney used in creating his own version.

In being cursed and cast out for his act of profanity against the Church (throwing the monk's psalter – Ronan's psalter – into the lake), Sweeney becomes (to my mind) liberated – already he gains insight in being 'mad' (the village idiot). Sweeney's violence 'violates' the rules Ronan sets for battle. Out of this contradiction (hypocrisy), a pacifist stance regarding the Toodyay violence arises – the breaking of the rules is not to engage in conflict/battle, bur rather to resist participating in the fight, not to wield guns, not to shoot roos (the 'sport' of it)… The ringing of the (peace) bell – flowers stop the violence. Bell heather rings across the bogs, dampening violence – moss is applied to wounds.

Sweeney Astray is Heaney's masterpiece. I usually doubt the smoothing of the rough edges in Heaney's poetic technique, in his thinking and his dealing with difficult moral issues, but he has done a superb interpretation in this case. On page 47 of the Faber edition, note Sweeney as 'mates' with the island/land. A beautifully wrought poem, yet not what I am looking for – it's the O'Keeffe I will look to.

Maybe it's the reformed alcoholic and addict in me that draws me to Sweeney.

Heard a tractor passing the house and looked out through the front (west-facing) arched window to see a tractor dragging an animal/livestock trailer. Peering out through its back grille were two cows looking desperate, forlorn and confused. Their eyes 'pleaded' outside and beyond any fears (you have to wonder why humans so fear it) of imposed anthropomorphism. Eyes are eyes, fear is fear, and fear so well-founded. The anthropomorphics are in the human usage of the cows, not in the 'pleading' of their eyes – the absolute awareness.

7 March 2014

Rare sunny day – just back from walk.

Ventured up Ardmanagh, then across to the Gubbeen Road and down to town, then on to Colla Road before turning down to the pier and back home.

The cows are still 'wintering' in their sheds – forlorn and defeated-looking. Spring 'turnout' for the milk cows should happen soon. There are warnings against doing so too early – the new grass can have 'wrong' balances of protein and sugars and cause illnesses. Farmers are also advised to ease cows into grazing, to graze areas for a few days at a time before changing, strip-gaze etc. This is the palimpsestic trail of the epics, of language here itself. The fate of cows.

Meyer Schapiro writes regarding Cézanne's 'Still Life with Compotier' (or 'Compotier, Glass and Apples'):

> Most original in the drawing are the ellipses of the compotier and the glass. Just as Cézanne varies the positions, colours, and the contours of the fruit, he plays more daringly with the outline of vessels. The ellipse of the compotier becomes a unique composition form, flatter below, more arched above, contrary to perspective vision and unlike the symmetrical forms of the glass.

This is what I want to achieve in a poem. The *contrary* vision. And to bring life through still life, to bring difference and variation through repetition. The 'same' is never the same.

Schapiro continues:

> In its proportion, it approaches the rectangular divisions of the canvas and in its curves is adapted to the contrasted forms of the apples and grapes, the straight lines of the chest, the curves of the fruit below, and the foliage on the wall. A line

drawn around the six apples on the cloth would describe the same curve as the opening of the compotier.[1]

I also note that the mouth of the glass trips perspective (especially in relation to the contents of the glass), leans out to take us in to the cool of the drink. Maybe you have to have lived long in a hot place to fully understand the coolness of this 'error', of this adjustment in the way of seeing. Aix's heat resonates in the spirit of this painting (wherever it was painted or viewed, the Aix need for coolness at the height of summer resonates through this painting for me). I am bothered into respect for this still life. It is as lively as stillness can be and as disrupted as a poem must be. It is an *ars poetica* – it understands disruptions to rhythm (substitution) and all its rhymes are perfectly slant.

A Riddle: who are those?

The horror of 'bovine genetics'.
Those who 'winter out' their cows.
Those who 'shed' them over the cold months.
Those who beef and those who milk.
Straws of profit. Liberty begins at home.

8 March 2014

Back from Cork City. Went to UCC library where I took out a dozen Muldoon collections and related works for my selection of his innovative/experimental poetry. Tracy took out an Italian language book so she can brush up for our trip to Italy in April.

We saw half-a-dozen whooper swans on the banks and edges of the Lee River in the western part of Cork City as we were heading home to Schull. They are so distinctly different from mute swans, which we see often. What I found fascinating was the way they clustered like an inward-looking star – all their beaks facing each other, floating near the green-grassed flood-banks (so recently flooded) in their formation like a pedalo being sailed to its mooring.

On the far side of the river are some remarkable 'Victorian-era' (a horrible indictment) buildings that repeat the same structures with towers over and over. Turns out it's Our Lady's Hospital which was a 'lunatic' asylum from 1858–90. It is apparently 'the longest building in Ireland' and the 'long corridors' were characteristic of asylums. [Information from a blog by Adeline Shorten – 'City Spaces'. She also notes the hospital had a large ballroom which was used for dances for the patients.] Whooper swans in the liquid light of…

A muted drizzly day with no sunshine. Tracy says that according to John D'Alton, it's what locals call a 'soft day'. Though Tracy says it was actually less than a 'soft day'.

1 http://www.ibiblio.org/wm/paint/auth/cezanne/sl/compotier/ (accessed 22 June 2016).

ON PAINTING AND POETRY

9 March 2014

My poetry has always relied on the 'visual'. I see 'landscapes' in terms of internal and exterior visual qualities, I see visual qualities in sound. I was surrounded by painting and art as a child. Not only was my grandfather a painter-signwriter, but my mother always dabbled (oils, watercolours, carving, china painting, puppet-making etc.), and my brother's great loves were/are nature, music and art. I also loved art-making, but in the end would often convert what I was painting, drawing or *making* into word montage, or at least pay as much attention to naming and describing the artwork I was engaged with/on as to the actual artwork itself. When I did an acrylics painting course at Fremantle Arts Centre when I was twelve, I was interested in the 'graphological' implications of the 'swirls' of acrylics on the paper.

My earliest poetry was either 'on' artwork/s or attempting to create a sense of an artwork with/in the poem (I remember seeing George Lambert's painting 'Across the Black Soil Plains' – my sympathies in the poem were with the horses dragging the heavy load). I loved going to galleries, and worked to recreate what I had experienced when viewing the painting or sculpture. I was keen on making an artwork out of an artwork rather than 'describing' what I had seen. This is how my early Lasseter-Nebuchadnezzar poems came out of seeing Arthur Boyd's *Red Nebuchadnezzar* in the Art Gallery of Western Australia. I went and sat in front of that painting day after day when I was eighteen, down from the country for university, and in all sorts of states of mind. From 'out of it' to clear as a bell, from 'happy' to 'depressed', I fixated on it. It seemed to me that the viewing was part of the narrative of the piece.

I recall seeing a book of commercial paintings as a child I deeply disliked, but I can still relate to their internal narrative. They were by Frank Pash, and about Christ's life. The 'style' didn't appeal, but the cumulative nature of art making or reflecting a story did. I only looked at them once or twice but I can still see (in a somewhat 'tacky' depiction) 'Christ' in my mind's eyes and recall the book's narrative structure. Sure, it's an expected narrative, but I am talking of the artist's visual interpretation of the narrative. I learnt that one can aesthetically reject something and still be affected by it.

I was just telling Tracy about the Pash book, mentioning that I think my mother bought it out of sympathy from a door-to-door salesman when I was a child, and Tracy says that her mum also bought the same book, possibly from a door-to-door salesman or via a newspaper, when she was a child! So she knows the book. She notes that it was called *The True Vine* with 'words by Brian Pash and paintings by Frank Pash'.

Be it my grandfather's paintings around his and my nanna's house and in Wheatlands farmhouse, or Albert Namatjira reproductions in my father's and his second wife's house 'up north', I absorbed all visual records and makings as forms of poems. Also influential on me were the illustrations in the *Reader's Digest Biblical World*, which my maternal great-grandmother gave me when I was about two. I can still see the lapis lazuli on the Assyrian king in his chariot. My grandfather's massive 'portraits' of Matthew Flinders, Captain Cook (that hung on the Barracks Arch) and of the newly crowned Queen Elizabeth II (the horror, the horror) are part of my psyche as illustration and narrative.

ALSO FROM A SCHULL JOURNAL

10 March 2014

Bright sunny day!

Went to Ballydehob this morning – Tim had to see the doctor there because Schull surgery had no free slots. I walked around the town and environs for an hour or so. Walked from the top of town down to the bridge over the inlet, then down to twelve-arch bridge – went under that and across the concrete and steel bridge, back (on the other side) to the twelve-arch bridge which I crossed, joining the walkway through patches of furze (in bloom and my hay fever is at full tilt), then on up the hill and past the church, back down to the main street of town. No swans on the inlet, though plenty of gulls. Saw three donkeys and a goat in a small field just outside town. Also a stonechat in furze bordering the field.

Ballydehob is like a relic of the hippy era, with a few locals still tripping from twenty or thirty (or more) years ago when it was a real 'alternative' zone, especially for English migrants. It still remains a hub of differing rural lifestyles.

Mum sent through scans from Grandpa's watercolour sketchbooks, from his youth and earlier years. Also scans from my great-grandfather's sketchbook depicting soldiers and a battle scene!

A magnificent and unusual-looking grey heron in Derreenatra Bog (which Tracy loves so much). Birds are not to be disturbed on these (very small) protected areas. Actually, I don't think it was a grey heron, but a (very rarely seen here) stork! If it was a grey heron, it has peculiarities likely to be linked with age, breeding 'status' etc. It was like a sculpture arising out of the bog – between hummocks, in the flooded zone. It was probably an old, large male grey heron illuminated by reflections off the bog-water, but it struck me (us – I think Tracy wondered as well) as different – also whiter than most 'grey herons'.

Tracy's just back from picking Tim up from school. They waited in the main street as a funeral cortege went past. Second time in a fortnight. The church bell is tolling constantly now. Very haunting and moving. Death is visceral and declared here in so many ways.

Looking through the Irish birds book, we have concluded that it was actually a large but immature grey heron, which accounts for the different head-feather patterning. Easy to jump to conclusions without all the information to hand. To misread by applying experience from elsewhere, and bird knowledges from a distance. The old was young, the bird looked rare in its highlighted posture, but was not 'rare' at all. Yet it was an intense, and dare I say, poetic moment. Which makes you question the validity of observation outside personal investment: the occlusion by self, the tyranny of the unified self.

Derreenatra Bog (small protected zone – a 'natural heritage area' – alongside a rubbish tip and small pine plantation – a residual 'moment in time' between Schull and Bally) is a lowland blanket bog consisting mainly of moss (80%), 'wet lawn' areas – white beak-sedge, bog asphodel and bogbean, 'pools and flushes' – marsh horsetail, sharp-flowered rush, watermint, bottle sedge and great sundew, 'on a bed of red sandstone', and including an array of 'regenerating cutover bog' and 'virgin bog'. You will also find ling heather, bell heather, purple moorgrass and slender cottongrass (only place in Cork for this).[1]

Postscript: There have been seven stork sightings recorded in Cork since 1846! I am more convinced that it was a large if 'immature' grey heron with the reflections of the bog-water and the fact that it was immersed in a flush distorting our way of seeing. That's the physical aspect of it. A freedom of seeing and of interpretation. And then questioning and research bringing doubt to how we see, how we interpret what we see, and what it means once context is understood and verified. There are many moments in the creation of a poem – its endless drafting – but first glimpses and first (mental/visual) drafts are valid as things-in-themselves.

Gustave Courbet said, 'I am fifty years old and I have always lived in freedom; let me end my life free; when I am dead let this be said of me: "He belonged to no school, to no church, to no institution, to no academy, least of all to any regime except the regime of liberty."'[2]

I don't vote. For years I have refused to even go into voting booths. Before that refusal, I would write 'Democracy in this form is slavery', or an anarchy sign, or 'voting is a placebo' across the ballot paper. But many, many elections have passed since I did even that – now I accept the fine (enforced voting in Australia – how liberated!) and stay out of the process entirely. Any form of participation strikes me as conceding that there is a centralised authority I should placate, I should perform for. I will not. The state is wrong, and I won't sign off on it. All those who serve the state serve its empowerment over the individual,

---

1 National Parks and Wildlife Services, 'Derreennatra Bog NHA', http://www.npws.ie/protected-sites/nha/002105.
2 *Letters of Gustave Courbet*, trans. and ed. Petra ten-Doesschate Chu (Chicago, University of Chicago Press, 1992), pp. 203–4.

and over subcultures and the many silenced groups and communities who are lost under the weight of majority will and tyranny.

The only election I have actually voted in over the last few decades was a local election revolving around an 'up-close' specific ecological issue, and I now consider that the wrong action because the process absorbed the impact of protest by placation, and resolutions were watered down and the system created excuses. This is linked to the liberty to see as we see, even if later we need to adjust (which we do) as we acquire more information. It's at the core of seeing, but also making art, receiving glimpses that are or become poems.

12 March 2014

Cézanne's *Pastorale (Idyll)* 1870

> For Cézanne is staging himself: it is he who meditates, outstretched, in the middle of that 'supernatural eclogue' of the Pastorale...[3]

Alex Danchev in *Cézanne: A Life* notes that Cézanne 'adored Giorgione's *Concert Champêtre* ('Pastoral Concert') (c. 1510). It hung in the Louvre, where he would often go and immerse himself in it...' Danchev then quotes Cézanne saying to Gasquet, 'The whole landscape in its russet glow is like a supernatural eclogue [*églogue surnaturelle*], a moment of balance in the universe perceived in its eternity, in its most human joy. And we're part of it, we miss nothing of its life.'[4]

Eglogues Surnaturelles ... idea for sequence of poems.

Went on a long walk this morning. Up Ardmanagh, across to Gubbeen Road, on to the Colla Road spur, then down to Colla Road, down alongside the cemetery and on to the pier, then up through town and home to Anchor Lodge. Felt great distress at seeing a slab of dead but still 'fresh' and supple starfish – all entwined and compacted into each other – slopped/dropped/placed on the edge of the pier looking out towards the mouth of the harbour.

Saw a chaffinch and numerous other birds, and was fascinated by ravens working their way among the 'de-shedded' jersey cows, and a pied wagtail busy with insects (appearing with the sun like spontaneous regeneration!) down on the shingle near the red sandstone rock channels and beds down below the Schull Sailing School.

Returned (just now) to the scene of the starfish crime and photographed it. Horrific images. For the record – mine an act of witness, not surveillance. I would not normally do this – it is a gruesome scene and the act is intrusive in so

---

3 See Gary Tinterow and Henri Loyrette, *The Origins of Impressionism* (Paris, Connaissance des Arts, 1994), p. 123.
4 Alex Danchev, *Cézanne: A Life* (London, Profile, 2012), pp. 224–5, citing *Joachim Gasquet's Cézanne – a Memoir with Conversations (1897–1906)* (London, Thames and Hudson, 1991).

many ways, but I felt it needed witnessing in literal image and in a poetic form/ sense as well. The sun was staring at/straining the camera's eye and a line of shadow segmented the starfish slab, but the truth will be buried in the images.

Tracy just discovered a seeming contradiction in that Damien Enright who wrote the local walking book (I have quoted from earlier) is a member of a bird-watching group who opportunistically ate a dead swan! I will be cautious reading anything he says about the natural world – his sensibilities may be blunted by his desires, and his curiosity may be fed by the same desire.

MORE 'WAYS OF SEEING'

13 March 2014

2.15 pm Day was foggy until 11-ish, then haze set in. Sun out now. Did the same walk as yesterday but with Tracy and it was terrific. One looks in different ways when walking and conversing with someone close. The furze was erupting – both the 'western gorse' and the regular gorse – the longer-thorned and shorter-thorned varieties.

Saw a rare Subalpine Warbler ('passage vagrant from Southern Europe' according to Dempsey and O'Cleary's *The Complete Guide to Ireland's Birds*, p. 183). Absolutely no doubt – saw it close-up before it hopped into a pile of hedge-cuttings and hid. It was a male with an explosively red patch on its chest. All is patches. The 'anatomy has no outlines' and sketches are not 'real', to paraphrase Cézanne.

We also saw (opposite Town Park field) the largest sheep we've ever seen (and that's saying something coming from the zone of giant merino rams!) Must tell Stephen. They stood four-and-a-half feet high and were heavy. White bodies and black heads. Tracy took photographs. It was reinforcing, having her record the walk photographically – a different visualisation which carries and creates its own narrative, with stops and starts that offer a different pacing, a different flow, intensity and angles of observing/seeing.

Danchev (I've just reached page 300) mentions Bridget Riley talking of 'near' and 'far' in painting (Danchev is drawing an analogy with Cézanne's practice). Not sure how this might correlate to my 'up-close'/*in situ* and 'at a distance'/'from afar' dynamics, but surely it does? Exciting. [see 'Agoras' essay earlier] Just looked up and read the Bridget Riley 'near and far'. Came across 1993: Bridget Riley Interviewed by Andrew Renton, 'Bridget Riley: Some things near and some things far', *Flash Art*, Vol. 26, No. 168, pp. 59–61.

Cézanne saw the body outside 'lines' – I see poems outside lines. It's the smudges and crossings-out, the 'bleedings' and coronas, that make up the poem as much as they make up the body of a person or animal (those scars, those blemishes) or plant.

14 March 2014

Mid-day – pre-walk… I want to think of the clouds as shutters to the sun's photographic eye as I walk today. I will close one eye and look with the other, then reverse to look with the other eye. I want to filter and over-expose light/ objects, to fragment and re-align in the way I observe. I want to see anew. Poems written to observe the rhythms of walking, in response to those rhythms. Coast to hinterland to hills to coast. A new route today.

15 March 2014

This morning we went to Lough Ine [also known as Lough Hyne] – up to 40 m deep and the most unique marine space in Ireland (one of the most unique in Europe). It was the first marine nature reserve in Ireland, established in 1981. There's a creek connecting/from the Atlantic that brings a tidal influx of saltwater. 'Highly oxygenated but warm seawater' (according to the Wiki entry). We walked the road on the western side of the lough – that is, on Knockomagh Hill which has 'original' yew forest (it is believed). Also, Tracy says that some of the walls around the lough were built as part of 'Famine relief' projects. Two magnificent mute swans at the northern end. The lough is remarkably clean.

This afternoon we caught the 2 pm ferry to Cape Clear Island. Remarkable and will write much more later and also when we (hopefully) return for an overnight stay soon. Passing Sherkin Island, I noted the dry-stone walls on very steep hillsides plunging to cliff faces with cows working to find their footings facing the Atlantic/Celtic Sea. On the return journey we saw two seals swimming the waters near Sherkin. Furze fires across the Mizen were evident from Clear Island where burnings were also taking place. Tim got to use a small amount of his Irish in the shop on the island.

17 March 2014

St Patrick's Day and the propaganda is in full flow. Will be avoiding all related activities. National days are offensive to me/us anyway, but one in which Church and state collude is particularly distressing.

The death of forests in Australia. The horror of Abbott's version of democracy. The might-is-right majority rules 'fairness' scenario. And the 'unlocking' of the Tasmanian forests is the triumph of Inferno. As Tracy says, regarding 'resistance' in poetry, 'It's the naturalists-who-eat-swans school of programmatic, conformist resistance.' Won't see them out there in the forests in front of the forests (or if we do, it will be just a glimpse before they return to their comforts).

'Explored' more nooks and crannies of the southern Sheep's Head Peninsula today. Poems emerging.

20 March 2014

Stephen and Dzu were married in a Muslim ceremony in Perth today. Mum and John, Dad and Shirley, and Auntie Lorraine and Uncle Gerry were there. Great day.

Awake much of last night listening to the trauma of a cow separated from its calf. 'Calving time'. Sick. The bellowing was of a pain-register one rarely hears outside one's own.

Jetsetting does not an internationalist make. Some are more internationalist without leaving their patch. It's a state of acceptance and willingness and respect and dialogue, not an art of 'visitation' or extracting what is useful to one's sense of 'worldliness'.

FROM A SCHULL JOURNAL

23 March 2014

Farmers in Ireland (Cork a focus) are 'burning, herbiciding and digging' their 'nature' habitats in revenge on the EU for not granting subsidies for un-farmed land. We're just back from a drive on the peninsula where we saw vast areas of burnt habitat – up almost vertical mountains and other places that can't be 'farmed'. Read an article in the *Independent* where one local farmer said how nice it was to see the animal and bird life in the furze on his property, but now he was going to 'burn, herbicide and dig' the lot out in order to punish the EU and make his point. It speaks for itself.

Yesterday, we drove to Kenmare via the 'interior' road across the Shehy Mountains. From Ballylickey via Coomhola Bridge to Kilgarvan. We passed over the mountains at about 1500 feet – snow on the peaks and wet-snow around us. Between Knockboy Mountain on the left and Conigar Mountain on the right. That is, up the Borlin valley, then over the spine of the Shehy chain and down into the Slaheny River valley. Despite such inclement weather, it proved to be one of the journeys of our lives. Even the sheep were close to the ground or hugging the red sandstone for protection from the wind and 'wintry showers'. It was around 1.5°C up there and about 8°C down in Bantry. Seeing the 'preserves' for the Bantry Shooting Club (carrying signs saying' no shooting' because they (p)reserve the right to shoot the 'game birds' they breed there for their own nefarious purposes/'sport') was sickening. 'Nature's' only permission to exist is when it meets the need of the human.

24 March 2014

Inclement weather.

Thinking a lot about coastal lookout/watch towers. Two on Rock Island near Crookhaven in particular. One is almost opposite the old coastguard houses on

Rock Island (now holiday chalets). These towers are tall and 'sleek' – well-made out of slate/sandstone. They were built in the late seventeenth century by the British military for coastal watch and as communication 'relays'.

There are also the Martello towers built during the Napoleonic wars for the same purpose. This network of towers plus lighthouses for a coastal communication makes an almost 'panopticonic' system. I am interested in the notion of them looking inwards as much as outwards – hold to task the population by keeping the French (facilitators of 'revolution') out. And the protection of trade through lighthouses (preventing wreckage of shipping and loss of goods) – the capitalism of occupation and the 'disturbance' this is/was. Further, Marconi ran his wireless tests from Mizen – i.e. from Brow Head. That tower is gone now (blown up in 1922 by Anti-Treaty forces) but those early 20th century communication sites were central to the colonisation of the biosphere and the damage done as a consequence. It was as damaging as the Industrial Revolution. Marconi experimented with ship-to-shore/shore-to-ship wireless, also tapping into the underwater cable to Cape Clear Island from Crookhaven to monitor his activities, with Fastnet the other point of his triangle or rhomboid or even pentagram in the context of the ship. The pattern/shape of communicating radio waves vs the line-of-sight of the watchtowers. A poem: The Towers – an 'undoing' of Yeats's securities?

I am fascinated by the interface represented by the towers, which are extreme symbols of occupation/surveillance in their origins and functions, but have now – to some extent – become local reference-points that have (re)joined the stone from which they were taken/made. The politics of the 'built' environment (just chatting about this with Tracy, especially regarding the destruction of the stately homes/big houses during the war for independence) are exemplified/focussed and intensified through these towers: communications = constraint, observation = restraint; the 'permeable wall' is more solid than the thickest stone wall or the barrier of coast/ocean itself. In these gaps between towers nothing passes unless it's part of the machinery of depopulation to increase control (and claim to the made-'uninhabited'/'vacated' – exploitation of an 'absentee' population by often-absentee colonisers). These towers work like valves, letting the colonisers in and keeping the threats to the occupation out … AND *letting* the 'population' (the unwanted – the 'native') out as migrations. Goods/produce out, luxury items for the colonisers in. Valves of stone and 'light'.

26 March 2014

The Route

Went for a long walk today with a new addition to the route. Up Ardmanagh, across the Goleen Road, right on to the Colla spur road, then right just before the end of the spur, and up the hill. It's a dead end, so I turned back and after a few hundred metres encountered an old local bloke (more of this shortly) then continued back to the Colla Road spur and down on to the Colla Road. I then walked down the path alongside the cemetery but turned back when I realised the harbourside paddock was now being used by cows (wanted to leave them in peace, which is not considered necessary because most locals just walk through regardless). Back to the Colla Road, towards town, then a right turn after the high school down through The Moorings, past the pier, and up into the village. Lengthy conversation in the main street with John D'Alton; then Sheila called me over to Whyte Books where she introduced me to a photographer who'd taken iconic photos of rock stars and the literati, including one of those stand-outs of late Beckett.

Encounter with an 'old man' halfway up the hill

You pass a B&B, a few houses, and then the road opens to bogland. As two vans approached from opposite directions I stepped aside into the bog and stood on a chunk of sandstone as water flowed beneath my feet (one always hears the sounds of flowing water in the hilly and mountainous parts of the region), while the descending van pulled into a slight 'layby' to let the other van pass. The road is little more than the width of a single vehicle.

I waited as the 'locals' opened their windows and had a chat, then when they'd finished, I moved back on to the rough/pitted bitumen and continued upwards. I came to a bend with an even smaller (grassed down the centre) road running off parallel to the coast before turning abruptly. I followed this road. On this side road which proved to be a cul-de-sac, I greeted an old man who was pruning damaged branches – perched on an aluminium ladder, fully extended. Precarious. His place/house – made of stone and boasting a 'shed' (on the opposite side of the road) that looked like a castle (complete with crenellations), was in itself perched on the hillside and surrounded by impressive gardens and walls.

As I rounded the hill, the road took me past fields and a 'private property' sign with a track climbing to the obscured summit of the hill. Looking back inland from the road towards the range one gets a real sense of the age and rigidity of Mount Gabriel and the entire range. Barnancleeve Gap is so defined it looks like a scored loaf of bread, with the Gap the score mark to snap off the end section of the loaf. I followed the curve around further until I reached a dead end, though there was a thin trail through bog back up over the hill.

Returning, I came across the old man again – down from his ladder. Somehow we started to chat and I told him who I was and where I lived and where I came from. As his trust and interest rose, he started telling me stories of the area. We swapped tales.

Later, in town, John would tell me how 'deposits' and 'withdrawals' work here, in terms of sharing/favours (he cited an American fiction-writer as an example). I mentioned to the old man not only my family name and connections, but also Tracy's (direct connections with Cork) and names of some of the people in the village I know. These points of reference allowed me/my entry into the fabric of local geo-history, especially as a writer recording 'the place'. He told me to ignore the 'private property' sign up the hill, because it's his land (inherited from his father), and said I should visit the memorial to sailors he'd built at the top of the hill – 'Go between the two boulders and you'll see the tower I made myself … and you'll see plaques commemorating sailors and others who have lost their lives in these seas.'

I tell him of my interest in lookouts, lighthouses and towers. He says that he was a sailor (fisherman and tugs) and knows every nook and cranny of this coast. He also told me that his mother's family lived (as one of only two families) on Calf Island (waves crashing over them) and that his father owned the elevated land above Colla Road and could look out over Calf Island. He discussed the history of smuggling and piracy and pointed out that the high point was always used for surveying the coastline and 'natural harbour'. His mother's family are O'R…s and his father's Gs.

What was remarkable was the increasing level of invitation and trust – which I value and appreciate. He told me to 'keep left' and walk to the back of his house – which I did – and as I walked he eventually appeared from the right (going around the other side of the house). We discussed the stunning view – I mentioned that it must be the best in Schull and he agreed and said that everyone thought so. The *detail* of the harbour, islands, Baltimore and so on, was astonishing. One could see *anew*. I brought up the Mizen Archaeological Journals and he pointed through his feature window and there, on the coffee table with a few other books in a pile, was volume two of the bound journals!

And then he began telling me how the original road of the Colla point/ peninsula area ran just below his home … That he had unearthed it years ago and confirmed its existence through using old maps. I should say that there are acres of landscaped garden ('only furze here before') – all stone ponds, walls, grassed banks with shrubs and trees. A remarkable place. He took me from the back through some grassed/boggy areas to an overgrown, very narrow and stone-walled road. He pointed out that there were large granite boulders (see Note 9) higher up so no horse and cart could have traversed it. They called it a Funeral Road back then because it was where they'd eventually carry out the locals in their coffins. He said this with an equanimity that leads me to think about those for whom the Church looks after the worries of a mortal existence, and for whom the certainty of deliverance brings calm to discussions of death. I can't say what he thinks – I didn't ask, but it's what I wondered at the time. Tracy has seen funerals passing through town – coffin carried up the main street from the church (the body having been viewed in the funeral parlour – a few houses from where we are living – the night before), shops closed and people respectful in their shop doorways. A really sacred and deeply felt moment for the entire community.

From the funeral road the old man took me through layers of the garden to show me the mortared stone walls of the old house where he'd dry-stoned with more sandstone to 'build up'. I connected with him over the beauty of red sand-stone used in the wall with its varicoloured play in the light – lichen, residues etc. He pointed out protruding slate which he said would have been a step or maybe a shelf for a lamp.

After showing me the storm-damage to his trees – many down, which he was cutting up, including a massive pine out by the roots – he discussed comparisons being made with the Big Wind/Great Storm of the nineteenth century.

I assured him I'd visit his memorial in coming days and that I'd say hello as I passed by – he asked me to do so. I said I'd bring my wife with me one time. And then I continued my walk as described earlier.

Considerations

Considering all of this, the conversation I had with John in the main street about locals being curious as to who you are, then accepting you (to an extent); of deposits, withdrawals and the necessity of adding something to the communal mix, I have also clarified my gaps and passes issue. What flows in and what goes out. This also connects with the valve notion of towers and observation points. What's allowed in and out; what's kept out and in ... the maintaining of lines of communication in very particular ways.

John told me no one can steal boats from the harbour, because everyone knows the individual boats and their owners. When someone committed a crime in town and tried to make their getaway in a boat, they were caught because of the boat being identified. We also discussed the issue of right of way and access to the land, how people feel about access rights. Much to consider in all this. I will write a poem 'Funeral Road'.

Notes that are part of the whole

Note 1: The old man said, 'The short furze is Irish furze, the big flowering furze is French furze.'

Note 2: The old man had gardening gloves on which were understandably dirty. He went to slap me on the shoulder in a gesture of friendship (reaching up!), but stopped and looked at his gloves and changed his mind.

Note 3: I mentioned my caution about going on to private property (though I am no believer in such a thing, I am a respecter of others' customs and beliefs) and he joked, 'It never stops the Americans!'

Note 4: He was interested in Famine migration and didn't see 160 years as being anything at all in the grand scheme of things – he still considered me/us as 'coming back'.

Note 5: Much not written here will manifest in poems.

Note 6: Insect and birdlife very active during the walk, especially around boggy areas and in the old man's landscaped garden.

Note 7: The old man strongly reminded me of the orchardist in Kelmscott/Clifton Hills I wrote about over twenty-five years ago (though in that case I talked with the old Dalmatian orchardist numerous times over many months). He was an unusual and determined individual with his own philosophy about the intersections between people and 'nature'. From the foot of the Darling Ranges to the hills of the peninsula here.

Note 8: The 'old man' (it has to have quotes … I don't feel I can use his family name and though over 50 I was the young man to his much older man!) referred to the Celtic Sea as opposed to the 'Atlantic Ocean' of the more Western parts. The 'Celtic Sea' has been a constant from circa 1923 not 'agreed upon' until the early 1970s. Prior to that it was called the 'Western Approaches'. It does form a specific area, though, and its western limit is marked by the east of the Mizen Head. So looking out from the Colla Road 'highlands', one is looking on to Schull harbour, Roaringwater Bay, the islands, the Celtic Sea and beyond to the Atlantic 'proper'. Though it is still all the North Atlantic in the broadest sense.

Note 9: I am sure the old man said 'granite' and not sandstone. There was a granite quarry near Dunmanus (now closed) and various walking guides talk of the granite spine of the nearby Sheep's Head peninsula. So granite boulders are possible, but up there on the Colla highlands it seemed to me to be all red sandstone. As an aside, I found some interesting details in 'Houses of the Oireachtas' documents online, coming out of a question by a Mr O'Driscoll asking the Minister of Industry and Commerce 'if he was aware that the Browhead granite Quarries near Dunmanus, County Cork, have been unworked since 1940…?' Mr Lemass replied: 'I am aware that the quarry referred to by the Deputy was in operation until September, 1939. There is little or no demand locally for the material, and the output of the quarry when working was, to a very great extent, exported to Great Britain. The immediate revival of the export trade is not practicable in existing circumstances.' [Dail Eireann Debate, Vol. 96 No. 20]

29 March 2014

Went out to Crookhaven this morning to examine the two lookout towers again. Thinking about them as a 'unique' pair in terms of that particular location and watching over the entry to the Crookhaven harbour, as opposed to the network of Martello towers built during the Napoleonic Wars in a coastal surveillance system. After Tracy photographed the two towers, we went across from Rock Island to Crookhaven itself where one has a clear view of the towers and the lighthouse on the promontory of Rock Island. The furthest tower looking from Crookhaven village appears slightly off the vertical – a leaning tower. Also many power poles – so lots of verticals or slightly out-of-kilter/off-centre uprights. And with the angling away of the sandstone, a strange sense of destabilisation pervades.

Also went to Galley Cove Beach with its centring view of Fastnet. And then up to Brow Head with its 'Marconi' tower in ruins. The original signal tower at Brow Head was built by the British in 1804 (potential French invasion), with the telegraph moving there in 1901 (Marconi's experiments). This theory of reverse-mirror, semi-porous, membranous model of towers I am constructing (or weaving), the Marconi 'tower' – lines of sight becomes lines of radio waves – is part of an effort to 'fill in the gaps', leave no stone unturned.

Network of Martello towers, signal towers/watch towers. Radar domes (Mount Gabriel), castles and keeps, Marconi's tower/Brow Head (also Lloyds communications with ships to America, flags and semaphore), other signal installations (Mizen Head), lighthouses (Fastnet – also site of Marconi's wireless equipment in 1904). Marconi proving that 'wireless signals' followed/bent to the earth's curvature. Arthur Nottage, assistant to Marconi, stayed on after the Marconi Wireless Telegraph Company left in 1914. And it's worth noting that Crookhaven had actually been pivotal to communications with America since 1863 when the telegraph line ran to Cork (established by Paul J. Reuter), becoming the last point of contact before ships crossed the Atlantic. Reuter would make contact with ships in the steamer 'Marseilles', then telegraph details/news back to Cork. [see GB4IMO International Marconi website.]

What so interests me in this is that such an apparently 'backward' place of the nineteenth century was actually in the vanguard of communications (for good and bad). Its last port-of-call/point-of-contact status, its sailing ships coming in from the New World, afforded it a special status and utility within capitalist empire-building. A staging-post of language (and not the 'local' language but the English that was rapidly becoming the lingua franca). So while local people suffered oppression and reduction, Crookhaven and environs became a vector for capitalist forces. Having said this, the New World did at least offer hope to the starved/oppressed and disenfranchised, giving the communications 'revolution' a radical application/manifestation. But it's a scenario of giving with one hand and taking with the other.

TERMS AND CONDITIONS OF WRITING PLACE?

After a brisk walk up Ardmanagh Road, with rain and hail predicted (though it doesn't arrive till 3 pm), the furze bristling with intense bumble-bee activity, I am thinking over the terms and conditions of engaging with and writing place, I've come up with a set of notions to consider:

1. If lifelong familiarity exists, or years of childhood are spent in a particular place, then there is an 'access' to its substance, co-ordinates and ineffable qualities that is focussed (even if unutterable at times or in certain circumstances), intense and ironically 'authoritative' in a variety of ways.
2. The dynamic and conditions of indigenous/non-indigenous relationships to place need to be constantly registered in terms of language and spirituality. An indigenous observer has immediate access and a self-defining legitimacy of presence. However...
3. ... place is not only an issue of legitimacy, as it's constantly changing and never stable. The person 'passing through' can see in a way the local (first generation or of many generations) might not. This is a tangential but essential component of international regionalism – the local being enhanced and intensified by listening to the views of the transient. In Ireland, the travellers in particular have the status of both 'temporary' and 'permanent' (in the expectation that they might pass through), creating a dynamic in which the local and the transient are in symbiosis materially, culturally and even in terms of self-identity.
4. Further, the longer-term visitor will take original impressions, change them over time and re-evaluate the place, reconsidering first encounters as they understand manners, language and 'tones' of that place. This feeds back, and is conveyed elsewhere through the personal webs/networks of friends, family etc.
5. The migrant offers other angles of access. A place becomes their place (as well) because of the permanence of migration (not only in the new location but 'loss' in so many essential ways of the old location, whatever ties

remain) – it is as legitimate as any other presence and way of seeing, though as with all incomers, respect for indigenous observers/presence/primacy is essential, along with an awareness of the collective knowledge of other, earlier (and following) migrants.

6. There is also the universal variable of 'place' – the effect that presence, participation and even the act of observation have on the entire biosphere (where all places are one, despite the patterns of air movement). The local is part of the whole, the regional part of the international, and whether one calls it the 'Butterfly Effect' or something else, presence and 'passing through' both bring/carry 'costs'. Place is a component of space. Rather than international regionalism, maybe more accurately: biospheric regionalism. The biosphere is extant, entire – the 'international' is a subset as much as the 'regional' is.

Conclusion

The indigene, the migrant (of today, yesterday, or generations back), the visitor, the 'passer-through', the transient, are all enactors of seeing/observing in place. All are participants. We need to compile, to gather together their 'seeings' to understand the nature of human presence in space, and its collective contribution to place. We also need to contextualise with and within animal-place, plant-place and the geological subset under/within the biosphere. A holistic picture that tracks consequences of presence and place.

Notes

Note 1: 'Indigenous' in this context 'means' having a 'pre-history' of association with a place – really, 'those who came before' or 'prior' if not 'first'. Not so much 'origins', but association with a region stretching far back beyond individual and family memory – preserved in collective/group memory through language, ritual, totemics of place, passed down over many ('uncountable', maybe) generations.

Note 2: 'Migrant' is used in terms of a migration from one place of belonging (if not origin, certainly 'originating' from…) to another – a new place in which the migrant seeks belonging. In polysituatedness, there is no ultimate and absolute leaving or arriving, as place is intrinsically connected and we carry all previous lives and experience in our presence. Even 'indigenous' presence has been about movement and micro-variations in connection and shifts in location, especially for 'nomadic' peoples and individuals within traditional societies. There are recent and long-established migrants – and there is the migrant who has migrated alone or with family or is awaiting family to come out and join him/her/other family; there's the person of migrant heritage who forms a relationship or has offspring with an indigenous person, with their offspring claiming multi-directional senses of belonging (even if most identify with their place and the traditions of the birth co-ordinates). Or the migrants'

303

offspring who, though 'native' to the new home-place, more strongly identify with ancestral origins, through a positive emulation of 'home' stories or a resistance to the place of their birth for social or political reasons.

Note 3: Eventually migrant heritage becomes naturalised and thus creates a self-defining permanence and sense of *entitlement* of belonging. Place is often read in terms of 'ownership', 'occupation', and denial of the indigenous by those subscribing to this version of 'home'-making.

Note 4: The 'nomad' suggests a broader sense of place, points of belonging (and all points in between), wherein movement becomes witness and observation – displacing and replacing as a 'continuum'. One might envisage a strong potential for a broader sense of impact of presence in many different forms on the biosphere. A spectrum of multiple and differing belongings.[1]

Note 5: 'The wanderer'/the 'transient' – often alienated but seeking connection on a temporary basis. Takes stories from one place to another, knits the whole.

Note 6: Refugees reveal the nature of place through displacement. The suffering undoes conceptions of belonging but also demands them.

Note 7 (a): To exile someone is to debase and fetishise place – to own and dictate it conceptually, even spiritually. To send someone into exile is an act (or enactment) of (dis)possession and control of/over place.

Note 7 (b): The 'blowback' – the returning 'native' – brings experience gathered elsewhere (in new homes, new places of belonging) to the originating 'home-place'. As Tracy mentioned regarding this dynamic/issue here in West Cork,

---

1 I envisage a departure from both the 'Nomadic waves or flows of deterritorialisation go from the central layer to the periphery, then from the new centre to the new periphery, falling back to the old centre and launching forth to the new…' of Deleuze and Guattari (Gilles Deleuze and Félix Guattari, *A Thousand Plateaus: Capitalism and Schizophrenia* [Minneapolis, University of Minnesota Press, 1987], p. 53), or Rosi Braidotti's 'The nomad's relationship to the earth is one of transitory attachment and cyclical frequentation; the antithesis of the farmer, the nomad gathers, reaps, and exchanges but does not exploit' (*Nomadic Subjects: Embodiment and Sexual Difference in Contemporary Feminist Theory* [New York, Columbia University Press, 1994], p. 25). There something disturbingly 'noble' about the 'does not exploit' observation, and I would certainly replace the convenient 'cyclical' (with its undertones of seasonal purity – this is not possible in a climate-damaged world, if ever) with a 'displaced/ replaced' dynamic (though never completely – 'replaced' is notional rather than actual: a desire, or maybe acts of spiritual wish-fulfilment?) Deleuze's and Guattari's model works well in text-play, but is diminished before the reality of cultural destruction that permeates, say, discussions of nomadism in Australia and the interference, even removal, of such cultural, social and survival modes since 'settlement'/invasion. In Emily Jeremiah, *Nomadic Ethics in Contemporary Women's Writing in German: Strange Subjects* (Rochester, NY, Camden House, 2012), p. 6, we read, 'Sara Ahmed raises further objection to Braidotti's concept. In *Strange Encounters*, Ahmed argues that in using nomads as a metaphor, Braidotti makes them something other than themselves, erasing the specificity and difference of particular nomadic peoples' [Sara Ahmed, *Strange Encounters: Embodied Others in Post-Coloniality* (Abingdon, Routledge, 2000)]. This seems strikingly obvious to me, and might be applied to all metaphoric or allegorical constructs dressed up as social critiques that use people and their communities to make points about privileged milieux.

and particularly on the Mizen, this can be resented by 'the locals' themselves. However, that resentment itself opens new, critical ways of seeing/observing, especially in terms of comparing 'here' with 'there', a comparative model of place builds.

Note 8: The cross-generational 'blowback' – our situation coming from Western Australia to Schull, Ireland for much more than a visit. Irish ancestry and 'returning' to live in Ireland for an indeterminate period (a measure of social belonging is 'your' child being in a local school). As both Tracy's and my families were 'Famine emigrants', the locals have a complex view of our 'return'. Our son's teacher used him and the Kinsella family as an example of 'having to leave' (conditions and hope for a 'better life' in the circumstances) and desiring, long after, to return. What also complicates the 'example' is the working-visa migration of local young folk to Australia (especially Western Australia) for work/economic reasons. It's almost an 'exodus' of youth, which brings entangled feelings of loss, guilt and hope in older folk here. A measure of this new presence in Australia – adding to the massive historic nineteenth-century presence – is the fact that Irish food brands are establishing themselves in Australia to meet contemporary Irish tastes. For example, a brand of potato chips (full of MSG) that carry a haunting inverted echo of the fate of many of their and our ancestors.

IRREDENTISM

In the context of 'Putin's Russia' (which it is not!) annexing the Crimea, the word 'Irredentism' is being bandied about. According to the *Guardian* newspaper of the 28/03/2014 in an article by Luke Harding, 'Talbott was referring to the doctrine that a country is entitled to control areas or territories outside its borders to which it has an ethnic or historical claim. The word comes from the Italian for unredeemed – *irredenta*. The Italian patriots who came up with it were referring to Italian-speaking territories at the time under the control of the Austro-Hungarian empire (Trieste, Istria, Dalmatia and so on).' The occupations and machinations of the Austro-Hungarian empire aside (if that's possible), the brutality and power-encased drive behind such reasoning are a destruction of the integrity of 'place' as a layered model of interaction and presence. As Harding goes on to say, 'The doctrine's most brutal exponent, of course, was Hitler.' One might add *every* country/nation-state that has had the military power to extend themselves. 'Historical' claims are rather flexible, and the empowered necessarily determine the historical terms themselves. Manifest Destiny and Irredentism seem to have more than a strong overlap. In essence, nation-states are antithetical to place. They are power structures arising out of exclusion, focussed on monitoring and surveillance, and about division and control of wealth by the few (including communist nation-states' party hierarchies) – in essence, concentrations of force. 'Place' is a cross-current outside imposed structure.

To belong and not to belong?

There's a photograph on the Schull Council website that shows 'Gypsies in the Quarry' (named 'Caravan and Quarry' on image). The photo shows 'Traveller' (my interpolation and likely anachronism) caravans on a road above Schull harbour, looking back to Mount Gabriel (from maybe near the present Colla Road). One person is looking out to the front of one of the caravans, which trail back into the distance. The photo looks early twentieth century, possibly late nineteenth century. What's relevant is the inclusiveness that still denotes separation. If one considers the argument that 'Gypsies' in Ireland have (also) been uprooted victims, sufferers, often made 'homeless' (caravan is one form of home, of course) and permanently on the move to survive, it disrupts the picture of nation even further. And if they were 'continental Gypsies' (Romany or 'Gaeilge' – origins are contested), then the crossings from *place* to *place*, the connection of points on the map, the routes, the construction of the Venn diagrams and equations of place and belonging bring us to this rudimentary equation:

$$\frac{place}{presence} = \frac{movement}{belonging}$$

thus to 'separate' off by defining *outside* community (and country and nation) becomes deeply problematic, especially given the history of British colonisation and its efforts to bend place and identity to its will and desire for profit and power (Ireland as its food-bowl).

Further notes

Note 1: Irredentism is one manifestation of the desire to control through identity and to override the specificities and idiosyncrasies of place (its dialect, its slight differences from neighbours, its slightly different geology, flora and fauna, all those things that make one village different from another, even if they basically share the same core language and ethnic origins!). It is racist (through 'inclusion' which also creates the excluded; also in denoting sameness across different places through notions of ethnicity-blood-race labelling). Place, large or small, defined by so many geo-social and eco-topographical variables, has finite limits. Maybe it's as far as a person can walk in a day, maybe as far as a shout can be heard or a weather event felt in almost the same way (in the big storm more trees came down in this immediate locale because it is open and up high – exposed – or fewer because it was sheltered … each location has its micro-events within greater weather occurrences) – all overlap and make Venn diagrams and lacunae in, of, and with place (and making 'new' places: subsets in subsets…).

Note 2: The 'Gypsies' and/or Travellers are othered as a reverse Irredentism with all its racist impact (not absorbing the race allotment!) In the othering programme of displacement, the Travellers are denied any place outside (a disputed!) 'origin', which is always vaguely defined by oppressing communal and governmental bodies as well as individuals and families seeking to 'move' the Travellers on. Where Travellers originate from is denied, ignored and turned into an anthropological contest (a perverse origin of species). Rather than carry stories and tales in the narrative of place – international regionalism – they are seen as disrupting those lines of story (right down to the deployment of their own vernacular). A purity cult of 'the tale' is a frightening part of denying the strength, brilliance and efficacy of the Traveller narrative. Intense in community and family loyalties (with all the attendant problems of 'blood' relations), the Travellers counterpoint the 'blood' bigotries of those whose (claims to) 'places' they pass through or camp in. Settlement, resettlement – displacement and replacement – presence and absence – and especially a continual postponement of settlement, and sometimes removal (by outside forces), are an unfixed dynamic, shifting, adjusting, adapting to social, economic and local cultural conditions (there is not the complete separation that bigots claim – that is an impossibility!) Is this 'nomadism'? Is this a process of displaced and displacing movement through space to define a fluid, Möbius-like *place*? And this is ongoing – its micro levels keep it outside national myths, investigations and restorations that come about through deconstructive studies.

*

Consider the overtly racist case of a 'blonde-headed' child being removed from Traveller parents under suspicion of the child having been kidnapped; the 'fair' and 'dark' displacement scenario. This actually happened twice in recent times, in Dublin last year and also in Greece. In the Irish case, the child was the Traveller-mother's offspring – the authorities used DNA (ultimate gesture of racism) to 'prove' the case (presumably against the mother?)

Further, the fact that a 2010 poll showed that 1 in 5 Irish people would refuse 'Irishness' to Travellers who (have long) lived here is alarming. A 'blowback' is acceptable to many, we have found, but not a Traveller with hundreds of years' traceable history in Ireland? Read the torrents of abuse meted out by townspeople to Travellers in Cambridge, UK, over the years we've lived there. The absolute fear and distrust of their temporariness, but also the refusal to have them settle for any period of time.

BEING BACK: PLACE, STORAGE, WASTE AND (UN)BELONGING

What *is* being back? We've just returned to Schull, West Cork, from Italy, Switzerland, France, England and Wales. Is *here* – Rosewood Cottage/ Schull – a substitute, a placebo for 'being back' at Jam Tree Gully in the Western Australian wheatbelt, our legal home in accordance with our 'nationality' (to which I don't subscribe) and 'place of permanent residence'? Is it another layer of 'home', a three-dimensional chess configuration of desired belonging? Are we 'just' visitors or because we want to stay as long as we can, are we in some way different? Does Irish 'heritage' mean we belong in some distant if disconnected way, does the feeling of empathy and connection with the land itself matter?

Poems are forms of connection, and poems are coming out of the place for us. Whatever arguments can be made for and against, we have 'returned' rather than 'arrived', and what we do is framed by that fact. Tracy and I are both writing sequences of poems connected to here, and I am mid-cycle in my exploration of epics and locality, mute swans and red sandstone. I feel connected – maybe culturally, but certainly in being an observer of the natural world, especially birds and plants. I record movements, comings and going, minute differences on a daily basis when here. My journals are a storage depot for these observations, for calibrations, for hypotheses arising from comparisons and patterns arising out of this data accumulated through seasons, over the many months.

We're now living next door to our previous abode, Anchor Lodge. Still on Ardmanagh Road, which is reassuring. Rosewood Cottage has an elaborate garden full of Australian plant species, an arboretum of exotica, a storage zone for the return mail of migration, colonialism and displacement. We assume, as do others, that the house's owners have some Australian connection. We don't know them; we rent through a local agent. The various gums (including lemon-scented) have recently been pruned back because of risk to the house from the waves of brutal storms that have been hitting Ireland over the last six months. Deeply distressing to see, after only three weeks' absence, that not only has much of the furze on Mount Gabriel been burnt but areas of general flora have been cleared (making new fields as vengeance against the EU because of its cut in subsidies for conserving 'wild' terrain?)

I look out through the kitchen window, across the heavily grassed fields (hay will be cut in a couple of months) towards the mountains, and get distracted by a ship in a bottle on the window ledge. This is the second one I've seen in the house. Anchor Lodge specialised in miniature lighthouses – things we would never collect and display or store, but things that will stay here during our residence and eat or flow into our psyches.

Waking between leopard-print sheets in this new 'let', which comes equipped with someone else's version of 'belonging'. Their home rented to us so it temporarily (and partially?) becomes 'our' home. In the 'temporariness' of abode, an ephemerality of house, the embedded transitory nature of 'renting' – 'home' leaks out through the cracks and aberrations in structure (despite the double-glazing). We wake to each other and talk over how we did or didn't sleep; we comment on the comfort or discomfort, especially with regard to the 'new' bed/s, make comparisons with other abodes and especially our previous rental in the same village/region. We affirm our love and friendship and push aside travel tensions, opting for some form of semi-permanence, of potential familiarity and certainty. We resonate in our togetherness and add to our stock of shared life experiences – it becomes our refuge, our repository of impressions collected outside and shared over meals, in the evenings.

This affirmation is part of 'return', even if mediated through the newness of abode and caution regarding its potential differences and surprises. This is a declaration of 'home' extended across 20,000 km to our wheatbelt sense of belonging (and unbelonging/intrusion/alienation). It's diasporic, place-specific, place overlaid and substituted, and about safety and determination to connect. Outside, maybe it is drizzling – that's familiar, likely. The blanket bogs (bog cotton, sundews, mosses), the saturated fields, the stream running out the back, emptying into Schull harbour.

Being here or anywhere is also likely to be about 'ancestry' (ours or not ours, but certainly those who have been in the place for a long, long time), ecology and welcome/alienation. At what level can we gain and maintain entry?

Though we know where we are born, we know little or nothing about where we will die. It could be in our/a temporary home/location as much as our long-term abode or region of residence. Should one pass away in a new or temporary home, one becomes part of that place in an undeniable way. Especially if 'remains' remain – the ground itself will store one's corpse or act as a bed for one's ashes, but also if they are 'returned'/'repatriated'/'taken back' (a residue of death both physical and spiritual). There's always the potential, and that means the present dwelling-place will resonate for family and others with an interest in who and what you are and were. It becomes, by association, part of them/ selves. And you become part of the spirituality of the place – your residue interacts with the residues of all that comes before. The essences blend literally and figuratively. It's why I always respect the spiritual beliefs of the people whose area I am part of – whatever the duration of my physical presence is. And I respect the places they choose as concentrations or foci of belief and connection and worship.

One might doubt or resent the domination of place by a religion, but its zones of worship are about the *people* who worship there (regularly and 'passing through'), and their desire to focus presence through place (the zone of worship) towards something more universal/transcendent and nodal. Which is not to say place in itself isn't transcendent and nodal, because it is. In many ways, it serves as a religious entirety in itself, outside the meddling of external power structures with their aim of self-embellishing. But these are personal issues of belonging and there is no prescriptive model of interaction between self and place, community and spirituality, even if we are often told there is! As Tracy observes, growing up in a large family she so lacked private space, however small, that she retreated into the 'interiority of the page'. For many, place becomes a negotiation of this need to write a private interiority and to communicate with community and, indeed, a transcendent spirituality.

STORAGE

Another batch of our 'stuff' (books, papers, kitchen items, clothes etc.) collected from the storage lock-up in Skibbereen where we placed all we had in Ireland while we were away and between rentals. Everything wrapped in plastic against the dust. In the boxes are our poetry manuscripts-in-progress, in a bizarre state of non-being. In the process of their unwrapping, their disinterring, there is something over-invested and painfully private. They're not *ready* and were stored in a half-dressed state. In state, but not decent. Encounters with our new place, interrupted by departure, unformed and unable to send their tendrils out to complete their growth, their grip on the place from which they are substantially (though far from exclusively) formed.

All neatly packed into the lightless, corrugated-iron room. Temporary space. We compact our '*here* lives', order the cell, the compartment, the windowless room without function outside that of storage. One of dozens, mostly the same, in a large, not particularly clean shed. Storage. Then transferred from there to Rosewood Cottage. A 25-minute drive. We will use the storage facility again, and again if need be. Packaging, unpacking, redistributing in different spaces. Objects of familiar function going out of usage and then coming back into usage in different contexts. Familiar, known, but changing in the (slightly) new 'ecos'. And the Ilen River at high tide with the pair of mute swans on small islets facing each other near where the river runs alongside the main road west of *Skib*. The river 'anglers' prey on in April and May, hungering after the sea salmon and the trout that trust its relatively clean waters. The swans know and inscribe their own versions of history – of flood and loss, of territory and food.

When we left Ohio in 2005, we left our/the car and boxes of 'possessions' in a ('paid-up') storage facility, not knowing if we'd return. Later that year, I went back to Ohio, to Mount Vernon and Gambier, for a few months, to sell the car and arrange for the boxes (mainly of books – there were a few poetry manuscripts, but most of the completed and published draft papers had been deposited in the Kenyon Library) to be shipped to Australia. During that time, I lived in a small college flat and wrote poems of absence. The storage facility was claustrophobic and echoed with collapse when emptied – a mirror to the fundamentalism of war (the polluting of my college office was no doubt linked to my anti-militarist stance), of religion in secular schools (a secondary teacher had branded a student in the name of Christ/God – the student was Jewish) and the fundamentalism of capitalism (embodied in *the car*, in truth). The storage facility filling and emptying embodied presence and loss and 'failure' to belong, though our son was born on American *soil*.

I have only recently become aware of the many reality television programmes that show the invasion of private space by claiming 'abandoned' goods in storage lockers, prying into people's lives to see what profit can be made from them. The bargain hunter as police of the private – it's not surprising many of these shows are set in America where notions of private and public space are fraught. Big Brother becomes you, and you can profit from others' decline or folly. Their loss is your gain. Their loss is your control over their privacy. When staying in my Ohio flat, I kept some of the stored material back from the lock-up to share my months alone. That never went to Australia with the main consignment – when I left, I gave the items away and carried the few books in my travel luggage. When the items arrived in Australia, part of our lives in America went into the Australian wheatbelt, where they became part of that place. They speak through all the texts I have written since in that place. I carry those texts in my head as well, to Schull, to Rosewood Cottage, without the encumbrance of material goods.

When young, I was a keen and committed philatelist. Then I stopped, and stopped for good – I shed my stored goods from their sheets, their albums. Stamp collecting was, for me, a type of storage – of gain, potential (for exchange), a harnessing of history (private and public), and even materiality. Storage became a mode of protection and curating, a museum in which the collected was the protected, a safeguard against loss. Less important was accumulation; more important was recording, filing and contextualising (historical, geographical, within the nomenclature of collecting – rare, common, a story attached regarding how an inverted watermark happened, and so on). And storage also became embroiled in loss – what is sold, exchanged, damaged, given away, deteriorated.

My mother keeps two stamp collections I inherited from my grandfather after his death: the Peace collection and the Coronation collections. I sold them to my mother back when I was a drinker, and she looks after them. The politics of coronation aside, these collections are in black card photograph albums, the mint stamps hinged in with my sign-writer grandfather's white painted headings over each – Antigua, Rhodesia, India, Australia … the language of colonialism. These were part of my grandfather's storage and are part of the storage of memories of him. They were what he was born in, what he migrated through, and what he looked back on.

He was not a sentimental man and if he thought he could turn a buck selling something – memories, autographs, stamps – he would. He liked a profit if it came without baggage. But his relationship with me was also based on stamps – we shared the interest and the passion. His passing them on to me was both an emptying and securing of the storage facility. It was a line of communication after death – an agnostic death.

As an alcoholic, I was not, as it turned out, a safe form of storage, but Mum 'insured' me in a sense, and I made the choice to sell to her rather than outside the storage unit of family. The storage ceased to be material and became conceptual. From all of this, an ethics opposing property and sole ownership forms.

The failure of storage: nuclear waste facilities. Ireland is nuclear-free, though there was an attempt to establish a nuclear power station at Carnsore Point in Wexford during the 1970s, but public opposition thwarted it.[1] But given the power plants and recycling facilities across the Channel in France and across the Irish Sea in Britain (the Windscale accident in Cumberland in 1957 was literally on the front doorstep of the most heavily populated areas of Ireland), it's far less 'free' than some may think. Nuclear waste is unsustainable as storage – a dissolutely temporary space in terms of containment, when talking of plutonium and many other 'by-products', a 'permanent' space in terms of longevity. A harnessing that unharnesses, a closure that will eventually open and release and cause the destruction of the storers (the hoarders?) themselves. Concrete, lead and steel cannot ensure the storage of radioactive materials in any safe way.

There have long been those who envisage Australia as a storage zone, or a location for storage – a nuclear Terra Nullius (where the Maralinga and Montebello tests have already contaminated vast areas): extract the uranium and replace it both conceptually and literally with residue, waste. From ex-Prime Minister Bob Hawke's call for Australia to profit from storing such waste, to Premier of South Australia Jay Wetherill's calling for a Royal Commission in the hope of stimulating what some have termed (approvingly!) a 'cradle-to-grave' enterprise, Australia offers itself as a colonial tract for the new colonialism of nuclear waste. With many Irish resident in Australia, maybe it makes for a strange kind of post-Famine anxiety – the degenerative blight and genocidal policies of an empire making the new destination as risky and deadly as the old origin. My family escaping famine to Ludlow in south-west Australia became part of the dispossessing pioneering. As nuclear experiments did at Maralinga, and as they will again in their various manifestations. The land is forced to store not only its traditional and ecological knowledges, but the legacy of imperial (capitalist, nationalistic, and centralised power structures') waste:

Maralinga

Hell is hollow, a gesture in a flat surface lipped in, the curve
upturned – no same point if you keep going in the same
direction; convex lore coated longer than words and longer
than belief. A weeping tree in flower, a minuscule tree among

1 See Chapter 7 of Liam Leonard, *The Environmental Movement in Ireland* (Galway, SSRC, National University of Ireland, 2007).

the saltbush and deceased. A camel skeleton hunched big-
boned against the track. Spirit-killer? It's a weapon they'd test
a few times at least. Watson siding as water only here was
apertured into lexical theft, before and after, to make the big
bang, negate and relegate the gathering tribes – a plan –
atomic warfare against a people so old they brought fear to
investors in peerage, shock wave propelling the train slightly
faster once out of Watson, where the first flock of birds seen
since yesterday overfly warning markers, pink and grey
galahs their chests shields worn in the x-ray rooms, all nature
is conflated in the atom and there's no half-life of logic to
ward off the insecurities. Clear sky thunder. The name retains.
A given name. A Christian name. Exposure to the energy
source of God by any sectarian configuration. Mirage of treed
islands run blue, like a leak from the sky, blue blood shining
over the expanse. Seriously, that's what you see: a spreading
blue across the Axminster texture of the plain, as they would
envisage it. Still holding the data, using it not an end in itself,
down the track. That line of hills to the north. What do they
hold back on the edge of the plain, the hollow bones.[2]

Degenerative toxic storage. Ships travelling the seas with barrels of toxic waste,
some pushed overboard, others bound for 'recycling' facilities. Suitcase-sized
desolation. Planting waste in the 'open spaces', in the 'nothingness' of Australia?
Space up for grabs. The recolonisation of the very particles of being. Total
intrusion and exclusion. Country as radioactive presence and exclusion. The
ultimate zone.

From the sublime to the ridiculous? Nuclear storage under North American,
European, Russian, Chinese, Indian … mountains? The suitcase as storage – for
travel, at home. Even at Jam Tree Gully I choose to 'live out of a suitcase' –
ready to go, so to speak, though I/we want to go nowhere. Habit from years
of travel? From wandering younger years without a home? I survive with few
clothes – I make them last. A small bag, and an overflow storage case. Things
shift due to priority, in and out of storage.

A journal is a storage facility. Computers, electronic data storage devices.
Indexing is somewhat different. Maybe the key is in the arrangement of data –
the flow of information from landscape into memory. But all are ineffective
storage devices when compared to the neural networks of the brain itself, and
the poem. The poem is a living, organic storage device with fuzzy indexing. Its
slippages can be generative. The poem, if memorised and passed on by word of
mouth, becomes a polyvalent and multi-layered storage device that reinvents
and replays with differing tone in different contexts, reinventing itself. The
stored line in memory is retold and changes. The key to the poem storage facility is both easy and complex – a riddle we all know and spend our time trying to

2 John Kinsella, *Armour* (London, Picador, 2011).

solve. We can memorise the poem, but we can't memorise the intent behind its composition if we didn't compose it. The poem is a paradoxical storage facility and faculty. Mnemonics, mimesis and mimeographics are components of that key as much as they are of the poem as storage entity in itself.

Inside the poem is Ohio, Rosewood Cottage, the nuclear power plant in Switzerland our train passed within a few hundred metres of. It's the uranium prospecting companies in the wheatbelt of Western Australia who hire as their publicist someone Tracy knew of who'd be a social being ready to shout the arts from the gallery boxes. It is Ireland and Australia. It's the seas of France oozing their dumped nuclear waste. It's the poem that says everything and nothing. It's the silence of the vacuum, the ultimate and yet vulnerable storage facility. It's identifying with a place and being forced to move on. It's identity in a place that can never be deleted, even by those trying hard to do so – radioactive fallout is an accident waiting to happen literally and conceptually. All that matters (to some) is where it happens. Which place. How does it affect … *our* place, some other place? *Horror vacui*…?

> There is scarce a little place to-day
> That I can recognise:
> What was on flood
> Is all on ebb.[3]

I read in *The Journals of John Cheever*: 'The idea is to get away from one place, but I never get away, I never reach another place. I try to struggle with things that bind me, but I forget the nature of the bonds.'[4] I think over Aristotle on place, that 'movement' equals 'changing place'. In Book III, Part 2, of *Physics*[5] we read: 'place, void, and time are thought to be necessary conditions of motion'. And in Part 5: 'It is the nature of every kind of sensible body to be somewhere, and there is a place appropriate to each, the same for the past and for the whole, e.g. for the whole earth and for a single clod, and for fire and for a spark' and 'Surely what is in a special place is in place, and what is in place is in a special place.'

3 From 'The Lament of the Old Woman from Beare', trans. Kuno Meyer, in *Selections from Ancient Irish Poetry* (London, Constable & Co., 1911).
4 John Cheever, *The Journals of John Cheever* (London, Vintage, 2010), p. 27.0
5 Aristotle, *Physics*, trans. R. P. Hardie and R. K. Gaye, http://classics.mit.edu/Aristotle/physics.html (accessed March 2014).

FROM STORAGE TOWARDS WASTE

Chatting over my notions of storage with Tracy on waking this morning, she mentioned hoards (not votive hoards) as a form of storage, which they are. She wrote a string of 'hoard poems' at Anchor Lodge, which she placed in storage in the Skib lock-up while we were away. They are out of storage now and in Rosewood Cottage. They will eventually travel back to Australia while the rest of our 'stuff' stays in storage in Skib (where it will return from Rosewood).

I was thinking over my grandmother's 'back room' (a bit like Saki's lumber room) and, later, her garden shed, as storage facilities that she alone was privileged to enter. She was wary of people trying to dictate what could be kept and stored and what couldn't. She had been a seamstress in her youth, and the back room which I was allowed to enter on occasion was full of buttons and cloth and dressmakers' mannequins, trophies for flower arranging and all the paraphernalia of that art, plus much more. Various family members felt the space should be cleared out somewhat, but I was sure that was investigative as much as controlling. The old photo albums, the items that would give clues to their own identities and lives. It was a repository and perhaps they wanted it opened, as if one's innermost thoughts and observations were broadcast on the cinema screen in front of an eager audience. I am reminded of lines from Tracy's poem 'Lost Property':

> ... to be immersed though not safe among the things
> that preceded you, immediate and limitless,
> everything already there, the way the world went on
> before you were thought of, that flux[1]

What interests me isn't the repository or the act of storage as much as its permeability, the slippage. In coming to Schull, we have no access to such

1 Tracy Ryan, 'Lost Property', in *The Argument* (North Fremantle, Fremantle Press, 2011), pp. 59–60.

repositories outside regional museums or the texts (such as the Mizen Head Archaeological Society bulletins) of place and community. Not of the local congregation, and in my case not 'of the religion', we have no access to the 'hoard' of collective identity ritualised through the Catholic Church. Nor the Anglican Church (here the Church of Ireland), with its history of domination and control of property and lives through money (but not the spirit), a colonial entity that will always be rebarbative in the context.

But even these storerooms are temporary, as was my grandmother's back room. When her stores overflowed, my grandfather erected a garden shed for the 'extras'. It was built over the area of the filled-in bomb shelter my grandfather dug during the Second World War. I have heard lots of bomb shelter stories. I have seen some of the Red Cross and other survival materials that were stored down there (my aunt still has them), and I have heard of all the 'stuff' that was piled-up down there when the war came to an end. Broken things are still down there, filled in and buried, including a broken porcelain statuette which was apparently quite beautiful and should have found its way into the back room. A failure of storage. The fetishisation of space, the acts of continuance and disconnection and smothering, the implications of the entombed breaking out with excavation. Storage or disposal?

Just outside Skibbereen is one of the mass burial sites of the Great Famine. Tracy and I may have ancestors in the same graves: Tracy's very possibly in this one or one nearby, because her people were from this region – mine from Carlow and Wicklow. A storage facility for bones, a concentration of trauma, of spiritual overflow. A resting place that is a disruption of history. A memorial. A witnessing. And horrific loss. Storage? And what access do we have? I feel trauma and guilt every time I pass by. Some of my ancestors made it to the south-west of Australia and became colonisers.

Storage has many disturbing resonances in this region, and for Tracy's and my Irish ancestors. The storage facilities were empty, the blight devastating the potato crops but there were also what amounted to genocidal 'laissez-faire' policies, formulated through the actions of Charles Edward Trevelyan, who was Assistant Secretary to the Treasury in London from 1840 to 1859, and who infamously described the Great Famine as a 'mechanism for reducing surplus population'.[2] Schull and Skibbereen are haunted by the dead, by oral histories recorded and still spoken of in disturbed voices that tell of such extreme

---

2 Trevelyan's letter to Thomas Spring-Rice, Lord Mounteagle, is one of the most telling reflections of British government attitudes and subtexts in the handling of relief (and extraction from) Famine victims in existence. The letter reads:

To the Right Hon. Lord Mounteagle
My Dear Lord,
I have had the pleasure of receiving your letter dated 1 inst., and before proceeding to the subjects more particularly treated in it, I must beg of you to dismiss all doubt from your mind of the magnitude of the existing calamity and its danger not being fully known and appreciated in Downing Street.

pain, anguish and death for family after family, that it is almost impossible to absorb.[3] Though having roots much earlier, contemporary Halloween

---

The government establishments are strained to the utmost to alleviate this great calamity and avert this danger, as far as it is in the power of government to do so; and in the whole course of my public service, I never witnessed such entire self-devotion and such hearty and cordial co-operation on the part of officers belonging to different departments met together from different parts of the world, as I see on this occasion.

My purchases are carried to the utmost point short of transferring the famine from Ireland to England and giving rise to a counter popular pressure here, which it would be the more difficult to resist because it would be founded on strong considerations of justice.

But I need not remind your lordship that the ability even of the most powerful government is extremely limited in dealing with a social evil of this description. It forms no part of the functions of government to provide supplies of food or to increase the productive powers of the land. In the great institutions of the business of society, it falls to the share of government to protect the merchant and the agriculturist in the free exercise of their respective employments, but not itself to carry on these employments; and the condition of a community depends upon the result of the efforts which each member of it makes in his private and individual capacity. ...

In Ireland the habit has proverbially been to follow a precisely opposite course, and the events of the last six weeks furnish a remarkable illustration of what I do not hesitate to call this defective part of the national character. The nobility and the gentry have met in their respective baronies, and beyond making presentments required by law, they have, with rare exceptions, confined themselves to memorials and deputations calling upon the government to do everything, as if they have themselves no part to perform in this great crisis of the country. The government is expected to open shops for the sale of food in every part of Ireland, to make all the railroads in Ireland, and to drain and improve the whole of the land of Ireland, to the extent of superseding the proprietor in the management of his own estate, and arranging with his tenants the terms on which the rent etc. is to be adjusted. ...

I must give expression to my feelings by saying that I think I see a bright light shining in the distance through the dark cloud which at present hangs over Ireland. A remedy has already been applied to that portion of the maladies of Ireland which was traceable to political causes, and the morbid habits which still to a certain extent survive are gradually giving way to more healthy action. The deep and inveterate root of social evil remains, and I hope I am not guilty of irreverence in thinking that, this being altogether beyond the power of man, the cure has been applied by the direct stroke of an all-wise Providence in a manner as unexpected and unthought as it is likely to be effectual. God grant that we may rightly perform our part, and not turn into a curse what was intended for a blessing. The ministers of religion and especially the pastors of the Roman Catholic Church, who possess the largest share of influence over the people of Ireland, have well performed their part; and although few indications appear from any proceedings which have yet come before the public that the landed proprietors have even taken the first step of preparing for the conversion of the land now laid down to potatoes to grain cultivation, I do not despair of seeing this class of society still taking the lead which their position requires of them, and preventing the social revolution from being so extensive as it otherwise must become.

Believe me, my dear lord, yours very sincerely,

C. E. Trevelyan. Treasury, 9 October 1846

Dublin, National Library of Ireland, Mounteagle, MS 13,397, in Noel Kissane (ed.), *The Irish Famine: A Documentary History* (Dublin, 1995), p. 51, as taken from http://multitext.ucc.ie/d/ Letter_of_Charles_Edward_Trevelyan_to_Thomas_Spring-Rice_Lord_Mounteagle. The reference to 'laissez-faire' and the 'mechanism' quote are from http://multitext.ucc.ie/d/ Charles_Edward_Trevelyan.

3 Later, after writing this, Tracy showed me her journal of the same period as my Schull

rituals become (dis)embodiments of the Famine horror, transitioning the unacceptable nature of truth into a ghoulish humour that barely brings it to the level of absorbability. The mass grave just outside Skibbereen – the Famine pit – holds unimaginable numbers (of the remains) of the dead. This is place that has been so displaced that it has constantly to reinvent itself even to continue the remembrance, contain the volatility of a narrative that can never be forgotten and should never be erased. When you see land or sky or even sea here, you see the shadows of mass death.

In an open letter written by two Oxford students, Lord Dufferin (also an Irish landlord) and the Honourable G. G. Boyle, published by J. H. Parker in Oxford in 1847, after a journey to Skibbereen during the Great Famine to act as witness to what was happening there, we read this:

> The coach was to pass through Skibbereen at ten o'clock, but upon its arrival we found it full; however, we determined to hurry on by any conveyance which could be procured, as we had seen quite enough to satisfy us, and a further stay would have been both painful and unnecessary. After a delay of three or four hours, we succeeded in hiring an outside jaunting car, to which an extra horse was attached. While this was being prepared, we sent out for an immense basket-full of loaves, intending to distribute them to the occasional starving beings we were sure to meet with by the way; but some of the people of the town had learnt our intention, and collected in a great crowd under the window to the number of 100 or 200, mostly women. It was a frightful sight to see those pale eager faces staring up at us,

---

journals, in which she wrote: 'What did my forebears do to evade those mass graves? (And John's forebears?) Of course they left – but how did they have the power and *means* to leave? ... Research quote, Schull and Skibbereen: "the two famine-slain slain Sisters of the South" ... Did they feel they had *no choice* but to go wherever they could – or did they feel they had a *right* to participate in doing to others what was done to them?'

Tracy's quote regarding 'famine-slain Sisters of the South' comes from this:

> This graveyard, looking out upon the restless waters from its quiet elevation, must remain for ages the most historic spot in the locality, although Skull is not without a history and historic remains. Many a castle and stronghold have the O'Mahonys and O'Donovans built among the crags of the rocky islands, which are grouped in such variety to seaward, the ruins of which are to-day full of beauty and interest for the tourist. But surely the day will come when those crumbling ruins shall be once again a portion of the common soil, nameless and forgotten; but distant though the day may be, Skull and Skibbereen, those two famine-slain Sisters of the South, must still be found on the page of Irish history, illustrating the great famine of 1847.

Daniel Donovan, *Sketches in Carbery, County Cork: Its Antiquities, History, Legends, and Topography*, https://archive.org/stream/sketchesincarber00dono/sketchesincarber00dono_djvu.txt (accessed March 2014).

It is also worth considering the disjunction/tension between this history and the fact that during the 1990s and up to the time of the collapse of the Celtic Tiger economy into recession in 2008 (following the global financial crisis), Schull was a playground for the rich visiting from Europe, America and further afield. See http://www.independent.ie/irish-news/everyones-gone-nuts-about-schull-26177904.html) (accessed March 2014).

uttering all manner of entreaties. Of course there was no hope of carrying off the bread, indeed it would have been cruel to have made the attempt; the only question was, how to divide it. At first we sent it down to the door, but the rush was so great, that that scheme became impracticable; and it only remained, to throw it out of the window. One can never forget what followed; the fighting, the screaming, the swaying to and fro of the human mass, as it rushed in the direction of some morsel, the entreaties and gestures by which each one sought to attract our attention to herself, and above all the insatiable expression of the crowd as it remained unsatisfied and undiminished at the exhaustion of our loaves – for what were they among so many! By two o'clock they announced the car to be ready, and it was with some difficulty that we got to our places amidst the crush and noise.[4]

The reclamation of old rubbish tips (such as in the Burswood river area in Perth) is an act of redefinition as much as repairing. Covering up the toxins with new-builds or the smiling faces of 'park' vegetation. But storage is usually with intent of access and reuse, with a sense of the temporary and a possible eye to permanence. Nuclear waste destabilises all the variables. Nuclear 'storage' is a euphemism for a desire to express usefulness and transience in waste when in fact it is pervasive, persistent, destructive and ultimately non-containable or non-restrainable. Disposal is the desire of nuclear storage but it cannot be achieved – no matter how deeply it is buried, no matter the 'buried sublime' under the mountain discourse of safety some might latch on to. Maybe the ineffective poem is one that becomes solely a repository for waste without effective and honest and 'transparent' qualities of storage?

4 See https://viewsofthefamine.wordpress.com/oxford-to-skibbereen-2/narrative/ (accessed 23 June 2016).

FINDING BELONGING?

'Returning' to another house has made the process of seeking belonging – or finding belonging – all the more difficult. If we'd been able to return to Anchor Lodge we would have felt more connected. This is not an issue of 'nation' or 'settlement' or legality, but of sense of interaction, connection and even, to a certain degree, 'acceptance'. Though I've never cared about 'acceptance', it is still an issue of mutual respect, and without it a vast amount of stored knowledge of place, accumulated through untold generations of familiarity, is kept securely locked away, with only snippets leaking out or falling through the cracks. It's a knowledge one needs access to even in order to understand the way plants and birds work the hedgerows, function on the roadside verges. When the Wren Boys[1] took the birds and glued them down for their rituals, they changed the ecology of the place. Why? I can read about it happening, but I want to know how and why. I want to understand the driving forces of landscaping. I don't want 'place' to be used as a word of location or how we relate to that location, but one in which all the instabilities of belonging, of the ongoing search for belonging, are present and active. Place is a set of dynamics of doubt, not certainty. Place is a category error – the GPS is the least of its certainties and the compass only one of its tools for translation. From the manuscripts stored in Skib, I rework my wren poem:

Wren's Electric Field Strength

Out of the furze and fuchsias
    to whisper sweet nothings,
wren pivots as fast and sharp
    as thought. With the domes
sending out high volts-per-metre charges,
    a house comes available.

---

1 See Mr and Mrs. S. C. Hall, *Ireland: Its Scenery, Character & c.* (London, How and Parsons, 1842), Vol. 1, p. 23.

Wren says, I'm resident year round,
   and will greet you here
on St Stephen's day. I won't die
   at your door, I will fly
below radar. And I say: I am not one
   for the old ways, and for
what it's worth, I'll watch out for you –
   nobody will put you
in a box, stick you on a beribboned
   holly branch, bury you
with a red cent. We never required
   Gothic in these parts,
says the Wren, the intricate vaulting
   of the hedges suffices,
and it always aspires up beyond
   the mountaintop. A gang
of boys passes by, striking hedges
   with hurleys, wary
of the girls walking ten steps behind.[2]

But today is Beltane, and outside the house I am thinking about the sun, 'cattle', furze fires, the activities of 'the others'. I walk up Ardmanagh Road towards the red sandstone and copper-seamed mountains, turning back to look at Roaringwater Bay, Cape Clear Island. I fall into the bay, into the island, the distance narrowing to an expression, a word. I head over to the road to Corthna, crossing the road that goes to Goleen (we must revisit the wedge tomb at Altar as soon as we can), and eventually looking back to Mount Gabriel and its radar domes, its communications between the Bronze Age and modernity. When we leave Schull for the town of Bantry (shopping, immigration…) we pass through Barnancleeve Gap and enter another world again. The concentration of Schull around its small harbour, the yachts and boats pinioned, swinging in the bay, seals and gannets and skuas and gulls on pylons. The magic mushroom graffiti along the wall near the fish factory. Tractors in the main street. The hard drinkers outside Hacketts and The Black Sheep. Tim at school. The draper talking to Tracy about his daughters living in Perth, his yearly trips to Australia. So many of the town's young – just out of school – head to the opportunities in Australia. The new migration. Then endless migration. The diasporic belonging – stored memories of home changing the nature of home itself. We are not quite blowbacks, but we are returnees via the mid-nineteenth century.

I store all these observations and add them to others. I will make poems in Rosewood Cottage. We've moved in and I am locating a space that works for me to write in, write out of. I am returning to my work on *Táin Bó Cuailnge*, that storage zone of naming, of identity, of place both far away and near to here, in which the massive violence (against animals and humans, especially given it's

2 John Kinsella, *Hiss* (London, Picador, forthcoming).

a cattle raid!) does not, for me, distract from the inherent processes of place-memory and assertion of language-presence. I am also intrigued by the issues of mobility and the storage of resentments, its catalogue of wrongs but also affirmations of the land itself fused with acts of spiritual and physical mapping that it contains (maps are prisons of storage and guides to liberation at once). It is taking us from home through alien places to where a new home might be configured in our deaths, or where our quest/purpose might begin:

> through Muicc Cruinb,
> through Terloch Teóra Crích, the marshy lake bed
> where three territories meet,
> by Tuaim Móna, the peat ridge,
> through Cúil Silinne, where Carrcin Lake is now – it
> was named after Silenn, daughter of Madchar;
> by Fid and Bolga, woods and hills,
> through Coltain and across the Sinann river...[3]

And this has me thinking again over the possibility – no, the necessity – of re-approaching the text from an animal-rights perspective, a pacifist perspective and from a crisis of (un)belonging. This is what I am writing, here at Rosewood Cottage.

---

3 *The Táin*, trans. Thomas Kinsella (Oxford, Oxford University Press, 2002), p. 63.

THE PLACE OF READING: THE GEOGRAPHICAL CONTEXT OF (RE)READING *THE JINDYWOROBAKS* AND SELF – FROM SCHULL TO AN IMAGINARY AUSTRALIA

1.

I picked up a copy of Brian Elliot's volume *The Jindyworobaks*[1] in a second-hand bookshop in Skibbereen. I am thrilled to have it as much as I detest (most of) the values of the 'Jindys' – I find it useful and generative re-encountering them *here*, in West Cork, Ireland. I am particularly taken with Rex Ingamells's (1913–55) 'Gum Trees in Italy'[2] where he quotes from Norman Douglas's piece on considering eucalypts 'planted some forty years ago' in Italy. Having called them 'abominations' that 'may look better on their native hearth', he continues, 'But I confess that this avenue of Policoro almost reconciled me to the existence of the anaemic Antipodeans.' This, though, is the reported Douglas comment I find useful and generative:

> Almost; since for some reason or other (perhaps on account of the insufferably foul nature of the soil) their foliage is here thickly tufted, it glows like burnished gold in the sunshine, like enamelled scales of green and gold. These eucalypti are unique in Italy. Gazing upon them my heart softened, and I almost forgave them their manifold iniquities, their diabolical thirst, their demoralizing aspect, precocious senility and vice, their peeling bark suggestive of unmentionable skin diseases, and that system of radication which is nothing but a scandal on this side of the globe.[3]

Now at first glance, this might seem a case of someone believing themselves culturally superior, and a predictable tangent to Eurocentric cultural imperialism; but rather, for all its bigotries,[4] it's more a case of general aesthetic imperialism. How one *looks* and what one receives back in terms of desires and (un)

---

1 Brian Elliot, *The Jindyworobaks* (St Lucia, University of Queensland Press, 1979).
2 An extract from Ingamells's *Conditional Culture* (1938), in Elliot, *The Jindyworobaks*, pp. 227–31.
3 Elliot, *The Jindyworobaks*, pp. 227–8.
4 Elliot, *The Jindyworobaks*, p. 227, with Douglas citing *The Dead Heart of Australia*.

fulfilled expectations is what's at stake here. It's fantasy fulfilment. It *might* be read as sexual in its vacillations and compelling because of this.

What Ingamells does with this is fascinating. He ironically identifies 'truth' in Douglas, plays with tones and intent. He asserts that it would be easy to caricature an oak and a weeping willow as loathsome examples of senility and obesity: 'it is a matter of point of view'. The shoe on the other foot, depends on ways of seeing. But Ingamells's 'ways of seeing' are as freighted as Douglas's. He is 'right' in saying, 'I mean the gum tree in its infinite variety of species and individuality', but then he goes on to identify, maintain and assert the 'beauty' – 'yet I am not alone in seeing a stark and vivid beauty about them even then'. Douglas has attacked (via Ingamells) the very foundation of cultural nationalism (without knowing anything really about that 'nation', the origin of the euca-lypts). I focalise this as a prototypical example of international regionalism, which is actually also epitomised by Ingamells's critic Max Harris and his Angry Penguins. Ingamells draws Douglas to his case, and thanks him with irony: 'Mr Douglas does relent for an instant, and catches a fleeting glimpse of beauty in the gum trees ... Thank you, Mr Douglas, for the mite!'

> It symbolises a first step. Before long, the strange unorthodox beauty of the Australian gum tree, and many other manifestations of beauty peculiar to this country, will find a sure place in the standards of general culture, which will be one stage nearer universality and so much richer.[5]

The 'elevation' of the 'Australian' to the universal is a cultural programme of 'independence', a *partial* decolonisation (in rejecting Britain and Europe as a source of cultural values), but not a decolonisation of indigenous space. Of course, there were those who considered the values of the Jindys' good reason to look back harder to the 'Old World', without issues of appropriation even being considered or understood in any of this. This is both fodder to the iden-tification of a cringe (later) and also the resistance to that same cringe. It's the two-way switch rather than the forked road of the movement. The issue has been seen but not fully acted upon in its implications for cultural nationalism, imperialism and, indeed, internationalism. This comes much later with the rise of the internet, and even then a regressive cultural nationalism, dressed up as cultural sovereignty but being an Antipodean Eurocentrism, will hold sway in print media and many literary canonical texts.

International regionalism asserts the local within the fabric of broader con-versations, yet not as Boosterism, but rather as assertion of difference. When Ingamells says 'general culture', is this the gridwork and palimpsests and cross-hatching of all ritualistic existence – a template? Maybe. The problem in the Ingamells equation is to be found in 'sure place' and 'standards' – that is, in his conservatism. Conservatism in the Jindyworobaks' manifesto is well attested, but I am referring to sexual deletion. For all their 'erect spears' and the like,

5 Ingamells in Elliot, *The Jindyworobaks*, pp. 227–8.

the Jindys and those they anthologised do not seem to allow for (or comprehend in any overt, textual way) the imperialism of sexuality and identity. Which is not to say they weren't individually aware (or 'in control') of their material, but certainly not in any collective sense (as a clique).

The word 'unorthodox' is relevant here as it both indicates a will to show Australia as different from Mediterranean/Western civilisation and thus 'unique' (the binary is a problem), and comments on the nature of orthodoxy in 'environment' in itself. Another paradox – it both subscribes and unsubscribes. One feels as if Ingamells couldn't quite articulate (any more than his critics!) what he could actually see/perceive. In his piece on 'Environmental Values', he writes of 'A fundamental break, that is, with the spirit of English culture, is the prerequisite for the development of Australian culture' and adds, 'Australian culture is at present in a nebulous stage because our writers have not come clearly to any such realisation.' He allows that 'Some of the greatest literature yet to be may have no local colour itself. Its settings may be in China, or Mars.' Considering the trade, cultural and regional 'contacts' between Australia and China of the present time (though they have in actuality long existed), the literary culturality of the two complex spatialities coexisting in whatever forms (e.g. in the poetry of Ouyang Yu), it seems odd to read this now. Ingamells ultimately believes that 'The real test of a people's culture is the way in which they can express themselves in relation to their environment.'[6]

Ingamells's desire for the 'distinct' and for 'sublimation' show (yet again) a wish to create Australia as desirable body, as a trophy and territory of one's imagined communal-self – one's own but also a collective identity to resist the cultural dominance of the European. He says in 'The Word "Jindyworobak"', 'Pseudo-Europeanism clogs the minds of most Australians, preventing a free appreciation of nature.'[7] I'd add that the clogging is to do with the complex of the unified self, the desire for agency, for capitalist security and related gain, for privilege over the indigenous in order to Frankenstein's-monster themselves into primacy. Ingamells's wish is to replace European 'thought-idiom' with a 'suitable thought-idiom' to break down inhibition and to 'release' Australian culture, to make it 'exist'. He would be its prophet, of course – the prophet of the new figurative language of 'his' ('our'!) place.

2.

I think W. Flexmore Hudson was the creator of a genuine pastoral-modernism in Australia. One could even argue for a pre-postmodern landscapism. He is a dynamic 'pastiching' and layering poet who could fuse urbane modernism with the Jindyworobak sense of place. I object to his later qualifications of nostalgia for 'primitivism' in looking to 'the Aborigines' and 'the Aboriginal' in the thrust of other Jindys' work – there is and was nothing 'primitive' about indigenous

---

6 Ingamells in Elliot, *The Jindyworobaks*, pp. 229, 230.
7 Ingamells in Elliot, *The Jindyworobaks*, p. 231.

Australian cultures. Rather, in reality, there *were* numerous parallels to the cultural/social and even technological achievements of other 'civilisations' (European achievements, for example). A knowledge of geology, geography, botany, medicine, seismology, cosmology and so on. Sure, a different *material* philosophy – one outside the thrusts towards accumulated profit and wealth, and accumulation of data to profit from as opposed to the accumulation of data relating to environment and cosmology for physical and spiritual application: the perfect science rests in its beneficial application for people, surely ... the art-map that is multi-dimensional, the tool that does precisely what it needs to do etc. Indigenous 'development' was concurrent if isolated in terms of the movements of other world cultures and their narratives.

Hudson gives 'place' an intertextual relevance, a true international regionalism – not one about 'travel' but about consciousness of the 'other', 'othering' and non-uniqueness. The poem 'Kirsova' ('written after a ballet performance in Melbourne during the New Guinea campaign') shows this in a disturbing and 'exemplary' way – it cross-hatches, creates strings of cause and effect, and ties event-history *in situ* with place of experience (i.e. seeing the event in an international contest that's personal and universal). His astonishing 'A hymn for the Dark Age' is possibly the best 'rewriting' of Christian mythology in the context of a contemporary horror that I have ever read. And this least 'Australian' poem doesn't require a paranoid reading for parallels with the Jindy environment of appropriating the indigenous, and dispossession, to be understood in that capacity.

In his introduction to *The Jindyworobaks*, Brian Elliott writes:

> Hudson had several styles, the best, in my opinion, being his landscape impressions ... This, which I call his 'Look! See!' landscapism, has nothing Aboriginal about it yet is intensely *actual* and no less strongly imbued with the 'Spirit of Place' (Ingamells's term). I would wish to call it site-magic. However, as that is an Aboriginal phenomenon, the term is not quite suitable.[8]

No, it is not 'quite suitable'; in fact, not suitable at all, especially given Hudson's way of seeing the Australian landscape seems to be 'becoming' (Deleuze and Guattari) *less* appropriative (despite its limitations and ultimate lack of knowing *how* to respect). Elliot is spot-on with his 'intensely actual', and maybe this sums up the best drive in non-indigenous readings of place vs. landscape vs. belonging in Australian(ist) threads of poetry? What interests me isn't 'Look! See!', but 'In situ! Experience!' followed by 'Contrition!'

Elliot says:

> Hudson was from the beginning as deeply committed to the intimacy and uniqueness of the Australian 'environment' as Ingamells was, but he took less kindly to the

---

8 Elliott, *The Jindyworobaks*, p. xliii, my italics.

imposition of an Aboriginal visionary scheme over the landscape. He chose rather to see with his natural eyes.[9]

This is Hudson's success and failure regarding mode/s of seeing – it is liberating and constraining, it is trapped; has 'cultural' origins and yet *no* appropriation; it is respectful *and* disrespectful. It is Hudson's paradox of seeing in which the 'non-indigenous' writer-reader/participant might find a way out, in a general sense, in writing 'country' in Australia sans indigenous authority (in whatever form of intimacy and 'permission' it comes).

Through this model I will also try to re-place, reread place and find new positions of viewing and participating here in West Cork. Moving up through Barnancleeve Pass (travelling to Bantry) and back through Barnageehy gaps/passes (in and out) through fog this morning, the blurred passage relying on memory (local knowledge) for clarity... To pass through and to belong, infused by the lack of clarity. Locals and visitors can have accidents in fog, especially at constrained points such as gaps/passes, but local knowledge provides some kind of protection if not immunity. Still, one can never account for the unpredictability of who might be coming the other way and what awareness they might or might not have.

As we passed one of 'Tracy's' beloved bogs she said that *underneath-speaking* they are neither truly dead nor alive. And Wendy (visiting us from wheatbelt Western Australia) added that the bogs are in limbo.

Eucalypts are found in Rosewood Cottage's garden. They're found in the Schull schoolyard, at Bantry House, the Bamboo Gardens and elsewhere. Decontextualised, they are exotica, at least *partially* contextualised, they are reminders of migration (the new Western Australian mining-boom work-visa demi-migration/travelling-work-visas/long holidays/new migrations post the collapse of the Celtic Tiger) or symbols of having been 'Down Under' – that is, focal points for reminiscences. They do not carry a sense of being 'invaders' here as they do in, say, Portugal (the Coimbra loathing of blue eucalypts I encountered among locals there in the late 1990s), or Norman Douglas's 'detestation' of them (without any real context of origins) in Italy. We might ask here if it would be different post the Second World War Italian migrations to Australia – those same eucalypts becoming a similar exchange/'reminiscence' symbol and conduit for locals with family 'Down Under' as for the Irish who have migrants to Australia in their families, or with a history of early migrations or convict deportations?

I think about this in the light of Tracy's reaction to a poem of mine just out in the Irish literary journal *Cyphers*. The poem, 'Post-Traumatic', is about the surprise of seeing lemon-scented gums in Rosewood's garden when we lived next door in Anchor Lodge, then, just before I could draw Tracy's attention to them, a gardener starting to cut them down (turned out to be heavily 'pruning') with a chainsaw. The chainsaw caused me deep upset, and its noise, and the smell of the

---

9 Elliott, *The Jindyworobaks*, p. xlii.

gums being cut, took me back to the trauma of seeing so much of the wheatbelt bulldozed and chopped up with chainsaws (though the lemon-scented gum is not a wheatbelt tree and is in fact from north-eastern Australia, many towns have it in their main street, and also many local gardens, and it has in fact become 'naturalised' in small areas – rather, it was the cutting of 'generic' eucalypts that stimulated this trauma). The whole issue of temporary and permanent (un)belonging came into focus and the local Australian term 'widow-maker' (lemon-scented gums being called that because of a tendency to drop limbs) became an irony for the cutting-off of/from 'home' for the migrant – the Irish planting in memory of those gone (or having returned from Australia) as affirmation, then chainsaws severing the connection (though ironically, it's the chainsaw that really caused me the shock of 'home'). When in the poem I mention Tracy 'says I will write about it', it's because she knows the sound of chainsaws deeply upset me. She was right.

However, Tracy just said that on reading the poem in *Cyphers*, and after reading an interview in the same issue with the late Seamus Heaney who categorically rejected the German reading of 'blood' with regard to his bog poems, pointing out that the German reading was to do with their own horrific history and not with what he was doing/saying, she felt/realised that without knowledge of my dialogue with Australian issues, my 'post-traumatic' could be read as a domestic commentary about dysfunctionality in the household. I used 'home' in quote marks to indicate 'Australia', but out of context 'home' might be read as the domestic home, which would be a 'wrong' meaning or at least one unintended by the writer (which doesn't invalidate it as a reading, but wasn't the intention behind its writing).

Now, all poets run the risk of their material escaping them, and every reading gives new meaning, and a 'paranoid reading'[10] exists in every poem *about* 'Australia' written (from a non-indigenous perspective/position) to my mind, but this interpretation of Tracy's took me by surprise. There is of course an obvious register in which the word 'spouse' might be read outside the 'spouse/widow' dynamic in the poem's diegesis, as the word is mentioned twice in the poem, and it contains a whole register of violent language that might be interpreted this way. My intention was to correlate violence with the aggression carried against the tree and what it symbolises.

Post-Traumatic

For days, I've been watching
the lemon-scented gums,
Australian eucalypts, swaying
through gales in the garden
of Rose Cottage next door.

---

10   Robert Ian Vere Hodge and Vijay Mishra, *Dark Side of the Dream: Australian Literature and the Postcolonial Mind* (Sydney, Allen & Unwin, 1991).

They have created a vicarious
connection with 'home'.
They are known as 'widow-makers' –
a propensity for dropping
limbs on spouses. Anyway,

I am feeling violently ill
because a bloke is chainsawing
the large 'specimen' in the back garden
down to the bone. Gums
and chainsaws. And the first

fine – crystal-clear – day
in weeks. The chewing at limbs
is the smell of southern summers –
the warnings, the bloodletting.
My spouse, Tracy, says, 'When

I heard that noise I knew
you'd have to write it out
of your system.' The lemon-
scented gum to be burnt
to ash with coal and peat.[11]

Tracy also pointed out that my other poem in the same issue, 'Grey Heron Is Not a Hood Ornament',[12] doesn't give context *outside* Ireland (though its tone

11 John Kinsella, *Cyphers*, issue 77.
12 **Grey Heron is Not a Hood Ornament**

The twelve-footer outboards in from the bay,
its ingress watched by gulls and the odd jogger.
The sea's a glasstop, so the chevrons from the boat's
passage tamp the harbour's walls. On its prow,
a grey heron, still as sculpture, staring down
the man tillering the motor. His haul under
wraps. The heron is in fully retracted mode,
compact and warping definitions of grace.
Its lack of animation prompts inanimate
comparisons: it looks more like a hood
ornament than a mascot. Patience
is another variable, with grey heron's
'stabbing' beak, its quick-as-a-flash
reflexes. All that immanence. A binary
relationship, a symbiosis, pragmatism
of hunger and symbols; whatever
works in the conditions. When the sea
is rough, such ornaments don't stick,
or don't try. The bird flies, though it will
come back if it lives another tide. One day

and language do for me) in terms of the 'Post-Traumatic' poem – that is, that the register of the other poem could be that of an Irish poet with nothing to do with Australia, and the bio note included with the poems does not refer to Australia. In localising content I cut threads that illuminate possible meanings? So the poem's symbols become personal symbols and without an Australian-migrational context become 'confessional' where there is no 'confession' being made. I think she has a valid point, but I also find this deeply informative about place and belonging and the cues of presence and entitlement to write about place that readers in a particular region or country might take to a text. It becomes an entirely different poem from the poem I intended. Should we consider this when choosing possible publication venues – and if so, frame the poem for its context (an epigraph or a contextualising bio note)? Context, it seems, always matters in some way or another.

One of my concerns is that I am in dialogue with an imaginary Australia – of believers and non-believers, of ecologists and destroyers, of supporters and 'enemies'. The poem exists in a context that persists/exists wherever I am in the world. I am always talking back, to or with (or from) an ecology of 'nature' and people. It's a redress. Even if, say, Jam Tree Gully or the wheatbelt or the desert or the jarrah forest or the coast are never mentioned. I take it all as implicit. The apparently self-contained poem always intentionally leaks and slips, trans-gresses, refuses and participates. It is part of a life-argument. I do not write 'curatorial' pieces for display – I write for outcomes (even if, as it turns out, the outcome might not be the one I imagined!)

So, are outcomes sidetracked or lost? No, but the use of the domestic refer-ence will always open 'wrong' doors (or, unwittingly, right ones – though I will say in this case they are wrong ones as the household is functioning very well!), as some readers desire the private, access to 'family' and gossip. They will not look for co-operation and functionality, but be piqued by dysfunctionality. They might well want the poem to be a mirror to their own fears and concerns (which is absolutely fair enough; it is also fair enough, given the poem begins with a title that references a psychological state and has an 'I' in the very first line and might be seen in post-Freudian castration-anxiety terms!) 'Widow-maker' can be personally ominous, but in this case is demographically-ecologically porten-tous and not *confessional* as such. I did actually write a poem entitled 'Widow-maker' sometime around 1993 which was an expression of personal angst – of a sense of loss of self. But that was in a different life, in a different register and far removed from the concerns of 'Post-Traumatic' which, when all is said and done, is about violence towards nature, undercurrents of loss brought about by wanton human violence inflicted on non-human life.

---

it just won't arrive, though another might,
enraptured by a semiotics of balance,
the stern riding low and unctuous,
a bellyful, a prow to be held in place.

Ingamells quoting Douglas[13] – 'Gazing upon them my heart softened, and I almost forgave them their manifold iniquities…' – is the dynamic of displacement (though anthropomorphising on an obvious level, and creating literary conceits out of nature to actually critique nature itself) that is so much at the core of Jindyworobakism itself. In bolstering a sense of belonging through annexing, appropriating – through creating a pragmatic and 'real' sense of participation in the 'soil' of place rather than the imports that decorate it (where does the migrant fit into this, as Ingamells and all the Jindys were with varying degrees of separation?) – Ingamells is trapped in the desire to contextualise, the need to validate. Douglas's comments are about intactness of the place he is living/staying in (a permanent exile from Britain for his sexual 'misdemeanours'), and about creating an 'other' to smokescreen his own otherness. Ingamells's is an act of finger-pointing and reclaiming to project the internalisms of Jindyworobakism out into an international sphere. The travelling-Australian trope, the extension of a real (the eucalypt) but also imagined Australia fighting for identity in a foreign context. It's international regionalism any way you look at it, which I hope demonstrates the nuancing of this theory, and that it's not merely a pat description of scale (small per large).

13 Maybe we should make a little more of Douglas's ironic patches in his piece!

HARVESTING THE GRASS (FROM A SCHULL JOURNAL)

29 May 2014

It's the time of mowing and hay-cutting here in Schull. Everywhere fields of cut grass ready for baling. Everywhere around the village the sound of whipper-snippers. I think of John's (the Guru's) report today from Jam Tree Gully (which he's been looking over in our absence): that there was 100 mm! (accumulated over a couple of weeks) in the rain-gauge. He planted 17 flat-topped Yates at the bottom of Bird Gully and will plant the rest of the tray of 30 next Wednesday when he's back there to 'supervise' the cleaning of the 90,000-litre rainwater tank by the tank-cleaning specialist. He says the wild oats are already very high there.

Which brings to mind grass-cutting at Jam Tree Gully, which has so defined our time there over the years. It is strange to hear and see and *smell* (hay fever!) the evidence of grass-cutting here and not be part of the labour. Here in Schull we live in a rental house, and someone comes in to cut the lawn and prune the shrubs, and we have no fields/paddocks belonging to the house to cut, though we live alongside a farm where there's constant 'grasswork'. To me, the lack of responsibility and *work* in terms of grass-cutting defines a kind of non-belonging. However, the grass-cutting here is for the animal-as-food industry, which I don't participate in anywhere or in any way, and if I was responsible for acreage here I wouldn't be cutting grass for that purpose.

At Jam Tree Gully we cut grass for safety reasons, because in the fire season it is a danger. Where we don't *have* to cut it we don't. So maybe it's not so much unbelonging as a different range of possible belongings that arise. Mowing *is* a pivotal act of connection, but it needs to be done in a way that minimises impact on ecology (taking into consideration at 'home' in Australia that the grasses are 'invasive' and 'introduced' in the first place).

I've been working through the 'Three Body Problem' (*an issue of gravity*). Position/mass/velocity of each of three bodies. The moon, the earth, the sun. Determine motion of each. Point in time. The Three Body Problem and

Moving. This is the poem. I think of occasions when I've accidentally flung stones with whipper-snippers and when I've been hit by stones flung. Recently, walking here in Schull, I was struck by a stone from a large mower/harvester, and bled into the soil. Machine – person wielding machine – the grass/ground/ stone. Maybe the poem is 'Distracted, the Mower Swings the Machine in My Direction' – In wounding me he makes/ me part of the system,/ the place. 'Blood and soil'/ absurdity –/ no grounds for cult of exclusion/ & possession.

> I bleed onto the soul
> but nothing miraculously grows.
> The chemical reaction
> leaves my claims out,
> though a bit more of me is here –
> like piss, spit & shit.
> We make deposits
> even when passing through;
> they are dispensed with
> & dispersed.

4.52 pm

In the fields behind Rosewood Cottage (same as those behind Anchor Lodge next door), the farmer is cutting the grass for fodder ensilage (the grass is chopped rather than cut into lengths that can be baled). About eight weeks ago the same fields were covered in a sludge of stinking slurry which drove us away from the house. The harvester cuts the grass (maize and mixture of other grasses, I'd guess) and it is poured out of the chute into a wagon dragged by a tractor. This is then transported to a silo. So … from forage harvester to wagon to silo where it will ferment over time and become cow-food. Some cut grass might also be placed under plastic sheeting to ferment – in other places, baled. Consciousness of compaction and possibilities of overheating (which must be prevented) is essential. If it is baled it needs partial drying-off in the field, which is not the case in the field behind us, so we know it is destined for ensilage.

In Ireland in the summer of 2012 and winter of 2013, there was so much rain that the fodder grasses wouldn't grow properly (low-grade) and couldn't be harvested until July 2013 (instead of late May/early July). This led to the 'fodder crisis' and much distress (including suicides) in the farming community. The inverse (but with the same results) of drought in Australia.

The farmer (as I write) is using a self-propelled John Deere 7400 Forage Harvester. There's also a Taarup Double Chop Harvester working nearby. Cut fields are appearing all over West Cork. Seems Strautmann forage wagons are being used (and John Deere tractors).

Just walked down into the village to get something to drink (vegan non-alcoholic grape juice) for tonight's dinner, and noticed chopped grass clumps and clots of mud along the road. The harvest on the way to silage – the tractors leaving their signatures. The sileage is being taken along the same route the slurry came in on. Then as I was walking back, a tractor appeared from the farm next door with a large forage wagon of chopped grass! The tractor (brand new) was being driven by a young woman I haven't seen around the village before – maybe a daughter home from university/college. She is carting with someone I assume to be her brother who is operating the other tractor and wagon and likely their father on the harvester. It's a honed operation. The process is so familiar to me from hay carting (the hay is cut not chopped) when I was young, and harvest. Reminds me of chaff-cutting (horror job I only ever had to do a few times), though at least the silage is still damp so you don't have the dust billowing everywhere.

Bizarrely, I am enjoying being amidst the mowing/cutting/storage of grasses, in inverse proportion to my recoiling disgust at slurry spreading. Still, in the end, it's only for the *temporary* wellbeing of the cows. It is really fuel to their suffering. To 'feed' their exploitation and agony in the death-camps that are, in reality, the farms. Still, I do understand the farmers, the processes of growing grasses, the 'harvest'. I understand even if I oppose.

LAST ENTRIES IN VOLUME THREE
OF A SCHULL JOURNAL

16 June 2014

On Saturday afternoon we travelled over to Tralee (Trá Li). It didn't greatly appeal to us, but we didn't get a chance to interact with it much. Tim and I caught a sliver – through the gates – of a hurling match, which was great. We saw the sliotar fly and someone scoop it on to their hurley and run with it. Tim was excited because he plays hurling at school and is a pretty full bottle on its history, teams, players and statistics. We drove over to Camp (under the mountains) and saw the bay – incredible wetlands/marshes and sandy beaches: a haven for birdlife.

Heading home, we turned at Killarney and drove north-east to Millstreet (under the wonderful Claragh Mountain on the edge of the Boggeragh Mountain Range) and then right across to Macroom before heading down to Bantry for a vegan Indian meal at the Moghul (they look after us well). It was a good day and we filled in some blanks in our knowledge of the geography (*in situ* as opposed to on the map) of Kerry and West Cork. Millstreet was a fascinating town – the railway to Dublin passes through it, and it has a very different feel from coastal West Cork and Kerry.

Just back now from a walk to the pier with Tim. He says school is really about being outdoors as it winds down to summer. There is so little dry sunshine (lovely notion) here that the teachers use every moment of it for the kids to have outdoor experiences. At the pier, kids are jumping off into the somewhat murky (at the moment) harbour (lots of boats in, and the fishing fleet is working from it again). Late last week there was a massive yacht in the harbour – an ocean-going schooner with two tall masts.

Tim wrote me a wonderful card – a poem on Millstreet for Father's Day (yesterday). We hope to return to Schull after the summer period (we are heading back to Australia) but that depends on so much.

As I near departure, I find it hard to write place – I remain bursting with eye-opening observation and drive, but when I feel something is closing off, I start to feel a lessening of the desire to record. What does this say about place (for me)? – when one can't be part of it, it loses its 'flashing lights'? Is non-place (Augé) really a sense of lost connection more than denied or occluded connection? For some, a car park *is* a connected place – a regular and consistent point of reference, a key to their day and their mode of living. I am reminded of the winter view from the Tesco shopping centre car park in Killarney – the snow-capped MacGillycuddy's Reeks – people just sitting in their cars and feeling connected despite the *non(-place)*, all the denials and occlusions implicit in the car (as viewing platform and manufactured object) and the car park itself. *Not* dead space entirely – changed and overlaid space, but still with vantage. It's disturbing and illuminating at once.

17 June 2014

Since summer has set in, I feel I don't connect in the same way. Maybe it's the immanence of leaving. Tourists and a different psychology of the weather – I don't get them/it. No writing, no connection. All displacement.

18 June 2014

Sunshine. Warmth.
Just back from my walk (Ardmanagh, Town Park, Colla Road spur, Colla Road). Saw a chough! Also a species of bird I didn't recognise. It was very upright on the ground and looked like a cross between a blackbird and an oversized thrush.

Dock is in its dark, brown-red seeded state – close to dropping its seeds. Hay has been cut and is drying in fields to be round-baled and wrapped in plastic. The cutters and hay-rakes are out. Many tourists appearing in town.

$$\text{Place} = \frac{\text{social units}}{\text{landscape}} \times \frac{\text{non-human ecology}}{\text{individual human}}$$

Place is the postcard as much as the day-to-day activities of a locale.

Place is the repair and the damage.

Place is the imposition – the rules imposed from the 'outside' on the 'inside' as much as those generated from within ('tradition').

I still want to write the dozen mute swans viewed through the Arch of the Ilen River Bridge and the Single Mute Swan at Ballydehob poems. So I still have some residue of spark!

19 June 2014

Unstable place

Reading bits 'n' pieces of de Certeau's work. Obviously I agree with the general gist of his argument regarding place vs. space, but overall it ties into entirely different co-ordinates from my notions of space/place. There seems to be a failure in locating 'nature' and its agencies (all too human and material for me).

Long walk today. Had to change route due to some guy spraying herbicide all over his property, verge and even the road. At the top of Ardmanagh, workers were baling hay as rectangular blocks. Now, that's something I know about and understand – it 'took me back' to a different time and place and spatiality in south-west Australia. Yarloop – 'south' more than 'wheatbelt'. Not surprising because that's also 'dairy country'. Strangely (to me), the bales were stacked as tripods/pyramids/'tepees'. These bales were being collected by hand and stacked into a 'livestock' trailer. The familiar in a 'strange' place (the uncanny) is a liberation (for the imagination if not the cows for whom the hay is being baled!) – the possibility of an *unstable* (as opposed to de Certeau's 'stability') model of place that incorporates the interstices of 'space'. As one passes through earlier associations – a visionary dreariness – evokes a connection across a lifetime that creates place in the imagination as real as anything else, and one to learn from.

Unstable place is made up of variables and co-ordinates over a life, and is adaptable, capable of 'learning' (acquiring knowledge) and sensitive to change. It recognises 'tradition' but is not bound to tradition. After all, not all tradition is good tradition. Unstable Place (I am capitalising!) is flexible and yet protective of the vulnerable (plants, animals, humans and even geological). It's an undoing model of place. 'Place' is displaced by a polyvalent, fluid model of interactions and interstices. Came across a reductive (and almost pointless) page on Heidegger (bridges) and de Certeau (fences) on the web:[1] a teaching tool of sorts that entirely misses the pragmatics of being out in the field where fences and bridges are acts of permission, rights and movement, not of conjecture. Out here, it is the hedgerow that plays the pragmatic cards, and, of course, lends itself to symbol and 'theorising': for plants and animals it is habitat, and one of the more diverse habitats around. It is real-world, though always unstable space. Farmers wish to preserve hedgerows in many places, but if hedgerows get in the way of expansion plans (protected or not), they become unplaces very quickly.

When hedges are cut back, their life and life they harbour is dictated to/controlled – ironically, from the municipal and agricultural perspective, cutting

---

1 A course page at the University of Central Florida: 'Symbolic and Structural Approaches to Place Michel de Certeau', https://pegasus.cc.ucf.edu/~janzb/courses/hum3930b/certeau1. htm (accessed 22 June 2016). I should note that I have no problem with the page in itself, and it's probably an appropriate teaching tool for the classroom – my issue is with the 'classroom' itself and the irony of the material being considered. Field of the page is field of activity, for me. As I move, as I 'migrate' back and forth from living place to living place (as with many 'species' of animals – and especially migratory birds – being 'temporary' in each place but always returning and building cumulative if interrupted knowledge or familiarity of...), I polysituate, and in doing so teach and learn outside fixed points (though those fixed points remain the terms of reference, the anchor points through which my 'error zones' and slippages operate as points of reference). I do not follow the 'seasons' (error zones) in my movements, but there are factors of climate, topography, family and work demography involved.

back is the desire for stable place, to control the unruly. Rather, let grow, they become a truth – Unstable Place (no positions to be maintained or resolved) is active space. A parallel: stories grow rather than become/are made grammatically and syntactically correct, properly structured and 'readable'. In the unstable place, it is the unreadable that is the rich, durable and truthful narrative.

de Certeau – 'tactics'/'strategy'
Heidegger – 'veiling'

De Certeau's tactics aim to undo the controlling powers by damaging them on a micro level. The use of time to delete where nothing material is removed. Inside Out. But it's not my take – mine is organic and comes out of ecology, out of the ecos. It creates its own micro-definitions. Visibility begins from the ground up and has no interest in or respect for the central/controlling powers. Fact is, they *do* see all below the threshold. That's their control – they control the micro in that they control the desires and needs of the 'worker', in terms of both materials and their use of the ecos. Threshold is state-businessocentric-materialist conceptualising of existence.[2]

Note: Animals, lost and gained time, de Certeau's 'tactics'.

Coming out of the rural, my view on the work of de Certeau (and others) will necessarily be particular. For me, loss of time doesn't mean a damaging of the 'disciplinary power' but the gaining of time for 'nature'. The worker sabotaging the slaughterhouse's profits through time-waste is not a gain in agency for the worker who will still *kill*, but the lengthening of the animal-to-be-slaughtered's life. De Certeau's 'tactics' are military because they are human – the only gain is in the side-effects of persistence and conservation of nature – lost time for humans is gained time for animals.

21 June 2014

Cloudy then sunny. Warm.

Went to Bantry this morning – it was very busy there.
  Bantry House is selling off 'its' possessions – the detritus of colonialism. Going, going ... gone. [NOTE: sale did not go ahead and there are moves to conserve the contents]
  Took Tim on one of my walks this afternoon – the rectangle of Ardmanagh up the lanes to the base of the range, then down to Town Park. The fields at the top of Ardmanagh with their collection of rectangular bales were busy with the stacking of bales from their pyramids on to trailers. I noticed that the bales were quite loosely compacted and also loosely strung, barely holding together.

2 See Jason Weidemann's essay at www.tc.umn.edu/~weide007/city.html, which as evaluation is fine, but whose premises I reject in every way!

Yet another death from toxic fumes in a slurry pit – not far from here, in Kealkill. The farmer was tragically overwhelmed by fumes and fell into the pit. It's death on death, year after year, in Ireland from slurry fumes. Something *must* be done about it. Slurry is dangerous and not just part of a 'traditional way of life'. It is not merely a benign and normalised part of the rural. Another rural disaster – sadly, it's a universal language.

23 June 2014

Place – 'landscape'

1. Pragmatic relationship to the land
2. Beauty – encounter and reaction/sublimity/arrival/departure
3. Visceral – imbued/'deep' connection beyond investment/profit/ownership

Tracy wonders if what we have – the manner of living and believing we share – is a form of (vegan) pantheism. It *would* probably have been called *pantheism* in the early nineteenth century.

CODA: CHANGING ROUTE (OCTOBER 2015)

The 'return' – or desire for return, or even fear of being forced to return when one has escaped a threatening situation – is inherent to polysituatedness. We return in our imaginations to reconfigure, to make different regarding where we've ended up, or where we've managed to reach (or escape) to. Many leave and hunger for the old place, the familiar zones of growing up or habitation. The migrant makes new reaching into the old, the place is reconfigured in part, and sometimes in great part. Even being in many places as part of a transitory life, or going out from home to make other dwellings to take back to your notion of where you come from, entails, necessitates, the folding of return into return into return.

From the day we arrived back in Schull, I've been re-acclimatising by walking. Picking up all my old points of contact and adding others. It's season and weather, but it's also change in micro and macro ways that come with time. The layering of the 'sense of place' is always polysituating, but so is the gathering of experiences in other places we've had since 'here last'. For ten days I walked my old routes up Ardmanagh and down across to the Colla Road, down to the Colla pier, looking out on Long Island and the Goats out to Fastnet, with variations taking me high and low, further and in an echoing circle gathering my connections in. I stand on the road above Carraiglea bringing in as many angles to Roaringwater Bay as I can; I am constantly falling into Cape Clear and its sense of the mainland as another country. Augmenting the walks, I have chatted with friends and re-opened our boxes of books, re-engaging with various histories and walking guides, and especially Peter Somerville-Large's 1972 volume, *The Coast of West Cork*. I have recorded all this in my journal and poems, but today's walk was one of those that bring a shift in direction, in a variety of ways and subtexts. My relationship to the *here* has changed in a distinct manner, for the manners of presence are at its core.

So, today I set off up Ardmanagh Road, intending to do what I call the rectangle walk, when I decided to take a side road up the mountain (to about

150 metres) that reaches a dead end. I've been up there before, but not for a long time. The view is magnificent; you can take in bay, islands, fields, walls, towers and Mount Gabriel itself, rising above you, manufacturing its own weather. You walk past cowsheds dark and slated and huddled into the mountain, radio playing for the cows, hurling finals fixtures being discussed, and you come across cows, sheep and horses in close proximity. Last time I was up there I wrote a poem of recoil at seeing mounds of white goods tossed in a bog, and also in crevices which are the stream-source of the small river that winds its way down, past where we live in Rosewood Cottage, to Schull harbour. This time, I was astonished and very pleased to find that it had been cleared up, and the land looked much healthier. Heather, foxglove, some wizened hawthorn trees and hedges of fuchsia looking much closer to winter than those on lower ground. Furze was sparky yellow under dull skies, and the red of the sandstone looked like old blood.

Standing looking out at Clear Island and the Gascanane Sound between Sherkin Island and Clear Island, I thought of the opening to Somerville-Large's chapter on Cape Clear:

> From Baltimore I took the mailboat to Cape Clear. Most times passengers face the Gascanane with dread, and are swept through white and bilious, Atlantic rollers pounding behind them. In the old days those who made the passage for the first time were expected to improvise a short poem to bring them luck and to distract them from sea-sickness.[1]

When we first crossed to the island in heavy swell on the *Dún An Oir II*, I didn't know about this old tradition, though I did compose a poem in my head as I went, as I always do when moving, and later transcribed it from the 'screen in my mind' on to paper. But it wasn't a poem invoking luck or preservation in that sense, though it was about ecology and preservation and respect and polysituatedness. What was I bringing to the island, what was I taking away? Later I wrote a poem on Clear Island to aid in the recovery of someone sick in Schull when we were at Jam Tree Gully. But today, standing on the heights at the end of a very local road, looking out at Gascanane, I improvised a poem of luck and 'warding off' for all those travelling there anew today. The wind was getting strong up there and I could see spray flying as small but tough waves hit Long Island and The Calves, and I knew it would be turgid out there. I said aloud:

> Watching the spray
> Leap from Roaring Water Bay,
> And following the way
> Through Gascanane's fray

1 Peter Somerville-Large, *The Coast of West Cork* (Belfast, Appletree Press, 1991 [1972]), p. 76.

> I wish the ferry
> Strength not to stray.

Okay, it's pretty corny and strains even to scan a little, but it was spontaneous and through its pouring-forth I had a genuine insight into the invocatory potential of poetry. I always knew it, and maybe practised it, but I felt it in a very tactile way. Be it in Bardic tribal land-grab and spiritual power play, or in a colonial Wordsworthian sentiment of poetry as 'spontaneous overflow of powerful feelings', the need to say something outweighed the desire to make a poem work in a variety of ways. The moment was more important than content or style and, in a sense, was the most *in situ* moment I felt I had been involved in. I compose *in situ*, I think *in situ*, but this time I was overwhelmed by a necessity – maybe because what I was seeing was probably four or five kilometres away, across the water. From a mainland mountain with its perverse radar domes scanning airspace, to the refusals and internalisations of Gaeltacht Clear Island.

Walking back down the mountain road, I moved aside (I ran into a field entry) for a van wider than the road, going to maybe the one or two houses up there; I waved and laughed, and continued until two voices called to me. I replied with a greeting. Are you visiting and taking a walk? a woman called out. I studied her from under my cap, and answered, We live here part of the year and are living on Ardmanagh and I am doing my daily walk. Been a while since I've been this way – my usual way takes me down to Colla and Croagh ... but the view from up there kind of called me. Ha, she replied, it does that. And then a man lifted his head from cutting turf with a sleán (I thought of Tracy's 'bog poems') and said, What do you do? I – We – are writers. They didn't ask what I meant by 'we', but nodded in semi-approval. Then I added, as there was a difficult silence, We're Kinsellas and O'Briens (and Egans and Kavanaghs and Sheehans, etc.) and feel some kind of connection with the place. Right you are then, they said as one. I will see you again, I said – I am adding it to my regular route for a while. Roots. Rhizomes. It's not because of ancestry I feel compelled to be here, but because of the plants and animals and old red sandstone. I feel healing can happen here, and that I can understand the damage being done through comparison with the Western Australian wheatbelt.

Yesterday I wrote a poem of experiencing the mountain as an inside turned out, as something growing outside the body of the planet, an ectopic pregnancy. Today, walking down the mountain, I stepped over the string of a washed-out tampon that had obviously been picked from rubbish – hooded crows were literally picking rubbish bags apart closer to town. I worried about gendering place, its implications in the polymorphous modality of body and place. I need Tracy's take on *here* to tune my own, maybe she needs mine? Maybe not. Not to balance or make a yin-yang equation, a gender binary – I don't believe this exists. Gender is fluid and unfixed, and always has been for me. But maybe another sensibility. A community of association and connection, even for an eremite like myself in my solitary wanderings, magnetised back to specific locales. I continued my walk thinking over the guardians of the mountain road that stopped a third of the way to the summit, of the elegiac commitment to 'being there', of occupation, presence and the sentinel, and also, distantly, the fixed foot of Donne's compass in 'A Valediction: Forbidding Mourning':

> If they be two, they are two so
>   As stiff twin compasses are two;
> Thy soul, the fixed foot, makes no show
>   To move, but doth, if the other do.[2]

And this all connects to an incident the other day as we drove (yet again) up the Famine Road over Tim Healy pass on the Beara Peninsula. Part of my journal entry for that day (4 September 2015) goes:

> [we were] confronted by a shillelagh-wielding old man ... The 'crazy man' stood in front of the car, waving his weapon and pulled us over. I opened the window a little and he tried to reach in but I kept distant. He asked if we were enjoying the/his mountain and was clearly about to exact a toll ... We said we live 'here' and he demanded where! The Mizen. Where were you from originally? Australia. And what do you do? I am a writer. He then looked at Tracy and said, And you? A writer. And then I added, And our son goes to school on the Mizen. He says – playing up the role he has established for himself to be 'crazy' for tourists (undoubtedly unwell, he was also ironising the 'authentic' for visitors ... to instil fear – indeed, we saw him pull over a car with three women, get them out of the car, and terrify them). He was playing Keeper of the Pass, and probably believed it as well. He looked threatening, hit the top of the car with his shillelagh, then smiled and said, I can see you are a happy family and I bless you and the car and you can pass on your way.

My entry continues:

> One must be careful with how one reads this interaction in retrospect – it was both serious and also 'play'. He played the part of a 'Sweeney', as the outsider but enhancing an authentic 'Celtic' identity, but he was also enacting an important critique of visitation and temporariness, of belonging and removal, of fleeting contact. He was going to make it either a case of exacting payment for contact – a toll – or a transcendent experience for the encountered, the intercepted. But as Tracy says, if she'd been on her own, as a woman confronted and 'held' in that way, she would have been terrified. Gender and the mountain. The shillelagh was weapon as sexual fetish, but also a weapon in itself ... Does he sell himself as transitional figure to The Others? A conduit, a medium? Playing the 'lunatic'[3] while being unwell and used as he 'performs'? I cannot say. But I did experience.

---

2 John Donne, 'A Valediction: Forbidding Mourning', at The Poetry Foundation, http://www. poetryfoundation.org/poems-and-poets/poems/detail/44131.
3 Just to clarify, I am talking of a trope and also literary convention of the 'lunatic' as

And a note I added later on the same day:

> The tourist who has his/her photo taken with the accoster, who 'sells' his/her expe-
> rience of isolation and difference in Ireland to the people 'back home', is part of
> the performance?

And this is the poem that came of it:

The Keeper of Tim Healy Pass

'the glen of *galts* or lunatics'
　　P.W. Joyce, *A Smaller Social History of Ancient Ireland* (1906)

As the 'lunatic' moves towards Glannagalt,
taking the roundabout route, the high road
and the loop, the rocky ways down the Beara
then back up to Kenmare and into Kerry,
as the 'lunatic' decides he's always
been the keeper of the pass,
and maybe he has, maybe he
has dwelt here lifetime on lifetime,
blocking the road, waving his shillelagh,
demanding to know if tourists are enjoying
the winding, narrow road with water rushing
through tunnels he hunches under, the sheep
who know him and eye him warily, their blue-
stained backs inflecting the sky, inflecting
his shouts of Stop, come here and be reckoned
with! as he makes his slow way up to the pass,
up the famine road, the lichen and old red sandstone
torn and repairing, torn and repairing, he calls us
in, waving his weapon, and asks us if we
are content on his mountain, where we're from,
what we do, why we live on the Mizen?
He taps the roof and blesses the car
and blesses us and allows us safe passage
down down as he moves towards Kerry,
towards 'the glen of *galts* or lunatics',
to drink pure well-water, to dine
on the 'cress along the crystal-clear
stream', to restore his sanity
and watch the old forest grow back,
finding relief from playing the Sweeney
for tourists in search of their roots, willing

---

manifested in figures such as Sweeney. I manifest my 'self' in this, in my ongoing sequence on
being an outsider in the rural community of which Jam Tree Gully is a part, entitled 'Village
Idiot Poems'.

to cough up, willing to photograph
a vista or furze-fire but not to keep
the well-water pure, the cress fresh,
to help keep them as a cure
for the lunacy they inflict.

To some extent we all perform 'place', and we all perform 'belonging', which
is not to weaken our bonds to where we feel connected, what locales make up
our real and imagined selves. We are of many places, we are many places, and
we can conjure many versions of ourselves *wherever*.

PART VI

Weirding place/Anti-bucolic

'BELOW THE SURFACE-STREAM, SHALLOW AND LIGHT' – TRANSFERENCES OF WEIRDING PLACE: THROUGH THE EYE OF RANDOLPH STOW'S 'STILL LIFE WITH AMARYLLIS BELLADONNA' WE APPROACH AND REPROACH THE PASTORAL AND ARRIVE AT A READING OF *STILL MOVING* BY MARC ATKINS AND ROD MENGHAM

Still Life with Amaryllis Belladonna[1]

In a sudden stillness
the Easter lilies she gave me
from her jungle garden
occupy the room.

Could she have known?

Eyes locked on eyes
hands locked on hands.

So was rapt Amyclae
undone by silence.

Two watches whisper
and on the table
a little scented pollen falls.

It was only shortly before the first Messenian war that the town was conquered by the Spartan king Teleclus. (Strab. p. 364; Conon 36; Paus. 3.2.6.) The tale ran, that the inhabitants of Amyclae had been so often alarmed by false reports of the approach of the enemy, that they passed a law that no one should mention the subject; and accordingly, when the Spartans at last came, and no one dared to announce their approach, 'Amyclae perished through silence:' hence arose the proverb *Amyclis ipsis taciturnior*. (Serv. *ad Virg. Aen.* 10.564.) After its capture by the Lacedaemonians Amyclae became a village, and was only memorable by the festival of the Hyacinthia celebrated at the place annually, and by the temple and colossal statue of Apollo, who was hence called Amyclaeus.[2]

---

1 Randolph Stow, *The Land's Meaning: New Selected Poems*, ed. John Kinsella (North Fremantle, Fremantle Press, 2012), p. 196.
2 William Smith, LLD, *Dictionary of Greek and Roman Geography illustrated by numerous*

26 Copy of Randolph Stow's handwritten draft (obtained by John Kinsella from Stow's sister Helen in 2011)

We wait for the Easter lilies at Jam Tree Gully, and they are a common sight (if not quite 'naturalised' around houses, or where houses once were, throughout the wheatbelt); being from the Western Cape of South Africa en route to Australia during the days of ship travel, they join many other migrant species of plant here. The Latin 'belladonna' is 'beautiful woman' and the 'Amaryllis' is from the Greek of Theocritus's ('amarysso' – to sparkle) and the Latin of Virgil's *Eclogues*.[3] Randolph Stow's 'late' poem is both a pure pastoral and an ironising of the necessity to position the cultivated or at least the harvested (picked, displayed in a room to embellish or enrich) as 'pastoral'. The positions of the observer and observed, the players and interlocutors through the traditions of pastoral dialogue, location of performance, and allegory of a real condition in the context of another real condition, are in play in this poem as a

---

engravings on wood, London, John Murray, 1854, http://www.perseus.tufts.edu/hopper/text?d oc=Perseus%3Atext%3A1999.04.0064%3Aalphabetic+letter%3DA%3Aentry+group%3D8 %3Aentry%3Damyclae-geo (accessed 22 June 2016).

3   Lover, love-object, the 'magic' of love, Amaryllis is a polyvalent female in Virgil's *Eclogues*, whose works are polyamorous, with *Eclogue II* (the 'Corydon Eclogue' portrays overt homosexuality, presenting *delicias domini*) transfiguring interpretations of love across the entire work. It is essential to consider Stow's poem in this light.

form of domesticated *deus ex machina*. The foreboding in the 'trivial', the laden 'pollen', the question of self-knowledge and awareness of fate – all are conscious 'devices' in the fluidity of a still-life, a set piece. They are 'stillness moving'.

The distance between reader and the 'stilled' action of the poem, its mode of presentation, its framing of history and interaction between players, make it an uncanny version of we might term a *preparatio culpa*. In the plane/plain of the poem – in the room where spatiality is measured by two watches almost silently conversing (echo-sounding – or reading blips on their mirror radars) the decorative lilies – brazen pink on their long thick-veined stalks – register the sounds, the emissions, the dimensions of the room and what is happening within it. It is a visual-aural register of the now, and of history and its recording as anecdote, making literature – *Amyclis ipsis taciturnior*.

We read in an essay by scholar Charles Lock:

> Distance is, in pastoral, figured spatially as well as temporally. Where Greek pastoral located itself in distant Sicily, Latin pastoral (above all, Virgil) would translate the ideal world to Arcadia. Panofsky, in his famous analysis of the Latin motto '*Et in Arcadia ego*', points out that for the Greeks Arcadia is an ordinary sort of place, and that it takes distance and the Latin language to give that name the lush and dreamy resonance that it still retains for us:
>
> > Virgil ... transformed two realities [Arcadia and Sicily] into one Utopia, a realm sufficiently remote from Roman everyday life to defy realistic interpretation (the very names of the characters as well as of the plants and animals suggest an unreal, far-off atmosphere when the Greek words occur in the context of Latin verse)...[4]

Lock argues, 'Pastoral and counter-pastoral are hardly to be told apart. Like utopia and dystopia, the pairing is not antithetical but, rather, bifocal: a question of blinking, a second glance',[5] and in essence, he is correct. An anti-pastoral might self-determine, but by definition requires an idyll to argue against. But really, what many eco-poets are wittingly or unwittingly doing is attempting to de-pastoralise discourse on the natural world by repositioning their creative and critical voices vis-à-vis the rurality they can't get around (organic or industrial) in terms of eating for survival, never mind value-added sustenance which is leisure and pleasure. Pastoral has an in-built critique of anything but a perfect world (*retro*-'Arcadia' via Sicily or Rome) for human habitation, and its need for an idyll is because things are always far from an idyll, so it's no surprise with changes to a rural world in, say, England (enclosure, the early effluvia of industrialisation, movement of populace to the city) that the agonies of rural life will become metatextual – entertainment is one thing, but an intellectual trade in awareness need go hand in hand. The arising of a lit-crit *culturality* necessitates

4 Charles Lock, 'The Pastoral and the Prophetic: Making an Approach to Geoffrey Hill', *Salt* 17.1, ed. John Kinsella (2003), p. 96.
5 Lock, 'The Pastoral and the Prophetic', p. 93.

both beauty and awareness, so the lack of human equality, the pain of starvation, the squalid will arise with the ideal manifestations of humans-in-nature. But the radical shift comes with an awareness of how both human leisure (more so) and human suffering (different) can damage and inflict only suffering (never leisure) on the 'natural' world. That's where the pastoral implodes, and we might call that a true counter-pastoral that doesn't make for a binary or a balancing act or two parts of the whole, but something different. And we can rename it as 'anti-pastoral', but this is semantics. Really, we are undoing pastoral as a way of talking of the rural, the natural and the idyllic.

Lock notes, 'In pastoral – and in literature generally – all that we "recognize" from our quotidian experience is framed by the conventions, and placed in a separate sphere.'[6] And also, 'Separation by frame is also the condition of that response which, according to Aristotle, enables us to enjoy the representation of what would otherwise give pain.'[7] He is right in this, but I personally have no interest in the reader's enjoyment. What concerns me is the need for a pastoral to reconfigure how we 'read' and then critique our own position as users of rurality, to be able to position ourselves as consumers of literature 'about' that rurality (real or unreal). It's about land usage. We have to critique our own positions as consumers, as well as that of the writer/artist/musician. As with the 'Grecian urn', what was idealised once in the form of art becomes a remonstration with the brevity and instant loss of the *now*, which becomes a perverse irony in its reference and recycling in the art of now – the poem that captures and comments and then will be read by a future undergoing the same crisis of a lost past. A past which has contained as much mixed fortune as the *now*. This is the paradox of the 'Cold pastoral!'[8] This is why I question Lock when he says, 'And yet, we still like to be seduced by pastoral, even as we appreciate its acknowledgement of our resistance to seduction.'[9] I reject any 'acknowledgement' of this 'like' as a sop and resist its seduction. It can be a fiery place, the pastoral, and we need to contemplate our role in its perpetuation (especially if we follow Lock via Bailey as it being 'all' literature in one way or another). With his exquisite (taste!) sense of irony, Lock notes, 'Pastoral is the name of the frame: of the threshold over which we are enticed, in front of which we stop, hesitating to pass by, but into which we cannot (for fear of kitsch) permit ourselves to step in empathy',[10] but as we look at the pastoral painting on the curated wall, we need to lift ourselves into the cleared fields of the poisoned paddocks and take action.

---

6 Lock, 'The Pastoral and the Prophetic', p. 100.
7 Lock, 'The Pastoral and the Prophetic', p. 100.
8 Lock, 'The Pastoral and the Prophetic', p. 94. Lock, talking of Paul Alper's landmark *What Is Pastoral* (1996), notes, 'Even more oddly, Alpers is constrained to write a 400-page monograph on pastoral without more than a single passing mention of Keats. There is, in Alpers, only silence where Keats is most pertinent: "Cold Pastoral!"' See Keats's 'Ode On a Grecian Urn'.
9 Lock, 'The Pastoral and the Prophetic', p. 101.
10 Lock, 'The Pastoral and the Prophetic', p. 101.

Under these conditions, and with a determination to refuse enjoyment and to reconsider the frame of the page, I approach Marc Atkins and Rod Mengham's devastating collaboration – photographs and text are what it is and is not – published by Veer in a landscape-format book in 2014. As Michel Delville says in his astute micro-essay 'Foreword', '*Still Moving* appeals to the five senses and beyond.' This is a book of gothixellation, of prophetic and preterapocalyptic synaesthesia – here is the odour of sight, as there is here where I write, with those flowering bulbs we call Easter lilies, Amaryllis belladonna,[11] long gone with a southern wheatbelt winter, but the memories of the singular profusion still redolent. This is a work of clinical observation with blurred aftertastes. Delville notes, 'The focus is on confrontation rather than juxtaposition, whether between structures and variables, motion and stasis, words and images, depths and surfaces, inside and outside, or reflection and speculation.'

The flowering of the Easter lilies here was when my copy of the book arrived and sat and gestated. Farmers are replacing their sheep with cows. Cows are more profitable (now). Mines are opening up in the rural zones. A bucolic is setting a frame for consumption of the item arrived as mail in a jet aircraft. And thus with Stow's poem of the absence of presence in mind, the ironic structures of pastoral tradition to allegorise any interaction – platonic, passionate, indifferent, circumstantial, strained, longed for – in mind, I read the book. I have a process. I will go through (it).

I no longer *believe* in surfaces. It's not just that they are a lie behind which to hide catastrophe, but that they don't exist. And never have. Whatever the intent behind the Atkins–Mengham collaboration *STILL moving*, it is this work of surface texture and textual investigation that has hoisted me over the line in coming to this conclusion. On the page is not the image. The image (and the text) are in spite of the page, but not a spite of the page. A negotiation, sure, but not about the reality, or not of surfaces.

What is made is not a surface. But there is making. It is claimed, there is evidence, and there are the residues of being exposed to making. But my not believing in surfaces is not a privileging of 'depth'. Rather, we are eternally inside the conditions of production. We can only imagine externals, surfaces, the depth by which we are subsumed. Russian dolls: the celestial sphere holding the performative space – a pastoral sphere.

In first approaching this Veer Books manifestation of the work, of the work of making, I use the 'flick' method I used when making cartoons in the corners of my exercise books at school. I watch the figure run through a history of the moment. Later, I read Atkins say in his 'A Word from the Makers', 'words

---

11 They have a different local name in the UK, which makes Randolph Stow's referencing of them as 'Easter lilies' all the more devastating re dislocations of place in the performative space of the pastoral: he had not returned to Australia for many years and his association of Amaryllis belladonna with that name perhaps reflects the years of his growing up rather than the decades of later life, whatever the locale of the poem.

pinned through a cartoon', and Rod Mengham evoke 'Words on the air with no frame'. Dungeness nuclear reactor on its 'sand and shingle' is a pressing image, *with an eye* for the care of 'cattle' who will feel its effects before they are killed and served up on plates. The maddest cows. Through the air and through other media the radiation, and the surfaces that would absorb or deflect not doing their job, other surfaces porous in so many different ways, the images seep through, and the pictures are always past. In the Marvel comic, in the holding up on super-8 film to see each frame – some damaged – I take the storyboard plate by plate towards its denouement. I hide, watching, behind *my* cloak of invisibility. Mengham knows – 'There are traces of heat in the air through which memories pass.' And those memories are altered by the presence, so many mirrors bouncing them back and forth they are lost. 'In the cubism of the dismantled lighthouse.' For you see, the efficacies of art are our marking time as well. Can one be anything but formalist and nihilist at once before the architecture of the nuclear power station? It belongs to no era in its utility, its attachment to the concrete and steel work of a particular time, government, company, factory specialising in … France. Across the Channel, the routes of the nuclear industry. Trains and trucks. All those ties, all those routes to 'constructivism of a shallow grave'. He said it earlier, slightly earlier – the paragraph, the stanza before: 'In the suprematism of a highway, joining the dots in a history of the Richter scale.' Threat? Urban wanderings to the 'End', as Atkins shows us – responds but not to tell us. These frames. How safe? Melange of populace or specificity of the hazed gaze? That was the urban bucolic. Theocritus looked to his home, Sicily, for his Arcadia. Arcadia for Virgil was, well, Arcadia. In Greece Arcadia is the ground broken by hooves. The crags. The heat. In the fields. Back in the fields. The naming: 'the stars come out on the Great Hungarian Plain, and Orion's belt acquires a notch'. We assume a travelling, but maybe not. 'As I live and breathe' but to break in, what do we breathe? Those rails – the armaments, the makers of genocide, the power-brokers of economy, the nuclear waste going to … the stars, the Zone, the illumination or glow looking in on itself, its own production – Melpomene far-looking, pensive/reflective and *steely* – what internal lights show through filters, lens, chemiluminescence – the grain of curves and the rails preventing centrifugal catastrophe. The book itself is centripetal? Why? The images accruing and axons will take me there when I dream: and this is not lush, any more than allegory in Virgil's eclogues, the fear and obsession with the God-emperor, the loss of estates and who gets what in the redistribution. But that was not Zimbabwe. The southern lands. Here, where I wrote to you, images and text … from. Which tunnel supplies us with roof flowers? Which texts denote the category of rectangle, the golden mean? As perspective is limitless in the curve, the tunnel takes us back to our beginning, though light at the end is not a spiral; it is a violent welcoming. You will emerge; others have. To toll or be told, to be marked in the crossing. There never was a liminal. We reject it: you can't escape this. They will force you out of the tunnel in the end. Just hesitate, you can do that. So, as Meliboeus says, 'nos patriam fugimus: tu, Tityre, lentus in umbra/ formosam resonare doces

Amaryllida silva'[12] ... and what a cheek of the privileged,[13] what a rubbing-it-in, for Tityrus to come back with:

> O Meliboee, dues nobis haec otia fecit.
> namque erit ille mihi semper dues, illius aram
> saepe tener nostris ab ovilibus imbuet agnus.
> ille meas errare boves, ut cernis, et ipsum
> ludere quae vellem calamo permisit agresti.[14]

which is not to deny the beauty under the blanket, the starlight in the lines of concrete, the window mirror statements, the textures if we look, the splendour in what is lost – taken – the clouds prophetic over the place of records, of servers – the two-thirds rule the strike from an orbiting fleet of more advanced beings with weaponry we could never envisage ... and bricks, which we cling to, from their scooping and baking and the piling up. '3 SOUNDING POLE'. Before encountering this 'deeply', I will consider that Mengham's poetry and essays have always had elements, at least, of the subterranean, of the snake escaped from paradise. Of burrowing and looking into the forbidden. And then there are details: labels, signs, conjectures on encounter. Certainty and questioning can be in the same word – but always knowledge, always information flowing in through the gaps caused by movement. What do we know, let's sound it out, let's apply the tuning fork to the resonating box, the white box on which we might check our images: 'no Falernian wine to mend your fortunes/ no chance of promotion to the fleet at Ravenna'. Where, the centres of empire? Wherefore 'a door opened and closed', and what of the qualities of light, the concentration of comparatives, the application of (false) binaries? We of the 'incomprehensible crowds'. Water carries the song of the blue whale for over 1,000 miles (I cite Tim's project on blue whales). Light reflected back can burn on a cold day. And the shore shifts and not only as the levels rise. What we know of living proof, of data we take with us into breakdown. A loss, absolutely. Don't doubt it. We read: 'The lights get carried away to the burying-ground by the harbour, where a necrotising linctus covers the eye. Off to the right, Seurat's bathers gradually depixellated.' We see: the materials of the made in the framing, the making in the binding of pixels, the pointillisms rendered to their fluid moment. This is no trick of light, no parsing of surface: where brightest and most full on the spectrum we realise lightlessness.

---

12 Virgil, 'Eclogae I', in *Eclogues, Georgics, Aeneid 1–6*, Loeb Classical Library (Cambridge, MA, Harvard University Press, 1999), p. 24.

13 Tityrus has spent a life enslaved and Meliboeus has had his land taken. The 'privilege' has shifted and we might ask if it's with sincerity and irony (imported by us? do we have a choice but to do so?) that Tityrus offers the warmth of the rural hearth, his hearth, his reward for his grey hairs, to the exiled (in essence) Meliboeus. This is the inbuilt contaminant of the pastoral and the obvious niche in which the poisons will pour and violate the seemingly immutable 'gifts' of 'nature' in the ruralised/cyclical engagement between 'civilisation' and the 'state of nature'.

14 Virgil, 'Eclogae I', p. 24.

This is illumination, a burial in dark matter, in the spaces between perception. The Arcadia resting place sings us – rough ground, burning hot, an ambush as quiet as a whisper when we've stopped mentioning the risk. Aggregated to the rising seas, acclimatised to the change. Loss in the cut eye, the *Un chien andalou* moment that is not gendered, but we see the cut of a woman, her silhouette. Who is speaking with whom? In the history of the modern pastoral is the argument of cinema: the moving stills, as every moment claims its point. Polarised, what we see are harmonics, the waves making sound. Whose song is whose? In the prism, the green strand. The plucked-from-the-poisoned-rainbow revelation. Thyrsis says, in *Eclogue VII*:

> Aret ager, vitio moriens sitit aëris herba,
> Liber pampineas invidit collibus umbras:
> Phyllidas adventu nostrae nemus omne virebit,
> Iuppiter et laeto descendet plurimus imbri.[15]

But the collation of signatures offers solutions: strange, uncanny, grotesque, weird, outlandish, off-beam, peripheral solutions. We read: 'There is nothing more strange than a signpost blown out to sea, drifting anywhere on the face of the waters.' On the face of an ontology: the mists of Merlin, the crisis of the Grail, a betrayal of Camelot itself by its constituent parts, its audience: the viewers? The Dragon's Breath? 'The mist of breath on a mirror passes away with the first word.' In the Beginning. 'So they talked to him freely, listening to their tales of men calling to a Maker, but with no hope of ever understanding.' This epic crossing, this navigation. In equipping the expedition, the argosy of exhibition, the storehouse of tales and their images. Bachelard says a lot of so-what, but he also says, 'When I was sick my father would light a fire in my room.'[16] I am here too, placing a mirror to the quiet, cold lips of pastoral, waiting for breath to mark it. The lenses of my eyes are thin, and thinning. It is difficult to retain the seeing contents. Become masters of our hearths, of our eyes. That's the translation. Don't fear. So much pleasure under the man-God's eye, these performances of the rural, these conquests of the soul of Greece? But not here, not in Mengham and Atkins's defibrillating pastorals which open the hands to release the images: they are aspirations, they are not enclosures. We do not have to remain trapped in the traps. The ash tree of M. R. James, outside 'rather dank little buildings'. Be wary. The possessions of the lone tree, the forlorn, the forest agitating in the blanks.[17] Ever the stately home or country

---

15 Virgil, 'Eclogue VII', p. 72.
16 Gaston Bachelard, *The Psychoanalysis of Fire*, trans. Alan C. M. Ross (Boston, Beacon Press, 1968), p. 8.
17 The witch-possessed tree. The gendering of the primeval. The clearing of superstition and mythology in favour of the utility of 'progress' and energy production. In James's story, we read: '"Well," he said, "my grandfather's Bible gave one prudent piece of advice – *Cut it down*. If that stands for the ash-tree, he may rest assured I shall not neglect it. Such a nest of catarrhs and agues was never seen."' From M. R. James, *Ghost Stories of an Antiquary*, https://ebooks. adelaide.edu.au/j/james/mr/antiquary/chapter4.html (accessed 22 June 2016).

manner in disrepair.[18] That smothering cloud, that breaking of meniscus. The unbalancing tomb as we allow US ALL to emerge, what we most fear. Anxiety and anticipation. The ghost bird-planes, the flotilla coming in late, those walks I take with thyroxine at dangerous levels bursting out of my gland. The light is that, in the tales. Cautionary. Nightfall. And the wavecall.

'WHERE SUNS LIE' in a sixth part – sharp and bold incipient catastrophe images, which caught me in my bucolic cartoon flickery. Sizewell B will echo. Dungeness is the Springwatch BBC programme I viewed at Rosewood Cottage in Schull, Country Cork – collectively intruding – the English awakening, were there eagles around the power station? Smew activities in radiation penumbra? Or the collection of poems by the film-maker, obit., I am sent by his anthologiser, his films and isolation and correlation of body event, and 'decline', in the shadows of the power station. I will read: 'The British nuclear industry is built on sand/ and shingle banks.' I will count the polishes of sea connecting and the waders picking amidst the structures offshore, 'The insatiable logic of nuclear architecture': now they're becoming one, the *Maker* and the *Maker*: a fearsome becoming. They see their consumption, the light of development (the computer light coming out at them, this familiarised exposure), and a meeting is held, a *quiet* collaborative spectacular of makers and viewers, all, one and all, listening to the goatherds sing *The Society of the Spectacle*. I read Debord (how much light shone on the page?): 'The image of the blissful unification of society…'[19] And always the sun, the power of the sun, as I sit here amidst my drafts of sun poems, and think about the poem of Randolph Stow's in which the 'Easter lilies' fill the room with the breakdown of tradition, as tradition never was. Just scaffold, like patronage, for that is pastoral and that is why *STILL moving* is aching with pastoral reproduction but is never-pastoral. If everything in literature is pastoral, this is unliterature and not photography. I will return to the sun and my disquisitions against 'place'. I will, even 'down here' where the mines bud into mines, and the first step on the nuclear train is taken (no metaphors mix), and the enriching plant at Capenhurst (Urenco) and the ponds at Malvési and the sacred land of Leonora, O sacred lands all sacred lands,

Danger
from windborne particles
contamination through
inhalation[20]

18 *STILL Moving* is a polysituated dialogue of history and mythology, geography and architecture. Place is specific and also archetypal, especially in the implications of (mis-)usage. Site-specific and grotesquely universalising in its consequences. The imposition of sameness makes a specific and general destruction and desecration at once. It is a paradox of the polysituated, which results in catastrophe.
19 Guy Debord, *The Society of the Spectacle*, trans. Donald Nicholson-Smith (New York, Zone Books, 1994), p. 45.
20 Marc Atkins and Rod Mengham, *STILL Moving* (Guildford, Veer Books, 2014), p. 57.

Yes, now I read – the facts. '6 metres a year'. Now. When the font was applied. 2097 decommissioning 'complete'. Yes, yes, it was Derek Jarman. Sophie sent me his poems. And the art. The art of shingle. Razors – mine always blunt on my chin, which is older and the bristles are white, wiry. Hemisphere crystal ball egg – 'Dorian nightingale'/'herald'/labouring God. *Pierians*.[21] On the shell, such a sheen – try getting the shutter speed spot-on, the point and retain of shadow, stark blocks. As if it were beauty against facts. X-rated.

What evidence have I supplied? Of pastoral, of surfaces? Do I have to come back in *STILL moving*? Do I expose or supplant or expect an archaeology? Hereabouts, it is funded by petrochemical companies. Chevron is big in the investment of petroglyphs. Matthew Arnold responds in 'Below the Surface-Stream':

> Below the surface-stream, shallow and light,
> Of what we *say* we feel – below the stream,
> As light, of what we *think* we feel – there flows
> With noiseless current strong, obscure and deep,
> The central stream of what we feel indeed.[22]

We take unto ourselves the colonial history, the patterns of teaching. Tim is home-schooled in wheatbelt Western Australia. Latin. Or the scroll-books in English, 'The Roman Mysteries' series. Dovering – like hoovering. A vacancy the bullies opened for us, in rightfulness. Arnold, Mengham knows in the room of upwardness, a warped mobility – 'a self-haunting reverie'. Yes, 'If England is rooted in the imagining of its chalk bulwark, then England is chimerical as a blue bird over the white cliffs.' I've seen it, departing the shores. Areva (via EDF) barely touched by Channel storms. Underways, overpass of particles both ways: swirl in such pristine, sharp images of now-as-history. To stretch a panorama is to make more of the picnic under fallout skies. A fence is a ledge. The roots of weaponry: defence/offence and then lips and failing teeth and the dentures of thumbnails. The frames are so specific and yet, the text is the teeth on the old film we place through the sprockets of the projector on which my grandfather showed home movies. They are always home movies and always were – the farm brought indoors on the screen that filled the curtained bay window, people moving fast, then slow, then waving awkwardly as the paddocks rolled by. And the industry of the rural continuing underfoot, *mise-en-scène*, as dust in the air. We breathe and see it all. Atkins and Mengham know this. Theirs is a collaboration appealing to our senses. It is a call to action in which history is not held in check by pastoral reckonings, their digital embodiments, the nuclear-electric hunger for reaction.

---

21 J. M. Edmonds (trans.), *The Greek Bucolic Poets*, Loeb Classical Library (Cambridge, MA, Harvard University Press, 1996); see Edmonds' *The Pattern-Poems* (Greek Anthology, XV, 21ff.), 'The Egg', p. 497.

22 Matthew Arnold, *Poetical Works* (London, Oxford University Press, 1969), p. 483.

WORKING WITH THURSTON MOORE ON THE POEMS OF *A REMARKABLE GREY HORSE* AND 'NEW STUFF': *ET IN ARCADIA EGO*, NOT

Trash Frost Ghost Saint Lullaby

Trash ghosts merge wasp galls
On lanky armed wattle tree
Far from city's inversion layer

Jack in the box
Hales dead halo
Lush about plush lips

Free frost flits like saint hair
Purses snatched by lips soiled
I lick your itch ok
Wonderful meeting

To flesh out & test
Centipede reflex
Or mess with fleeting
Invectives, love's prospect

Whip it on me goldboy
First thought is predestined desire
You know
Nothing was (sun always s/peaking)

Trucked across wastes
Nothing was gross as the moon
So we hailed
The lost to rise up & come to us

Off to bed
Blues heart the reminder
All is
OK

Above is the latest in a string of poems I have co-written with Thurston Moore. As with others we've done, it started serendipitously, and after a break of no email chat for some time. I said hello and sent a few lines, and a few lines came back. Where I was it was winter, and about 8 am. Where Thurston was it was London night-summer, I'd guess by the time signature on his email, but I am only guessing – I didn't ask. The poem did the asking and answering or avoiding. Readers might be able to deduce. It would have been about 2 in the morning. The times matter. Swapping lines via email till dawn. The aubade (to icons and iconoclasts) and the laments and the sleeping times. The wry tones of our lines and stanzas, that weave or add in to existing lines and stanzas, are given pique or refreshed by the circumstances we are respectively in. We are each largely unaware of the domestic life of the other. These blinkers help. 'Life' is sublimated through the lyric, and the poems become not only cultural and social commentaries, but maybe inflections and reflections of where we are at personally.

These are poems about slippage between conjecture and actuality, between an imagined real and an almost bubble-like immunity to the other poet's personal zone. Which is not to say there isn't caring or empathy – of course there is – but the poems are enough and do their work within themselves; they don't need the personal details, they don't need cushioning. What is diary or journal or observation or participation in them is hidden, and what is surreal, drawing into the dream or nightmare, what is dipping into reading or hearing or seeing or experience, is always in question.

So just now, I look out the window and set off and wonder about what might come back, and am surprised, and that sets me off in another direction. A mood always prevails. Early/late. A lullaby. Between, I send another message saying I am listening to Son House, and that filters in as gesture rather than as something literal. Son House isn't in there, but the manner and state of listening are. But even then I am not sure. Maybe, in some way. But the essence, for me, is a sensibility and an expectation. I don't find anything random in the process – in fact, these factors, and a knowledge of Thurston's vast array of creativity, almost make this interaction narrative and the poems stories. There's a dialogue, of course, but they are also lyrical stories that set their own agenda. Maybe the largest traversal is across the 'natural' and the 'made', across the urban and the rural. But there's no binary, and other stuff is constantly filtering or forcing its way in. And often the tension between the body and the head, desire and the spirit, brings about a coalescing, and the dialogue becomes one of body and soul in which neither of us owns a role.

Thurston and I are not privy to each other's writing process – how Thurston writes lyrics to his music has been much written about, and he and other members of Sonic Youth have discussed process which ranges from collage to one line, then the next from chunks to the whole – process is a living thing and music speaks with words. But these poems work in their own way, and each of us provides prompts to the other in the form of lines and stanzas and a group of poems such as those in our chapbook *A Remarkable Grey*

Horse[1] bounce off each other and necessitate not only call and response within a poem, but between poems. The existence of one poem necessitates another. What we're listening to, reading, where we are … the movies and 'stars' and icons and catchwords whose familiarity we share, growing up in different parts of the world in different ways. Thurston has been to Perth, Western Australia, and I have heard him perform there (with Sonic Youth); I know New York, we both know London, he has performed his poetry (without music) in Cambridge and I have chatted with him in public about his poetry and poetry-making process. We share a fascination for the small poetry publication, for the space of the page and the affect and effect of the poem as object. It's language in the end … all language. The language we share in part, the language we hear everywhere as difference, the words that leap across cultural difference and become 'buzz' words or even 'buzzkill'.[2]

Are these poems 'lyrics'. To music? I think so, I can hear the music that would go with them and I am sure Thurston can. He could make that music, but that's not what he's doing, we're doing. The poems generate their own discords and melodies all at once. A line rolls and then clashes; it endstops and enjambs at once. This is noise poetry that can be mellifluous; it is a clash of registers that 'marries' itself. It is collusive and rebarbative. Maybe we always need to reset the way we hear? Some of this is written in Ireland on the south-west coast during wild storms, some on the road in America while touring with new solo material and a new band, some of it comes out of Irish legend, some out of a pedagogical ecology of the Naropa University, Boulder, Colorado. And we have our personal interactions, our worries and delights, and these poems become conduits for all that. They are much larger to us than they seem on the page, but they are also there, then gone, to reappear and disappear again and again.

Speech is about how we hear. I hear Thurston's overhearing. I am familiar with his music – have been for thirty-five years now. I know his hearing as it manifests in art pretty well. But I don't know his hearing when he first hears it. I don't have that intimacy or knowledge of him, as he doesn't of me. Yet we get ideas through each other's work, inputs into this. Speech is what we are and overhear. The idiom he talks in, and the way he overhears across languages and geographies and cultural inflections, in venues before and after shows, in his day-to-day life. And the idiom 'of the bush' I am part of and collect and repro-duce, mediated by my ear-experiences and attempts at imitation of speech elsewhere. Both of us are always coming and going and seeing and hearing but refer back to who we are and how we learned to speak and hear. This is in the poems.

Our poems have been composed in a variety of ways, and more ways of com-position are being added. Sometimes a line adds to a line, other times a stanza

---

1 Thurston Moore and John Kinsella, *A Remarkable Grey Horse* (Montreal, Vallum Chapbook Series, no. 16, Vallum Society for Arts & Letters Education, 2014).
2 See poem in *A Remarkable Grey Horse*, pp. 17–18.

follows a stanza, and on other occasions lines or fragments of lines cut into what has come before. There might be rearranging and resetting as a 'whole' evolves. Punctuation may change, or a point made for retaining a certain spelling or syntax. Fairly quickly in the process of a poem a modus operandi is established, though one 'surprise' word 'late' in a poem can change this and lead the other to 'rethink' what the poem was about. Building and wrecking and building.

Our poems are installations and performances. They are also quiet moments. Exchanges. They sing-speak-clash and hopefully smoulder and spark and sleep and wake and perform their daily tasks. Both of us have been involved in many forms of collaboration over the years, and I am sure I can speak for both of us in saying that collaboration is inevitably generative and stimulating to solo work. This has been a special collaboration for me in the sense that both Thurston's solo work and his work with Sonic Youth play as a soundtrack in my head when I am writing my parts of the poem, which are so often in a different register from Thurston's, but speak with familiarity because of this soundtrack. We are very different artists, but also, I think, share a lot of artistic sensibilities. There's a desire to 'control' the mediums we work in on a technical level, but also let the art (poetry-music-visualisations) 'happen', to suggest their own paths, energise in their own right. Words always do the work, and we follow, ears and eyes open, ready to taste and sense everything they have on offer!

I'll finish with a short poem we wrote during the months we were composing the poems of A Remarkable Grey Horse, but which didn't find its way into that chapbook. It's actually in a slightly different 'key' from the rest of the poems of that period, but it also connects with them. I always found a wistful sadness to a poem closing off when working with Thurston – as if the air had been sucked out of the room I was in, leaving me giddy and disorientated and 'out of it'. It wasn't a bad thing. Sounds weird to say, but it's true. Like when Tracy and I heard all of Daydream Nation played by Sonic Youth by the Swan River under the gaze of King's Park and the mining towers of Perth: surreal, extra-natural, slightly incongruous, but brilliantly and excitingly a trashing of the pastoral. That's what I like about this process: streetwise Cage undoing Arcadia, death being overtaken by the zip of life. Buñuel, surrealism, Dada, Doris Day, performance, skateboards, punk love, sex, city meets country, Warhol and heavy weather in the Guggenheim. I am not really sure what my part is, but I am also there, with my forms and screens and ecologies and eclogues.

Ramshine

Rising on the kraken wave,
a hulahoop of a break,
the skaters set their low-
riders for a sunset dip,
a slip into smooth lingo;

Lowerlips bad mouth kissing
cigs, eyes skipping pavement
honey, wild time may last
only so long, but who dares
Care? Time to slip through.[3]

3 Thurston Moore and John Kinsella, 2015.

ECLOGUE FAILURE OR SUCCESS: THE COLLABORATIVE ACTIVISM OF POETRY – WORKING WITH CHARMAINE PAPERTALK-GREEN[1]

This process begins in exchange – a building of a single poem or maybe shorter poems adding to a whole – between myself Charmaine Papertalk-Green. I have Anglo-Celtic heritage that connects with the 'pioneering south-west', Charmaine is a Yamaji (Wajarri-Badimaya) woman who grew up in Mullewa and lives just outside Geraldton. I went to high school (last three years) in Geraldton and have retained family connections there to this day. My father ran a farm for a time outside Mullewa – a 30,000-acre spread ruled by massive machinery and vast quantities of superphosphate. In conflation and *débate*, in *tenso* but without *conflictus*. It is a rewriting of the terms of engagement with the rural. My brother is a shearer who lives about 20 km outside Geraldton and shears from Eneabba to Kalbarri, and deep inland across where land changes in form and language. Many shearers in Western Australia have indigenous heritage, and thus he works alongside many indigenous people who have a substantially different notion of the 'rural' within their country. I don't state this as a vicarious 'credential', but as a fact of slippage: what he experiences I in some way experience through him, and what is essential is that country is negotiated on many levels as a result of an ongoing colonisation, as a result of 'primary industries'.

Charmaine and I have communicated for years. We often exchange messages about the rapacity of mining companies, most recently over the companies' manipulations over uranium 'deposits' around Wiluna. And the closing of 'isolated' communities. By agreement, we are both 'troublemakers' (to lift a word from an email of Charmaine's), and find it necessary to be so. Our anti-mining stances predominate in our discussions. I have written many poems contesting righteous talk of mining companies 'benefiting' all Australians. And Charmaine has been deadly in her tackling of their claims to largesse:

---

1 With poems by Charmaine Papertalk-Green and John Kinsella – Charmaine's poem are reproduced with her permission.

Mining destroys

Why do Yamaji
Still trust mining companies?
They trick the Elders
With their fancy talk
They trick younger people
With flash of money
Then they go ahead and do
What ever they want with the land
Regardless of what is signed or said
My brother said "poor old Tallerang"
that's the way it is now
scattered along railway tracks
between Mullewa and Geraldton
I go to the railway lines near my house
I can pick up a piece of iron ore
From Tallerang – How sad is that
My brother said "poor old Tallerang"
And I guess he was right.[2]

We plan a book of poetry and stories and non-fiction pieces around our views and frustrations over the paternalistic colonisations of mining companies. Charmaine writes,

> I have been thinking about this further ... I have seen visuals within the community which I would like to include in some sort of way – for example at the Perth airport there is a huge huge billboard about mining and WA being a gateway for the resources (or something to that effect) – I want to weave around this and talk about my feelings and thoughts, how not all of us have been mesmerized or 'fallen in love' with digging up the land for the mighty dollar. (7 May 2012)

I reply with my personal connections to a mining industry I resist:

> It relates to my great-grandfather on my maternal side being a gold miner (being foreman of a gold mine in the late nineteenth century) and my grandmother (his daughter) being brought up at Kookynie. And the other work relates to my father working for Dampier Salt for many years. All the work critiques mining in various ways and explores the politics and impositions of it. (5 May 2012)

Charmaine comes back with a message about her own familial connections to the world of mining and the complexity of holding her views when those close to her are working for mining companies or those who help service them. For neither of us is it a case of being 'outsiders' or commenting from the outside.

2 Charmaine Papertalk-Green, 'Mining Destroys', in *Just Like That and Other Poems* (South Fremantle, Fremantle Press, 2007), p. 48.

We're both implicated. And in Charmaine's case, it's her community lands being done over again, or the lands of fellow first-nations peoples. I reply,

> It touches us all. Your family, and mine. And when I was a young alcoholic bloke, I worked in the CSBP factory making fertiliser (mined from Christmas Island)! I think it's important we trace our own lines here. The fact is, the mining companies rule all and people end up jobless without them. That doesn't make them right, and there should be alternatives. One of the (many) issues is that there are not – your blokes are in the position because that's the position they're offered. That's the thing. We need to wrestle with these contradictions. That's what we can do. (7 May 2012)

So we wrote and exchanged some poems, then the line went quiet for a variety of reasons. But then, after a year, another poem sequence emerged, which might eventually feed back into the overlapping concerns related to mining. Connections between the old collaborative idea/approach and the 'new' will, I hope, become apparent.

I write poems about the appropriations and intrusions of the religious (was Anglican and became Catholic) architect, Monsignor John Hawes. We contest him. If not flytings hurled in his direction, or towards the magnificent buildings he designed, imposed and built from the pre-existing architecture of other cultures – the gouging-out of land that operated as spiritual meeting place, that carried its own iconography – then certainly voicings of anguish and reservations.

This pastoral discussion that goes beyond any anti-pastoral, well beyond, also has rhizomes in a discussion I had with the American poet Rosanna Warren years ago about Virgil and the pastoral. While recognising that through allegory, the decays and traumas of the age were expressed against a backdrop of rurality that is lauded, I expressed scepticism at the actual purity of the rural as backdrop. There is no Arcadia even to wish for. But I think I lacked clarity in some of my points, and just today wrote Rosanna this email:

> I was just reading back over our earlier dialogue and thought – years later – I should offer a clarification (or, rather, a clarity). When I said I was thinking about Virgil's Eclogue 1 in the old stone post office building in the country town of York, that I was thinking of the villa and seats of power (the emperor in Rome), I wasn't suggesting that was the setting of Eclogue 1! Of course, it was a reflection on looking out from an edifice to outside/without the town, to the deeper 'rural' of the fields/paddocks. Tityrus talks of the 'bigness' of Rome – that it wasn't like the country market town, but something much larger and more powerful. And it is there that the emperor has bestowed the land (back?) on him (or as a slave, maybe, granted…), and it is from the villa (office in its thick stone walls) I was *thinking out of*, so to speak. Rereading, I feared I might have given the wrong impression. Is this the case? I ask because I can run on my own lines thinking I am crystal clear when it's not the case … or the case itself! Meliboeus's loss of land, his exile, his passing through, were being juxtaposed to the new security of Tityrus, whose world also

might come unstuck with the arrival of 'outside' forces (Rome, new soldiers). I was reacting to the xenophobia – that what 'we' have in peace and tranquillity (smoke of the neighbour's … bees etc.) can always be taken away, and Meliboeus's fate (is his loss really Tityrus's 'gain'? Probably not) become our own. (11 August 2015)

The eclogues of Virgil seem relevant here. In the messianic prophecy of the child who will lead humanity (i.e. the Romans) to a Golden Age (IV), or the loss and gain of Eclogue 1, the background of Virgil's pastorals bears much resemblance to Canberra's machinations in its desire to defeat those who claim that rapid climate change can be slowed by better, more environmentally minded human practice, and its desire to put profit (coal mining, uranium) above and beyond the health of people, the environment in the sense of the local, and the entire biosphere.

In implanting their conservative interests in all facets of life in Australia, the Federal government and also State governments, controlling vast areas (closing of communities, altering of environmental laws or working around them to 'develop' – get rid of 'green tape'), enact a perverse manifestation of polysituatedness. The presence of many places in each self and as multi-layers through community means all place is absorbed through control of the individual, small communities and the country as a whole. There's an interminable interconnectedness in the argument of the common good, in which what is claimed as good for all of us is in inverse proportion to how many it is actually good for. More vote to cede rights to fewer people, and think they are breaking free of the constraints of green 'control' and deprivation of their liberties (the liberty to use and waste and pollute).

Environmentalists too easily become involved in a poetry contest in which insults are hurled, songs are sung and the media decide (weighted) who is the winner. The distraction of the selfie – that liberty that conveys the self as liberated and yet conspires to present itself in the light of self-regard – feeds the breakdown by creating communities of those who think they are individual but who have ceded their rights to groupthink. Trying to progress a protest is more limited by social media than it is expedited: awareness and witness, promotion and achievement are confused. The replacement of one moment with another dilutes impact, and when it comes to the evolution of mining it is astonishing and bewildering what is actually happening out there in terms of exploration and start-ups. Witness the non-disclosure (by a foreign company) of the search for gold below the streets of Kalgoorlie city itself.

In theorising place, we offer up tools for the abuse of land, and to create terms of land usage which become levers at the bargaining table. The 'global/local' ('think globally, act locally') dynamic becomes a useful tool for exploitation; the linguist's skills in recreating assaulted and damaged language roots become tools to extract with a return of 'identity'. But these things only last as long as companies need them to last. Like funding the arts.

It is not the place of this essay to give yet another rendition of the life and works of Hawes – this essay is concerned with forces at work that merely found their expression and even personification through the 'eremitic' architect.

But in order to give some context I will cite a couple of paragraphs from the *Australian Dictionary of Biography*:

> In Rome Hawes met Bishop William Bernard Kelly from Western Australia and was recruited for his Geraldton diocese. The dual role of outback missionary and architect with a commission to design a cathedral appealed strongly to Hawes's two major enthusiasms. Arriving in Geraldton in November 1915, he took up a temporary appointment in the Murchison goldfields parish of Mount Magnet and Cue, but started work on his Geraldton cathedral next June. By August 1918 the nave was opened for services but the Cathedral of St Francis Xavier was not completed until 1938, owing to lack of funds and the hostility of Dr Richard Ryan who succeeded Bishop Kelly in 1923. The cathedral is Hawes's most important building: frankly eclectic, a mixture of Romanesque and Californian Spanish Mission styles, but with a roughcast simplicity and dignity totally in harmony with the surroundings.
>
> Of Hawes's other buildings in Western Australia, the most interesting include his highly individual parish church of Our Lady of Mount Carmel, Mullewa, again largely Romanesque and built of local stone mainly through the architect's own labours, and the adjoining priest's house (1927). There are also churches at Morawa (1932), Carnarvon (1934), Northampton and the Utakarra cemetery chapel (1935), and Perenjori (1936); and he designed chapels at Yalgoo, Bluff Point, Nanson and Melangatta homestead.[3]

The key reference points with regard to what follows are the cathedral in Geraldton, Our Lady of Mount Carmel in Mullewa and the church at Northampton. The Hermitage in Geraldton is also relevant. Other buildings will become foci as Charmaine and I work our texts, but these are to come. Hawes's biography is of relatively little interest to our project, though it is of some, as all information and data affect how we see and interact with an edifice and its cultural fallout, but our concerns are primarily with what these buildings delete and obfuscate. These foci of Rome as symbol of colonial power are not a specifically anti-Catholic act, but an anti-colonial one. Our work is not negating belief, but challenging the Church's colonial attack on other beliefs and the space they inhabit. In the setting-root in and occupation of space the Church (and its 'architects') work in conjunction with political and commercial forces. The 'villa' I mention above is the *building* itself – be it dwelling or church or office – the claim on space by creating the panopticon that connects with another panopticon and builds a fortress of presence. In other words, 'architecture' in our context comes to represent dispossession and invasion.

Our collaboration began with this exchange of emails, in ecologic fashion:

> JK: We should write a series of Hawes poems. I could start – a short poem, and you could respond and we could do a few of those. A collaborative poem. Can be about mining and colonisation and imposition of religion and resistance and ownership

---

3 See the *Australian Dictionary of Biography*, http://adb.anu.edu.au/biography/hawes-john-cyril-6601 (accessed 22 June 2016).

and country and all. Not just Lord praise the wonders of Hawes and all he did for … whom? He did make some good buildings but they were good because of the stone and earth he made them out of. Maybe that's how I'd begin:

1.
The church Hawes made in Mullewa
was great in its stone and earth.
The white folk praised its shape
of God out in the hot zone.
He got a lot of credit.
A lot of praise.
His altar had believers
kneeling on ants.
Red-tailed black cockatoos
sit on its edges. Visitors
don't know their names.
JK

And Chairmaine responded:

2.
Galloping in bible and cross in hand
Hawes God's intruder
Altar stone of the earth
Intruding on our barna
In the name of catholicity
Bow your head and conform
For this is now the whiteworld
Hawes God's intruder
Onto our barna
A campsite – home
A place of living
A place of our ceremonies
Long before it was
called "Mass Rock"
Hawes God's intruder
CP-G

And so on:

3.
Coming in from the 30,000 acres,
eyes fixed on the ornate structure,
as if two towns – or more – divided
like the biblical sea, shearing teams
drinking the red fleeces away.

Not our church, someone said,
and we wondered, as Dad
got his supplies of beer

from the Railway Hotel,
his hands oily from the dual-wheeled tractors,
burnt from working in the superphosphate shed,
the fog of occupation over the fortunes of country,
not his, not the millionaire's
whose farm he managed.

That priest, England in his veins,
converted the 'midwest', diocesan vision
of souls gathered under one-roofs.
A Spanish breeze drawn
under the arches. Mount Carmel.
Where? Romanesque?
What did he write: 'My heart
is in these stones'? His European
heart? His heart of … home?

And we as kids, outsiders,
jumping from one side of the tracks
to the other. The Mullewa,
train to Perth, discontinued
a few years earlier.
(Saturday, 2 August 2014)
JK

I think that's the best way to start the poem … and some of the stone from the quarry was behind the Aboriginal reserve in Mullewa and some of the Yamaji men helped build the Mullewa church.

What road was the farm on? – Morawa, Mingenew, Geraldton or Yalgoo Road?
(Sunday, 3 August 2014)
CP-G

Yalgoo if I recall correctly, C. It was bloody Alan Bond's farm!!! My father managed it for a few years. A bunch of my poems are set there.

If in part 2 you mention the stones etc, then we're on our way with the poem.
(Sunday, 3 August 2014)
JK

4.
Living on the Mullewa fringes
Became my people's place
When a colonial township emerged
Like a pimple amongst the wildflowers

Foreign church structures rose
Dominating the landscape
Family showed me the quarry
From which rocks were taken

Building the Whiteman's worship place
Close to the Mullewa Reserve
Mullewa – Morawa Road nearby
Aboriginal hands helped build that temple
Their energy and sweat is in them rocks
Their heart is in them rocks
Hawes didn't do it on his own
Wonder if that is written anywhere?
As a child I peered into that temple
Curious why gargoyles watched the entry
Frightened to look at the statues inside

Our playgrounds included train tracks,
Wheat silos, the Common and looking into the dam
Our family had died in there – as local kids we would
Peer through the big wire fence at the dam
Wildflower season meant tourist buses
We chased the bus from Our Lady of Mount Carmel
To the Lesser Hall for the promise
Of left-over sandwiches and cakes.
CP-G

5.
On the steps of the Big Church
I hesitate, unsure of what's inside
for me. I have the sand and wheat
ships in my head, and wonder
how far they might stretch the scene.

Mum is a teacher at the high school,
and my nickname there is Dictionary.
I write poems in a laboratory.
I work weekends and holidays
in the shadows of the mineral sands
factories, preparing samples
that show the quality of the land
pouring through the capitalist
hourglass, shifting the spirit
to metals and plastics and paint.

It was rocket science. The birds
stayed away and their songs
ignored by too many. Shifting
sands. Gunslits in 'settler' buildings.

We ride our bikes from Town
to Drummond's Cove where crayfish

bristle below reefs and reef sharks
patrol the gaps, snapper glinting,
brightening the underworld.

We live opposite the prison
in a limestone house
that was home to nurses,
an old colonial mansion
taken over by the Education
Department, a statement of possession
we know is haunted, distressed.
We weather a cyclone,
we find old coins fallen
through the wooden boards.
We are part of something
we can't quite piece together.
Mum volunteers to teach prisoners
written English, to listen to their lives.

Now, where house and yard
and Moreton Bay fig stood,
is Coles Shopping Centre
carpark. Beneficence?
For the people?

Down from there, trains
rounded on themselves,
head-to-tail on the turntable,
and the sea against the seawall,
and the curve of beach
reaching to Saint George's
(what did he have to do with it?)
and the cobbler's sting that undid
my nerves and had me shrieking
the agony of Champion Bay
I didn't understand. The school
was busy re-enacting Grey's
expedition but I knew
that wasn't part of my vision,
though later I'd rewrite it
as a poem of decolonisation.

When I return to Geraldton,
to what part of me is there,
I rest in a dry creek bed
and listen to the river redgums,
I go to the bottomless pool
and watch the swallows

defy gravity. I know sunsets
make a coast and I listen
hoping my errors
will find redress.
JK

6.
Growing up I lived opposite the Catholic Church
"Our Lady of Mt Carmel" in Mullewa
Every day I walked past Monsignor's house
I knew nothing of their beliefs and customs
It was just a playground to take pictures
Get a cool drink from the water fountain
The gargoyles perched at the entrance did
Frighten me at night as I close my eyes
And sprinted past the church to get home
I didn't understand why these monsters
Were on a church building – roof at that
I still don't care they just looked out of place

During the celebrated wildflower season
We would pose – 'cute little Aboriginal kids'
For the tourist as we waited for rewards
of cakes and sandwiches leftovers from
Their morning and afternoon teas
They probably felt sad for us – who knows!
We just got our feed and waved to them

I wrote poems and stories in a little diary
You know the ones with lock and key
And cute little girly covers
Each time finding new hiding places
From intruding little relatives and the rest
Each time having to tear up and throw away
My words, thoughts, emotions, feelings
Because there were no hiding places

The big church in Geraldton on the sand hill
was not part of my world in Mullewa
It was there but meant nothing to me
I don't remember it as a child or a teenager
Why should I had no business with it?
Our SDA church sat staunchly
On Maitland Road waiting for its family
We got bags weetbix, oranges, and apples
Saved us from really starving so
That's something I guess

But that big church in Geraldton
What a poser standing there like a temple
My mum went to a wedding there in 1940's
An Aboriginal wedding at that – Catholics
I have a pic of mum leaning on outside wall
All young beautiful and a tea maid
Mum had a permit to work in Geraldton
At West End of Marine Terrace
From the Native Protection Board
Or should I say her Employer had the permit
That's the way it was – Aboriginal people
Were controlled and couldn't move freely

Even as a teenager coming across to the
Aboriginal basketball carnivals
Or at the Maitland Park footy oval
I don't recall the Big Church
It didn't make a lasting impression
It just didn't belong to my world

Later in life I moved to Geraldton
And the big Church was in my face
I drove past it, I walked past it
I stared at it from the QPT lawns
I couldn't escape its physical presence

And what I did learn about it made me sick
The space it so grandly took over
Was once a traditional campsite
Is it coincidence that the Aboriginal
People living at the campsite were

Moved to other locations including
Moore River Native Mission?
At the same time the big takeover
colonising church was to be built.

Oh yes the big church is grand
They pray and worship their god
Tourists come from everywhere
With their cameras to make memories

All I can think about when I see it
Is of the campsite taken over
Of our people displaced and alienated
From traditional country
Colonised space it became and stayed.
CP-G

What is church? What is refuge? What is channel to an omniscience, a sense of purpose and belonging? The overlays and exclusions and sheer arrogance of the act of replacement is attested in the texts and needs no embellishment. But it does seem relevant to me to talk of the narrative in which one is trapped in creating such texts. In trying to gain leverage, to move from one spatiality through another that has cluttered the vista with blocks hewn from other blocks, that has restyled forms to suit other controls,[4] one runs up against the limitations of the colonial language. This can be broken into and broken up (Lionel Fogarty, to various degrees) or it can be redeployed to clearly act against its own (self/ selfie) interests. Language is liberty, and yet it is also our greatest constraint. Break too far away from its conventions and rules, and we risk being accused of speaking 'nonsense'. To speak no sense does not mean one believes no sense or will act with no sense. But to use 'nonsense' (which is NOT no sense – nonsense is what is not understood, usually wilfully) in the eyes of those whom the texts are aimed at 'undermining' serves little purpose. To stand up in a community meeting and contest the mining representatives requires either speaking in/ on their own terms, utilising some form of translation, or using advocates. This should not be necessary. Poetry impacts and compacts all possible outcomes, and poetry becomes the narratorial lever in the activist's tool kit.

Which brings to mind Daniel Punday's comments on 'corporeal levers' in *Narrative Bodies*. Citing Elaine Scarry from *The Body in Pain*: 'In the attempt to understand making, attention cannot stop at the object (the coat, the poem), for *the object is only a fulcrum or lever across which the force of creation moves back onto the human site* and remakes the makers.'[5] This is the case with poem as activist tool, though one could argue that the poem can, on other levels, become a cascading event in which space opens on space, infinitely. That's *ostranenie*, and the defamiliarisation of paratactically active poetry can achieve this. But the poem serving an activist purpose is a lever within the narrative of human activity: the fulcrum to stop the mine, not to adorn conversation; the tool to *unbuild* the church (without violence), or rebuild it as an aware space that gives ground back to what has been taken. This is repair, if not reconciliation. It is land usage that is not total and obliterating – what mining companies so often purport to be doing, but there's no trust where there is profit. Profit means someone is losing somewhere. Punday himself notes,

> Critics have long recognised that the very principle of narration is founded on praxis and the explicit attempt to manipulate the reader to some end. Garrett Stewart has recently argued that we can read the history of the modern British novel as an attempt to define and organize reader agency.[6]

4 Speaking of Rome, the infallibility of the pope speaking *ex cathedra* is weirdly tested by his own cardinals when *he* challenges the global-warming powers!
5 Elaine Scarry, *The Body in Pain* (Oxford, Oxford University Press, 1987), p. 307; Daniel Punday, *Narrative Bodies* (London, Palgrave, 2003), p. 179.
6 Punday, *Narrative Bodies*, p. 180.

The poem can be seen as part of a narrative of activism in the face of abuse; as a space in the narrative that opens doors into other spaces in which we might reconstitute the opening, the introduction, even the prologue to what was to come. Cascading spaces of meaning but also of application, of praxis. The poem as propaganda? Maybe, but also of progress and movement in the narrative on which mining companies (material) and churches (material-spiritual) build their stories, collect their souls, sell their wares. The poem parallels, operates as a mirror and as a shadow to the narratives of control – it's not just an affront, not just a lever to move back to 'the human site', but co-determinate. It is ephemeral, yet once uttered becomes a part of what it has critiqued or debated. It is an ecological tool, permanently contesting, with the golden age only possible when the power-site is disabled or pulled back into real dialogue with interests outside itself.

This, sadly, is rare. The poem as socio-political activism too often relies on the singer, the storyteller, the minstrel, the performer, who occupy space with their 'selfie' presence which, like the 'selfie', can be methodologised into 'distance', but is entirely self-interested and subjective. We all have our own bodies and what-ever else that constitutes the self to think of, to negotiate, to please, to answer to, to rely on. Self inhibits action, and yet, paradoxically, it is the source of action. So the poem must connect with other poems and the self, the performative self, the actor, 'shared', or made stronger through the anonymity of community.

The collaborative poem, the anthology, the group reading at a contested site, become far more potent than even the 'famous' individual poet for whom the cause becomes identified with an ego-I, no matter how non-unified the self of the poems. Language is private, no doubt, but it is also ultimately public. To co-write poems: retaining identity (very necessary in the case of the 'white' bloke and the Yamaji woman), yet speaking to each other and also to a world at large, is a dynamic that becomes part of a narrative that can connect spaces without obliterating them.

Charmaine and I primarily deal with the non-city (though Geraldton is now considered a small city), and in my case the overtly rural, but what we traverse is country that exists outside city-country. It was country. It is country: and that's not just polite acknowledgement on my part and visceral association for Charmaine, it is a fact of spatiality, of people who have spent thousands of years aurally and visually mapping in a multi-dimensional way. In her great (if increasingly contested and essentially 'middle-class white of the wealthy new world') work, *The Death and Life of Great American Cities*, Jane Jacobs offers many terms we can translate without an advocate for our immediate activist purpose. She opens the chapter 'Salvaging projects':

> One of the unsuitable ideas behind projects is the very notion that they *are* projects, abstracted out of the ordinary city and set apart. To think salvaging or improving projects, *as projects*, is to repeat this root mistake. The aim should be to get that project, that patch upon the city, rewoven back into the fabric – and in the process of doing so, strengthen the surrounding fabric too.[7]

7 Jane Jacobs, *The Death and Life of Great American Cities* (New York, Vintage, 1992), p. 392.

This can sound like an apologia for integration in the context of this essay-poem. Or it can be adapted to the purpose of this essay in an activist way – it can be co-opted into a textual argument around space. The project becomes the space taken by the church or the mine, and the city's fabric is country itself. Rather than integrating country into church, mine or, indeed, city, let's read the other way and integrate the church, mine, or city back into country. Land rights. The wrongness of the colonial (and ongoing colonial) act/s does not mean violent retribution, but it does mean some form of dialogic tool needs to be established that necessitates land rights by the act of usage. Poetry can be this tool. A conservative poet might use a poem to 'say' the mining companies are right (and there are many poems from the 'gold-rush' days of Western Australia that do just this), but in the end they rely on gain at the cost of land. You cannot have land gain and the human gain greater – the equation doesn't work. There's an inbuilt default in which the conservative ('right-wing') activist poem undoes its own fabric by supporting its own desires (material gain, manifestations of power, mythical roots that are co-opted to build an identity of power and so on) so overtly.

So we are left with a telling in the space of our experience, an observing in the space of our experience, extrapolation in the space of shared or 'heard' experience, and the question of how to use these variables in bringing positive change. The indigenous poet might come of one skin, various skins, and draw on European, Asian, African, Oceanic or other heritages. In the polysituated self, the experience of all that has come before, of all that is seen and read and heard, an ever-expanding echo, a narratalogical cascade in which origin stories become anchors of identity, we isolate what it is that has 'made us' the singers or speakers or protestors we are. We offer evidence, we lay ourselves bare, we offer proof. This is beyond any confessional, and yet is not a fetishised selfie or claim to 'fifteen minutes'. It is an excoriation put out there to mirror and shadow the damage being done. To say this is who and how we are is to offer a lens for listeners or watchers to position themselves, become aware of their own polysituated responsibilities.

Another paradox: we have no rights over someone else's space and yet that space is part of who we are. Local actions have global effects. The regional *is* the international. And yet we have spaces in which it is appropriate to speak, and spaces in which it is appropriating to speak. But this doesn't mean silence – it is the eclogue, a contesting in a way that looks for the best possible outcome, not to defeat the opposition. I do not wish to devastate mining companies; I wish them to become aware! We need the right to *choose* ('eklegein') our directions, but to do so with all consequences of that choice realised and experienced. Damage brings pain.

When I think of the eclogue, I think of the false sense of its meaning as 'Goatherd tales.'[8] I think of my brother shearing sheep – an advocate for the

8 See Alex Preminger, Terry V. F. Brogan and Frank J. Warnke (eds), *The New Princeton Encyclopedia of Poetry and Poetics* (Princeton, NJ, Princeton University Press, 1993), p. 317: 'The spelling *aeglogue* (or *eglog*), popularised by Dante, was based on a false etymology which

rights of sheep, a vegetarian and animal rights person – in complex social environments, at the nexus of farm and industry, of animal and human. I think of the politics of invasion and work in the context of work for Aboriginal men in Western Australia, especially in the mid-twentieth century. I think of the poem as activist tool that speaks at cross-purposes, that advocates contradictory outcomes. The poem is never about clarity; it's about those cascading spaces and endless doors and windows leading to endless doors and windows. But ambiguity does not mean loss of purpose or focus, and the drive to get to a positive end to the space-on-space is the *raison d'être*, the reason.

To write poems of mutual protest does not mean we need to see 'eye-to-eye' in everything – no one can – but the poem allows for such narrative digressions while always returning to the main storyline. And in these poems, Charmaine and I share concerns about dispossession and colonial behaviour that are obvious, if personal and maybe (maybe!) more 'private' concerns that are less obvious.[9] That is the poem, and that's why as an activist tool it is so effective: it says, and does not. It is a statement and a vehicle for private or 'closed' concerns. Indeed, it shifts and changes with context, and eventually it might leave its paralleling and become one with its subject – that is, when it has been 'effective' and 'affective'.

7.
The night I was beaten so badly
the cops and ambulance arrived
at the Geraldton Drives to carry
me away from my comfort zone,
I gained a weird respect from
a Yamaji guy who stood watching
while a white boy who hated
my guts pounded my head
into the bitumen, chips of blue
metal lodging in my scalp
like a sick halo lit-up by
the flickering images
of The Who's 'Pinball Wizard' –
Tommy playing on the big
screen like out of control
dreams and imaginings.
The Yamaji guy said
to his white associate,

---

derived the word from *aix* (goat) and *logos* (speech) and was construed to signify, as Spenser's "E.K." argued, "Goatherd tales"'.

9 In these poems is a lot of 'confessional' detail which doesn't need recounting in prose. But as said earlier, that does not make the poems 'confessional': in fact, these details are being used as factual levers, as evidence of participation, as vehicles that engender questions of witness and experience of site-specific acts/places in the spatiality of overlapping if distant (and even totally unaware) and unfamiliar experiences. The 'disorientation' offers a different mode of focus.

You better stop, mate,
(there was only the mateship
of being out at night and searching
for action in the dead rural suburbs,
the beaches just too far away
to catch the echoes of waves)
he said, there's too much blood,
you can't even see his face
it's so messed up. It's mush.
I heard him speak as cars
of whites sat watching
without losing a beat,
the 'crazy flipper fingers',
and the guy doing the punching –
a schoolmate – got a few extra
in and then gave it away,
my brother screaming,
restrained by others
in the group – the 'gang'.
That beating changed my face
and my life. I'd climbed over the fence
with my brother and a friend,
and spread a blanket up front
with a speaker next to us,
swigging green ginger wine.
We'd offered the boys
who'd come in the same way
from a different angle,
a drink. Then the Dictionary-
'teacher's-son'-stuff came out
and it turned bad. When the cops
wanted names they weren't interested
in the white kid who'd done
the damage, but wanted to know
if there'd been any 'black bastards'
in the 'gang'. I said no, just whites,
and didn't name names. For some reason
I wondered if they'd been pines
planted alongside the drive,
inland, to hide the screen.
What sort of trees were they?
I asked, and the cops thought
I had brain damage. I can't
remember even now, though
my brother would live for years
near where the old screen had stood,
still glowered. Years later,
the Yamaji guy I mentioned
saw me in the streets of Geraldton

and came up and said, You're a legend, bro –
we – we – know you didn't tell the cops
anything. I know you kept me out of it.
If you hadn't, my whole family
would have paid and would still
be paying. In your name crimes
beyond imagining would
have been committed.
JK

8.
Aah I remember the sickly taste
of green ginger wine
Sitting in the tall grass sipping
or on the hill behind the Club Hotel
Yarning about young girl things
Sipping, giggling, getting light headed
Now I ask myself
How did 13 year old girls get grog?
Where did we even get the money from?
Cant remember all I know it happened
And I seen some pretty good smashes
Back then – you know 'real fights'
Out across on medicine square
When fair fights happened
And fights were picked up at sun up
To satisfy someone's need to be satisfied
Not this mobbing bar rushing shit
With gings, bottles and stones
Or the kicking in the head business
I seen men and women take it away
Clean and fair and with handshakes
No white kids in sight or with us
I think they had their own craziness
happening elsewhere in town
They really weren't my concern
My space was quite a blackout
If you know what I mean
A few of the Yamaji girls from the reserve
Looked out for me – Never forgot that
That kind of respect lasts a lifetime
Even when they died far too young
CP-G

9.
We were in Northampton recently
and families were sheltering from the sun
under shop eaves – we crossed the road
to study the gothic of Hawes' St Mary's

in Ara Coeli and his Sacred Heart Convent
and then back across to where the old tennis
court brooded and now native vegetation
has been planted as if it was never there
in the first place. I think of the Tennis
Court Oath, the meeting of the Third
Estate locked out by Royalty, their pledge
to meet until a constitution was drawn-up
and I imagine a *Serment du jeu de paume*
at Northampton as the town's stone buildings
summon the lead ore from the ground
to contaminate so much further than
the strongest eye can see, and I think of
the t-shirt you designed now hanging
in the Geraldton Maritime Museum
where the white woman selects the little one
in the middle but any one will do! her
own revolution in taste and vanity, in ownership and 'protection' and 'doing them a favour'
rewriting of love and family, as architecture
is to poets and spiritual tourists, to miners
and collectors of Australiana. Then I am
back thirty-seven years doing the school
marathon trials up behind Geraldton Senior
High School – up into dunes beyond
Shenton Road, down to the back beach
where time rips apart certainty, sandshoes
slipping in sand, and back past what
I now know is Hawes's Hermitage,
built in 1936 for his retirement
before he retreated to Cat Island
in the Bahamas… but we knew it
as the 'place where weirdoes live', a haunted
hellish place we jogged past fast, where
bullies pushed you closer and a face
never defined peered at you from
the unnatural window in its gabled roof.
I read now its design was influenced
by the Arts and Crafts movement
of his home country, that it's what
architects call 'Inter-war Old English
style', and that it is a national treasure.
Our fear, the unspoken poisoning
of water by lead disturbed in the ground,
the stripped paddocks surrounding Northampton,
the surveying and renaming and theft
of bodies and souls are not treasures.
Families were sheltering from the sun
under shop eaves, and I swore

a non-violent oath where
the tennis courts
had played their role.
JK

10.
Hawes stone piles Mooniemia placed
Tidyness of a town – village with rolling hills
Standard creek for frogs to amuse
Hawes Mooniemia stone construct
Forcing eyes to look upon its face and body
Like a sulking teenager demanding attention
Looking out of place and knowing it
Fleeting glances from car windows
Is as close as I ever get – passing by
Unwelcoming I imagine ghosts of the pasts
Doing all the things White people do as
they conformed to the rules of their society
I also wonder if Aunty Dolly (rip) went in there
Hawes stone pile stamping Nhanda land for the settler
Where did the stones come from?
I think what our old people told us
"dont take that rock or stone from there"
"leave it dont take it away – no good"
Hawes with his religious amour
Quarried where ever he wanted so
that people will speak his name forever
To ensure fame is bestowed for the
stone constructs strategically placed
The Yamaji architects with the clay and mud huts
placed on the same land pre settler times
Is forgotten, not talked about, ghosts of the past
Explorer Grey did document for us to find
To remind people of the first architects here
The Nhanda, Naaguja, Amangu, Nhandagardi
Whilst Hawes stone piles cry out for attention
Through out the Midwest and Yamaji areas
I feel sad about that – he will always have
His societies religion, a fan club of architects
Whilst our Yamaji culture and history is still
not celebrated or appreciated for its place on the land
How can it not be does over 50,000 yrs mean nothing!!
I wish our peoples constructs could have been
National Treasures instead of on pages in
Surveyor accounts of land good to steal and claim
As a teenager in Mullewa I ran home past
Our Lady of Mount Carmel – this was my marathon
After school every day for many years
A fast sprint at night thinking of the gargoyles

With their wings and ugliness coming to get me
They played their role in keeping us out.
CP-G

Inasmuch as Charmaine's work reclaims and affirms identity and presence, enfolding stories of belonging that stretch from the dreaming to the pragmatics of engaging with an ongoing colonialism, so my poems vocalise a deep-felt anxiety of presence. My narrative is one in which stories of presence and origins draw on a distant ancestral space and reinvent them where a relationship with land has been constructed out of longing and need. Between the two of us, we make our own narratives, but narratives that converse and reach for understanding, comprehension and respect.

PART VII

Appendices

APPENDIX 1: SOME ANSWERS TO MISSING QUESTIONS

What follows are responses to an array of questions by journalists and interviewers – the answers serve as an overview and introduction to my thought and practice.

On personal and public issues of censorship and liberty

I was born in South Perth, Western Australia, I have spent a lot of my life in rural areas, especially the Western Australian wheatbelt, where a lot of my poetry is 'set'. I have also lived for many years in Cambridge, and later in Gambier and Mount Vernon, both in Ohio. I have lived in Ireland, and spent much time in various places around the globe, including extended visits to La Réunion and even lived on the Cocos and Keeling Islands in the mid-1990s. In my youth, I worked on farms, in a fertiliser factory, market gardens and laboratories. I have lived as a vegan anarchist pacifist for over thirty years, including stints in shacks without electricity or mains water, growing veganic vegetables. I am an animal rights and environmental activist, and our place in the Western Australian wheatbelt, Jam Tree Gully, is a place of tree replanting and refuge for wildlife. Along with anti-nuclear activities, and forest protection, I am an absolute believer in indigenous land rights. I am committed to a non-nationalistic, equitable, communal and small-scale model of living. From dreadlocks and the forest to professor of literature is not much of a leap as far as I am concerned.

*

Someone (who was being censored) recently asked me if I'd ever been censored as a poet. Never by my book editors or publishers, but I have been in many other ways – including by literary and other journals who have dropped overtly politicised poems 'on advice' (having actually accepted them in the first place). And I had a 'rewording' issue for legal reasons with another journal (to do with my anti-genetic-modification-of-crops position). Whether one starts with arrests for vocal objection to nuclear power and the military, or to threats of violence for objecting to the treatment of refugees in Australia, especially during the 'Tampa crisis', I have experienced censorship in many forms. But the Australia of today is even more extreme – the limitation on reporting of things considered a threat to the nation has frightening implications. The ability to tap into emails and web traffic. Apart from the inherent wrong in this – without liberty of expression we are slaves to the military-police state – the fact that words can be lifted from context (though I don't doubt this would be denied) leaves anyone who is a target vulnerable to accusations of being a threat. I won't ever forget being told by a quasi-official figure in a different context many years ago that the fact I was a pacifist was threatening to a state in itself! But the government impositions on journalism, internet and personal liberties are only part of a complex picture of suppression. There are many Australians who censor each other, oppress their fellows by demeaning their religious, social, identity and political freedoms. Maybe you have to live in rural Australia to see this, where being a 'greenie' has you treated with contempt in many overt and subtle ways. Fear of the 'other' is strong – largely come out of misinformation or the tone of discourse such as that coming from the Federal government regarding Islam, Australianness and other white nationalistic ploys. The desire to reshape the national education school curriculum is an example – more white history, less indigenous, more Christian 'origins'. This is seen as history, as fact. Too often the right in Australia claim that they are ideology-free, that ideology is what the left deploy. As someone once said, 'Ideology is what others have'. You've got to understand that in Australia the fearing and loathing of refugees, especially those who arrive on boats, is so deep that you can see young people in public wearing 'bomb the boats' t-shirts, that major supermarkets can sell xenophobic hatred t-shirts, that fly-in-fly-out mining translates via a popular t-shirt and bumper sticker acronym (FIFO) to 'fit in or fuck off'. Now this offers perverse takes on censorship – while attempting to prevent a presence and articulation of cultural difference (even if people have been driven from their home places by wars Australia itself eagerly participates in), it is free to incite racial hatred via such labels and sayings. Censorship is selective in Australia.

*

Though the situation is getting worse, free expression in Australia has always been limited. The Ern Malley/Max Harris/Angry Penguin obscenity trial of the 1940s is a case in point. What worries me, as I said, is the communal policing of opinion. The bullying at school and by one's peers. In critiquing Australia's obsession with masculinity and its manifestations, I in turn get bullied for highlighting such bullying. The current Federal government, the most conservative and right-wing government of modern Australia, is a manifestation of broader social attitudes.

*

I consider myself an activist poet. I write to bring awareness, hopefully to offer insights into the damage being done, the human impact on place. I use all 'methods' in my poetry, from the lyric to the rant, from figurative language to factual details. I don't wish to 'tell' anyone how or what to think, but rather to prompt discussion and concern, to open different ways (maybe) of seeing and hearing. Each of my books has been an engagement with ecology and the politics of presence, often mediated through visual art and issues of representation. I am interested in how language comes out of place and how place is affected by language. Articulation and the rights attached to expression (and 'seeing') are pivotal to my work. I think my poems are acts of witness.

*

The poems 'Delicate Balance' and 'Warrant: Pssst' are direct indictments of the loss of rights to an increasing militarisation of Australian society. The removal of rights in indigenous communities during the 'intervention' (done in the name of removing the paedophile threat) was a case of invasion, colonisation (again – it has never ended in Australia), control and censorship. One manifestation of many. Now, as indicated in these poems, the rhetoric of 'it's for the country's good' – to give away our freedoms so that we might be safer from the 'threat'. Out of fear, Australians let their rights go because they are told every day what kind of threat they face, how they will suffer and be hit where and when they least expect it. Whether it's banning the burqa, or various processes of enforced integration into white capitalism. We sign our own death warrants, we give away what seems intangible. We *let* the Federal forces control us – the conservatives' idea that 'smaller government means more liberty' is a ploy ... rather, it's handing more power for money-making and control to corporate Australia, to business people, while taking away freedoms of expression and behaviour. Less government but more power over the people. What seems a small piece of legislation or utterance to the media by a government representative has massive effects down the track. Too many buy into the notion that some oppression is needed to fight oppression – this government is enforced by the Murdoch press and increasingly by other right-wing media outlets (the miners in this country control many modes of public expression). We have a situation where one major mining figure is seeking to guide social policy, especially with regard to indigenous people. This is frightening. It is a triumph of the corporate police state written into the theft of minerals from country.

*

Too many Australian writers are cautious, scared or policing of their fellow writers. Too often, review-culture is praise or hate, and is driven by fear that Australian identity (that is, the nationalist version) will be undermined or especially shamed overseas. There is a common idea that the poem in particular is demeaned by political content, or, should I say, overt 'ranting'; that aesthetics and 'craft' should guide the poem, culturising it within an acceptable curatorial space. Connecting it with a tradition it often doesn't belong to, or rejects. There's a fear of the postmodern in some circles, and a strict policing of the text's authority and integrity. It must be an example of creative (personal) vision, engage with a unified self, and so on. Now, there are many exceptions to this - many poets who write against it - but most are wary of attacks from the textual conservatives (who sometimes nonetheless see themselves as socially/ politically left).

*

What disgusts me most recently is Australia's desire to be a 'middle-ranking power' with clout. To project its military into policy-making. As someone who believes in peaceful regional integrity and rights in the context of international discourse (what I have termed 'international regionalism'), I find it appalling that security and policing are linked. Basically, by contributing to military efforts elsewhere, 'we' might prevent problems developing in our region. I don't need to provide statistics to show the impoverishment and exploitation of Australian indigenous peoples – mining companies have become very adept at manipulating and claiming rights where they should have no rights. It is indigenous land, and usage needs constant negotiating. Of course 'we' are all part of the place now, and we have rights, but those rights should not occlude or deny the rights of traditional peoples. And once these issues are mediated through government structures, the people whose land has been stolen will always come out with less and less. I have recently written a novella looking at the history of Afghan cameleers, gold mining in Western Australia and the outbursts of racism in the wheatbelt when refugees were being brought into the area a few years ago; all this against a background of such extreme racism to indigenous people that it's hard to visualise. It's real, it was part of this country and it remains so. No changing of educational curriculum will alter that. And I might add that one of the 'authors' of the new curriculum proposal, Professor Barry Spurr, is undergoing scrutiny at the moment for allegedly having sent horrific racist and bigoted emails privately to colleagues.

*

It should be added that as part of the Grand Censorship that is contemporary Australia, vital issues such as human-induced climate change are written out of the equation by the Murdoch papers and their government minister-deniers. Funding is being cut, the debate hijacked. The prime minister recently spoke of coal being 'good for humanity'. This is the country of newspeak, of turning truths upside down. Pollution is something to be attained. Hunting and gun rights parties are on the rise. The liberty of damage, if you like. Their 'liberty' means the loss of liberty for so many others! And budget cuts to social services go hand in hand with what amounts to an open budget for military deployment in Iraq and Syria.

*

Well, as an anarchist vegan pacifist, I think only smaller units of self-governance are the way forward. But outside that model (which is realisable – it's an issue of consensus rather than abdicating our rights to elected representatives who cannot know most of whom they are 'representing'), I think that liberties of belief and expression need restoring and enhancing; we need land rights recognised in a meaningful and non-compromised way, the country de-militarised, a more compassionate view of the 'refugee', environmental protections rather than erosions, and a de-monetarised 'society' and sharing of wealth, religious and spiritual freedom. It's a long list! But I believe anything is possible. Change can come, even if slowly. And however it comes, it needs to be just, non-violent and not of the mentality of sacrificing anyone. One needs to listen to everyone and be inclusive, but in the end liberty, fraternity and equality need to be the values we hold highest.[1]

On the writing of poetry

Most often poems appear in my head and I see them – on a kind of internal screen. I also compose poems while walking, as I find the rhythms of walking very compatible with organising words, phrases, lines and stanzas. I usually handwrite a draft in my journal, or on a scrap of paper, and if I can (depending on where I am at a given time), write up my next draft on a manual typewriter before taking it across to an electronic document. Sometimes I compose directly on to a manual typewriter because, as with walking, I find its rhythms helpful and conducive to composing. In a sense, when I write or type I am copying lines of the poem from the 'screen within my head'. It's actually quite a visual experience for me, and when the aural aspects combine with this visual experience, I feel the poem is going where I want it to go. Poems are very spatial for me. I don't think of a poem as an object (and do not like *objets d'art*), but it is certainly tactile and malleable and part of a wider world. It is organic. I utilise what I term an *in situ* approach to creating a poem – I prefer to draft (mentally or physically) at the moment of event, and take it from there. Even when writing something from memory, I find a need to be in an environment that stimulates that memory, either through being similar or dramatically different to create sharp juxtaposition. I am interested in gaps and slippage – a poem often occurs in the disjunction between what I envisage something to be and what it very likely is.

*

I consider myself an activist poet. I write to prompt scrutiny, witness, and hopefully change. I write for the here and now, not for a vague posterity. A poem only has worth to me if it energises the reader into (re-)considering their givens, their certainties. Art must have purpose, to my mind. My prime concern is the health of the biosphere, of the environment. My concerns are human, of course, but always in the context of how humans respect (or don't) the 'natural' world. I am driven by a belief in small communities interacting with each other and lessening human impact on ecologies. A poem is part of the fabric of the natural

---

1 These paragraphs were originally written responses to a journalist's questions for a feature in the December 2014 issue of *Index on Censorship*.

world and is a form of exchange. A poem can be giving as much as emphatic and challenging. It's a means of rectification. I will use any poetic 'technique' to get to this modus operandi. I am not interested in the packaging of ideas and aesthetic impulses for arts consumerism. I do not wish to be pretty and handsome or neat or tidy. I wish to create poems of witness, and am prepared to be damned for writing things as I see them. I am culpable myself. Sometimes I write out of myself and address 'us', me included.

*

My poetic influences? Most poets would say 'many poets and it's impossible to tell'. I fit this, but I do have a number of 'historic' poetic voices that have shaped my way of seeing and hearing poetry since I was a child. Doesn't mean I 'like' them, but that they are part of my fabric. But I respect most of them greatly, and learn many things every time I return to them. That list includes Milton, Blake, Virgil, C. J. Brennan, Frost, Zukofksy, Malcolm Lowry, Lawrence, Plath, Hughes, Michael Dransfield, Randolph Stow, Wordsworth, Dante, Whitman, Rimbaud, Baudelaire, Emily Brontë, Judith Wright, Hart Crane, Peter Porter and Shelley. But there are many others. And among the living poets, the list is a long one. And I'd also include musicians such as Leadbelly and Robert Johnson in there. But in terms of literal influence, if I had to name a single poet, I would cross the contemporary J. H. Prynne with Judith Wright. They are the poets who have had the most dramatic impact on how I think about the meaning and language of a poem.

*

Poetry is a means of expressing the inexpressible, as I often say. But it's also a positive means to change and is always alive – new conditions of reading make different poems out of the same material. Main thing is that it stimulates us to question the world as we know it, accept it and live in it.

*

A poem is never finished. It's one possible point along a diverse set of paths. It's more 'chaos' than it is a straight-line journey from point A to point B. I always have problems with major rewrites of poems in selected and collected poems because poems are of their moment. I guess that suggests a kind of completion on 'publication' ... but I don't mean that, rather I mean an original version should exist and have the possibility of being read as much as later versions (extensive revisions of the 'original') as something about the here and now is being said in both (or the many) versions. Poetry is never static for me, but living. I am not interested in creating curatorial objects and never read the poems of my contemporaries in this way. I always expect their poems will change, but the original is still part of who I am and who we all are.[2]

2 See http://www.picador.com/blog/december-2014/a-poem-is-never-finished-john-kinsella-in-our-poets-on-poetry-series (accessed 22 June 2016) for original context.

Diversity, against constraint and international regionalism

There are easy answers to this and somewhat more entangled ones ... It's easy to say that poetry is part of any artistic practice and that poetry itself draws on, even relies on, many sources for its existence, and work in other genres is there-fore a logical extension of my work as a poet. Further, the inclination to find poetry in other genres/forms necessarily means that those other genres/forms are inherently poetic, and that what one discovers in them in terms of practice is essentially part of poetic practice anyway.

For example, when I write for the theatre, it tends to be verse dramas – for radio or stage, long forms and shorter forms. The pieces work as poems in voices with an emphasis on dramatic action and with awareness of performance in mind, but ultimately they are extensions of poem-making. And I'd say the same of my collaborative work – with writers I create poems or poetic texts, with musicians I tend to work on creating either poems or texts that will fuse with sound/performance, and with artists, either poems or poetic texts that dialogue with artworks, or maybe suggest artworks.

The more entangled answers involve the question of 'chicken-and-egg' poetics – does the interest in short stories, long fiction, plays, cross-genre work, music, art, essay etc. create the desire to 'make' the poem more flexible, less constrained, or does the poem absorb these forms from the start? I have always been interested in the formal aspects of expression, and I suppose music theory and, say, the rules of perspective or chiaroscuro directly influence how I might structure a poem. All prosodic approaches to making a poem are of interest to me – from rhyming four-line stanzas through to open forms that combine reportage, emphatic expression, lines based on musical notation, variations in typography – and this necessitates drawing on all fields of artistic expression.

Poetry has never been a straitjacket for me (though some critics might prefer it were so!) and when I wrote the first draft of my experimental novel *Morpheus* in 1980–82 it was interlaced with original poems and poetic fragments. The main character's poetry was inseparable from his life and his narrating of that life, even when he was discussing theatre with an older friend (and theatre/play-script becomes part of the novel as well). And every essay I've ever written since being at school has been informed by the act of writing the poem, and unsurprisingly in this light, I had many early poems entitled 'An Essay on...' and the like.

*

I call it international regionalism, and it has underpinned my practice for the last twenty years. I am an anti-nationalist who believes in using poetry and artis-tic forms to facilitate dialogue between 'places', between locales and regions, between zones of habitation and consciousness. For me, a poem is a porous entity – into the poem can feed the materials of the place in which it is written, but also the place in which it is read and articulated. It can become an embodiment of both affirmation of presence and also a space for the challenging of occupation and dispossession. It is a complex and organic 'machine' of negotiation. Poetry isn't a means; it's a necessity for opening lines of communication between 'difference' while maintaining intactness. Poems are 'devices' of respect, interaction, mediation, witness, confrontation and also healing. They are activist.

Where I write from in the wheatbelt is as much a 'centre' as anywhere else. In a sense, there are no peripheries (and no real 'centres'). One can be isolated or 'removed' in a city as much as out here, where we are certainly at a greater distance from groups of people: population is sparse and 'spread out', with small towns as points of concentration/shopping/communal activities. It strikes me as strange that Australia constructed itself as isolated – it's not isolated to those whose relationship is with the earth, the place itself, and for those with indigenous heritage, country.

*

Landscape is about human impact – I am a (one) witness to that human impact and I regard it as my responsibility to record what I see. The personal and the public are implicitly linked – one doesn't exist without the other. Eco-poetics is just a packaging of what has been around for a long time – the poem as a means of scrutinising human interaction with the natural world, and its costs. In *Redstart: An Ecological Poetics*, Forrest Gander and I scrutinise the term and the tools proffered by 'eco-poetics'. It's a means of identifying an epistemological approach to a condition of human habitation, not an end in itself. I am interested in action – in witnessing, bringing to attention, and letting the poem prompt debate and discussion. For me, the poem can be wielded in a pacifist way to stop damage being done. It can be declaimed at protests against the logging of forests, it can halt chainsaws. I am not interested in writing for entertainment or for aestheticist reasons. Eco-poetics is only useful as a rallying call, not as an idea in itself. It's just a means.

To write place, to write the 'land' as we see it, to mediate between 'here' and 'there' not as a binary opposition but in dialogue, has long been my way. I need to touch, taste, see and hear where I am. I need to hold myself accountable for my presence, and a poem is a means of recording this while adding the ambiguities and 'unsayables' of any negotiation of place and presence.

*

I don't like the digital aspect of blogging (at *Mutually Said* with Tracy Ryan) – in fact, I think the web and computers make a large contribution to the environmental damage being done. They use vast amounts of power, lead to the destruction of ecologies in the mining of materials to make hardware (and provide an 'ecology' for the software) and much more. Given this, as with flying, I keep it limited and weigh up the pros and cons (I would never fly where I could travel some other practicable way). So I do appear online every now and again (I used to a great deal, and didn't for a few years at all – i.e. directly, myself) when I consider that the cause in some ways counters the costs/impacts (which it can never truly do, to be honest).

'Mutually Said' is a creative activist space – even if it's a vegan recipe, it's saying something about making a less damaging world. We are both very concerned with protecting the rights of animals (for example), and that's a good means of communicating to a diverse and often distant group of people. The poems I post on 'Mutually Said' are about witness, commentary, intervention and sometimes lament. Rather than publish them in journals, I want them to go out into a more public realm – not an 'edited' space, but an active (and interactive to some extent) space. Things are read differently on a blog – they are read as the personal declaring itself in the public ... there's an aspect of the challenge about them, not just private thoughts made public. They come out of a need for immediate expression, a compulsion to say something in the moment. That's a form of activism, to my mind, that complements the act/s of the text itself.

*

Anthologising is a negotiation between the requirements of the generic category under which the anthology is being created (the rubrics of whatever), pushing against those constraints (for example, an 'Australian' anthology that is anti-nationalistic – yes, it's possible), and one's own personal likes and 'dislikes'. It's an act of mediation, self-awareness and, sometimes, responsibility. I suppose these qualities apply to anything we write or do, be it a poem or taking a walk.

*

My first collection actually appeared in 1983 – *The Frozen Sea* (published as John Heywood). It was a short collection, a *livre composé*. I suppose you could say, using 'poet parlance' (that most dubious would-be *sub rosa* language), that *Night Parrots* was my first 'full-length' collection – it was actually finished in 1987 but took a couple of years to appear (though I revised some poems over that interim period).

In some ways this is by-the-by, but in others, not. The early 1980s were very different from the end of the 1980s, with the constraints of distance even more prevalent in the west. There certainly was a perceived east–west divide which still exists today, but was overwhelming in the 80s. Rather than Sydney-Melbourne vs. the rest, I think it was more like Western Australia vs. the Rest. You can tell where I come from, and why, indeed, I went travelling at an early age and developed the various threads of my 'international regionalism'. In some ways, it was out of necessity. 'Isolation' (which is a limited term in the context) is a variable, not a constant. How you see yourself as much as how you are seen by others is part of it. Living in Geraldton and going to high school there, I felt I was way outside the conversations of art and culture that were relevant. Now, at 52, I think in many ways the key conversations were being had there and I hadn't yet realised it. The issues of ecology and 'settlement', of dispossession and language, are as impacting now as they were then.

But that's not the poetic landscape you are talking about, I guess, though I'd say it was the real poetic landscape – the issues of place/country/culture as what make a poetry. But in terms of camps and cliques and so on, well, ever was it

so. Whether it's the colonial poets looking back to the Old Country or the literary rivalries of the 1960s and 1970s in Sydney (which were less about formal
issues than many claim, and certainly less about American influence because
most poets writing in English were influenced by some American poet/s or (an)
other/s, and more about how one *lived* and *behaved* in Australia itself). I am sure
all there would agree it's really secondary to their own practice, and even the
'movements' or 'collective' groupings of fellow poets they were associated with
or gravitated towards. Influence works in terms of shared interest (and poetics),
but also in defining 'against', and valuing that 'against'.

Aside from personal dislikes, many of these poets had more in common than
not (ranging from ethnic origins to their more Epicurean likes and dislikes).
Don't get me wrong, I am not saying you can't chart different poetic threads,
but rather that in the end they are more similar than different. Now there
are wonderful, generative differences that actually bring things even closer
together. A more pluralistic and 'diverse' social backgrounding to the poetry
has brought about more 'internationalist' arguments about what constitutes
an 'Australian' poetry, but there's also an increasing awareness of the need for
respect for difference, challenge and sharing regional space. All of this against a
knowledge that many of us live on stolen land and there are linguistic and material consequences. And for those writing whose land has been stolen, poetry has
become a powerful means of redressing in language wrongs done, and hopefully they will achieve restitution. This was all there in the 1980s (I am editing a
volume of Jack Davis's poems at the moment and it says much about this), but it
has become more emphatic across poetry readerships and has brought positive
change.[3]

3 The original interview was conducted by Robert Wood for the small publisher Work &
Tumble and can be found (with Robert Wood's questions) at http://www.workandtumble.net/
blog/?offset=1425695053014 (accessed 5 July 2016). This website has since been deactivated.

APPENDIX 2: MANIFESTO AGAINST RAPACITY

1. This is a distillation of many other manifestos I've written over the last quarter of a century. Sounds like a long time, doesn't it? It's expressed to sound that way, but it isn't a long time really.
2. There is no need to eat or use animals. We can manage without doing so. Exploitation begins with our use and abuse of animals.
3. Animals have rights, equal to our own. Accommodating those rights is our ethical zenith.
4. The world wasn't *made* for humans.
5. Humans don't have to experience everything. The ability to exclude some experiences is part of an ethical system. It doesn't preclude knowledge or even curiosity. It doesn't mean we need to leave things to the imagination, but the imagination is one expanding universe we can explore with minimal damage to other entities. There's plenty to feed it without colonising.
6. The paradox of this manifesto: suggest by example, not by instruction. Without free will there is no choice; without choice there is no ethics.
7. 'Technology' is propaganda. It is often greed and damage. Work is purpose.
8. Barter and non-profit means-of-exchange are feasible, working in conjunction with interactive small collectives supporting common property (outside those personal markers of identity), 'governed' by real consensus where every vote carries equal weight and no democratic tyranny of the majority rules.
9. Violence contains so many contradictions, it cancels itself out. It is wrong on all levels. To take a life for a life is violence. Both are crimes.
10. Power resides in all living things. It is 'shared' equally among all living things. Power resides alone in no individual, group or people. We become empowered to annul concentrations of power. To be 'powerless' is to be empowered in the face of oppression.
11. There is no ownership, there are no ownerships. But this is not an argument for theft. Non-property is not about removal but about sharing and

negotiating. If none is entitled to more than another, 'property' ceases to have meaning.

12. Racism, sexism, gender bias, misogyny, homophobia are obviously all contradictions of the above, and wrong. However, it's not as simple as making a list. It is even contradictory (in a non-generative way) to say one shouldn't judge character on the basis of difference. One shouldn't hierarchise in any way in the first place.

13. When do we cede a right to a say in consensus? What level of crime denies rights? The inflicting of violence upon living things seems a self-evident example. And who is to deny those rights? Without violence (constraint, confinement), those in whose community the crime is committed. Violence extends to the land as well. Wanton destruction carried out in spite of an understanding that it is damaging is different from destruction of land that is not understood as such. There are degrees. Understanding those degrees is an act of education. We are mutually responsible, and all culpable.

14. There are no judges and no juries. Natural justice. We are all responsible for outcomes. No police forces, no armies, no surveillance.

15. Culture is about definition and relationship with place and others. Culture is a paradox – a liberation and tyranny. But it is to be respected, and will always be the source of negotiation and hesitation.

16. Religion is a tyranny and colonisation of the spiritual. But the choice of it is to be respected, and will always be the source of negotiation and hesitation. The principles of faith and respect, of humility and sharing, of valuing the non-material, are admirable points. But not when some seek empowerment in the maintenance and affording of those points. Any system of belief that offers rewards (in afterlives, next lives, or this life) materialises the 'spirit'. This is where capitalism in its many forms finds its succour – in the deal done with those who empower themselves to speak on behalf of the spiritual world. This is not characteristic of one particular religion, but of 'religion'. Having said this, some 'representatives' (of all religions) are more sincere than others, and are worthy of respect for thinking outside satisfying the 'self' (but if they're expecting a reward, they *are* thinking of the self!)

17. Mutual aid. Mutual respect. No greed. No rapacity.

18. Science most often serves the scientist, and those who fund it.

19. Medicine is often a smokescreen for greed and excess, for cruelty and inequality. It need not be.

20. The thirst for energy is the watershed of existence. People want to consume suns.

21. Pollution speaks for itself.

22. When poetry, music, art and other creative endeavours seek to control, they lose volition. But their expression of empathy and antipathy is a necessity. Such activism can bring change without violence. Creativity is aspiration, qualification and consideration of all that we are. All of us.

APPENDIX 3: LANDFILL: A CONVERSATION BETWEEN JOHN KINSELLA AND MCKENZIE WARK

Date: 28 September 1999
Place: British Airways aircraft; flying between London and Toulouse[1]

John: There was actually a rubbish tip there and they went in and 'reclaimed' the ground – reclamation and re-occupation are two quite different things! It's worth noting that they also reclaimed sections of the Swan River to build the Kwinana Freeway, which I find darkly amusing because it's the Perth tourism trade's number one asset (closely followed by King's Park). They filled it in to develop other aspects of Perth ... using landfill, of course. A paradoxical act in the eyes of the local balance of payments, maybe. And two things are interesting ... where the landfill comes from and how they reclaim an area in the first place.

Ken: It's characteristic of human activity particularly in the New World. You dig a hole and then you fill the hole in from somewhere else. You notice it in my part of the east coast in the freeway (that used to be the tollway) between Newcastle and Sydney. This huge gash is gouged through hills, the rubble from which of course you then use to fill in the valleys so that the roads create this whole new, this geological feature that is 100 miles long and much the same level from one end to the other. This smoothness is a great characteristic of New World topography. A smooth straight line connecting property to property.

John: So what you do is you strategically locate your places of extraction. For example, take the Dawesville Cut/Channel, an engineering 'feat' in Western Australia near the 'tourist town' of Mandurah, where they cut a channel between the ocean and the Peel Inlet so they could flush it out because it used to get algae-ridden in the summer, making the area fresh and wonderful and

---

1 I flew frequently during the 1990s and through to 2008 when I stopped flying as much as possible for ecological reasons. JK

consequently more attractive to residents, investors, commercial enterprises utilising the resources of the inlet. The cut is quite massive, and as a consequence a massive amount of landfill was extracted – stone, soil, etc. One might assume that they took that extracted material to other places for building purposes. So, if they plan 'wisely', they can turn the whole loss/gain thing into a true profit-making capitalist enterprise. But lack of planning leads to unwanted holes and too many piles…

Ken: Yeah I'm thinking this loss/gain thing even transcends the space of the continent. I remember as a teenage growing up in this house where there were these quite distinctive stones that were the walls around the edge. And they were a very, very dark blue stone. Newcastle is mostly sandstone, so this igneous rock was really distinctive. I remember having it explained to me that the blue stones were ballast stones off the ships from England. So you can imagine: ships bringing rocks all the way across the other side of the world for no particular reason, other than to load up with cargo to take back to the other side…

John: Upsets the equation that reads: natural produce and materials go out of the Antipodes, minerals and so on, to the industrial centres of the world … manufactured goods back. One of those neat and highly fallible equations economists love to use at press conferences and that primary schoolteachers fob off on the kids. Of course, in the early part of this century, the equation was quite specific to Britain. There wasn't quite the same random variable there is now. Or, indeed, even when Pig Iron Bob did his notorious deals with Japan just before the Second World War. I found it fascinating going into Australia House in London for the first time, as people pointed out the various hardwoods had been brought in from Australia to timber the place. It was built during the First World War, and even stone used there was from Australia as well. Now here's this massive war going on and they were concerned about bringing building materials from Australia so they were occupying 'valuable' cargo space with a vanity product.

Ken: That's my whole approach to modernity. I think it always starts from the periphery. When you look at the construction of modern Europe it seems to me to be made from the materials of the periphery – made from the landfill of somewhere else. The gold was from somewhere else. Even the tea that stirred the metabolisms of Europe's labouring classes, as they laboured with the materials from the colonies, was from the colonies. Modernity is shifting landfill on a global scale.

John: What's interesting is that centre/fringe construction, and that peripheral construction is an entry point into British society. When we first moved to Cambridge, Tracy and I attempted to construct all our conversations in terms of 'this is the fringe come to the centre', and we're going to occupy it and 'take over' as a defensive mechanism. As the last few years have passed, that centre/ fringe construction is entirely gone and as far as we're concerned our centre is in fact the place we've left and we now live on the fringes. And really and honestly in many ways that's quite the case. That whole peripheral construction is something that can be manipulated according to personal perspective.

Landfill is also a kind of cultural filling in. In Britain, in trying to 'promote' Australian poetry or Australian literature, the idea is that we're filling in a space that they don't occupy – but the potential for reception is there. Historically, they made the hole long ago. But rather than a law of diminishing returns they're getting something rich and complex back, that has outgrown them and that flows over into other spaces. This spreads all over the world – it grows and represents the complex amalgam of voices that constitute Australian 'identity'. The trick is, once you start occupying the space they allow you to fill, you start rhizomically spreading through their culture and affecting the centre's 'culture' as well. So landfill actually becomes something quite dangerous (in the centre's eyes) and mobile, and it doesn't just get moved from one space to another, it actually spreads above and below the surface in a rhizomatic way.

Ken: Can you fill that space in the landscape and still occupy one in Australian landscape? There's a danger in the Australian cultural space of being constructed as either/or, as one of us/not one of us.

John: Yeah. There's two things one could say to this. The first, in the removal of raw materials from Australia, particularly minerals and for example the smelting of the iron ore, be it Japan or the United States or Britain, you change the nature of the materiality of place. They might represent Australia in the same way a souvenir does, but they no longer have the complex set of references (i.e. comparisons) that make landscape. They are denuded of that meaning and given others. Though, of course, they can still symbolise aspects of the landscape they're extracted from. Of course.

Secondly, as we send satellites into space and pass a particular barrier – leave the earth's atmosphere and consequently what we define as 'ours', doesn't it affect the whole psychogeography of the earth? Doesn't it affect the way the earth's conceptually 'held together'? Even the symbolic value is lost – that is, there are no points of references relative to the individual and cultures. But maybe that's what science fiction's for! And the eternal 'our universe' type shows that saturate television. Patrick Moore's *Sky at Night* programme has been going for decades in Britain. He's tolerated because he's speaking about something entirely disconnected from most people's reality. The man is an absolute bigot and misogynist. His racism would not be tolerated under any other circumstances in so public a position. (Though one sometimes wonders about certain members of the police force/s in public relations positions.)

In the same way, the removal of Australian raw materials has always bothered me, to put it mildly … that it would cause a total unbalance … Interestingly, most indigenous peoples invariably say that the removal of any of the materials of place … of the land, causes distress and disrupts it … the Ranger uranium project is a good example … that the elders of the area said at the time that any interference with that particular space would cause an imbalance and poisoning.

Ken: Well it's the difference between a traditional and a modern relation to space. The modern idea is that space can be abstract. That anything can be in any one place or it can be in another place – it can be moved. You can construct any relation whatever between one place and another, or one resource and another. Or in other words, in the modern world, there's nothing outside the vector. There's no outside-vector. Things only exist in their productive relations to other things. Which is why I wonder about the grand plan to put traditional, indigenous communities on a self-sustaining economic basis. I sometimes wonder if outback tourism might be more of a curse than mining, in the way it makes the most intimate parts of traditional culture 'sustainable' only at the price of being a useful 'resource'.

John: You know, talking about spatiality … Have you read Jan Appleton's 'Darwinian' theory of prospect and refuge? Extending the notion, within the context of landscape theory, prospect is what you can see in many different points in a landscape – your vista, your horizon, and actually what exists in between the point of seeing and the point of absolute perspective. Refuge is the 'shelter' or hiding place within the landscape – it's the place you go internally that you can't see out of and consequently can't be seen within. Now, we're talking about processes of extracting, taking materials from a particular place and using them as landfill elsewhere.

   Well, in terms of that model, by taking something that's part of an entirety, a complete picture, a 'wholeness', and with respect to traditional uses of land versus modern uses of land, you're actually destroying any ability to gain refuge. Landscape becomes pure prospect. You're actually destroying the internal space of the land – its interiority. You're creating an increasing perspective of prospect that equates with productivity and absorbs refuge. Refuge becomes a marketable idea. The house, the swimming pool. Refuge as marketing concept. Check out 'Barnley Heights' … our prospects offer a variety of refuges…

Ken: Refuge as prospect – how perverse. Or as Paul Virilio says, there's nowhere left to hide. If the whole surface of the earth … is mappable then in a sense the line of sight becomes a line of force. The vector of perception doubles as a vector of exploitation. Although of course Virilio has never been in the Western Desert, so his thinking doesn't really fit. He's too much of the centre, he doesn't see things from the periphery, which to me is the point of view from which you see how things move. You see the prospect in Australia, at a time when in Europe there's a lot more loose talk about losing a privileged refuge, I think.

John: There's two interesting points to bring up here – one is that we're in an aircraft that is actually a composite construction of global components … and certainly global technology; the second that as we shift from English-speaking space to French-speaking space, the cross over of languages and the removal of languages and using languages of landfill in the construction of new languages should come into consideration. Should always be under consideration!

Moving 'back' to Australia: There's also – thinking about the Western Desert and the making of sand paintings that dissolve after a period of time and represent a particular, not only in a symbolic sense but also in a quite literal sense, mapping of both physical space and conceptual space. The plane – and the aircraft! – in some very abstract sense, almost hijacks mobility and fluidity and preciseness in crossing particular spatial zones.

Ken: Yes, now you've got me thinking about the way Stephen Muecke thinks about the difference between Aboriginal space and white fella space, in his book *No Road*. In white fella space you can connect any point to any other point. But what makes this possible is the ability to divide any point from any point. This is the instrument of private property: any point can be closed off and owned, and having been made distinct, can be seen as potentially connected, along any available vector, to anything else. Or in other words: roads and fences. Abstract, meaningless relations.

As I read Muecke, he's saying that Aboriginal space is one where you can't automatically connect any point to any other. It has to be negotiated, every movement is singular and meaningful. But there is no private property – nothing is blocked off absolutely, everything is a site of rival and related claims. To effect movement in this landscape, you have to negotiate, and negotiate again each and every time you want to effect a relation. It's a brilliant system for preventing abstraction from taking hold, the abstraction that allows power and wealth to accumulate.

John: I'm also thinking of ownership, say, along the Canning Stock routes and using that as a closed European construct of that particular area. But you see a gnamma hole becomes particular watering space and a signifier of voice and identity, a mythical exchange point where different stories move in and out of each other, which anthropologists then usurp and impose as registration. One of the things that came up in Daisy Bates' 'investigations' of mythologies and customs revolving around gnamma holes is that distinct sense of 'ownership' and space. That it didn't exist anywhere else. (I'm reconstructing an argument almost not made to make the point, making utility where it shouldn't be made, but…) Because in that particular region water places were the only reserve of life. Particular peoples did feel strongly about their usage and there was a kind of debt incurred when a particular place was 'invaded' or used. And this goes against the whole notion of nomadism and so on…

Ken: Well yes and no. I think Deleuze and Guattari's *Anti-Oedipus* has not been well understood on the subject of nomadism, particularly in the centre. It takes a 'peripheral' writer like Stephen Muecke or Eric Michaels to find the still-workable materials in their work and release them. What you often don't get in the celebrations of nomadism is an understanding of debt. Deleuze and Guattari talk about the savage relation of debt – only the French could use language like this in this day and age! But there is something in the way they distinguish the privatised, monetised, abstract debt of modernity from what they call a debt to the earth. A debt that is always quite particular. It could be owed to quite particular places to quite particular symbolic figures.

Besides this so-called savage debt there is despotism, where debt is accumulated and subordinated as debt to the sovereign. The sovereign could also be the dictator – Kim Jong Il or Saddam Hussein. In comparison to despotic debt, private debt really does seem more conducive to liberty. Debts are contracted singly and abstractly, always in the same coin. But while the Cold War was won by the system of private debt, which really was I think much more conducive to liberty than debt to the sovereign, the state, the party, the relation between private, quantitative, abstract debt on the one hand, and social, qualitative, particular debt on the other emerges out from under the shadows of the Cold War as a more fundamental problem.

John: Interesting subtext to this – I'm thinking of processes of reterritorialisation for example…

Ken: Which is exactly what debt does – it reterritorialises. It connects a prospect, a potential, a resource, to something that limits and directs it. Or in other words, the problem of 'reconciliation' can be seen as a problem of conflicting practices of debt. To what does who owe what? Only once you see it as qualitatively different kinds of obligation, it's no longer so easy to talk glibly about reconciling them. There's no middle road between landfill and a sacred site.

John: There is an analogy I can make with the draining of the fens in the southeast of England centuries ago. They brought drainage engineers across from Holland to put the canals and ditches in to drain the area, to make it fertile and profitable to farm. It had been primarily under water and was occupied by eelers and people who hunted wild fowl. By gradually releasing areas, 'reclaiming' them, by draining and by setting up wind pumps and dykes to keep the water under control, the Crown and Parliament and others stimulated the processes of accumulation and profit – the potential increase in material wealth became very specific and measurable.

So as each place was cleared, its value obviously increased. But more interestingly, because the 'mythological map' – that of spiritual and cultural identity – was being changed, instead of overlaying, landfilling, covering things up, they were actually exposing, unearthing. In many senses, a dual process took place. Drainage literally revealed a lot of lost items. From potlatch to missing treasures. So some people reclaimed that history – they gained wealth because they were able to claim the lost and forfeited, the offered and the taken. But they lost their identity in the same process of revelation. So this kind of revelation/enclosure thing was constantly going on. There's a huge metal detector craze in Britain – this obsessive reclaiming of the past, or getting lost wealth back. Of exacting 'rent' from invaders, particularly the Romans.

Enclosure worked in the same way. Works in the same way! Getting control over the usage of public land, of the unobtainable – say so-called Crown Land in Australia, as opposed to returning it to its rightful custodians. Obviously wealth was increased in a general sense through drainage and enclosure, but there was also a diminution of the local people's individual prospects, of their capacity to earn, to maintain control over the negotiation and reception of their mythologies as well.

I don't know how you translate that in the whole gnamma hole context, and, in fact, it may be undesirable to do so. But there's certain obvious theoretical correlations that can be made.

Ken: Well, maybe one has to make the attempt, even if only as conversation, to connect these things. In the New World there's a kind of repressed similarity in some way to things that have always existed in English space and the Old World in general. There always were these pockets of traditional property right, there's always been something like 'native title' in England. There has never been an absolute form of private property – it's always negotiable at some point … with things like right of way and so on. So we suddenly rediscovered that – that, ah hello!, here are all these previous complex, quite subtle, unreadable and in a sense non-negotiable rights. How do you negotiate between them?

John: We're talking about the genocide of people with their landscapes. The two become indistinguishable. The destruction of one leads to the destruction of the other. A 'terrible' symbiosis. Thinking of the fens, they actually removed the landscape, they altered it, they changed it. Theoretically if all the pumps stop, and the dykes overflow and so on, and no-one repairs it, Cambridgeshire might return to something like its previous form. But the people who were part of it have long gone. But that's not completely true, fenlanders always claim difference and speak against outsiders. The threat of flooding, of water, makes them different. Those on the Norfolk Broads in particular, but also in Cambridgeshire. They always remember the great floods!

I find this interesting, Lionel Fogarty, the great Murri poet, actually gets inside the English language and dismantles it from the inside out. Mudrooroo has called this his guerrilla tactics. Instead of using a kind of Pidgin English or a construction of a hybridity, he is actually taking words and dismantling them through using his Murri tongue as the colonising language, and not the colonised language. He reverses the hybridising relationship. He's re-mapping a landscape that has been entirely removed from his people. He's reclaiming it through speech, through words. The 'control' of language is power. He's rejecting the coloniser's linguistic claim on that space… He's saying that you've come into our space and we're fighting you with your own language. So he's entirely reversed that victim/coloniser binary. He's reclaiming space.

Ken: In a less 'literary' way, that's the story of Aboriginal country music and of 'settlement rock'. A sort of oral guerrilla culture inside the language and harmonic language. We were discussing earlier whether modernity begins on the periphery or the centre. Or whether these terms make any sense once you explore the play between them. Likewise, I think there's a sense in which colonialism begins at the centre and not the periphery. So 1745, before Australia's even 'discovered', the colonisation of Scotland gets going full bore. There's a sense of which, seen from without, you tend to think about the Old World as the centre from which modernity radiated. But without the resources set free in the periphery, the whole process would never have got off the ground. The whole process began at home already, already in Cambridge, already in Scotland, this process of internal colonisation had already been going on.

What an act of colonisation does is deterritorialise and reterritorialise. Land and people are broken free from their debts and set loose, only to be subordinated to a qualitatively new kind of grid. Only in the process, some resources, particularly people, are set loose to colonise again. The Scots were great colonisers in the New World, having been set loose by the dispossession of their traditional relation to land. My ancestors and probably a lot of yours were themselves 'landfill'.

John: One thing that shocked me when I first moved to Britain was the reference to Australia as the New World, uncritically. New to whom? Using an old term for a new process without question. Any comment on that?

Ken: I still like the expression in the sense that it has been used in the Americas. The New World has a sense of hope, something that has yet to be constructed. I think it's hard to have that optimism in the face of the continuing existence of the *Ancien Regime* in Europe, but it's something that Australia, in a more low-key way, does share with America. That sense of constructing the world – and still trying to get it right. An open modernity rather than a closed – and enclosing – one, perhaps.

John: We're flying in over the fields and roads of a Euro heartland right now. One thing that's interesting about this particular conversation, because we're in a plane, and because we're about to land, it induces stress. I'm certainly finding that my thought patterns aren't as linear, I'm reacting under a kind of stress to answer a question I've been asking myself about what constitutes the occupation of place and what do you take away from place when you physically leave it. If we weren't about to land would I ask such a question? What your obligations are as a human as a citizen in movement?

You've come from Sydney to London and then to Cambridge and back to Toulouse then you'll go back to London and back to Sydney and you'll do it all over again. And what are your obligations in the removal of cultural discourse or whatever cultural participation into that space and then to the next space. Acts of appropriation. The tourist thing. The destruction of regional boundaries. In the same way we criticise those who make the holes in order to fill other ones they no longer want, what are your responsibilities?

Ken: Interesting question. Though why is it the movers rather than the unmoved who are supposed to have a responsibility? What are the responsibilities of people who don't move. There's a sense in which you're supposed to be exempt. I'm curious as to why. It is always so-called 'globalisation' that is called upon to justify itself. It's amazing how old leftists and the far right share this totally uncritical sense of the rightness of the national boundary nowadays. And the left can't even see how defending protectionism might be just as racist as restricting immigration. At least the right aren't hypocrites! They know they are against foreigners prospering, whether by coming to 'our' space or selling their goods into 'our' space.

So, perhaps perversely, I wonder why staying put and valuing staying put should be exempt from ethical questioning. 'Cosmopolitanism' was a term of abuse used by the Nazis, and sometimes by Stalinists, too. Sometimes 'cosmopolitan' was a code-word for Jew, but sometimes I wonder if Jew might not have been, and still be, a code-word for cosmopolitan. It's a refusal to accept identities constructed on the run, on the move, along the vector, rather than within the territory.

John: 'Exemption'? My grandmother on my father's side never, ever, ever left the south of Western Australia. Her husband was a state forester of Western Australia, and there is actually an area called Kinsella in the south-west named after him. The naming was a reward for his services in the forests to the state. Such namings are all about usurping and totally obliterating indigenous occupation and ownership. And for him it would have been an honour. I don't know if he thought about its implications.

My paternal grandmother basically went through a process of denial. She felt there was no point, say, returning to visit her British 'roots' as it would be destroying identity a lot of people had gone to a lot of trouble to create. She was a 'Western Australian', and that was that. Time was not the issue, presence in place was. Immediate family was the signifier, the marker of presence and place. So she felt it was morally bankrupt to travel, to leave one's space, and she criticised my mother when she took my brother with her to Bali when he was 13. She was indignant, absolutely outraged. I stayed at home so I could sell more stamps, actually. She respected my profit-making enterprises, I think. Not sure though. We didn't really discuss it. But it kept me 'home', so I guess it did. Home was actually Geraldton then – five hundred kilometres north of Perth – but still in WA! She was indignant because she actually felt that by travelling, especially at such a young age, he would be corrupted and turn against his home, that he would actually weaken the ties of place.

APPENDIX 4: NOTES ON GLOBALISATION AND NEO-LUDDISM

International regionalism is a rejection of globalisation. Words have only ever been as global as the language that carries them. Translated, they become new texts, but their meaning and intention often shines through. Any form of communication with others relies on effective translation, even within the same language group. Google Translate is the 'globalised' to the human translator's 'international' in this (false) binary. The point is that language and especially literature, especially the poem, can carry the complexity of the local, the iterations of the idiolect, across language barriers into a shared experience. The poem that is maybe just signs and symbols, sounds when read aloud, can still impart meaning through tone, and take that meaning close to the intention of the words themselves. This is the key to international regionalism – the retention of idiolect in an international context, whereas globalisation will pursue the path of least resistance to overcome and adapt what it encounters to its own (market/ profit) needs. Sadly, this can also be a truism when applying international 'necessities' through the machine of globalisation – such as with health and aid. A pandemic then becomes a vehicle of infiltration and a broadening of markets for the country-companies that contribute and assist.

Globalisation is the capitalist inflection of imperialism, and can be as much the engine of a one-party state as of a so-called liberal democracy. Globalisation is foreign policy mediated through large and small corporations. It is the surface privatisation of exchange that is a front for the militarisation of worldwide means of exchange.

As an anarchist I believe in barter and local 'produce' wherever possible.

The internet is the vanguard, espionage, factory, middle person, shopfront, public and private face/s of globalisation. Those who 'oppose' it can still easily become its vectors and its tools by mere participation in the worldwide web. Only hackers can contest this role, and they so often operate out of self-gain – either financial or malicious. It pleasures them, even if perversely.

The market is a place of inequality. To swap things of comparative 'worth', taking into account the 'value' one places on an item in one's situation of need or excess, is a relatively positive use of the marketplace, but so often someone will eye off an exchange that places them in a superior position and allows them to grow their exchange-base. This inequality is intrinsic to the idea of the market; but kept within its locale and self-regulated by consensus, its impact remains limited. Expand it and the degrees of separation mean less protection for the exploited and more protection for the exploiter. Globalisation relies on this dynamic – expansion into less privileged markets means goods gain a fetish-worth they would not hold elsewhere. Further, the labour that has gone into creating these goods is often extracted at next-to-nothing from the very people whom the global corporations are exploiting to manufacture their goods. Head office in one of the major cities of the world is a long way from the sweatshops or contaminated and contaminating factories that produce the goods. Heidegger's spinner[1] might not dwell in the building in which she labours, but she might very well live in its basement or near her machine, a slave to labour and hand-to-mouth survival, for whom the qualities of *living* are divorced from habitation. A dwelling without life-quality. Globalisation is built on exploitation and the destruction of the local.

In 2009 I wrote an article for the Australian Broadcasting Commission website declaring my non-violent neo-Luddism and plans to withdraw as much as possible from the digital world. I managed this for some years before developing a strained relationship with the global modern. I oppose it, I reject it and I am at least partially entrapped by it. *Mea culpa* is not enough. The Trojan Horse argument is not enough. These decisions we make on a micro level every day. To use an imported product because it allows a comparatively 'non-cruel' and 'non-exploitative' (say, towards animals) eating outcome is participation. But if the company creating the product is small, traceable, committed to ethical outcomes, does it compensate for the ecological impact of importation? Partly – one encourages and searches out the local. It's about reductions of

---

1 An odd 'connection' here with an article published in the *Guardian* newspaper in 2002 that attempted to demystify 'globalisation' and ended up saying nothing in particular. We read: 'Low-paid sweatshop workers, GM seed pressed on developing world farmers, selling off state-owned industry to qualify for IMF and World Bank loans and the increasing dominance of US and European corporate culture across the globe have come to symbolise globalisation for some of its critics. The anti-globalisation movement is famously broad, encompassing environmentalists, anarchists, unionists, the hard left, some of the soft left, those campaigning for fair development in poorer countries and others who want to tear the whole thing down, in the same way that the original Luddites attacked mechanised spinning machines. Not everyone agrees that globalisation is necessarily evil, or that globalised corporations are running the lives of individuals or are more powerful than nations. Some say that the spread of globalisation, free markets and free trade into the developing world is the best way to beat poverty – the only problem is that free markets and free trade do not yet truly exist' (Simon Jeffery, 'What is Globalisation?', *The Guardian*, 31 October 2002, http://www.theguardian. com/world/2002/oct/31/globalisation.simonjeffery [accessed 22 June 2016]). And regarding Heidegger's comment, 'the working woman is at home in the spinning mill, but does not have her dwelling place there', see Martin Heidegger, *Basic Writings*, ed. David Farrell Krell (London, Routledge, Kegan and Paul, rev. edn, 1996), p. 347.

impact and blunting the impact of the global greed movement. Here's the bulk of that article:

Neo-Luddism

Technology isn't the deliverance of humanity; it is its damnation. 'Progress', used as a noun, becomes the linchpin of technological propaganda. Computers aren't a tool of liberation, but of destruction – look to the power they are chewing, the materials that go into making them, the pollution engendered in their manufacture, especially of batteries for laptops, despite the propaganda of 'greener' models, the radiation they emit and the health risks associated with associated wireless technology being constantly debated.

As an anarchist, I believe firmly that 'small' is necessary (or, as Andrew Fleming on his anarchist blog notes, 'local', or what I might call 'regional'), that rights are best protected on a community level and without centralised hierarchies as delivered by the state; that rights come out of consensus (all members of a community having an equal say and all members' agreement being necessary to making 'change' within the community – we might understand this within the usual dynamic as a shift in 'policy', but it is fundamentally different).

Computers, especially in their networked web manifestations, allow *modes* of bypassing of normal state media constraints (for example, through sites such as those managed by the various IndyMedias around the world), but they also become the tools of the state – the multinationals and governments themselves thrive on the manufacture of hardware, and the web allows for a dissemination of their own propagandas, often disguised by the sense of freedom engendered through surfing the net. Further, as the state and its corporate and criminal affiliates monitor traffic – 'read' emails, track movements, 'cookie' people's lives – participants become inured to what they know is happening. A belief that the 'freedom' they gain outweighs the freedom they concede. I find this horrifying in its implications for liberty.

Propaganda is embedded (to use *their* military metaphor) in so many ways. Technological advancement is sold as both an affirmation of the state (or statelike corporate bodies) and an individual's right to a better, more productive life. Technology is apparently better health and longer life, more 'leisure', and creates more 'leisure time', safer living conditions … all in all, it is for our own good. We are told. We assume ourselves.

As an anarchist, I incline towards the more positive 'mutual aid' rather than the 'survival of the fittest' excuse for getting ahead. But there is something, to my mind, even more insidious, and that is the notion of 'progress': that in some way the next model will always be better than the one preceding.

Humans are seen as getting faster and better, and our early ancestors are seen as steps on the way to this desirable 'advancement'. Why? It's relative, according to these rules. What we are now is no better than what we were before. Technology is a tool of profit-making, of control and of monitoring how we behave. It has never been about liberty.

The Luddites were violent in their class challenge to the new weaving technologies, and as a pacifist I don't condone their actions. But I defend the reasoning behind their objection to the new technologies: livelihoods were threatened, the abilities to direct one's life within even that marginalised context of choice further reduced.

Ultimately however, and this was not their concern, my personal identification with this resistance is on the level of ecology. The more sophisticated a technology, the more damage it usually inflicts on the environment – the more 'resources' (a word that denotes human ownership of a world that is owned by no one and no things, to my mind) it uses.

The only way I can justify my usage of a computer to write this and contribute to the consumption of power and materials (and all else I write and send out via the technology) is to say that come October, I will, outside my university work (and I will lobby that for change), go entirely offline and off computers and off-grid.[2] I've always written by hand or on a manual typewriter anyway (a 'lesser' technology and hopefully less damaging – they certainly last longer, the typewriters I use are decades old), so it won't be hard at all.

---

2 This remains an eternal aim and desire for me.

APPENDIX 5: GRAPHOLOGY MUTATIONS 11: RECLAIMING 'DWELL'

'Poetry is the original admission of dwelling.'
   Martin Heidegger[1]

Poetical Man dwells fulsome on cloyed earth
making four quarters knot together, glide
in sea to peruse crevices, dig deep
to upend leisure centres, bring
home the building, inhabit
submarine desires.
And so from the roof
under a ceiling of sky,
and so the grit you might
fall into, breaking your meritorious
neck, the baubles of worship
littered, a signing to heaven:
words without roots.

     *

Cultivating the vista
a sudden rush uninspires
the poet who won't
build anything and thus
no longer dwells in or inhabits
her poem. It's as if she never
wrote in the house of a journal
she carries everywhere with her –
going from one place to another,
her essence a blank if filled page.

     *

1 Martin Heidegger, *Poetry, Language, Thought*, trans. Albert Hofstader (New York, Harper and Row, 1971), p. 227.

My father knows Kenworth trucks
inside out and was going to live in one
to be fleet of foot and the new sleepers
can house a six-foot MAN and maybe
even a six-foot WOMAN. The Dead
Kennedys' 'Winnebago Warrior'
is a creature to be wary of,
as is the snail with its shell
as is literature housing
the Western Poems
which we know incorporate
words forward and back of Australia.

*

Heidegger says, 'We do not dwell because we have built, but we build and have
built because we dwell, that is, because we are *dwellers*.'[2]

In the collective lean-to
windbreak anorak of openness
poems rush in on an Antarctic wind.
A speechless peace is a peace nonetheless.
It spares us, this peace. But who is to
be spared, peacefully? A route
to OUR language ruling us? Listen:

'Poetically, man dwells':

'Cultivating and caring (*colere*, *coltura*) are a kind of building. But man not only
cultivates what produces growth out of itself; he also builds in the sense of *aedi-
ficare*, by erecting things that cannot come into being and subsist by growing.
Things that are built in this sense include not only buildings but all work made
by man's hands and through his arrangements.'[3]

*

Where the bridge
touched the lips
we set up our senses.

Locale is not where we kissed.
The *quality* of dwell on the lips. Habitat.

In the space of the poem
we build massive tangents to affection.

2 Martin Heidegger, *Basic Writings*, ed. David Farrell Krell (London, Routledge and Kegan
Paul, rev. edn, 1996), p. 350.
3 Martin Heidegger, *Philosophical and Political Writings*, ed. Manfred Stassen (New York,
Continuum, 2003), p. 268.

The bridge-building destroyed the signs
of earlier building far more
integrated into surroundings.

Surround sound is the resonant poem,
not a home theatre necessity.

Sound permeates the boundary
unfolding of tolerance
as one locale bleeds into another

and there are noise abatement orders
motivated by building waves
of objection.

                    Class action
might be the same. An utterance
building building ... made into law,
making new structures.

                    But here
they campaigned for a new bridge across
the Avon River because the old one
was unsafe and eventually mining royalties
were applied so we might all *benefit*.

Spatium and *extensio*.

There you go.

              *

The mortality rate amidst our things
is devastating. Space in the grave
is. Tree roots reach in and feed off us.

                    *

I made a poem written in rooms of a house
and displayed in front of invigilators: they said,
This will make a good project. It will make him
a 'more poetic poet', and maybe even more
of a man. In need of being more of a MAN,
I made words in different rooms and brought
them together where granites emit radon,
but then, prepositional statements got in the way
and I ground jam-tree seeds into a flour.
Extracting them from pods was the only
pleasure. I worked alone. But not in a vacuum.
I was, atypically, abundant.

*

'Authentic building occurs so far as there are poets, such poets as take the measure for architecture, the structure of dwelling.'[4]

Measuring my absence in the line
I take from Schull to Jam Tree Gully –
a wavy resonant line – incapable
of death, but 'counting the beat'.

I pick up barnacles as I journey.
They are scoured from my hull
with viscous chemicals. This
is nature poetry, but not
the poetic nature. In the stones
is the God I acknowledge
but don't know and can't worship.

It's a residue of my time
in the Hölderlin House, years ago,
by the river and in his room
and taking down the sky's manifest
and wondering what silent prejudices
filled the dovecote, each room
of the conference. Its imprint remains,
and the blue was a different blue.

Not a trace of azure. And so many
faces reflected back. Strangely,
I can't remember where I slept,
the room I slept in. Rooms
were so important to Tennyson.
Writerly security. Love. And housing
what's important to us: protecting
it from the elements and certain
divinities. Prying eyes.

                    I was up
on the roof, repairing troughs
and peaks of corrugated iron.
Technically, *the pans* are where
water runs. There's a way to walk,
where to put the feet. On a roof.

I thought about roofs everywhere.
Roofs you can't step on in extreme heat.
Or climb on in snow – those steep,

4 Heidegger, *Philosophical and Political Writings*, p. 276.

mountainous peaks. Avalanches.
That's the measure of me, a poet.

*

Appropriating, yet again, *the authentic*;
I am the body and mind of Hölderlin,
I am near and far from him. We are distance.

*

In gutters I discover clusters
of leaves though I cut away
the overhanging branches
at the start of summer.
Leaves have accrued
from elsewhere as the cut-back
tree is dormant. In gutters
which have sides and two exit-
points for any content (well, not leaves,
but certainly rain which gathers
as flow – a wave of water),
which are what we call downpipes.

When downpipes clog with leaves,
the thingness of things, water
can't find the way we want it to find
and it breaks the meniscus of the gutter,
spills over, roughly flows – cascades –
and I have to think ahead.

Leaves
cannot dwell in gutters though they catch
earth – dust and sand blown up on dry days –
and make a semi-fertile bed for growth.
You find ants up there. And other insects.

Seeing is not to witness your annihilation,
though in the distance – say twenty ks away –
neither near nor far but seeming near
as high explosive shells go off
at the Bindoon Army Range;
you see the problem?
You see?

*

Gutters gushed.
Gushing was damaging.
It was no offering
I could relate to: though
the suddenness altered topography
around *our* dwelling. I recalled

other instances: during Storm Darwin
on the Mizen Peninsula. A gushing
then a flooding then a need
for preventative action.
So *far far* away.

       *

Getting ready to go outside this house
to work on the block, to carry and pour,
to shift and nurture, I think that only
'Nearness preserves farness'.

I can tell you, there are fewer birds
showing themselves in recent days,
though I can hear weebills close by.
Their chatter is similar to but different
from birds heard far from here.

In other locales. People around here
shoot birds. Maybe not weebills.
But other birds. Especially corellas.

And all birds are beautiful.
I object to these shootings,
and not only because
it leaves my poems
imageless.

     *

'To die means to be capable of death as death. Only man dies. The animal per-
ishes. It has death neither ahead of itself nor behind it.'

'… the world's worlding…'[5]

We sometimes find birds
arrive at a place to die.
That same place will be
valid for some time. Old
birds whose territory
remains the same from
the moment they break
away from home. They
die in a chosen place,
just outside their space,
seeing the corpses of
other birds who have
chosen the same way.
Death echoes out,

---

5 Martin Heidegger, 'The Thing', in *Poetry, Language, Thought*, pp. 176, 177.

touching their egg-lives
and their earth-life,
just feathers beak & claw
on the surface. Ants.
When I die, I will perish.

*

My eyes have been
further damaged by
the *mirror-play* of
the silver roof. A
tearing away of
what's left. What
I have seen I won't
see the same way
again. But I can still
determine the objects
from the trees. I
don't hunger
for things,
nor the glare.

BIBLIOGRAPHY

Acker, Kathy, *Kathy Goes to Haiti* (London, Flamingo, 1990)

Acker, Kathy, *Blood and Guts in High School* (New York, Grove Press, 1994)

Acker, Kathy, *Pussy, King of the Pirates* (New York, Grove Press, 1996)

Acker, Kathy, *In Memoriam to Identity* (New York, Grove Press, 1998)

Acker, Kathy, and McKenzie Wark, *I'm Very Into You: Correspondence 1995–1996* (Los Angeles, Semiotext(e), 2015)

'Advertising', *The Inquirer and Commercial News* (Perth, WA), 30 April 1856, p. 2, http://nla.gov.au/nla.news-article66005007 (accessed 27 March 2015)

Ahmed, Sara, *Strange Encounters: Embodied Others in Post-Coloniality* (Abingdon, Routledge, 2000)

Aitken, Adam, Kim Cheng Boey and Michelle Cahill (eds), *Contemporary Asian Australian Poets* (Sydney, Puncher and Wattmann, 2013)

Alizadeh, Ali, and John Kinsella (eds), *Six Vowels and Twenty-three Consonants: An Anthology of Persian Poetry from Rudaki to Langroodi* (Todmorden, Arc Publications, 2012)

Anderson, Sherwood, *Winesburg, Ohio* (Toronto, Dover, 1995)

Apollinaire, Guillaume, *Alcools*, bilingual edition, trans. Anne Hyde Greet (Berkeley and Los Angeles, University of California Press, 1965)

Apter, Emily, 'Radical Pastoral – *Peripheral Light: Selected and New Poems* of John Kinsella', *Boston Review*, April/May 2004, http://bostonreview.net/poetry/emily-apter-radical-pastoral (accessed 22 June 2016)

Aristotle, *Physics*, trans. R. P. Hardie and R. K. Gaye, http://classics.mit.edu/Aristotle/physics.html (accessed 22 June 2016)

Armand, Louis, and John Kinsella, *Synopticon* (Prague, Litteraria Pragensia, 2012)

Arnold, Matthew, *Poetical Works* (London, Oxford University Press, 1969)

Ashliman, D. L., *Folk and Fairy Tales: A Handbook* (Westport, CT, Greenwood, 2004)

Astill, James, 'Congo rebels are eating pygmies, UN says', http://www.theguardian.com/world/2003/jan/09/congo.jamesastill (accessed 4 June 2015)

Atkins, Marc, and Rod Mengham, *STILL Moving* (Guildford, Veer Books, 2014)

Augé, Marc, *Non-Places: An Introduction to Supermodernity*, trans. John Howe (London and New York, Verso, 2008)

Bachelard, Gaston, *The Poetics of Space*, trans. Maria Jolas (Boston, Beacon Press, 1964)

Bachelard, Gaston, *The Psychoanalysis of Fire*, trans. Alan C. M. Ross (Boston, Beacon Press, 1968)

Bardon, Jonathan, *A History of Ireland in 250 Episodes* (Dublin, Gill and Macmillan, 2009)

Barthes, Roland, *The Pleasure of the Text*, trans. Richard Miller (New York, Hill and Wang, 1975)

Batchelor, John, *Tennyson: To Strike, To Seek, To Find* (New York, Pegasus Books, 2013)

Baxter, James K., *Selected Poems*, ed. J. E. Weir (Oxford, Oxford University Press, 1982)

Beddoes, Thomas Lovell, *Death's Jest Book* (1829), ed. Michael Bradshaw (Manchester, Carcanet, 2006)

Beeliar Boodjar: An Introduction to Aboriginal history of the City of Cockburn based on existing literature (Spearwood, City of Cockburn, 2011)

Bennett, Bruce, *The Australian Compass* (South Fremantle, Fremantle Arts Centre Press, 1991)

Bennett, Bruce, and Jennifer Strauss (eds), *The Oxford Literary History of Australia* (Melbourne, Oxford University Press, 1998)

Biarujia, Javant, 'X Marks the Parataxis: Louis Armand, John Kinsella and Jessica L. Wilkinson', *Cordite Poetry Review*, 1 May 2014, http://cordite.org.au/essays/x-marks-the-parataxis/ (accessed 22 June 2016)

Bloom, Harold, 'Introduction', in John Kinsella, *Peripheral Light: Selected and New Poems* (New York, W. W. Norton, 2003; North Fremantle, Fremantle Arts Centre Press, 2004)

Bourdieu, Pierre, *Distinction*, trans. Richard Nice (London and New York, Routledge, 2010)

Braidotti, Rosi, *Nomadic Subjects: Embodiment and Sexual Difference in Contemporary Feminist Theory* (New York, Columbia University Press, 1994)

Brooks, David, and Noel Rowe (eds), *Southerly: The Poetics of Space* 65.3 (2005) (The Journal of the English Association, Sydney)

Brooks, David, Noel Rowe and Jennifer Rutherford (eds), *Southerly: Shared Space Brokered Time* 66.2 (2006) (The Journal of the English Association, Sydney)

Burke, Edmund, *A Philosophical Enquiry into the Origin of Our Ideas of the Sublime and Beautiful* (Oxford, Oxford University Press, 1998)

Carey, Peter, *True History of the Kelly Gang* (London, Faber and Faber, 2000)

Celan, Paul, *Selected Poems and Prose of Paul Celan*, trans. John Felstiner (New York, W.W. Norton, 2001)

Chamley, Santorri, 'On the Shores of Malawi's Lake of Stars, Activists Raise Uranium Fears', http://www.theguardian.com/global-development/2015/jun/03/lake-malawi-activists-uranium-fears-paladin (accessed 4 June 2015)

Cheever, John, *The Journals of John Cheever* (London, Vintage, 2010)

Chesson, Keith, *Jack Davis: A Life Story* (Melbourne, Dent, 1988)

Clark, Manning, *Henry Lawson: The Man and the Legend* (Carlton, Melbourne University Press, 1995)

Clay, Henry, *Two and Two: A Story of the Australian Forest by H. E. C., with Minor Poems of Colonial Interest* (Perth, 1873)

Collard, Len, Sandra Harben and Rosemary Van Den Berg, *Nidja Beeliar Boodjar Noonookurt Nyininy: A Nyungar Interpretive History of the Use of Boodjar (Country) in the Vicinity of Murdoch University* (Report for Murdoch University, 2004)

Cook, Mercer, 'Auguste Lacaussade', *Phylon* 2.3 (1941), pp. 260–74.

Danchev, Alex, *Cézanne: A Life* (London, Profile, 2012)

Darlington, Robert, and John Hospodaryk, *History Alive 7 for the Australian Curriculum* (Milton, Qld, John Wiley, 2012)

Davis, Jack, *The First-born and Other Poems* (Sydney, Angus and Robertson, 1970)

Davis, Jack, *Jagardoo: Poems from Aboriginal Australia* (Sydney, Methuen, 1978)

Davis, Jack, *John Pat and Other Poems* (Melbourne, Dent, 1988)

Davis, Jack, *A Boy's Life* (Broome, 1991)

Davis, Jack, *Black Life: Poems* (Brisbane, University of Queensland Press, 1992)

Davis, Jack, *The Dreamers* (Sydney, Currency Press, 1996)

Davis, Jack, *The Poems of Jack Davis: A Retrospective*, ed. John Kinsella (Broome, forthcoming)

Debord, Guy, *The Society of the Spectacle*, trans. Donald Nicholson-Smith (New York, Zone Books, 1994)

de Certeau, Michel, *The Practice of Everyday Life*, trans. Steven F. Rendall (Berkeley, University of California Press, 1988)

'Derreennatra Bog NHA', *National Park & Wildlife Services*, http://www.npws.ie/protected-sites/nha/002105 (accessed 22 June 2016)

Deleuze, Gilles, and Félix Guattari, *A Thousand Plateaus: Capitalism and Schizophrenia* (Minneapolis, University of Minnesota Press, 1987)

Dempsey, Eric, and Michael O'Cleary, *The Complete Guide to Ireland's Birds* (Dublin, Gill & Macmillan, 2nd rev. edn, 2002)

Derrida, Jacques, 'Everything is a text; this is a text', https://prelectur.stanford.edu/lecturers/derrida/

Dissanayaake, Wimal, and Rob Wilson, *Global/Local: Cultural Production and Transnational Imaginary* (Durham, NC, Duke University Press, 1996)

Donovan, Daniel, *Sketches in Carbery, County Cork: Its Antiquities, History, Legends, and Topography*, https://archive.org/stream/sketchesincarber00dono/sketchesincarber00dono_djvu.txt (accessed 22 June 2016)

Dransfield, Michael, *Michael Dransfield: A Retrospective*, selected by John Kinsella (St Lucia, University of Queensland Press, 2002)

Drewe, Robert, and John Kinsella, *Sand* (poetry, fiction, and memoir) (North Fremantle, Fremantle Press, 2010)

Edmonds, J. M. (trans.), *The Greek Bucolic Poets*, Loeb Classical Library (Cambridge, MA, Harvard University Press, 1996)

Eliot, Ian, *Moondyne Joe: The Man and The Myth* (Nedlands, University of Western Australia Press, 1978)

Elliot, Brian, *The Jindyworobaks* (St Lucia, University of Queensland Press, 1979)

Enright, Damien, *Walks of Ballydehob and Schull* (Balbriggan, Merlin Press, 2004)

'Everyone's Gone Nuts About Schull', 20 August 1998, http://www.independent.ie/irish-news/everyones-gone-nuts-about-schull-26177904.html (accessed 22 June 2016)

Fegan, Melissa, *Literature and the Irish Famine, 1845–1919* (Oxford, Oxford University Press, 2002)

Ferriter, Diarmaid, *The Transformation of Ireland 1900–2000* (London, Profile Books, 2005)

Fitch, Andy, 'Forrest Gander and John Kinsella with Andy Fitch, an interview', *The Conversant*, October 2012, http://theconversant.org/?p=1469 (accessed 22 June 2016)

Fitter, Chris, *Poetry, Space, Landscape: Toward a New Theory* (Cambridge, Cambridge University Press, 1995)

Foster, R. F., *The Oxford History of Ireland* (Oxford, Oxford University Press, 2001)

Foucault, Michel, *The History of Sexuality, Vol 1*, trans. Robert Hurley (London, Penguin, 2008)

Frost, Robert, *Collected Poems, Prose, and Plays*, ed. Richard Poirier (New York, Library of America, 1995)

Gander, Forrest, and John Kinsella, *Redstart* (Iowa City, Iowa University Press, 2012)

Gantz, Jeffrey, *Early Irish Myths and Sagas* (London, Penguin, 2000)

Genette, Gérard, *Narrative Discourse: An Essay in Method*, trans. Jane E. Lewin (Ithaca, NY, Cornell University Press, 1983)

Gilbert, Kevin (ed.), *Inside Black Australia: An Anthology of Aboriginal Poetry* (Ringwood, Penguin, 1988)

Gorton, Lisa, *The Life of Houses* (Sydney, Giramondo, 2015)

Green, Neville, *Broken Spears: Aboriginals and Europeans in the Southwest of Australia* (Perth, Focus Education Services, 1984)

Gregory, Derek, and John Urry (eds), *Social Relations and Spatial Structures* (Basingstoke, Macmillan, 1985)

Hall, Mr and Mrs. S. C., *Ireland: Its Scenery, Character & c.* (London, How and Parsons, 1842)

Hallam, Arthur, 'On Some of the Characteristics of Modern Poetry, and On the Lyrical Poems of Alfred Tennyson', *Englishman's Magazine*, August 1831

Hardacre, Paul, *liber xix: differentia liber* (Sydney, Puncher and Wattman, 2011)

Harvey, David, *The Condition of Postmodernity* (Malden, MA, and Oxford, Blackwell, 1990)

Hay, John, 'Literature and Society', in C. T. Stannage (ed.), *A New History of Western Australia* (Perth, University of Western Australia Press, 1981)

Heaney, Seamus, *Sweeney Astray* (London, Faber & Faber, 1984)

Heidegger, Martin, *Poetry, Language, Thought*, trans. Albert Hofstader (New York, Harper and Row, 1971)

Heidegger, Martin, *Basic Writings*, ed. David Farrell Krell (London, Routledge, Kegan and Paul, rev. edn, 1996)

Heidegger, Martin, *Philosophical and Political Writings*, ed. Manfred Stassen (New York, Continuum, 2003)

Henry, Brian, 'Poetry in Review: *Peripheral Light: Selected and New Poems* by John Kinsella', *The Yale Review* 93.1 (2005)

Hewett, Dorothy, *Collected Poems* (South Fremantle, Fremantle Arts Centre Press, 1995)

Hewett, Dorothy, and John Kinsella, *Wheatlands* (Fremantle, Fremantle Arts Centre Press, 2000)

Hodge, Robert Ian Vere, and Vijay Mishra, *Dark Side of the Dream: Australian Literature and the Postcolonial Mind* (Sydney, Allen & Unwin, 1991)

The Inquirer and Commercial News, 15 June 1881, p. 2, http://nla.gov.au/nla. news-article65958465 (accessed 29 March 2015)

Jacobs, Jane, *The Death and Life of Great American Cities* (New York, Vintage, 1992)

Jeffery, Simon, 'What is Globalisation?', *The Guardian*, 31 October 2002, http://www.theguardian.com/world/2002/oct/31/globalisation.simonjeffery (accessed 22 June 2016)

Jeremiah, Emily, *Nomadic Ethics in Contemporary Women's Writing in German: Strange Subjects* (Rochester, NY, Camden House, 2012)

Keats, John, *The Complete Poems* (London, Penguin, 1977)

Keeping, Charles, *Charley, Charlotte and the Golden Canary* (Oxford, Oxford University Press, 1968)

Keneally, Thomas, *The Chant of Jimmie Blacksmith* (Sydney, Angus and Robertson, 1972)

Kinsella, John, *Full Fathom Five* (South Fremantle, Fremantle Arts Centre Press, 1993)

Kinsella, John, *Syzygy* (South Fremantle, Fremantle Arts Centre Press, 1993)

Kinsella, John, *The Silo: A Pastoral Symphony* (South Fremantle, Fremantle Arts Centre Press, 1995; Todmorden, Arc Publications, 1997)

Kinsella, John, *Genre* (South Fremantle, Fremantle Arts Centre Press, 1997)

Kinsella, John, *Poems 1989–1994* (South Fremantle, Fremantle Arts Centre Press, 1997)

Kinsella, John, *The Hunt and other poems* (South Fremantle, Fremantle Arts Centre Press; Newcastle upon Tyne, Bloodaxe Books, 1998)

Kinsella, John, *The Hierarchy of Sheep* (Newcastle upon Tyne, Bloodaxe Books, 2001)

Kinsella, John, *Peripheral Light: Selected and New Poems*, selected and introduced by Harold Bloom (South Fremantle, Fremantle Arts Centre Press; New York, W.W. Norton, 2003)

Kinsella, John, *Doppler Effect: Collected Experimental Poems*, introduced by Marjorie Perloff (Cambridge, Salt, 2004)

Kinsella, John, *The New Arcadia* (South Fremantle, Fremantle Arts Centre Press; New York, W.W. Norton, 2005)

Kinsella, John, *Disclosed Poetics* (Manchester, Manchester University Press, 2007)

Kinsella, John, 'Poetry as Means of Dialogue in Court Spaces', *Cultural Studies Review*, 13.2 (2007), pp. 98–114

Kinsella, John, *Contrary Rhetoric: Lectures on Landscape and Language*, ed. Glen Phillips and Andrew Taylor (Mount Lawley and North Fremantle, Edith Cowan University and Fremantle Press, 2008)

Kinsella, John, *Divine Comedy: Journeys through a Regional Geography* (New York, W.W. Norton, 2008; St Lucia, University of Queensland Press, 2008)

Kinsella, John, *Comus: a dialogic masque* (Todmorden, Arc Publications, 2008)

Kinsella, John, *Shades of the Sublime & Beautiful* (North Fremantle, Fremantle Press, 2008; London, Picador, 2008)

Kinsella, John (ed.), *Penguin Anthology of Australian Poetry* (Ringwood, Penguin, 2009)

Kinsella, John, *Activist Poetics: Anarchy in the Avon Valley*, ed. Niall Lucy (Liverpool, Liverpool University Press, 2010)

Kinsella, John, *Armour* (London, Picador, 2011)

Kinsella, John, *Rapacity: A Death's Jest-Book Intertext* (Cambridge, Equipage, 2011)

Kinsella, John, *Redstart: An Ecological Poetics* (Iowa City, University of Iowa Press, 2012)

Kinsella, John, *In the Shade of the Shady Tree: Stories* (Athens, Ohio University Press, 2012)

Kinsella, John, *Jam Tree Gully* (New York, W.W. Norton, 2012)

Kinsella, John, *Vision of Error: A Sextet of Activist Poems* (Melbourne, Five Islands Press, 2013)

Kinsella, John, *Morpheus: A Bildungsroman* (Buffalo, Blazevox, 2013)

Kinsella, John, *Spatial Relations*, 2 vols (Amsterdam and New York, Rodopi, 2013)

Kinsella, John, *Firebreaks* (New York, W.W. Norton, 2016)

Kinsella, John, *Hiss* (London, Picador, forthcoming)

Kinsella, John, and Niall Lucy, *The Ballad of Moondyne Joe* (North Fremantle, Fremantle Press, 2012)

Kinsella, John, and Thurston Moore, *A Remarkable Grey Horse* (Montreal, Vallum Chapbooks, 2014)

Kinsella, John, and Tracy Ryan, *Mutually Said* (a blog at http://poetsvegananar chistpacifist.blogspot.com.au/)

Kinsella, John, and Tracy Ryan (eds), *Western Australian Poetry Anthology* (North, Fremantle, Fremantle Press, forthcoming 2017)

Kissane, Noel (ed.), *The Irish Famine: A Documentary History* (Dublin, 1995)

Lacaussade, Auguste, *Les Salaziennes* (Paris, 1839), http://www.poesies.net/augustelacaussadelessalaziennes.txt (accessed 22 June 2016)

Lacaussade, Auguste, *Poèmes et paysages* (Paris, 1852), http://www.poesies.net/augustelacaussadepoemesetpaysages.txt (accessed 22 June 2016)

Lacaussade, Auguste, *Les Épaves* (Paris, 1861), http://www.poesies.net/augustelacaussadelesepaves.txt (accessed 22 June 2016)

Lawson, Henry, *The Penguin Henry Lawson Short Stories*, introduction by John Kinsella (Ringwood, Penguin, 2009)

Lea, Bronwyn, *The Other Way Out: New Poems* (Sydney, Giramondo, 2008)

Lefebvre, Henri, *The Production of Space*, trans. Donald Nicholson-Smith (London, Blackwell Publishing, 1991)

Leibniz, Gottfried Wilhelm, *Political Writings*, ed. Patrick Riley (Cambridge, Cambridge University Press, 1988)

Leonard, Liam, *The Environmental Movement in Ireland* (Galway, SSRC, National University of Ireland, 2007)

Lewis, Sinclair, *Arrowsmith* (New York, Signet, 2008)

'Local and Domestic Intelligence', *Perth Gazette*, 6 August 1856

Lock, Charles, 'The Pastoral and the Prophetic: Making an Approach to Geoffrey Hill', *Salt* 17.1, ed. John Kinsella (2003)

Macalister, Robert Alexander Stewart, *Lebor gabála Érenn: The Book of the Taking of Ireland* (Dublin, Published for the Irish Texts Society by the Educational Company of Ireland, 1938), https://archive.org/details/leborgablare01macauoft (accessed 22 June 2016)

Mateer, John, *Elsewhere* (Cambridge, Salt, 2007)

Mateer, John, *Emptiness: Asian Poems 1998–2012* (North Fremantle, Fremantle Press, 2012)

McAdams, Janet, *The Island of Lost Luggage* (Tucson, University of Arizona Press, 2000)

McAdams, Janet, *Feral* (Cambridge, Salt, 2007)

McAdams, Janet, *Seven Boxes for the Country After* (Wick Poetry Series, Kent State University Press, 2016)

McCooey, David, 'Lines in the sand', review of *Activists Poetics: Anarchy in the Avon Valley*, *Australian Book Review* 336 (2011), pp. 61–2

Mead, Philip, 'Connectivity, community and the question of literary universality: reading Kim Scott's chronotope and John Kinsella's commedia', in Peter Kirkpatrick and Robert Dixon (eds), *Republics of Letters: Literary Communities in Australia* (Sydney, Sydney University Press, 2012), pp. 137–56

Mengham, Rod, and Glen Phillips, *Fairly Obsessive* (South Fremantle, Fremantle Arts Centre Press, 2000)

Meyer, Kuno (trans.), 'The Lament of the Old Woman from Beare', in *Selections from Ancient Irish Poetry* (London, Constable & Company, 1911)

Mizen Journal (Mizen Archaeological and Historical Society, 1993)

Morgan, Sally, *My Place* (South Fremantle, Fremantle Arts Centre Press, 1987)

Newkirk, Pamela, 'The man who was caged in a zoo', *The Guardian*, 3 June

2015, http://www.theguardian.com/world/2015/jun/03/the-man-who-was-caged-in-a-zoo (accessed 4 June 2015).

O'Brien, Sean, 'Sean O'Brien reviews *Peripheral Light: Selected and new poems* by John Kinsella', *Times Literary Supplement*, 30 April 2004, p. 32

O'Keeffe, J. G., *Buile Suibhne* (London, Pub. from the Irish Texts Society by D. Nutt, 1913)

Oldenquist, Andrew G., *Moral Philosophy: Text and Readings* (Prospect Heights, IL, Wavelands Press, 1978)

Oppen, George, *The Collected Poems of George Oppen* (New York, New Directions, 1976)

O'Reilly, John Boyle, *Moondyne: A Story of Convict Life in Western Australia* (1879) (Australind: The National Gaelic Publications, 2010, being a facsimile edition of the George Robertson Publication, 1880)

Ouyang Yu, *Fainting with Freedom* (Melbourne, Five Islands Press, 2015)

Palmer, Nettie, *Fourteen Years*, in *Nettie Palmer*, ed. Vivian Smith (St Lucia, University of Queensland Press, 1988)

Papertalk-Green, Charmaine, *Just Like That and Other Poems* (North Fremantle, Fremantle Press, 2007)

Perloff, Marjorie, 'Introduction', in John Kinsella, *Doppler Effect* (Cambridge, Salt, 2004)

Pierce, Peter (ed.), *The Cambridge History of Australian Literature* (Cambridge, Cambridge University Press, 2009)

Plato, *Crito*, trans. Benjamin Jowett, from *Dialogues of Plato* (New York, P.F. Collier & Son, 1900), http://caae.phil.cmu.edu/Cavalier/80250/part2/Crito.html (this text is in the public domain, released August 1993) (accessed 4 July 2016)

Plato, *Phaedo, The Last Hours Of Socrates*, trans. Benjamin Jowett, Release Date: 29 October 2008 [EBook #1658] Last Updated: 15 January 2013, http://www.gutenberg.org/files/1658/1658-h/1658-h.htm (accessed 1 May 2016)

Pound, Ezra, *The Cantos of Ezra Pound* (New York, New Directions, 1996)

Preminger, Alex, Terry V. F. Brogan and Frank J. Warnke (eds), *The New Princeton Encyclopedia of Poetry and Poetics* (Princeton, NJ, Princeton University Press, 1993)

Prynne, J. H., *Poems* (Edinburgh and London, Agneau 2, 1982)

Punday, Daniel, *Narrative Bodies* (London, Palgrave, 2003)

Renton, Andrew (interviewer), 'Bridget Riley: Some things near and some things far', *Flash Art*, 26.168 (1993)

Ricks, Christopher, *Tennyson: A Selected Edition* (Harlow, Pearson Longman, 2007)

Robertson, Joshua, 'Murrumu charged after driving with licence issued by his Indigenous nation', *The Guardian*, 27 May 2015, http://www.theguardian.com/australia-news/2015/may/27/murrumu-charged-after-driving-with-licence-issued-by-his-indigenous-nation (accessed 28 May 2015)

Rukeyser, Muriel, *The Book of the Dead* (1938), http://murielrukeyser.emuenglish.org/writing/the-book-of-the-dead/ (accessed 22 June 2016)

Rutherford, Jennifer, 'Editorial', *Southerly: Shared Space Brokered Time*, 66.2 (2006), pp. 5–6.

Ryan, Tracy, *The Argument* (North Fremantle, Fremantle Press, 2011)

Samlong, Jean-François, *Une Guillotine dans un train* (Paris, Gallimard, 2012)

Scarry, Elaine, *The Body in Pain* (Oxford, Oxford University Press, 1987)

Schapiro, Meyer, 'Still Life with Compotier', http://www.ibiblio.org/wm/paint/auth/cezanne/sl/compotier/ (accessed 22 June 2016)

Scott, Kim, *Benang: From the Heart* (South Fremantle, Fremantle Arts Centre Press, 1999)

Scott, Kim, *Kayang and Me* (South Fremantle, Fremantle Press, 2005)

Scott, Kim, *That Deadman Dance* (Sydney, Picador, 2010)

Selections from Ancient Irish Poetry (London, Constable & Co., 1911)

Sidney, Sir Philip, *The Old Arcadia* (Oxford, Oxford University Press, 1999)

Smith, Beverley, 'Early Western Australian Literature: A Guide to Colonial Life and Goldfields Life' (MA thesis, Department of History, University of Western Australia, 1961)

Smith, Stan, *Poetry and Displacement* (Liverpool, Liverpool University Press, 2007)

Somerville-Large, Peter, *The Coast of West Cork* (Belfast, Appletree Press, 1991 [1972])

Stewart, Susan, 'Poems Containing History', *Oxford Poetry* 13.1 (2009), http://www.poetrymagazines.org.uk/magazine/record.asp?id=25201 (accessed 22 June 2016)

Stokes, Whitley, *Revue Celtique* 9 & 10, http://sejh.pagespersoorange.fr/keltia/immrama/maeldun_en.html (accessed 2 May 2015)

Strahan, Clare, 'Writing is Always a Political Act: An Interview with John Kinsella', *Overland*, 21 September 2011, https://overland.org.au/2011/09/writing-is-always-a-political-act/ (accessed 22 June 2016)

Stow, Randolph, *The Land's Meaning: New Selected Poems*, ed. John Kinsella (North Fremantle, Fremantle Press, 2012)

'Symbolic and Structural Approaches to Place: Michel de Certeau', https://pegasus.cc.ucf.edu/~janzb/courses/hum3930b/certeau1.htm (accessed 22 June 2016)

The Táin, trans. Thomas Kinsella (Oxford, Oxford University Press, 2002)

The Táin, trans. Ciaran Carson (London, Penguin, 2007)

Temperton, Barbara, *Southern Edge: three stories in verse* (North Fremantle, Fremantle Press, 2009)

Tennyson, Alfred, *Alfred Tennyson: A Critical Edition of the Major Works*, ed. Adam Roberts (Oxford, Oxford University Press, 2000)

Tennyson, Alfred and Charles, *Poems by Two Brothers* (New York, Thomas Y. Crowell & Co., 1900)

Tennyson, Hallam, *Alfred Lord Tennyson: A Memoir by His Son*, Vols 1 and 2 (New York, Macmillan, 1897)

Thoreau, Henry David, *Walden and Civil Disobedience* (London, Penguin, 1986)

Tinterow, Gary, and Henri Loyrette, *The Origins of Impressionism* (Paris, Connaissance des Arts, 1994)

'To the Editor', *The Perth Gazette and West Australian Times*, 2 May 1873, p. 3, http://nla.gov.au/nla.news-article3752307 (accessed 29 March 2015)

Views of the Famine: Contemporary newspaper articles and illustrations from the Great Hunger in Ireland, 1845–52, https://viewsofthefamine.wordpress.com/oxford-to-skibbereen-2/narrative/ (accessed 22 June 2016)

Viner, Katharine, 'Hand-to-brand combat', *The Guardian*, 23 September 2000, https://www.theguardian.com/books/2000/sep/23/society.politics (accessed 22 June 2016)

Virgil, *Eclogues, Georgics, Aeneid 1–6*, Loeb Classical Library (Cambridge, MA, Harvard University Press, 1999)

Walker, Charles, *Irene. A Tale. In Two Cantos. And Other Poems* (London, Saunders & Otley of Conduit Street, 1853)

Wark, McKenzie, *Virtual Geography: Living With Global Media Events* (Bloomington and Indianapolis, Indiana University Press, 1994)

Wark, McKenzie, 'The Sailor Turned into the Sea' (Salt online, 2008)

Wheatbelt Noongah: Recording Traditional Knowledges (Literature Review For Avon Basin Noongar Heritage And Cultural Significance Of Natural Resources by Murdoch Project Team, Principal Researcher Sandra Harben, Cultural Consultant Leonard Collard, Kura, Yeye, Benang, Kalykool *Past, Present, Tomorrow, Forever Ngulla Budjar Our Country*)

Wilson, Rob, 'From the Sublime to the Devious: Writing the Experimental/Local Pacific', *Jacket*, 12 (July 2000), http://jacketmagazine.com/12/wilson-p-pomod.html (accessed 22 June 2016)

Wright, Judith, *The Human Pattern: Selected Poems*, introduction by John Kinsella (Manchester, Carcanet, 2010)

Yeats, William Butler, *Writings on Irish Folklore, Legend, and Myth* (London, Penguin, 2002)

Yinjibarndi Aboriginal Corporation website [http://yindjibarndi.org.au]